# Bloom's Modern Critical Views

*Bloom's Modern Critical Views*

# JOHN DONNE AND THE METAPHYSICAL POETS
## *New Edition*

*Edited and with an introduction by*
## Harold Bloom
Sterling Professor of the Humanities
Yale University

BLOOM'S
LITERARY CRITICISM
*An imprint of Infobase Publishing*

8/17/10
WW
#45—

**Bloom's Modern Critical Views:**
**John Donne and the Metaphysical Poets—New Edition**
Copyright © 2010 by Infobase Publishing
Introduction © 2010 by Harold Bloom

Bloom's Literary Criticism
An imprint of Infobase Publishing
132 West 31st Street
New York NY 10001

**Library of Congress Cataloging-in-Publication Data**
John Donne and the metaphysical poets / edited and with an introduction by Harold Bloom. — New ed.
    p. cm. — (Bloom's modern critical views)
    Includes bibliographical references and index.
    ISBN 978-1-60413-590-9 (alk. Paper)
Donne, John, 1572–1631—Criticism and interpretation. 2. English poetry—Early modern, 1500–1700. 3. Metaphysics in literature. I. Bloom, Harold.
PR2248.J593 2010
821'.3—dc22                    2010006448

You can find Bloom's Literary Criticism on the World Wide Web at
http://www.chelseahouse.com

Cover design by Alicia Post
Composition by Bruccoli Clark Layman
Cover printed by IBT Global, Troy NY
Book printed and bound by IBT Global, Troy NY
Date printed: May 2010
Printed in the United States of America

10 9 8 7 6 5 4 3 2 1

This book is printed on acid-free paper.

# Contents

"Hac ex consilio meo via progredieris":
    Courtly Reading and Secretarial Mediation
    in Donne's *The Courtier's Library*      175
    *Piers Brown*

Ecstatic Donne: Conscience, Sin, and
    Surprise in the *Sermons* and the Mitcham Letters      209
    *Gary Kuchar*

HAROLD BLOOM

# *Introduction*

## JOHN DONNE AND THE METAPHYSICAL POETS

### I

Abraham Cowley is a poet remembered today only by scholars, and I doubt that he has a dozen readers a year among them, whether in America or in Britain. In the later seventeenth century he was regarded as a canonical poet, hugely influential, very much the Ezra Pound of his era. Though faded by Samuel Johnson's day, he was still famous enough to lead off Johnson's *Lives of the Poets,* where he, rather than Donne, is regarded as the founder and chief ornament (rather dimmed) of the Metaphysical school or line of wit, the bad old way superseded by Dryden and Pope.

Literary history, particularly the history of criticism, has a habit of making ludicrous many of a period's firm judgments. When I was young, Shelley was ignored or deprecated in literary and academic circles, and Donne was considered the paradigm of poetry. In the age of Eliot (or the Pound Era, if you prefer), you were dismissed as barbaric or eccentric if you believed that *Song of Myself* was the central American poem, or that Hart Crane was a permanent poet, and W. H. Auden perhaps something less than that.

Johnson himself thought his *Life of Cowley*—the best of the *Lives,* since his discussion of the Metaphysical poets (he took his name for them from Dryden) was a pioneer venture. It may be unfashionable to believe this, but Johnson's discussion of the school of Donne seems to me still the most adequate we possess, despite the perpetual Donne revivals which go on continuously, from Coleridge through Arthur Symons in the nineteenth century, and endlessly in our own.

1

Johnson, whatever his blindnesses and flaws, remains the most fecund and suggestive literary critic in the language, with only Hazlitt and Ruskin as his near rivals. It could hardly be expected that he should have preferred John Donne to Alexander Pope; I do not, and in any case Johnson's analysis of Metaphysical poetry still seems to me more just than any of the modern defenses, down to the persuasive attempt by Louis Martz to substitute "the meditative poem" for "the metaphysical poem" as a category. Martz gives a very useful account of both terms, and of their complex interaction:

> Meditation points toward poetry, in its use of images, in its technique of arousing the passionate affections of the will . . .
>
> For critical and historical purposes we should, I believe, attempt to distinguish between the "metaphysical" and the "meditative" qualities in this poetry . . .
>
> ["Metaphysical"] poems tend to begin abruptly, in the midst of an occasion; and the meaning of the occasion is explored and grasped through a peculiar use of metaphor. The old Renaissance "conceit," the ingenious comparison, is developed into a device by which the extremes of abstraction and concreteness, the extremes of unlikeness, may be woven together into a fabric of argument unified by the prevailing force of "wit."

This is responsible and lucid, though a long way from the fierce verve of Johnson on the same matter:

> Wit, like all other things subject by their nature to the choice of man, has its changes and fashions, and at different times takes different forms. About the beginning of the seventeenth century appeared a race of writers that may be termed the metaphysical poets . . .
>
> The metaphysical poets were men of learning, and to shew their learning was their whole endeavour . . .
>
> If the father of criticism has rightly denominated poetry . . . an imitative art, these writers will, without great wrong, lose their right to the name of poets; for they cannot be said to have imitated any thing; they neither copied nature nor life; neither painted the forms of matter, nor represented the operations of intellect.
>
> Those however who deny them to be poets, allow them to be wits. Dryden confesses of himself and his contemporaries, that they fall below Donne in wit, but maintains that they surpass him in poetry.

If Wit be well described by Pope, as being "that which has been often thought, but was never before so well expressed," they certainly never attained, nor ever sought it; for they endeavoured to be singular in their thoughts, and were careless of their diction. But Pope's account of wit is undoubtedly erroneous: he depresses it below its natural dignity, and reduces it from strength of thought to happiness of language.

If by a more noble and more adequate conception that be considered as Wit, which is at once natural and new, that which, though not obvious, is, upon its first production, acknowledged to be just; if it be that, which he that never found it, wonders how he missed; to wit of this kind the metaphysical poets have seldom risen. Their thoughts are often new, but seldom natural; they are not obvious, but neither are they just; and the reader, far from wondering that he missed them, wonders more frequently by what perverseness of industry they were ever found.

But Wit, abstracted from its effects upon the hearer, may be more rigorously and philosophically considered as a kind of discordia concurs; a combination of dissimilar images, or discovery of occult resemblances in things apparently unlike. Of wit, thus defined, they have more than enough. The most heterogeneous ideas are yoked by violence together; nature and art are ransacked for illustrations, comparisons, and allusions; their learning instructs, and their subtilty surprises; but the reader commonly thinks his improvement dearly bought, and though he sometimes admires is seldom pleased.

Wit is, for Johnson, as he says: "strength of thought" and not mere "happiness of language." Though he went on to deny Donne and his followers a share either in "the pathetick" or "the sublime," Johnson gave them what was, for him, a measure of true praise:

Yet great labour, directed by great abilities, is never wholly lost: if they frequently threw away their wit upon false conceits, they likewise sometimes struck out unexpected truth: if their conceits were far-fetched, they were often worth the carriage. To write on their plan, it was at least necessary to read and think. No man cold be born a metaphysical poet, nor assume the dignity of a writer, by descriptions copied from descriptions, by imitations borrowed from imitations, by traditional imagery, and hereditary similies, by readiness of rhyme, and volubility of syllables.

In perusing the works of this race of authours, the mind is exercised either by recollection or inquiry; either something already learned is to be retrieved, or something new is to be examined. If their greatness seldom elevates, their acuteness often surprises; if the imagination is not always gratified, at least the powers of reflection and comparison are employed; and in the mass of materials which ingenious absurdity has thrown together, genuine wit and useful knowledge may be sometimes found, buried perhaps in grossness of expression, but useful to those who know their value; and such as, when they are expanded to perspicuity, and polished to elegance, may give lustre to works which have more propriety, though less copiousness of sentiment.

Reading and thinking are activities Johnson always recommended to poets, particularly at his own moment, yet these paragraphs of praise are qualified by the absence of Johnson's deepest veneration, which is for wisdom and its poetic refinement through elaborate invention. Johnson is careful to deny Cowley (and Donne, his master) invention, the essence of poetry, though his care is uneasily qualified by an implicit realization that is made explicit in *The Rambler No. 125:*

Definitions have been no less difficult or uncertain in criticism than in law. Imagination, a licentious and vagrant faculty, unsusceptible of limitations, and impatient of restraint, has always endeavoured to baffle the logician, to perplex the confines of distinction, and burst the enclosures of regularity. There is therefore scarcely any species of writing, of which we can tell what is its essence, and what are its constituents; every new genius produces some innovation which, when invented and approved, subverts the rules which the practice of foregoing authors had established.

We cannot fault Johnson for not seeing Donne as such a new genius of innovation, and not merely because we would excuse the critic's blindness as a product of the vagaries of taste. Toward Donne, Johnson is both puzzled and respectful. His Donne is "a man of very extensive and various knowledge," "abstruse and profound," "indelicate," whose work, when improper, "is produced by a voluntary deviation from nature in pursuit of something new or strange." But this Donne troubles Johnson, as Cowley does not. What Donne calls into question is Johnson's criteria of the general or the universal, and the natural, and to have provoked the great critic in regard to those criteria is to have manifested indubitable poetic strength.

## II

Johnson had a great distrust of devotional verse, which I suspect was a hidden element in his ambivalence toward the Metaphysical poets. Even in the *Life of Cowley*, the distrust is evidenced, when Johnson discusses Cowley's frigid religious epic, the *Davideis:*

> Sacred History has been always read with submissive reverence, and an imagination over-awed and controlled. We have been accustomed to acquiesce in the nakedness and simplicity of the authentick narrative, and to repose on its veracity with such humble confidence, as suppresses curiosity. We go with the historian as he goes, and stop with him when he stops. All amplification is frivolous and vain; all addition to that which is already sufficient for the purposes of religion, seems not only useless, but in some degree profane.
>
> Such events as were produced by the visible interposition of Divine Power are above the power of human genius to dignify. The miracle of Creation, however it may teem with images, is best described with little diffusion of language: *He spake the word, and they were made.*

Two very diverse judgments, moral and aesthetic, uneasily mingle here. "Submissive reverence," with one's imagination "over-awed and controlled," is hardly a proper stance for any critic, let alone the strongest critic in Western literary tradition. This moral position is curiously reinforced by Johnson's keen aesthetic apprehension of the sublime economy of style manifested by the Authorized Version of the Holy Bible, much of it the work of the preternaturally eloquent William Tyndale and of Miles Coverdale. Poor Cowley has little hope of sustaining close comparison to Tyndale, but that is his Johnsonian punishment for daring to provoke a great critic into "submissive reverence." At that, Cowley fared better than the unfortunate Edmund Waller, whose Sacred Poems stimulated Johnson to the most powerful strictures against religious verse ever written:

> Contemplative piety, or the intercourse between God and the human soul, cannot be poetical. Man admitted to implore the mercy of his Creator, and plead the merits of his Redeemer, is already in a higher state than poetry can confer.
>
> The essence of poetry is invention; such invention as, by producing something unexpected, surprises and delights. The topicks of devotion are few, and being few are universally known; but few as they are, they can be made no more; they can receive

no grace from novelty of sentiment, and very little from novelty of expression.

Poetry pleases by exhibiting an idea more grateful to the mind than things themselves afford. This effect proceeds from the display of those parts of nature which attract, and the concealment of those which repel the imagination: but religion must be shewn as it is; suppression and addition equally corrupt it; and such as it is, it is known already.

From poetry the reader justly expects, and from good poetry always obtains, the enlargement of his comprehension and elevation of his fancy; but this is rarely to be hoped by Christians from metrical devotion. Whatever is great, desireable, or tremendous, is comprised in the name of the Supreme Being. Omnipotence cannot be exalted; Infinity cannot be amplified; Perfection cannot be improved.

The employments of pious meditation are Faith, Thanksgiving, Repentance, and Supplication. Faith, invariably uniform, cannot be invested by fancy with decorations. Thanksgiving, the most joyful of all holy effusions, yet addressed to a Being without passions, is confined to a few modes, and is to be felt rather than expressed. Repentance, trembling in the presence of the Judge, is not at leisure for cadences and epithets. Supplication of man to man may diffuse itself through many topicks of persuasion; but supplication to God can only cry for mercy.

Of sentiments purely religious, it will be found that the most simple expression is the most sublime. Poetry loses its lustre and its power, because it is applied to the decoration of something more excellent than itself. All that verse can do is to help the memory, and delight the ear, and for these purposes it may be very useful; but it supplies nothing to the mind. The ideas of Christian Theology are too simple for eloquence, too sacred for fiction, and too majestick for ornament; to recommend them by tropes and figures, is to magnify by a concave mirror the sidereal hemisphere.

How well do Donne's devotional poems, or Herbert's, or those of Crashaw, Vaughan, Traherne withstand this formidable theoretical assault? Do the meditative poems of the Metaphysical school escape the indictment that their tropes merely "magnify by a concave mirror the sidereal hemisphere"?

Perhaps Johnson could be accused of overstating the aesthetic risk of devotional verse, yet he is refreshingly original and all but unique among critics in addressing himself to this difficult, and for him painful matter. It should be noted that Johnson's exalted praise of Milton, extraordinary in a critic who opposed Milton in politics, religion, and cultural vision, is founded upon the critic's conviction that Milton almost uniquely overcomes the limitations of a religious poetry:

> Pleasure and terrour are indeed the genuine sources of poetry; but poetical pleasure must be such as human imagination can at least conceive, and poetical terrour such as human strength and fortitude may combat. The good and evil of Eternity are too ponderous for the wings of wit; the mind sinks under them in passive helplessness, content with calm belief and humble adoration.
>
> Known truths, however, may take a different appearance, and be conveyed to the mind by a new train of intermediate images. This Milton has undertaken, and performed with pregnancy and vigour of mind peculiar to himself. Whoever considers the few radical positions which the Scriptures afforded him, will wonder by what energetick operation he expanded them to such extent, and ramified them to so much variety, restrained as he was by religious reverence from licentiousness of fiction.

It is by the standard of *Paradise Lost* as a Christian poem that Johnson found the meditative poetry of the school of Donne unpersuasive and uninteresting. As readers of Donne's sublime hymns, or Herbert's *The Temple*, we rightly are convinced that Johnson's sensibility was surprisingly narrow when he read the Metaphysicals. On the basis of his quotations from Donne in the *Life of Cowley*, Johnson seems to have shied away from Donne's divine poems, and he avoids quoting from Herbert. What seems an overwhelming virtue of Metaphysical devotional verse, its detailed imagery and highly individualized figurations, must have offended Johnson's Horatian passion for the universal. Certainly he had little patience for the minute particulars of the Metaphysical trope:

> The fault of Cowley, and perhaps of all the writers of the metaphysical race, is that of pursuing his thoughts to their last ramifications, by which he loses the grandeur of generality; for of the greatest things the parts are little; what is little can be but pretty, and by claiming dignity becomes ridiculous. Thus all the power of description is destroyed by a scrupulous enumeration; and the force of metaphors is lost, when the mind by the mention of particulars is turned more upon the original than the secondary sense, more upon that from which the illustration is drawn than that to which it is applied.

## III

Frank Kermode, a foremost contemporary critic of Donne, accurately remarks: "It remains true that to write of the fortunes of Donne in the past seventy years is, in effect, to write less about him than about the aesthetic preoccupations of that epoch." I would amplify Kermode's observation, fifteen years later, by suggesting that the years 1915–1955 had very different "aesthetic preoccupations" than the years 1955–1985, or than subsequent years are likely to have. Eliot, as Kermode says, sought to associate his own poetry with the mode of Donne, but Eliot's poetry, as Kermode does not say, in fact derives from Tennyson and Whitman. *The Waste Land* has far more in common with "Maud" and "When Lilacs Last in the Dooryard Bloom'd" than it does with *The Second Anniversarie* or "A Nocturnall upon S. Lucies Day." Kermode associates the restoration of Donne "to his place among the English poets" with the restoration of "wit to its place in poetry." Johnson associated wit with poetry and Pope. I myself find more wit in the Shelley of *The Triumph of Life* than in Donne, but then I am of a different critical generation from that of Kermode.

I doubt that future defenses of Donne and of his school will organize themselves as Modernist celebrations of a Metaphysical agility in wit. Donne seems now as archaic as Spenser, and as specialized as Ben Jonson. The Eliotic vogue for him is now over, and with it is gone the New Critical notion that every good short poem must follow the paradigm of a Donne lyric or meditation. Johnson's powerful critique of the Metaphysicals may not be the last word, but it has recovered a good part of its force during the past thirty years. The recent essays reprinted in this volume manifest a serious attempt to appreciate the school of Donne on a basis very different from the one that extends from Eliot to Kermode. Donne and Herbert do not seem to me poets of the eminence of Spenser and Milton, and a critical epoch that preferred them to Spenser and Milton was certain to pass away as an almost grotesque interlude in the history of taste. But they are the principal devotional poets in the language, hardly equalled by Hopkins or by the Eliot of the *Quartets* or the later Auden. Whatever Johnson thought, the sacred Milton was anything but a devotional poet. A sect of one, Milton persuasively redefined Christianity almost as drastically as William Blake did. Curiously enough, it was rather Donne and Herbert, and their fellows, who merited Johnson's praise. For them, the good and evil of Eternity were not "too ponderous for the wings of wit."

## DONALD RAMSAY ROBERTS

# *The Death Wish of John Donne*

In the darkest time of the long period of poverty, illness, and dependence that followed his imprudent elopement, John Donne wrote in a letter to Sir Henry Goodyer in September, 1608:

> Two of the most precious things which God hath afforded us here, for the agony and exercise of our sense and spirit, which are a thirst and inhiation after the next life, and a frequency of prayer and meditation in this, are often envenomed and putrified, and stray into a corrupt disease. . . . With the first of these I have often suspected myself to be overtaken, which is with a desire of the next life; which though I know it is not merely out of a weariness of this, because I had the same desires when I went with the tide, and enjoyed fairer hopes than now; yet I doubt worldly encumbrances have increased it. I would not that death should take me asleep. I would not have him merely seize me, and only declare me to be dead, but win me and overcome me.
>
> When I must shipwreck, I would do it in a sea where mine impotency might have some excuse; not in a sullen weedy lake, where I could not have so much as exercise for my swimming. Therefore I would fain do something, but that I cannot tell what

*PMLA*, Volume 62, Number 4 (December 1947): pp. 958–976. Copyright © 1947 Modern Language Association.

is no wonder. For to choose is to do; but to be no part of any body is to be nothing. At most, the greatest persons are but great wens and excrescences; men of wit and delightful conversation but as moles for ornament, except they be so incorporated into the body of the world that they contribute something to the sustentation of the whole.[1]

In this quotation two sentiments are to be noted which are unusually significant for our knowledge of Donne. One is his conviction that "no man is an island," that every man must find and fulfill his vital function in the world of men, a conviction which had much to do with his decision to enter the Church, and even more to do with his subsequent success as the most admired preacher in England. Some years after these words were written he found in the ministry the opportunity of "contributing something to the sustentation of the whole" which to him was a necessity of life.

More noteworthy, however, is the confession, only thinly veiled beneath the commonplace euphemism of "the next life," of a positive wish to die. That Donne had such a wish, that it was persistent, even lifelong, and that a full understanding of this wish throws considerable light not only upon Donne's temperament and certain of his actions, but also upon certain aspects of his work and philosophy, is the thesis of the present study.

Certainly there is abundant evidence in the poems, letters, sermons, and other works, that the desire for death was a permanent element in his psychic life. Occasionally we come upon an open confession, and at other times we need only read between the lines. If we can trust in the letter to Sir Henry Goodyer, Donne had been preoccupied with thoughts of death even in the youthful and outwardly careless years before his disastrous marriage ("when I went with the tide, and enjoyed fairer hopes than now"); and in several poems of that period there is in fact to be observed a certain morbid absorption in the physical conditions of the grave which we shall see recurring at the time of his death over thirty years later. In the painful period of insecurity between his elopement in 1601 and his entry into the Church in 1615, Donne's expressions of this sentiment are often infinitely pathetic. "As I would every day provide for my soul's last convoy, though I know not when I shall die, and perchance I shall never die,"[2] is a typical remark. In one letter which tells that Donne and his whole family are ill and destitute, and he is bowed down by the death of his children, he writes: "I flatter myself with this hope that I am dying too, for I cannot waste faster than by such griefs."[3] On recovering from an illness, he could attempt a modest conceit on the subject: "I begin to be past hope of dying; and I feel that a little rag of Monte Mayor which I read last time I was in your chamber, hath wrought prophetically upon me, which is, that Death came so fast towards me that the over-joy of that recovered me."[4] Two months later he reported that he had "relapsed into good degrees of health," and that his "cause of sorrow" was that he had "fallen from fair hopes of ending all."[5] In the later period of his priesthood, he judged death as "at the worst indifferent and to the good, good." In 1623, writing under the stress of illness, he says, "If man knew the gain of death, the ease of death, he would solicit, he would provoke death to assist him by any hand which he might use."[6] The candidest of all his words on this subject, however, are those of the preface to *Biathanatos*, where he avows not only a wish for death, but a temptation to suicide: "Whensoever any affliction assails me, methinks I have the keys of my prison in mine own hand, and no remedy presents itself so soon to my heart, as mine own sword." These are only a few of innumerable utterances which might be cited, all of which indicate, obliquely or directly, Donne's fixed private attitude toward death. The negative evidence is equally strong. I should venture to assert that there is no utterance in the whole canon of his works that can legitimately be interpreted as evidence of a personal fear of or aversion to death.

With this hypothesis in hand, it is desirable to re-interpret the macabre drama of the last months of Donne's life, of that death that he was clearly determined to see as a "*mortem raptus,* a death of rapture and ecstasy." All his acts at that time bear out the hypothesis. The facts are well known through Walton's biography; for it is evident, both in the length and detail of Walton's account, and in his tone of awestruck piety, as well as in the title of the first edition ("The Life *and Death* of Doctor John Donne"), that to the author one of the principal events in the career of his subject had been his mortal decease. Donne died a slow death, probably from cancer, and the inevitable progress of the disease must have been apparent as early as a year before he finally succumbed; his death was widely rumored several months before it actually took place. (Donne appears to have been less disturbed by this than by the contrary rumor that he was feigning illness.) His letters of this last year are full of references to his coming "dissolution." Three months before he died, refusing a milk diet, he told his physician that he "was so far from fearing death, which to others is the king of terrors, that he longed for the day of his dissolution"—a state of mind revealing something more than appropriate Christian resignation. About six weeks later, now visibly in the throes of fatal illness, he overruled every protest to preach his customary annual sermon in Saint Paul's Cathedral on the opening of Lent. The sermon was intensely dramatic; Donne evoked horrid imaginations of corruption in the grave, exalted death as an inescapable principle at work even within the bounds of life itself, and expressed feverish longings for the glories of the resurrection. Three weeks before his death he acceded to the request of his friends for a memorial, but had his own plans in the matter. When the painter came, Donne disposed himself with his eyes closed and a shroud about his head. The resulting grave

image (well known to many from the sculpture later made from the painting)
he then set beside his bed to contemplate—with what kind and what intensity of satisfaction we are free to conjecture—for the few remaining days of
life. His last words, according to Walton, were, "I were miserable if I might
not die," and his last living act was to close his own eyes and arrange his body
in the conventional posture of the grave, doing an office he had doubtless
performed many times for others. In all this, though the impression may be
obscured by Walton's tone of pious homage, do we not clearly discern the actions of a man playing out a drama to signalize to the world that death holds
no terrors for him, but is rather the consummation of a lifetime of longing?

It is true that Donne's lack of reticence is partly a reflection of contemporary attitudes. Seventeenth-century Englishmen recognized death as an
important event in one's religious life, and surrounded it with more ceremony
than we do today. Death was a commoner event in everyone's experience; it
often struck at the young and came in the mass in the form of plagues. It
might almost be said—and the observation is borne out by the prominence of
the subject of death in literary and philosophical speculation—that the very
fact of death was more generally accepted than it now is. Certainly the occasion of it was more public, social, and ceremonious. It required an elaborate
and formal religious preparation. Confession and repentance were often an
extensive business, seriously undertaken and carried through. In confession
the sick man might attempt to unbosom himself of all the sins of his life;
confession should properly be followed by sincere repentance. Next the sick
man should arrive at a proper state of resignation, and when he had done
so he might make a semipublic testimony of his condition of faith. To give
such a "testimony" was doubtless part of Donne's purpose in his last sermon.
Arrived at such a state, the faithful might then legitimately look forward to
the joys of the hereafter. Thus Donne's acceptance of death would have appeared less *outré* to a contemporary observer, when such an acceptance was
the usual and necessary duty of a Christian. What marks his conduct off from
the expected and contemporary is not his general line of behavior, but certain
episodes that betoken not only a negative acceptance, but a positive desire.
Contemporary ritual demanded no such presumptive measures as preaching
one's own funeral sermon, arranging one's body for the coffin, and preparing
a posthumous monument.

But though Donne's throes were enough in accord with contemporary culture to have seemed less extravagant in the seventeenth than in the
twentieth century, there yet remains about them a quality still unaccounted
for, the histrionic and romantic quality which captivated Walton and which
has piqued the curiosity of modern critics. Donne's essential motive in thus
dramatizing himself requires explanation. Gosse ascribed his behavior at
this time to a Renaissance love of pageantry, and compared his death scenes

with those of Bernard of Palissy and Sir Philip Sidney. I would suggest that Donne's model and avatar was the early Christian saint and martyr. A better comparison than Gosse's is that of the early fathers of the English Church, whose deaths are described by Bede in his *Ecclesiastical History* with liturgical monotony: each one predicts the day and hour of his death and then lies down in perfect resignation at the appointed hour and is wafted to the bliss of heaven. There is evidence that Donne envied the saintly simplicity of his early predecessors in the Church, though he was mistaken in supposing that the same quality could be recaptured by him in his own more sophisticated era. As will be shown later, Donne had a peculiar sense of affinity with the Church martyrs, and his self-imposed pattern and example in later life was Saint Stephen, "Christ's protomartyr," who like himself had been both a convert and a preacher. As every student knows, such a sentimental mimesis of antiquity as this interpretation implies was most common in the early seventeenth century. Nor will those conversant with Donne's egoism believe him incapable of the impertinence of entertaining such a notion of himself—if, that is, it is indeed an impertinence. To the student who knows only the youthful Jack Donne, the erotic poet and "visiter of ladies," the notion of John Donne as a saint may seem extravagant; but to Donne himself on his deathbed, as to Walton his hagiographer, who understood well his intention in this regard, that figure had long been submerged and atoned for. Viewed as a whole, the life of Donne does in truth conform to an established pattern of sainthood (of which Saint Augustine is one of many examples): a youth at least relatively worldly and wicked; a long intermediate period of retirement and penitential suffering; then the emergence, after a renunciation of the world, into an illustrious career as preacher of the faith and spiritual guide to the people. Had he lived a thousand years earlier, when the appreciation of spiritual vitality was livelier and less philistine, who is to say that Donne would trot have been canonized? Of course, the drama he was playing did not quite come off. Despite Walton's attempt to celebrate it, it appears to have failed in large degree with his contemporaries, just as it fails with us. But the failure was due to historical realities that Donne and Walton were powerless to change.

To his contemporaries the most striking event connected with Donne's decease must have been the delivery of his last sermon. He appeared in the pulpit of the great cathedral showing a "decayed body and a dying face," and with tears and in a "faint and hollow voice" delivered to the distinguished congregation, which included the king himself, a passionate sermon on the text, "And unto God the Lord belong the issues of death." His auditors judged his intention rightly when they said that he had preached his own funeral sermon; and even today the text produces a powerful impression, instinct with terror and horror, when it is read with the circumstances of its delivery in mind. As for its theme, to the pious view this work would appear to be an unusually eloquent exhortation to Christian resignation in the face of death. In another view it appears as an impassioned glorification and justification of death, in which the subjective bias of the preacher is only too evident in outcries such as, "How much worse a death than death is this life, which so good men would so often change for death!" Even after a certain change in taste in such matters between Donne's time and our own is discounted, there is in some passages more than a tinge of morbid absorption in the physical decay that accompanies death.[7]

> We must all pass this posthume death, this death after death, nay, this death after burial, this dissolution after dissolution, this death of corruption and putrefaction, of vermiculation and incineration, of dissolution and dispersion in and from the grave, when these bodies that have been the children of royal parents, and the parents of royal children, must say with Job, *Corruption, thou art my father, and to the worm, Thou art my mother and my sister.*[8]

It is for its intellectual rather than its personal implications, however, that this sermon is most significant. The central idea is indicated by the title of the printed edition: "Death's Duel, or, a consolation to the soul against the dying life and the living death of the body." It is, that all earthly life is but a form of death, a continual progress toward the grave (together with the corollary, which concerns us less at the present moment, that death, through the promise of a resurrection, brings hope of eternal life). This theme, conventional though it is in theology, Donne develops far beyond the Christian commonplaces of contempt for the world, and with the aid of his rare and splendid rhetoric makes of it a mighty paradox, in which the wit of the poet and the ingenuity of the theologian serve only to underscore his passion and deep seriousness. The paradox that life is in reality a death is declared in the most grave and terrible words, far more intense than those of Hamlet in the depth of their disgust with life:

> this whole world is but an universal churchyard, but our common grave, and the life and motion that the greatest persons have in it is but as the shaking of buried bodies in their graves, by an earthquake. That which we call life is but *hebdomada mortium,* a week of death, seven days, seven periods of our life spent in dying, a dying seven times over; and there is an end. . . . all the way, so many deaths, so many deadly calamities accompany every condition and every period of this life, as that death itself would be an ease to them that suffer them.[9]

Even more paradoxically, Donne maintains that the very beginnings of life in the womb are a form of death.

> In all our periods and transitions in this life, are so many passages from death to death; our very birth and entrance into this life is *exitus a morte*, an issue from death, for in our mother's womb we are dead, so as that we do not know we live, not so much as we do in our sleep . . . this issue, this deliverance, from that death of the womb, is an entrance, a delivering over to another death, the manifold deaths of this world; we have a winding-sheet in our mother's womb which grows with us from our conception, and we come forth into the world wound up in that winding-sheet, for we come to seek a grave.[10]

Now this sermon, it must be remembered, is the fruit of a lifetime of meditation, and its subject, moreover, is one of the most widely explored in the history of religious speculation, and was especially dear to the age in which Donne lived. One should not expect too much novelty in a seventeenth-century sermon on death. To define and trace back to their traditional origins Donne's thoughts on the subject of death might be an interesting task, but it is outside the scope of the present inquiry, which is directed at the living source rather than the dead pattern of the idea. And in turning from a consideration of the unconscious motives which governed Donne's attitudes toward death to a consideration of his conscious speculations, on the intellectual plane, on that subject, my purpose is only to disentangle a single thread from that rather vast fabric and follow it from its origin. This thread is found in the "funeral sermon" in the form of a conception of *the existence within life of a contrary destructive principle, an anti-life or death principle*.[11] It is perhaps more obscured than otherwise, from a philosophical point of view, by the intermixture of theological conceptions and by the brilliance of the rhetoric in which it is clothed. But the ardor of Donne in expounding it shows that it possessed a peculiar value for him. In order to trace the history of this conception through Donne's intellectual life, it is necessary now to consider earlier evidence.

As is not uncommon with persons of a neurotic cast of mind—and not at all universal with poets—John Donne was a constant, careful, and clearheaded student of his own psyche. Indeed it is perhaps this quality of self-knowledge, together with a corresponding candor about himself, which accounts in large degree for Donne's great popularity in the present century. A letter of about 1608 reveals his inquisitiveness about the workings of his own mind, and also a lively sense of the danger of subjective error in this kind of study.

> If I knew that I were ill, I were well; for we consist of three parts, a soul, and body, and mind: which I call those thoughts and affections, and passions, which neither soul nor body hath alone, but have been begotten by their communication, as music results out of our breath and a cornet.
>
> And of all these the diseases are cures, if they be known. Of our soul's sicknesses, which are sins, the knowledge is to acknowledge, and that is her physic, in which we are not dieted by drams and scruples, for we cannot take too much. Of our body's infirmities, though our knowledge be partly *ab extrinseco,* from the opinion of the physician, and that the subject and matter be flexible and various, yet their rules are certain, and if the matter be rightly applied to the rule, our knowledge thereof is also certain.
>
> But, of the diseases of the mind there is no criterion, no canon, no rule, for our own taste and apprehension and interpretation should be the judge, and that is the disease itself. . . . I still mistake my disease.
>
> And I still vex myself with this, because if I know it not, nobody can know it. And I comfort myself because I see dispassioned men are subject to the like ignorances.[12]

This letter shows clearly that at one time at least Donne was concerned with questions of what we now call abnormal psychology, and that he felt the lack of systematic knowledge on such questions.

It was doubtless from the introspection implied here, supported by data from his immense learning, that Donne drew the conclusion, as early as thirty years before the final sermon we have been examining, that a death wish such as he recognized in himself is a universal manifestation in nature. This conclusion is stated in two of the "paradoxes" in the little book called *Paradoxes and Problems.*[13] Most of the pieces in this book were composed before 1600. In one he maintains "That only cowards dare die," that suicide is an act of cowardice rather than courage, or, to paraphrase him in modern terms, a surrender to a lower instinct. In another, entitled "That all things kill themselves," he clearly formulates a universal principle of self-destruction.

> To affect, yea to effect their owne death, all living things are importun'd, not by Nature only which perfects them, but by Art and Education, which perfects her.

He argues further, in a passage which is both a statement of the Elizabethan theory of "cosmic decay" and an anticipation of certain modern theories of cosmic history, that this principle is inherent in the nature of the world.

If then the best things kill themselves soonest, (for no Affection endures, and all things labour to this perfection) all travell to their owne death, yea the frame of the whole world, if it were possible for God to be idle, yet because it began, must dye. Then in this idlenesse imagined in God, what could kill the world but it selfe, since out of it, nothing is?

These are daring speculations, and their significance has been over-looked only because the *Paradoxes* have generally been regarded as exercises in wit, as intellectual bagatelles. These alleged bagatelles, however, contain the first clear enunciation of a theory that nature partakes of an impulse toward suicide. This theory, as applied to the world of human beings, Donne worked out more fully in the book on suicide which he wrote in 1608: *Biathanatos. A Declaration of that Paradoxe, or Thesis, that Selfe-homicide is not so Naturally Sinne, that it may never be otherwise. Wherein The Nature, and the extent of all those Lawes, which seem to be violated by this Act, are diligently surveyed.*[14] Since the seventeenth century, when it provoked some theological controversy, this book has not been regarded by scholars as important for its own sake. Gosse regarded it as an apologia, intended to justify Donne in the event that he should give in to the "sickly inclination" to suicide which he confesses in the Preface. Mrs. Simpson repeats the trivial judgment of Canon Jessop that it is a scholastic exercise in dialectic, an academic defense of a thesis like those practiced in the medieval universities. More recently, Professor C. M. Coffin has argued its value for interpreting the intellectual life of Donne, but without attributing to it any significance in the history of ideas. It is time, therefore, that this book should be examined for its substance in the light of our knowledge of today.

The title, with its emphasis on the word *naturally*, indicates the germinal idea of the work, though with a certain diffidence such as might be expected in the presentation of so heterodox a notion. In the book itself, Donne examines the question of suicide from three points of view: "the law of nature"; "the law of reason"; and "the law of God." It is in the first of the three parts corresponding to these divisions of the subject that Donne develops the thesis that self-destruction is a natural phenomenon. A brief summary of the First Part of this little-read book will serve to indicate the main lines of Donne's argument.

The first Distinction (subdivision) of the First Part is an examination of the moral imperatives of suicide: Donne argues that suicide does not invariably proceed from motives that can be stigmatized as unworthy. In the second Distinction he attacks the law of self-preservation, maintaining that this alleged law is not universal in its application either in the animal kingdom or in the world of humanity. He cites examples from the animal world (bees and

pelicans) where self-destruction is a part of the normal life-cycle. From this
point on we have a learned and penetrating study of the place of suicide in
human history. Donne first points out, with cool logic and learned data, that
human custom outside Christianity has often differed in its view of suicide,
and in fact has often sanctioned it. He cites the ritual suicide practiced by Roman gladiators, the self-immolation on the husband's funeral pyre of "wives
in the Indies," the practice of "the Samanaei priests in the Indies," and the
Germanic custom of the immolation of warriors upon the death of their lord
(the Soldurii of ancient France). Without overlooking the obvious example
of Roman custom, he gives an imposing list of illustrious Romans and Greeks
who took their own lives, and figures on the large number of suicides in antiquity. Donne does not regard these and similar phenomena as the perverted
practices of barbarians, but as evidence of a universal and deepseated desire;
and draws the triumphant conclusion in respect to suicide that "in all ages,
in all places, upon all occasions, men of all conditions have affected it, and
inclined to do it."

Christianity failed to eradicate this desire. Although Christian doctrine
forbade suicide and stigmatized it as a sin, man's natural lust for his own ex-
tinction was not to be denied, but was merely transferred in the Christian era
to a new outlet in the form of martyrdom. "After Christianity had quenched
those respects of fame, ease, shame, and such, how quickly naturally man
snatched and embraced a new way of profusing his life by martyrdom!" Thus
Donne looked upon the mania for martyrdom which swept over the Christian world in the fourth century as the manifestation of a suicidal impulse.
Martyrdom was encouraged at first by the Church fathers, and the desire for
it was much stimulated by the famous example of Ignatius, bishop of Smyr-
na, with his inordinate appetite for death. Donne describes the provoking
of magistrates by would-be martyrs, and the arising of heretic martyr-sects,
some of which, like the Donatists and the Circumcelliones, dispensed with
the troublesome ritual of martyrdom and were frankly suicidal. "It becomes
any ingenuity to confess," he concludes, "that those times were affected with
a disease of this natural desire of such a death." At length the Church was
compelled to discourage martyrdom and to distinguish the true case from
the false. Gradually the illicit passion for martyrdom abated; in Donne's own
day it is to be observed only in the Jesuits—an accusation he was shortly to
develop more at length in his pamphlet, *Pseudo-Martyr*. "Only the Jesuits
boast of their hunting out of martyrdom in the new worlds, and of their rage
till they find it. . . . So that, if this desire of dying be not agreeable to the
nature of man, but against it, yet it seems that it is not against the nature of
a Jesuit." This interpretation of the early Christian lust for martyrdom, ending with a condemnation of the Jesuits on the same score (a fact not without
significance, as will be shown later), is especially remarkable for the shrewd

manner in which Donne distinguishes conscious from unconscious motives, and for his perception that the means may be altered while the motive remains the same.

In the fourth and last Distinction, Donne notes that suicide has been sanctioned in highly civilized countries, and condoned in special cases by thinkers so humane as Plato and Thomas More. Thus, "laws and customs of well-policed estates having admitted it, it is not likely to be against law of nature."

In this summary, the scholastic dialectic, the numerous citations of authors, and the discussion of doctrinal questions—all of which make this a somewhat thorny book—have been ignored in order to make clear the author's central thesis: that the desire of death is native to humanity. Donne returns to this thesis again and again with stubborn insistence, with terms like "this desire of death" (p. 61), "that natural desire of dying" (p. 91), "propenseness to martyrdom" (p. 58), "a natural infirmity of despising this life" (p. 67), "that desire of dying that nature had bred" (p. 68). And the nature of these terms indicates that he considered this desire as on the order of an instinctual phenomenon, rooted in the human mind and emotions.

Thus the First Part of *Biathanatos* is to be regarded as a primitive essay in psychology. Donne's treatise, moreover, is of special interest to the twentieth-century reader because of the new dignity and sanction that have been given to the theory of a death instinct in recent times. The modern theory, which has its classical statement in Sigmund Freud's *Beyond the Pleasure Principle* (1922), although it still remains in the twilight realm of scientific hypothesis, has now become so widely known and so generally applied in the interpretation of human behavior that few educated persons are ignorant of its implications. It is not extravagant to describe Donne's essay as a clear anticipation of the Freudian theory. It is true that the latter, which posits the existence of two contrary, complementary, and virtually all-inclusive instincts—a life (Eros) instinct and a death instinct—one creative and one destructive, claims a domain for the death instinct which is far broader than Donne envisioned for his relatively modest discovery. In judging the value of Donne's work, however, we should remark that he does much more than express a vague intuition. He gives a competent, penetrating survey of the death wish in history; and one needs only to compare in detail his interpretation of the fourth-century craze for martyrdom with the interpretation of the same events by Dr. Karl Menninger in his recent book on suicide, *Man Against Himself* (1938), to appreciate Donne's prescience and the depth of his intuition. His view of martyrdom is wholly corroborated by this eminent psychiatrist of the present day. Donne perceived also that a self-destructive impulse could express itself indirectly in various forms of self-punishment, and in fact came close to defining the concept of what is known as masochism: in particular he noted not only martyrdom, but fasting, self-mutilation, and the sacrifice of one's life for another. In thus identifying a single cause of diverse phenomena he was working the true vein of scientific discovery.

Donne appears to have had a special fondness for *Biathanatos*. Although he did not print it during his lifetime, probably because of its quasi-heretical views (he even hints at a death wish in Christ himself), he sent it for criticism to scholars of "both universities," who, according to Walton, "could find no flaw in it." When he travelled to Germany in 1619, he sent two copies to friends as a precaution against loss of the manuscript, forbidding either its destruction or its publication ("Both the press and the fire"). He shows a similar attachment to the theory expounded in it, and there is little reason to believe that he ever abandoned the essential idea of a death instinct. If we look for any fruitful development of this idea in his later writings, however, we are disappointed. There existed no adequate science dealing with such matters—only the empirical observations and untested theories that Burton collected so zealously in the *Anatomy of Melancholy*. Consequently Donne's theory undergoes no further development along the naturalistic line of inquiry he pursued in *Biathanatos*. Instead, it is transferred from the realm of psychology to that of theology; the concept of a principle of self-destruction appears now in theological rather than naturalistic or scientific terms, and it has been assimilated to conventional doctrine. Here is a significant utterance from a sermon:

> Was not God's judgment executed speedily enough upon thy soul, when in the same instant that it was created, and conceived, and infused, it was put to a necessity of contracting original sin, and so submitted to the penalty of Adam's disobedience, the first minute? Was not God's judgment speedily enough executed upon thy body, if before it had any temporal life, it had a spiritual death; a sinful conception, before any inanimation? If hereditary diseases from thy parents, gouts and epilepsies, were in thee, before the diseases of thine own purchase, the effects of thy licentiousness and thy riot; and that from the first minute that thou begannest to live, thou begannest to die too?[15]

In this passage there are several interesting notions, all characteristic of Donne's later expressions on this subject: the destructive principle is now equated with—or adapted to—original sin,[16] and this is paralleled with a physical principle of destruction or decay which is inherent in the body. Between the latter principle and the contemporary popular theory of "cosmic decay" (see note 11) an obvious association is to be made: they are variants of the same doctrine (or should we say judgment?), applied in one case to the individual and in the other to the cosmos. Probably we should be wise in this inquiry to content ourselves with noting these things. If we were to pursue these questions further, we should be in danger of finding more than is properly to be found in the productions of a mind which is not the systematizing mind of the philosopher. In summary, let it be said that Donne's later works, his sermons in particular, show him frequently concerned with several conceptions: a death instinct; original sin, considered especially as the source of spiritual death; and a principle of corruption and decay, universal in the material world, operating both in the individual and in the universe. Finally, that these conceptions are loosely connected in Donne's mind, and together they form a significant and dynamic element in his thought.

The persistence, in one form or another, of the idea of a death instinct in Donne's intellectual life may be attributed to the fact, which accords with the rule in such matters, that a wish for death was a permanent and constant element in his psychic life. Unlike literary and cultural influences, which may be transitory, it was always present, varying only in that it was now more and now less morbid or intense. It comes to the surface and breaks out in words in times of illness and depression. Of the three periods into which Donne's life divides—so conveniently that it is almost inevitable to follow this division—in the first the death wish is concealed under a hard ambivalence; in the second is discernible at times a feverish mood, close to surrender; and in the third a greater confidence and a calm resolution to bear the ills of life. Doubtless Donne's entrance into the ministry helped to fortify his resolution, but some of his moral struggle is also implicit in *Pseudo-Martyr,* a book written in 1609, not long after *Biathanatos,* and equally overlooked as a source of Donne's spiritual biography. In this tract against the Jesuits, Donne argues that the deaths of the Jesuits by execution in England are not genuine martyrdoms, because their motive is not the legitimate desire for the propagation of their faith, but rather a lust for self-destruction, which Donne now is coming to view as morbid and perverse. The development of this thesis from the interpretation of martyrdom in *Biathanatos* is obvious. This judgment of the Jesuits and what he saw as their pursuit of martyrdom was a settled conviction with Donne, and is more than once repeated in the sermons. But in so condemning them, not only was he condemning members of his own family (which, according to his Preface, could claim as many Jesuit martyrs in its number as any other of the same extent); he was also condemning something in himself, and announcing his victory over it.

Conquered or controlled though it may have been, his death wish was not destroyed or forgotten. In the transparent egoism often evident in the sermons—for which he has been duly rebuked by Mr. T. S. Eliot, and for which he once rebuked himself as "mingling a respect of myself in preach-

ing Thy word"—we can discern the zeal of the reformed sinner to tell of his
sin and his redemption. Not infrequently he engages in little homilies on
whether a Christian may desire death; whether he may legitimately court
death, as in a time of plague; whether suicide is ever permissible. Indeed
a certain irony attaches to the spectacle of Donne before those Jacobean
and Caroline congregations, who must have been robustious enough and
quite adequately devoted to this life, gravely arguing the moral imperatives
of these questions, and reproving "them in whom a weariness of this life,
when God's corrections are upon them, or some other mistaking of their
own estate and case, works an overhasty and impatient desire of death."[17]
In the numerous sermons (including many of his best) which have death
as their subject, although there is sometimes a note of horror and fascination, we look in vain for any genuine sentiment of repining or protest at
the fact of death. This is true even of the sermon Donne preached directly
after the death of his wife—doubtless the one person on earth to whom he
was most deeply attached. In the choice of a text ("I am the man who hath
seen affliction by the rod of his wrath") the personal note is inescapable;
but the sermon itself is a grave and impersonal call to Christian resignation.
The well-known sermon on the text, "What man is he that liveth, and shall
not see death?" ("the King being then dangerously sick at Newmarket"),
is less a prayer for the safety of his sovereign than an adjuration to receive
death calmly and in Christian temper. Other notable sermons on the subject are those on the deaths of Lady Danvers and of King James, the sermon
preached during the plague in 1626, and the last sermon. The solemn, reasoned conviction that governed Donne's later years is best expressed in the
grave and impressive sermon preached at Whitehall, February 29, 1627/8,
which is especially rich in autobiographical overtones. "Every man is bound
to do something, to take some calling upon him"; secondly, "to do seriously and sedulously and sincerely the duties of that calling"; and thirdly,
"the better to perform those duties, every man shall do well to propose to
himself some person, some pattern, some example whom he will follow and
imitate in that calling." Donne's own pattern for all—and for himself, we
may be sure—is "Christ's earliest witness, his proto-martyr, his first witness
Saint Stephen, and in him that which especially made him his witness, and
our example, is his death."[18] The theme of the sermon, significantly, is that
of Jeremy Taylor: how to live in preparation for death. Thus, finding spiritual satisfaction in preaching and solace in thoughts of the resurrection,
Donne expresses well his mature attitude toward death in *La Corona:*

> For, at our end begins our endlesse rest;
> The first last end, now zealously possest,
> With a strong sober thirst, my soul attends.

As for the question of the origin of Donne's death wish, it will be well, instead of elaborating conjectures, to seek again his own testimony. In the Preface to *Biathanatos* he suggests several possibilities, in a passage which, though already quoted in part, deserves to be quoted again more at length.

> I have often such a sickely inclination [to suicide]. And, whether it be, because I had my first breeding and conversation with men of a suppressed and afflicted Religion, accustomed to the despite of death, and hungry of an imagin'd Martyrdome; Or that the common Enemie find that doore worst locked against him in mee; Or that there bee a perplexitie and flexibility in the doctrine it selfe; Or because my Conscience ever assures me, that no rebellious grudging at Gods gifts nor other sinfull concurrence accompanies these thoughts in me; or that a brave scorn, or that a faint cowardlinesse beget it, whensoever any affliction assailes me, mee thinks I have the keyes of my prison in mine owns hand, and no remedy presents itselfe so soone to my heart, as mine own sword.

The only one of these suggestions that would recommend itself to modern thought on the subject is that which lays his suicidal tendency to early association with the fanatical Jesuits of his family. Though Donne turned away from their religion, and came to condemn their example, there is every reason to suppose that the effect of this contact on his young and sensitive mind was powerful and disturbing.[19] Martyrdom in particular was a special concern of Donne's throughout his life, as can be seen in his choice of Saint Stephen as his pattern and example. He had not in him the aggressive or destructive capacity that would have made suicide a possibility, and martyrdom probably remained his secret aspiration. His "meditation of martyrdom" is much in evidence in the sermons; and he was well aware of the element of pleasure in the sufferings of the martyrs: "certainly the joys that the martyrs felt at their deaths would make up a far greater body than their sorrows would do."[20] This poignant outcry in the poem "The Martyrs" would seem to express his own deeper feelings:

> let their blood come
> To begge for us, a discreet patience
> Of death, or of worse life: for Oh, to some
> Not to be Martyrs, is a martyrdome.

The period of Donne's boyhood—let us say about 1580—is precisely the period when there were many portents of the ultimate failure of the Roman cause in England; when consequently the Jesuits in their attempt to effect a counter-reformation had reached their most desperate, intransigent, and fanatical state of mind. We may count John Donne as in some degree an innocent victim of this historic struggle. The apparent contradiction in the suggestion that Donne was psychically infected by Jesuit fanaticism (or what he indubitably regarded as such) while at the same time he consciously rejected the cause and purposes of the Jesuits, is not a real one. The conscious and unconscious minds can readily take divergent paths.

The later history of Donne's religious sentiments corroborates the belief that he reacted emotionally to Jesuit influence. It is probable that we have here, in his consciousness of a private grievance against the Jesuits, the real reason for his abandonment of Roman Catholicism. In his conversion to the English Church he never became anti-Catholic. Grierson has remarked that the poem, "Show me, dear Christ, thy spouse so bright and clear," composed in 1617, reveals Donne still doubtful, after two years in the Anglican ministry, whether his choice had been right. In preaching he often took the position that it is relatively indifferent by what road or what faith one finds his way to God; such tolerance was pretty rare in those days. His theology was almost perfectly orthodox, according to the conclusion made by Husain in a detailed study; such orthodoxy, in an intellect so singularly independent as Donne's, is a sure sign that he was not fundamentally interested in the intellectual basis of religion, in doctrinal differences. If he was not anti-Catholic, however, he was firmly, even violently, anti-Jesuit. His antipathy to the Jesuits, some evidence of which has already been cited in this study, can be seen everywhere through his works; it is significant that it was against them that he directed the two polemical pamphlets we have from his hand, *Pseudo-Martyr* and the bitterly satirical *Ignatius his Conclave*.

The question which will be of greatest interest to students of Donne is the effect of the death wish on the creation of Donne the artist and poet. Here, although the taboos against the expression of sentiments such as Donne entertained were even stronger then than now, both direct and indirect effects can nonetheless be traced. It is true that death most commonly figures in the poems, as a conventional metaphor for departure or absence; and that naughtier metaphor so much fancied by the Elizabethans also occurs frequently. But in certain poems death figures in a more vital way. Donne's obsession with the physical conditions of the grave comes to the fore at times. In "The Funerall" he pictures himself dead by his mistress' scorn, and asks those who come to shroud him not to touch the wreath of her hair on his arm. "The Relique" has the same theme; the bracelet of hair is found on Donne's skeleton when, in the distant future, his grave is dug up to make room for a new occupant. "The Dampe" begins with the cheerful imagination of an autopsy of the poet's body. In "The Apparition," one of the most savage of the poems in its bitter hatred, he pictures himself dead, his ghost returning to plague his faithless mistress in another's bed. These poems have a quiet, untheatrical horror that is thoroughly in the baroque manner. The clearest revelation, however, is to be found in the second of the two *Anniversaries*. These poems, long something of a puzzle to critics because of their medieval amorphousness, have been described by Grierson as a *de contemptu mundi* and "an impassioned and exalted *meditatio mortis*." Although this is a good description of their content and purpose, we should look beyond their analogues in theology to their more personal origins.

Thus in the *Second Anniversary*, when it is stripped of religious exhortation and conventional sentiment, there remains a clear and poignant expression of a longing for death. Some lines have a fevered, frenetic quality, like those where the poet exhorts his soul to welcome "Gods great *Venite*":

> Thirst for that time, O my insatiate soule,
> And serve thy thirst, with Gods safe-sealing Bowle.
> Be thirstie still, and drinke still till thou goe
> To th' only Health, to be Hydroptique so.
> Forget this rotten world . . .
> Be not concern'd: studie not why, nor when—

In a sustained passage of thirty-five lines (85–120) he urges his soul to think gladly and eagerly of death, conjuring up in a succession of grisly images all the intimate circumstances of his deathbed. These are passages that criticism has tended to pass over in favor of the later parts, where Donne attains a note of confidence and affirmation in speaking of the intercession of Christ and of the Resurrection; but their tendency and impulse cannot be ignored.

Beyond these more direct and obvious expressions, we now have a key to some of the motives of Donne's love poetry more meaningful than the facile notion that he represents a "reaction" to an outmoded fashion in sentiment. The protestations of indifference and callousness, the disparagements of women, the exaltation of carnality, the impudent praise of inconstancy, the vituperation of the hate poems—in fact, much of the alleged "realism" of Donne's treatment of love may have its explanation in these words of a modern student of the mind: "Persons prone to suicide prove upon examination to be highly *ambivalent* in their object attachments, that is, masking with their conscious positive attachments large and scarcely mastered quantities of unconscious hostility."[21] To those better informed in such matters than the present writer, the death wish may well be the clue to what has often been regarded as the enigma of Donne's personality.

Lastly, a few words by way of summary and conclusion. I have attempted to trace a single impulse in John Donne's unconscious mind, its origin and its effects. I have tried to show that it accounts for certain aspects of his conduct and his work that criticism has hitherto tended to shy away from; that it reveals the true base of a good deal in his complex of ideas; that it supplies a key to motives of his art and aspects of his personality that are less immediate, and that Donne was a powerful and original thinker on subjects that have been thoroughly explored only in recent times. In the story that has been told there is much that is unpleasant and even painful. Indeed, to those who, like Gustave Aschenbach, lack "sympathy with the depths," it may even appear unseemly that such a story should be told at all. Then too, it might be objected with some justice that such a study, with its inevitable emphasis on sickly phenomena, might distort our judgment of a man whose career, seen in a larger view, was actually one of vigorous accomplishment. But it is open to question whether any discredit is reflected at last upon John Donne. For the story is that of a struggle which is among the bitterest and most heroic in human experience: carried on through a lifetime, not against an outer, but against a silent inner enemy, and it ended in the main in victory. It was carried on with an unrelenting earnestness. Sentiments such as Donne's have been felt by other poets and in other ages, and it is instructive to compare his christianly courage with the mood of later poets in expressing similar feelings—with the dilettantism of Keats (in "Ode to a Nightingale"); the self-abasement of Leopardi (in *A Se Stesso*); the defiant impudence of Swinburne (in "The Garden of Proserpine"); the pagan abandon of Whitman (in "Out of the Cradle Endlessly Rocking"). It can be said in the twentieth century, which in some respects is better informed than the nineteenth, that Donne, in rejecting such self-indulgence was wiser and sounder than any of these.

## NOTES

1. Edmund Gosse, *The Life and Letters of John Donne* (New York and London, 1899), I, 190–191. Hereafter referred to as Gosse.

2. Gosse, I, 173.

3. Gosse, I, 189.

4. Gosse, II, 15.

5. Gosse, II, 45.

6. John Donne, *Devotions upon Emergent Occasions together with Death's Duel* (London: Simpkin, The Abbey Classics, n.d.), Meditation 16.

7. Hugh I. Fausset, *John Donne: A Study in Discord* (London, 1924), describes vividly the manner in which Donne's mind was possessed by the image of death in his later years. His explanation of this prepossession, however—that Donne dwelt upon that image in order to mitigate the horror that death held for him—is interesting only for being an exact inversion of the true one.

8. John Donne, *Devotions upon Emergent Occasions together with Death's Duel* (London: Simpkin, The Abbey Classics, n.d.), p. 176.

9. *Ibid.*, p. 171.

10. *Ibid.*, pp. 167–170.

11. Charles Monroe Coffin, *John Donne and the New Philosophy* (New York: Columbia University Press, 1937), chapter xiv, "A Sensible Decay of the World," discusses Donne's thought in relation to the conception here described in the popular form which it took in the early seventeenth century of the theory of "cosmic decay." This theory supplies the main theme of Donne's *First Anniversary*. But Professor Coffin's conclusion, that "it is . . . dangerous to regard Donne as an apostle of the doctrine of the world's decay" (p. 279), is based upon a somewhat belabored interpretation of a single passage in a sermon of about 1621, from which the conclusion is drawn that Donne abandoned this theory; it ignores the repeated expressions of the idea, in one form or another, from the *Paradoxes and Problems* to the last sermon. As will be shown later, it is probably unwise to consider the theory of cosmic decay apart from other cognate elements in Donne's thought.

12. Gosse, i, 184.

13. John Donne, *Juvenilia, or Certain Paradoxes and Problems*, facsimile edition (New York: Columbia University Press, 1936).

14. Reproduced by the Facsimile Text Society (New York, 1930).

15. Henry Alford, editor, *The Works of John Donne* (London, 1839), v, 461–462 (hereafter referred to as Alford). This sermon is dated 1616.

16. Donne often describes original sin as a principle or cause of spiritual death. It is not the idea, which is a commonplace ("The wages of sin is death"), but the directness of his language, the verbalism, which is interesting.

> It is not Adam, which is another name of man, and signifies nothing but *red earth;* let it be earth red with blood (with that murder which we have done upon ourselves), let it be earth red with blushing (so the word is used in the original) with a conscience of our own infirmity, what wonder that man, that is but Adam, guilty of this self-murder in himself, guilty of this inborn frailty in himself, die too? (Alford, i, 502–503.)

> Every sinner is an executioner upon himself. (Mistranslated from Augustine; Alford, ii, 105.)

> Man by sin induced death upon himself at first . . . Death then is from ourselves, it is our own. (Alford, vi, 53.)

> Of the shadow of death wherein I sit there is no cause but mine own corruption (Alford, v, 472.) death . . . is produced from me and is mine own creature (*Devotions upon Emergent Occasions, Meditation,* xv.)

> My heart is by dejection, clay,
> And by self-murder, red. *(The Litany.)*

17. Alford, i, 303.

18. Alford, v, 605.

19. See Alfred Adler, *The Neurotic Constitution* (New York, 1921), p. 208: "The most powerful psychic hold originates from the thoughts of death in childhood which produce a constant predisposition to suicide by shaping the psychic physiognomy under the influence of the egotistic idea."

20. Alford, I, 149. *Cf.* also I, 328–329.

21. Dr. Karl A. Menninger, *Man Against Himself* (New York: Harcourt, Brace and Company, 1938), p. 32.

PHOEBE S. SPINRAD

# Death, Loss, and Marvell's Nymph

It may not be so simplistic as it sounds to say that Marvell's "The Nymph Complaining for the Death of Her Faun" is a traditional poem. Indeed, so many strands of tradition are woven into the poem that the reader may easily overlook the completed fabric in following the various threads of convention. And thus critics have interpreted the poem as a political, religious, or romantic allegory; as a metaphoric lament for innocence, an old order, Christ, or love; and as a literal lament for a pet or—in one reading that borders on self-parody[1]—for a child.

Paradoxically enough, all these interpretations are both true and false. That is, none can be taken alone; each must be combined with seemingly contradictory patterns to form one larger pattern that includes them all. Therefore, in tracing the development of these theories, I raise objections only to the sole validity of a particular subpattern, not to its validity within the overall pattern.

One theory arises from the very first lines of the poem: "The wanton Troopers riding by / Have shot my Faun and it will die."[2] This image is a markedly contemporary one; the fawn has been "shot" rather than slain with an arrow, and the "troopers," as both Nicholas Guild and Earl Miner have pointed out, are most likely Cromwellian soldiers, of whom the word "trooper" was first used. Although Miner incorporates the political overtones of

---

*PMLA*, Volume 97, Number 1 (January 1982): pp. 50–59. Copyright © 1982 Modern Language Association of America.

"Troopers" into a more generalized lament for innocence and the pastoral order, Guild sees the entire poem as topical: a thinly disguised elegy for the old order in England, coupled with a grateful recognition that the old will indeed yield place to new. Both critics base a good deal of their argument on a passage in Book vii of the *Aeneid*, in which the slaying of Sylvia's deer by Iulus leads to war between the Trojans and the Latins and to the subsequent establishment of Rome in Italy.[3]

But if Marvell had wished to affirm the implacable destiny of Cromwell's new Rome, he would hardly allow his nymph, a sympathetic figure in the poem, to state so definitively that the troopers are "wanton," "guilty," and incapable of salvation or forgiveness. Of course, Marvell may be creating a naive persona in the nymph, one whose political innocence about the coming of the new order will evoke the more sophisticated reader's enlightened pity. But it may be helpful to look more closely at the *Aeneid* itself before accepting this reading.

Sylvia's deer (not a fawn, but a *cervus*, a grown deer) is both tame and wild. Its antlers are decorated and it returns home when it is wounded ("nota intra tecta refugit" 'he returns in flight to his familiar dwelling'), but it is in the habit of ranging the countryside for food and sport. When it does return wounded, it clamors for attention, and Sylvia, taking up the clamor, shouts for help until all her rough kin gather and prepare for war: "palmis percussat lacertos, / auxilium vocat, et duros conclamat agrestes" 'she beats her arms with her hands, cries for help, and calls her countrymen together' (vii.503–504).[4]

The tone of this passage is singularly unlike that of Marvell's poem. Although both contain a dying animal and a young girl, and although Sylvia's cry for help seems to be echoed in the nymph's "O help! O help! I see it faint" (l. 93), the similarities end there. Vergil's poem emphasizes the noise and uproar that surround the death of the deer and echoes the tumult in a series of clanging spondees within the verse. Marvell's poem follows the nymph's cry with an insistence on the calm demeanor of the dying fawn and a static display of its slowly dropping tears—a deliberate slowing down and softening of the action. Even the calls for help are dissimilar. Sylvia fully expects a response to her outcry, as well as rapid action to avenge both her personal injury and the affront to her people, and the Latins fulfill her expectations on a grand Vergilian scale. The nymph, however, is crying out in a solitary desperation that knows it will receive no answer, and she has specifically waived any demand for vengeance in the first twenty-four lines of the poem. Sylvia's is a cry of anger; the nymph's, of helpless grief.

While the political upheaval in England may have moved Marvell to write a lament, the political allegory alone is insufficient to account for this difference in tone, for Sylvio's behavior, and for the specifically Christian symbolism surrounding the fawn in parts of the poem. The various religious

interpretations may come closer. But even here, the amorous exchange between Sylvio and the nymph in lines 25–36 partakes too much of the often
trivial wordplay of the love sonneteers to be applicable to such a subject; the
deliberate toying with the emotions in this passage is out of place in a discussion of conceptual matters such as churches and doctrines.

To account for such amorous conceits and for the erotic imagery in general, some religious allegorists identify the fawn with Christ rather than with
the Church, relying for their exegesis primarily on the Song of Songs just as
the political allegorists rely on the *Aeneid*. This is perhaps fitting, since it is a
standard theological exercise to interpret the Song of Songs as an exemplum
of Christ's love for his Church, but there may be some problems in trying to
use a metaphor of a metaphor as a literal text.

There is certainly no lack of Christian symbolism in the poem. And
Donald M. Friedman, who sees the religious parallel almost to the exclusion
of all others, even attempts to deal with the blood imagery in lines 83–84
("Upon the Roses it would feed / until its Lips ev'n seem'd to bleed") that
some of his colleagues ignore. The bloody lip prints, he says, connect the fawn
and the nymph by a "serious metaphor" distinctly Christian in its foreshad-
owing of the fawn's "martyrdom," which the nymph, or Christian, must share
with Christ. This is a good attempt to deal with a rather disconcerting image,
but Friedman's insistence on limiting the "serious metaphor" to a Christian
one causes further problems in his delineation of the garden. He remarks, for
example, that the colors of the flowers are "the commonplace visual signs of
carnal beauty in the female"; then, by a sort of free association, he declares
that the flowers can therefore "only be reminiscent of liturgical imagery of
Christ and, most particularly, of the 'beloved' in the Song of Songs."[5] This non
sequitur is difficult to understand.

Furthermore, if the "wanton Troopers" are to be taken as killers of
Christ—in either the literal sense of Roman soldiers or the metaphorical
sense of sinners—then the blood imagery becomes confused. The nymph's
words appear to deny the traditional Christian image of the soul's cleansing
by the blood of Christ:

> Though they should wash their guilty hands
> In this warm life blood, which doth part
> From thine, and wound me to the Heart,
> Yet could they not be clean: their Stain
> Is dy'd in such a Purple Grain. (ll. 18–22)

The lack of cleansing efficacy in this blood hints of a sin beyond redemption, a suggestion that is alien to the Christian concept, particularly if the
fawn is taken as a specifically Anglican Christ. In fact, if the next two lines

did not reintroduce the image of the Lamb (or fawn) of God, the ineffectual washing of the hands would be more reminiscent of Lady Macbeth or the assassins in *Julius Caesar.*

It is interesting to note other ways in which Marvell undercuts his Christian imagery by juxtaposing it with more secular imagery. One of the most obvious, of course, is the nymph's rapid transition, in lines 24–25, from the Lamb of God to "unconstant Sylvio." Again, the contrast between the fawn's love and that of "false and cruel men" (ll. 53–54) is brought back to a secular level—one that is almost as poetically fashionable as Sylvio's puns—in lines 57–62, where the fawn's physical attributes are compared with those of the nymph and "any Ladies of the Land." What might have been a consideration of the degrees of divine and earthly love has here been reduced to a Petrarchan convention.

During the actual death of the fawn, too, Marvell alternates Christian and classical images. To be sure, pagan symbolism was often Christianized in the period, but seldom is the contrast between the two traditions as deliberately pointed as it is here. And the animal in an afterworld is pagan not only in imagery but in doctrine. It may be argued that if the fawn is a symbol of Christ, the Holy Spirit, or the Anglican church, then it would very likely go to an "Elizium," along with the saints who are poetically metamorphosed into swans, doves, lambs, and ermines; that in fact the "vanish'd" of line 105 may suggest the rising from the tomb, or the Ascension. But the design of the nymph's tomb, focusing not on the fawn but on the weeping statue of the nymph, denies any linking of the fawn with Christ crucified or risen. The fawn, lying at her feet like a faithful dog on a tombstone or a symbolic animal at the feet of a goddess in a classical frieze, is, by the end of the poem, perhaps still an extraworldly creature but certainly not Christ.

Geoffrey H. Hartman, in dealing with the Christian allegory, takes a tentative step toward a more comprehensive understanding of the poem, recognizing some of the psychological stages through which the nymph goes: the substitution of one love object for another in a series of losses that can never be quite compensated for. But he places this sequence only in the religious context of the progress of the soul, thereby postulating the fawn as the Comforter, or Holy Spirit.[6] Unfortunately, this reading forces him into the unlikely position of further postulating Sylvio as Christ, since Sylvio is the giver of the Comforter. No matter how much Hartman then tries to skew the unfavorable description of Sylvio into theologically acceptable terms (Sylvio-Christ only *seems* "unconstant" and "wild" because the earthbound soul cannot grasp his divine nature), the analogy remains incongruous.

As for the religious symbolism of the fawn and the garden in the Song of Songs, one can only agree that the imagery is similar to Marvell's, although Marvell's use of it may raise certain questions about real differences between the nymph's garden and the biblical one; for instance, the "beloved" in the Song "feedeth among lilies," whereas the fawn feeds, as will be seen, among some rather ambiguous roses. But the imagery in the Song of Songs is also common to a certain type of love literature, and to claim religious significance for it wherever it occurs is to reason backward. (One might just as easily claim that after John Donne all references to fleas must imply a love union.)

Still, attempting to produce a love allegory by interpreting the Song of Songs analogue secularly does not seem to suffice either, and within the allegory of lost love the critical view of the nymph herself sometimes becomes rather disapproving. Harold E. Toliver, for example, decries the nymph because the world she tries to create is false and thus vulnerable to any intrusion on her fantasy. She herself is partially to blame for the death of the fawn, he suggests, as well as for the departure of Sylvio, because she will not mix any warmth with her "cold passivity." Even Rosalie Colie, who sees the nymph more as a pastoral artist than as a jilted young woman, regards her as "myopically self-regarding," adding that "her garden and her pet are, in the end, projections of herself and her own strongly aesthetic needs." And Lawrence W. Hyman, who does attempt to incorporate some of the religious imagery into his dichotomy between "innocent love" and "adult passion," still sees the nymph as somehow insufficient, in that she has tried to create a Garden of Eden that is no longer accessible to humankind.[7]

One of the dangers in dealing with the love allegory is the temptation to base too much of one's argument on the question of sexuality. Hyman in particular appears to see sexuality in everything surrounding the nymph: her play with the fawn, the flowers in her garden, the troopers, and even her tears. For such critics, whether Sylvio has seduced the nymph becomes an important matter of speculation, as though a woman could not have her heart broken unless she had first had her maidenhead broken. Therefore, although these love allegorists begin to approach the major pattern of the poem, they are hampered by a different sort of exclusionary vision.

Leo Spitzer and Earl Miner seem to come closest to the whole pattern.[8] Spitzer in particular sees that something about the nymph and her fawn is doomed within the context of the poem, but instead of placing his emphasis on the nymph's physical purity, he refers to "the superhuman that is present in the physical" (p. 240), the quintessential purity of beauty itself. Such a view helps to explain the juxtaposition of syntactic simplicity and metaphysical wit in the poem; it reflects, he says, "the contrast of sadness and beauty" (p. 243).

Earl Miner takes a step further in this approach. The political, the religious, and the romantic interpretations of this poem are all possible simultaneously, he says, because what is lost or dying is innocence itself—not sexual purity, not the old world order, not pure religion, not even Sylvio or the fawn or the nymph herself, but all of these. Things must naturally progress from simplicity to complexity and in doing so must necessarily draw other things after them (pp. 10–11). Hence the fawn must eventually die, either physically or symbolically; as the girl becomes a woman, the fawn becomes a deer, and existence itself necessitates change. What Miner calls "the death of innocence," then, begins to emerge as the age-old theme of mutability and the transience of all things.

Because of the universality of this pattern, I want to develop it in a somewhat unorthodox manner: by citing analogues not only in the classics, Renaissance literature, and folklore but also in the literature of later centuries. It is always dangerous, of course, to compare the productions of one period with those of a later one (as in the standard joke about the critic who demonstrated T. S. Eliot's influence on Spenser); but since I contend that the overall pattern is timeless, I must use these later writers—some of whom deliberately returned to the Renaissance for their imagery—if only as interpreters or elaborators of Marvell's theme. And surely the critical understanding of these poets should be given at least as much weight as that of twentieth-century scholars.

But before I pursue the important point about mutability, I should like to examine the poem not as an allegory but as a psychological journey through the nymph's mind. And here another pattern becomes recognizable: a depiction of the human response to death—the death of a loved one or of oneself. Again, this depiction is not to be taken as the sole pattern, only as one of many, though perhaps, like the missing piece of a jigsaw puzzle, the one that will bring all the other pieces together.

In brief, the nymph's mind goes through a series of responses. At the first confrontation with death or loss, the mind goes into an initial and transitory shock as it states the situation to itself (ll. 1–2). This response is followed quickly by the secondary shock, or disbelief, in which the mind refuses to accept what it has stated (ll. 3–6), and then by bewilderment and a sense of injustice (ll. 7–12), which in turn lead to anger and protest at the injustice (ll. 12–24). The first movement toward philosophical acceptance (ll. 25–54) begins with a forced remembrance of the thing lost, along with an attempt at sardonicism about *all* loss (ll. 25–36). This sardonicism leads to the next stage, a focusing on the self as just in contrast with a world that is unjust (ll. 37–46). But the tone is wrong for comfort; unnaturally brittle in the first stage, it becomes cynical in the last stage, a speculation on what might have been and the possible unworthiness of the thing mourned (ll. 47–54). Since this answer is both untrue and unacceptable, it is rejected (ll. 53–54).

Once realism has turned for support to cynicism or to syllogisms that will not hold, the mind then allows itself to dwell on the merits of the thing lost and to idealize it, perhaps in apology for having maligned it (ll. 55–92). This reminiscence, which is less forced than the initial one, takes three stages: first the thing lost is seen as a static display in relation to the self (ll. 55–62);

next the thing lost is seen in motion as it lived, with the beginning of recognition that its nature is to move away from the self (ll. 63–70); and finally
the thing lost is elevated to an emblem of life itself (ll. 71–90). This final
reminiscence, like the first one, culminates in another speculation on what
might have been, this time in an idealized version that is as faulty as the
cynical one (ll. 91–92).

Idealism and cynicism both having failed, the mind returns with a shock
to the reality of loss (ll. 93–94), seeing with a magnifying vision the small
physical details of the thing that is slipping away (ll. 95–100). The search for
comfort now begins in earnest (ll. 101–122), first in attempting to fix per-
manently relics of the thing lost (ll. 101–104), next in seeking immortality
in an afterlife (ll. 105–110), and finally in seeking an earthly immortality in
monuments, often in art (ll. 111–122). But a recognition that the monuments
themselves hold a potential for loss runs concurrently with this last search
for immortality (ll. 117–122), and so the mind returns full circle, having been
comforted only partially, and then primarily through catharsis.

That this pattern of mind is ageless and universal is evident in the way
the poem's imagery and turns of phrase show up in all literary genres, from
the earliest to the most recent. The very opening of the nymph's complaint
echoes a child's nursery rhyme. Her bewilderment already beginning to surface in her first statement of fact—if the troopers are "wanton" and only "riding by," there is no purpose to their act—she blurts out her distress ("... Thou
ne'er dids't alive / them any harm") in the phraseology of "Ding Dong Bell":

> What a wicked boy was that
>     To drown poor little pussycat
> Who never did him any harm
>     But chased the rats from his father's barn.

It is interesting to note how the nymph rephrases this elementary response in her first, cynical reminiscence:

> How could I less
> Than love it? O I cannot be
> Unkind, t'a Beast that loveth me. (ll. 44–46)

She has progressed here from the nursery rhyme to the Book of Job: from
the concern for another to the concern for self (Job, after all, never spared
much sympathy for his stricken family and livestock), from sorrow to self-
justification. These lines, significantly, form a bridge between her attempt
to speak like Sylvio and her less successful attempt to indulge in "sour
grapes" about the fawn. Having mentally linked Sylvio with the troopers,

both of whom have destroyed something beautiful, she unconsciously becomes one of them; she begins to be "unkind," if only verbally, "t'a Beast that loveth" her.

Paradoxically enough, this disparaging of the loved one is a necessary stage in the acceptance of loss. The forced remembrance that precedes it reflects the natural tendency of the mind to link the present loss with all losses; to see death and pain as part of the human condition, something that the child's rhyme cannot do. But the nymph's self-justification, an attempt to place herself outside the human condition of *giving* pain, works just opposite to her intent and increases her own pain.

It is a sign of her discomfort with this line of reasoning that she has begun to speak in the conditional mood and to qualify her statements with such phrases as "I do not know / Whether" (ll. 47–48) and "I am sure, for ought that I / Could . . . espie" (ll. 51–52). She is learning, if only subconsciously, that there is no comfort in denying the need for comfort and that, given the universal nature of grief for loss, any attempts to magnify the self and diminish the thing lost not only fail to explain the real pain that she is feeling but add to the universal store of pain.

Since the pain cannot be reasoned away, the nymph gives in to it and dwells on the beauty of the thing lost so that she can analyze her grief into something logical enough to be dealt with. Her description of the fawn's beauty has proved the richest hunting ground for critics seeking allegories and for later poets searching for images with which to describe their own grief at the transience of beauty.

In these lines, when divorced from the more blatant political and religious overtones of the trooper passage, the fawn itself begins to take on a more folkloric quality than before. Its speed, grace, and whiteness and its capering on "little silver feet" (l. 64) suggest the evanescence of the unicorn, that mythic symbol of innocence. (The conjunction of "silver" with "feet" may also suggest quicksilver, another emblem of evanescence and, as I show later, of poison.) Certainly the recurrent emphasis on the fawn's whiteness strengthens the suggestion of innocence, since whiteness has always been a Western symbol of purity. But since purity in this sense is an absolute, any diminution of it necessarily destroys it; hence purity becomes so vulnerable that it is almost dangerous to itself. It is this feeling of danger, of beauty poised on the edge of destruction, that Yeats captures perfectly in a passage from *Coole Park and Ballylee, 1931* that might be an illustration of Marvell's poem:

> Another emblem there! That stormy white
> But seems a concentration of the sky;
> And, like the soul, it sails into the sight
> And in the morning's gone, no man knows why;

And is so lovely that it sets to right
What knowledge or its lack had set awry,
So arrogantly pure, a child might think
It can be murdered with a spot of ink.[9]

This is the "Tarry, thou art so fair!" of Goethe's *Faust*; but it must be remembered that at the moment of trying to fix beauty in place Faust calls down destruction upon himself.

Folktales are filled with this dangerous beauty. One tale after another speaks of magic castles and gardens that will vanish if the hero tries to speak, touch them, or look too closely at them. To be inviolate, the beautiful thing must remain external to the self and must be allowed to move at will, whether away from or toward the watcher. It is the sad face of this paradox that the beauty *will* in fact be lost, whether it moves away of its own volition or vanishes at the "spot of ink," the touch of the incautious hero. An interesting variation on this theme occurs in *Through the Looking Glass*, where the fawn runs away as soon as he and Alice have emerged from the wood where things have no names. The act of naming is in itself an attempt to fix the nature of beauty.

The fleetness of the fawn is itself a traditional image. Any of Marvell's readers who have even a passing acquaintance with the classics are immediately struck by the echoes of those fleeting years in perhaps the most famous of Horace's odes: "Eheu fugaces, Postume, Postume, / labuntur anni" 'Ah, Postumus, Postumus, how the fleeting years slip by.'[10] And this fawn, like the years, is always in a state of slipping by, of running from the nymph and remaining uncontrollable and external to her. Only when it stands and touches her does the dangerous "spot of ink" appear.

Much critical attention has been given to the nymph's garden, and indeed almost any interpretation of it is possible. It is both tame and wild, echoing the antithesis of tameness and wildness in the nymph's discourse on Sylvio (l. 34). Its lilies are formally bedded (l. 77), but the garden is also "over grown" into "a little Wilderness" with them and with those puzzling roses (ll. 72–74). Critics who decry the artificiality and insularity of the garden may find it helpful to recall that, though pastoral poets of the time sometimes admire a natural state of growth, in Renaissance drama the "wilderness" or untended garden is often a symbol of corruption. The unweeded garden in *Hamlet* has certainly become famous, and equally famous is the Duchess of Malfi's "I am going into a wilderness."[11] But something else has begun to appear in these unweeded gardens and wildernesses, an image of that spot of ink which is present in both the nymph's garden and the gardens of later poets.

Shortly before the Duchess of Malfi speaks of going into her wilderness, her brother Ferdinand cautions her: "You live in a rank pasture here, i' th' court; / There is a kind of honey-dew that's deadly: / 'T will poison your fame . . ."

(1.i. 306–308). This image of the poisoned flower, usually a flower associated with love, is virtually inseparable from the roses that make the fawn's lips seem to "bleed" (ll. 83–84). Although Leo Spitzer assumes this bleeding to be merely a manifestation of the traditional lover's "bleeding heart" (p. 237), the rose being an emblem of love in the language of the flowers, there is surely more to the image than this. The only other blood imagery in the poem is associated with the fawn's death in the passage about the troopers: the fawn there is bleeding to death; its blood will not cleanse the troopers' guilty hands; and those hands are stained "in such a Purple Grain" with blood, blood, blood. The connection of blood with death is too firmly made to allow it to take on an entirely different meaning in the later passage.

There is something poisonous about these roses, something that Keats recognizes in his "Ode on Melancholy":

> She dwells with Beauty—Beauty that must die;
>     And Joy, whose hand is ever at his lips
> Bidding adieu; and aching Pleasure nigh,
>     Turning to poison while the bee-mouth sips. . . . [12]

Something, too, that Hawthorne develops in "Rappaccini's Daughter," where the "print" of those beautiful, bloodstained lips is the kiss of mortality. And something, as well, that Tennyson sees in *Maud*. His young man, whose motivation is as ambiguous as that of Hawthorne's hero, unquestionably seems to be thinking both of the "honey-dew that's deadly" and of the nymph's fawn. Speaking of Maud in what he later discovers to be an erroneous metaphor, since he himself is the destructive force in the garden, he says:

> And most of all would I flee from the cruel madness of love,
> The honey of poison-flowers and all the measureless ill.
> Ah Maud, you milkwhite fawn, you are all unmeet for a wife. . . .
> You have but fed on the roses, and lain in the lilies of life.[13]

Later in the poem, when the young man (like the troopers or Sylvio) has destroyed the innocence and integrity of the garden, he makes the same connection between roses and blood:

> But I know where a garden grows,
> Fairer than aught in the world beside,
> All made up of the lily and rose . . .
> It is only flowers, they had no fruits,
> And I almost fear they are not roses but blood. . . . (p. 342)

Roses and lilies, as any critic will be quick to point out, are traditionally used together to represent the Petrarchan ideal of feminine beauty; the roses, separately, carry overtones of youth; the lilies, of purity. Even in folktales, Rose Red and Snow White are often inseparable sisters. But, associated with blood, the roses may perhaps be glancing at another literary convention: the flower as an emblem of the shortness and futility of life, as in countless seventeenth-century carpe them poems and this sixteenth-century "May Song":

The life of man is but a span;
  It blossoms as the flower.
It makes no stay: is here today
And vanish'd in the hour.[14]

In this regard, the roses make even the lilies seem ominous, and the fawn's delight in folding "its pure virgin Limbs . . . / In whitest sheets of Lillies cold" (ll. 89–90) after eating the roses may suggest that the cold sheets of lilies are winding-sheets.

"Lillies without, Roses within" (l. 92) is probably one of the most exqui-sitely beautiful images in English poetry. But one of the things that make the line so beautiful is its poignancy: it cannot exist. The nymph has returned here to her contrary-to-fact conditionals: "Had it liv'd long" (l. 91), it would have come to this, but it will not live long. This is the same phrasing that the nymph uses in her earlier, cynical reflection (l. 47), and neither speculation is valid.

That the lilies and roses are almost like matter and antimatter, self-doomed from the start, is apparent in almost all the imagery surrounding the nymph, her fawn, and their garden. The nymph cannot remain childlike; the fawn, "had it liv'd long," must have become a grown deer; and the "Spring time of the year" (l. 75) must turn to winter and the flowers die. The bleeding lips of the fawn are a symbol of mortality, and the "Lillies without" carry their own death within; they "dwell with Beauty—Beauty that must die."

This realization, too, is a necessary stage through which the mind must pass in learning to deal with death and loss: to understand their universal necessity and to develop a unity with all pain. The thing lost is a symbol of all loss—and paradoxically, mourning for the individual loss soothes the hurt of all the losses that have gone before. In this respect, seeing the fawn as a surro-gate love, the love allegorists approach the larger pattern, but the image of the dying fawn absorbs into itself more than the death of a lover; it epitomizes the passing of all "quick bright things [that] come to confusion."[15]

Seeing the nymph as self-centered and as exaggerating her loss, Rosalie Colie appears to miss the point in decrying the nymph's ensuing grief ritual: "Niobe after all lost *all* her children; this girl has lost a single white deer" (p. 131). Samuel Johnson is more perceptive about the matter:

We always make a secret comparison between a part and the
whole; the termination of any period of life reminds us that life
itself has likewise its termination; when we have done any thing
for the last time, we involuntarily reflect that a part of the days
allotted us is past, and that as more is past there is less remaining.
. . . [B]y vicissitude of fortune, or alteration of employment, by
change of place, or loss of friendship, we are forced to say of.
something, *this is the last*.[16]

What Colie sees as the nymph's unnecessary pother over her own and her
fawn's tears is actually a valuable lesson that the nymph must learn and that the
poet is leading the reader to learn: by universalizing the idea of pain, she will
be able to transcend the thoughtless cruelty of the troopers and Sylvio—not
by imitating it, as she tried to do in her cynical stage, but by understanding
the pain of things outside the self. Like any other human creature, the nymph
does attempt to salvage physical relics of the thing lost in a last effort to fix the
transient beauty, but it is interesting to observe what she does with her vial of
tears, her own pain and the fawn's mingled in the Vergilian tears of things.

In all the controversy over "*Diana's* Shrine" (l. 104), two relatively important points seem to have been overlooked. Diana may represent the chas-
tity or purity violated in the killing of the fawn, or Innocence, and Diana is
the goddess of the hunt, a point that has caused some critical bemusement.
But the two objects sacred to Diana are the deer and the cypress tree, and
in discussing the deer Cyparissus accidentally slays in Ovid's *Metamorpho-
ses*, most critics seem to have overlooked the significance of the cypress tree:
that Cyparissus' transformation became sacred to Diana, not because he had
killed a deer, but because he felt grief for its unnecessary death. In the same
way, critics who mention Diana's revenge against Actaeon—her turning him
into a deer who is killed by his own hunting dogs—find unanswerable the
question this allusion raises; they fail to see the implications in the legend
that Actaeon is not only punished but taught a lesson about the sanctity of
things connected with Diana, including her sacred deer. In some versions of
the legend, Actaeon-turned-deer is even described as weeping while he dies,
like the nymph's fawn.

Diana's shrine, then, is a perfectly logical place for the nymph's vial of
tears; the offering attempts to rectify the injustice complained of earlier in the
lament and bears out the nymph's first instinctive cry: "ev'n Beasts must be
with justice slain" (l. 16).

Once the relics are obtained and the offering made, the mind, by a natural human instinct, grasps at the possibility of immortality, whether in a divine
afterlife or in earthly monuments. Don Cameron Allen notes the prevalence
of laments for pets in the seventh book of the Greek Anthology, in which

they are described as roving the Elysian Fields,[17] but in adding that "Marvell's readers would be more likely to remember Catullus' lament on the death of Lesbia's sparrow," he quotes only the description of the sparrow's domesticity, omitting the following lines on its passage to the afterworld:

> Qui nunc it per iter tenebricosum
> Illuc unde negant redire quemquam.
> At vobis male sit, malae tenebrae
> Orci, quae omnia bella devoratis;
> Tam bellum mihi passerem abstulistis.
> O factum male! io miselle passer!
> Tua nunc opera meae puellae
> Flendo turgiduli rubent ocelli.

> . . . who now travels through the shadowy way to that place from which none may return. But woe to you, grim shades of Orcus, that devour all lovely things; for you have torn from me my lovely sparrow. Oh, wicked deed! Oh, oh, unhappy sparrow! Because of you, my love's dear little eyes are red and swollen with weeping.[18]

This passage is interesting in that it compresses into eight lines the grief, the railing at injustice, the universality of pain, the transience of beauty, and the image of almost excessive weeping that occur repeatedly in laments of this sort, including the nymph's. Also interesting is Catullus' use of the double diminutive in line 18 ("turgiduli . . . ocelli"), in which both the noun and its modifying adjective have diminutive suffixes, a device that Catullus uses in only two other places.

Such pathetic diminution occurs regularly in the Greek Anthology and all the "dapper little elegiac verses" (in Louis MacNeice's phrase) that were patterned on the Anthology, including those of the twentieth century.[19] It is a way of translating the bewilderment and sense of injustice into unequivocal terms by making the thing lost utterly blameless and pathetically insignificant in the grand scale of things. MacNeice himself, in his poem "The Death of a Cat," perhaps comes closest of all the critics to explaining why the nymph is so distraught and why Marvell gave her a fawn to mourn:

> Sentimentality? Yes, it is possible;
> You and I, darling, are not above knowing
> The tears of the semi-, less precious things,
> A pathetic fallacy perhaps, as the man
> Who gave his marble victory wings
> Was the dupe—who knows—of sentimentality,

Not really classic. The Greek Anthology
Laments its pets (like you and me, darling),
Even its grasshoppers; dead dogs bark
On the roads of Hades where poets hung
Their tiny lanterns to ease the dark.
Those poets were late though. Not really classical.

(Collected Poems, p. 321)

The same impulse that makes poets bang "tiny lanterns" in commemoration of loss makes the nymph and all her human kin build monuments to their sorrow. Erecting a monument is not only a way to "ease the dark" but an attempt to convince the self that the thing lost is still alive in some way. From the makers of the earliest grave markers to the builders of the most elaborate statue-adorned tombs, human creatures have taken a certain comfort in viewing poor reproductions of the dead; from John Donne to Clarissa Harlowe, they have gained some satisfaction in planning their own tombs; and from the writer of the first classic "go, little book" to the subjects of the clippings in the modem newspaper morgue, they have hoped that their art or accomplishments would gain them some sort of immortality in this world.

Planning one's own or another's funeral is certainly a literary commonplace of the sixteenth and seventeenth centuries, from Juliet's "when he shall die, / Take him and cut him out in little stars" (*Romeo and Juliet* iii.ii.21–22) to such popular songs as this anonymous poem that John Dowland set to music in *A Musical Banquet* (1610):

In darknesse let mee dwell, the ground shall sorrow be,
The roofe Dispaire to barre all cheerful light from mee,
The wals of marble blacke that moistned still shall weepe,
My musicke hellish jarring sounds to banish friendly sleepe.
Thus wedded to my woes, and bedded to my Tombe,
O let me living die, till death doe come.[20]

Othello's and Hamlet's dying instructions about their reputations are part of this tradition, as is Aspatia's famous and somewhat soggy funeral plan for herself in Beaumont and Fletcher's *The Maid's Tragedy:*

As soon as I am dead,
Come all and watch one night about my hearse;
Bring each a mournful story and a tear,
To offer at it when I go to earth;
With flattering ivy clasp my coffin round;
Write on my brow my fortune; let my bier

Be borne by virgins, that shall sing by course
The truth of maids and perjuries of men.

(ii.i.101–108)

Sentimentality? Yes, it is possible. But in the face of death and loss, when human life seems insignificant, there is a need to reaffirm one's own reality—if not importance—by building such pitiful monuments. Even folk ballads are filled with characters ordering their deathbeds to be prepared, from Lord Randall to the dying lovers in the Sweet William songs, including one whose opening stanza makes a connection between a "milkwhite sheet" and death:

O mother, go and make my bed;
    Spread me that milkwhite sheet,
That I may go and lie down on the clothes
    To see if I can sleep.[21]

Or the stricken lover may order a grave for the beloved:

My love shall have a coffin
    And the nails shall shine yellow,
And my love she shall be buried
    On the banks of Green Willow.[22]

The nymph's tomb partakes, too, of the classic tradition of metamorphosis hinted at in the reference to the Heliades and of the religious and folkloric legends of weeping (or bleeding) statues. And of course the monument is also a symbol of the artist's work, which is expected to live on when he or she is gone. But even here, as in the garden, there is a spot of ink: the first stirrings of suspicion that such immortality is itself insufficient. The alabaster statue cannot capture the white essence of the fawn, and the very tears that flow from the monument will erode the marble itself.

So the poem comes full circle, and it would seem that mutability has won. All things must pass—the fawn, the old world order, pastoral simplicity, love, innocence, and all the surrogates that humanity seizes on in compensation for the latest loss. But, as in the Mutabilitie Cantos of *The Faerie Queene*, mutability does not have the last word after all. By coming to see the inevitability and universality of change and loss, the nymph and her reader have attained, if not comfort, at least catharsis; if not relief, at least a sort of marble repose; if not a defense against future loss, at least an enlarged understanding of it.

"The Nymph Complaining for the Death of Her Faun," then, is a traditional poem. Like all art, it confronts the questions of time, death, loss, and mutability—and finds no answers, only a new and more beautiful way to state the questions, always in terms of the questions that have gone before.

## NOTES

1. Evan Jones, "'The Nymph Complaining for the Death of Her Faun,'" *Explicator*, 26 (1967), item 73.

2. The text of the poem is that given in *Major Poets of the Earlier Seventeenth Century*, ed. Barbara K. Lewalski and Andrew J. Sabol (New York: Odyssey, 1973); hereafter cited parenthetically in the text.

3. Guild, "Marvell's 'The Nymph Complaining for the Death of Her Faun,'" *Modern Language Quarterly*, 29 (1968), 394; Miner, "The Death of Innocence in Marvell's *Nymph Complaining for the Death of Her Faun*," *Modern Philology*, 65 (1967), 9–16.

4. The text used is *The Aeneid of Virgil*, 2 vols., ed. T. E. Page (1900; rpt. London: Macmillan, 1970); translations mine.

5. Friedman, *Marvell's Pastoral Art* (Berkeley: University of California Press, 1970), pp. 108–109.

6. Hartman, "'The Nymph Complaining for the Death of Her Faun': A Brief Allegory," *Essays in Criticism*, 18 (1968), 113–135.

7. Toliver, *Marvell's Ironic Vision* (New Haven: Yale University Press, 1965), p. 136. An interesting pattern emerges from this book. Toliver, perhaps unconsciously, seems to look askance at any of Marvell's female figures who show a reluctance to go to bed with, or surrender emotionally to, the male personas. Colie is quoted from her *"My Ecchoing Song": Andrew Marvell's Poetry of Criticism* (Princeton: Princeton University Press, 1970), pp. 89–90; Hyman from his *Andrew Marvell* (New York: Twayne, 1964), pp. 24, 25.

8. Spitzer, "Marvell's 'Nymph Complaining for the Death of Her Faun': Sources versus Meaning," *Modern Language Quarterly*, 19 (1958), 231–243.

9. W. B. Yeats, *Collected Poems*, 2nd ed. (New York: Macmillan, 1956), p. 239.

10. *Q. Horatii Flacii Carminum Libri IV*, ed. T. E. Page (1883; rpt. London: Macmillan, 1956), p. 52 (Bk. ii, Poem 14, ll. 1–2).

11. John Webster, *The Duchess of Malfi*, Revels Plays, ed. John Russell Brown (Cambridge: Harvard University Press, 1964), i.i.359.

12. *The Poetical Works of John Keats*, ed. H. W. Garrod, 2nd ed. (Oxford: Clarendon Press, 1958), p. 275. It is possible that Keats may have had in mind such diverse images as the "deadly honey-dew," the "rose-kiss" of the fawn, Ariel's "Where the bee sucks" (*Tempest* v.i.88), and Othello's "O thou weed / Who art so lovely fair and smell'st so sweet / That the sense aches at thee, would thou hadst ne'er been born!" (iv.ii.67–69).

13. In *Poems of Alfred Lord Tennyson*, ed. Stephen Gwynn (London: Oxford University Press, 1950), p. 305.

14. Cynthia Gooding, *Queen of Hearts*, Elektra Records, EKL-131, 1953.

15. *A Midsummer Night's Dream* i.i.149. It would be futile in an essay such as this to try to compile a list of references to mutability in Renaissance literature. Their name is Legion.

16. *Idler*, No. 103, in *Rasselas, Poems, and Selected Prose*, ed. Bertrand H. Bronson (New York: Holt, 1971), pp. 214–215.

17. Allen, *Image and Meaning*, rev. ed. (Baltimore: Johns Hopkins Press, 1968), p. 166.

18. *Catullus*, ed. Elmer Truesdell Merrill (1893; rpt. Cambridge: Harvard University Press, 1951), pp. 7–8 (Poem 3, ll. 11–18). My translation.

19. *Autumn Journal* IX.49, in *Collected Poems of Louis MacNeice*, ed. E. R. Dodds (New York: Oxford University Press, 1967), p. 118. Echoes of and references to this lyric by Catullus occur in such poets as Edna St. Vincent Millay, Sara Teasdale, and even Dorothy Parker.

20. In *An Elizabethan Song Book*, ed. W. H. Auden, Chester Kallman, and Noah Greenberg (Garden City, N.Y.: Doubleday, 1956), p. 127.

21. "O Mother Go and Make My Bed," in Gooding.

22. "The Banks of Green Willow," in Gooding.

CAROL ANN JOHNSTON

# Heavenly Perspectives, Mirrors of Eternity: Thomas Traherne's Yearning Subject

[Holy Days] are Heavenly perspectives wherin we behold the Mystery of Ages, Mirrors of Eternity wherin we feed upon Revelations and Miracles.

—Thomas Traherne, "Book of Private Devotions"

Before, Behind, and evry where, Faith is,
Or sees, the very Masterpiece of Bliss.
All Its Materials are a Living Tomb
Of Glory, striking the Spectator dumb
And there our GOD is seen in Perspective
As if he were a BODY and alive.

—Thomas Traherne, "Article" in *Commentaries of Heaven*

The chance appearance in a London bookstall of Thomas Traherne's manuscripts of poems and meditations[1] early in the twentieth century coincided with Modernist interests in seventeenth-century poetry.[2] This coincidence naturally included Traherne in Modernist studies of lyric poetry. Modernist ahistoricism, however, relegated Traherne to a secondary place among already established poets such as Donne, Herbert, and Marvell: his work did not conform to standards that established poetry as "classic," such as compressed metaphors, double entendres, "telescoping images," and

*Criticism,* Volume 43, Number 4 (Fall 2001): pp. 377–405. Copyright © 2002 Wayne State University Press.

47

formal unity. In his essay "Mystic and Politician as Poet" (*Listener* 3 [1930]: 590–591), T. S. Eliot exercises his Modernist detachment from cultural context, deeming Traherne "more a mystic than a poet,"[3] a writer attentive to contemporary religious and political ideology at the cost of language and form. Thus, Eliot dismisses Traherne from the pantheon of worthy poets. Ironically, while modernist requirements for inclusion into the canon eschew historical and cultural circumstance, the cultural circumstance of Traherne's discovery is the very criterion that placed him in Modernist sight lines. Further, precisely due to circumstance, and in spite of steady critical activity and the recent discovery of several new manuscripts,[4] Traherne's language and *ars poetica* remain among the most maligned among anthologized seventeenth-century poets.

A further irony encompasses the critical judgments expended upon Traherne's *oeuvre*. While Modernists found his work too imbedded in culture, attempts to place it specifically within that culture have proven difficult indeed. Comparatively little is known about situations in which Traherne wrote his poems and prose meditations, or about Traherne's life. Traherne's biographers have largely based their accounts upon readings of his poetry and prose, which seem ecstatic and childlike. Placing Traherne's spiritual autobiography into biographical lacunae is one method of organizing the scant information that we have about him: he was born in Herefordshire in 1637, a shoemaker's son; attended Brasenose College, Oxford, at 15, earning his B.A. at 18; was ordained in 1657 as a Puritan minister to the rectorship of the parish of Credenhill, near Hereford; earned his Oxford M.A. in 1661; became one of the conforming clergy in 1660; served as the Anglican chaplain to Charles II's Lord Keeper of the Seal, Orlando Bridgeman by 1667; died in 1672 at Bridgeman's house in Teddington. Yet, even these few biographical facts suggest that Traherne did not withdraw to the world of naive ecstasy that his biographers find in his spiritual autobiography, but that he engaged in the intellectual and political life of the period. A literal reading of the "I" in Traherne's poems and meditations creates a tautology: critics build a fiction of Traherne's life out of the fiction of his work in order to clarify the known facts about his life, which in turn will clarify his work. His biographer and editor Gladys Wade codifies this identification of cause and effect when she concludes in 1942 that Traherne is "one of the most radiantly, most infectiously happy mortals this earth has known."[5] Recent articles have attempted to rescue Traherne from the legacy of his early biographers, placing him in a political context. Both N. I. Matur and Julia J. Smith connect Traherne to political events during his lifetime, and the recent discovery of Traherne's long political poem sanctions such a reading.[6] A political reading of Traherne however, remains somewhat problematic, since Traherne was in the employ of both Puritan and Anglican factions at different stages of his career. Because of these contrary loyalties, Smith deems Traherne a political "conformist," one who wants to fit in and keep those around him happy, a position not so far removed from Wade's diagnosis of a happy man. The benign view of a cheerful Traherne, then, remains largely unchallenged even now.[7]

The obstacle to critical judgment created by the mixture of Traherne's late discovery and his biographers' over-determined reading of his work remains easier to diagnose than to cure. Traherne's radical experimentation with language, coupled with our lack of information about his life, presents a reading problem of greater complexity than almost any other in seventeenth-century studies. Each issue, the linguistic and the cultural, seems to require an individual methodology; one, a study of his language apart from Modernist assumptions, and the other, placement of Traherne's work within a cultural context greater than those offered by theological debate or political struggle. Yet, while these two critical problems are distinct, they also are inextricably linked: language from Traherne's culture organizes that of his poetry. One cannot be addressed without also addressing the other. To consider language and the linguistic culture it forms requires taking the kind of middle ground between fields of study common for a student such as Traherne in the mid-seventeenth century. Traherne received the standard Oxford education, studying "Logic, Ethics, Physics, Metaphysics, Geometry, Astronomy, Poesy, Medicine, Grammar, Music, Rhetoric, . . . Arts, Trades and Mechanisms."[8] As fluent in these subjects as poets such as Donne and Herbert, Traherne's use of the language from these subjects nonetheless has seemed to many readers at best subdued or even absent. Yet I believe that his awareness of the history and development of "poesy" and the fine arts grounds Traherne as deeply in the theoretical issues of his art as he is grounded in Biblical exegesis and theology. Rather than writing a non-poetic verse in which he elaborates a personal ecstatic vision, Traherne attempts to write poetry that synthesizes poetic theory and painting theory. This synthesis, I argue, accounts for his abstract and non-metaphorical language, language that has seemed more like prose than poetry to his readers. His quest to strike a new kind of language from issues resonant in poetics and painting forms the extraordinary theoretical substructure of his work.

Uncovering that theoretical substructure is my task in this essay. I argue that Traherne engages poetics and painting at atypical theoretical angles. He addresses specifically the evolution and general use of metaphor in the tradition of Petrarch and the English anti-Petrarchan tradition, while also interrogating the technologies of three-dimensional perspective and the clear-reflecting mirror that dominate Renaissance painting. Examining both the Petrarchan construction of metaphor and Renaissance theories of linear perspective allows Traherne to engage in a discussion with a particular ideological issue that both share, the issue of subjectivity. This exchange with poetics and painting results in Traherne's forging a unique poetic language, one predicated upon the non-representational metaphor,[9] and one that attempts to devise a poetic middle ground between subjective and objective representation that maintains what he sees as desirable qualities in each. Such a conversation shows that Traherne's obsession with vision is that of an intellectual visionary who attempts to reclaim poetry from its central role in a cultural narrative that mistakes subjectivity for objectivity. Despite his strong efforts, however, Traherne's poetry represents a failed engagement with cultural hegemony. Ultimately, Traherne cannot redirect the powerful ideological trajectory that would take western thought to the subjective idealism of Berkeley and Fichte and the subjectivism of Kant.[10]

## Snapshots of the Petrarchan Past

Traherne claims ownership of a new kind of language in the preface of his *Poems of Felicity*,[11] one that spurns the poet's most useful tools, the metaphor and the image.

> No curling Metaphors that gild the Sence,
> Nor Pictures here, nor painted Eloquence;
> No florid Streams of Superficial gems,
> But real Crowns and Thrones and Diadems!
> That Gold on Gold should hiding shining ly
> May well be reckon'd baser Heraldry.[12]
>              ("The Author to the Critical Peruser," lines 11–16)

Literally, Traherne's lines tell us that his poetry will not be representational in the usual sense: no metaphors, no "pictures" or descriptions, just the objects themselves. Such a verbatim reading, however, yields something fantastical: Traherne claims invention of an idealized unity between objects and the words that describe them. Because such poetry is obviously not possible (an ideal only approximated in ancient pictographic languages, where words literally were pictures), we must read these lines at less than face value, and within the context of the anti-Petrarchan movement that held that poetry in the tradition of Petrarch (1301–1374), particularly in its understanding of metaphor, had become confusing to the point of absurdity. Strong anti-Petrarchan sentiments were voiced in such works as Philip Sidney's simultaneously Petrarchan and anti-Petrarchan sonnet sequence, *Astrophil and Stella* (begun in 1581), Shakespeare's *Sonnets* (1609), and George Herbert's *The Temple* (1633).[13] Critics have put forward various hypotheses to explain the longevity and intensity of Petrarchan and anti-Petrarchan rhetoric—politics, gender issues, and so forth[14]—but at its core, anti-Petrarchan poetry vilifies the

Petrarchan use of elaborate metaphor, and we must place Traherne's claim within this important context.

The guileless hyperbole of poetry typical of the end of the Petrarchan era in the English Renaissance validates the poet's impulse to attack such poetry. Stock versions of late anti-Petrarchan poetry focus upon poetry written in the manner—but not with the style or dexterity—of Petrarch. In the hands of a Petrarch *manqué*, the startling metaphors that he used to introduce the sonnet form become comic in their over-ripeness.[15] Much of this late Petrarchan poetry is simply outrageous in its use of metaphor, and merits Traherne's description of its "curling Metaphors that gild the Sence." But anti-Petrarchan poets, too, are capable of making outrageous claims about what they *will not* do with metaphor. In one of the more famous of these claims, Shakespeare's speaker asserts, "My mistress' eyes are nothing like the sun—" (Sonnet 130). While Shakespeare indicates here that he finds Petrarchan metaphor absurd in its hyperbole, his closing lines—that he loves his mistress more than those who write hyperbole love *their* mistresses—may in fact be the most hyperbolic claim of all. In a move typical of anti-Petrarchan poets, Shakespeare uses metaphor to spurn metaphor. Anti-Petrarchism uses metaphor to make a kind of understated overstatement. Yet poets claiming to simplify metaphor and structure do so with a wink and a nod; after all, if poets were to take anti-Petrarchism literally, they would deprive themselves of the variety available to them within complex metaphor and structure, and thus make writing poetry almost impossible.

The figurative strategy of anti-Petrarchism argues for metaphor with less distance between the subject of comparison and its analogy. Along the continuum of anti-Petrarchan contention, the extremity of Traherne's position is almost matched by George Herbert's in his two "Jordan" poems (*The Works of George Herbert*, ed., F. E. Hutchinson [Oxford, 1941]). Each of Herbert's poems exists vestigially in Traherne's poetry: Herbert's well-known phrase in "Jordan (II)"—"Curling in metaphors a plain intention"—yields Traherne's "no curling metaphors that gild the sense;" in "Jordan (I)," Herbert's argument about poetic styles, rather than his language, prefigures Traherne's position. Traherne's use of Herbert in this instance, however, illustrates Harold Bloom's "map of misreading," a misreading understandable when we examine Herbert's rhetoric in "Jordan (I)." One of the few poets whom Traherne quotes in his notebooks,[16] Herbert adopts in "Jordan (I)" a strategy of arguing for "truth," a condition that places the word as close to its referent as possible. He opens this first of his two famous *ars poetica* with an anti-Petrarchan claim that seems very close to Traherne's: "Who says that fictions only and false hair/ become a verse? Is there in truth no beauty? / . . . . Must purling streams refresh a lover's loves?" ("Jordan I," lines 1–2, 8). Unlike Traherne's bald statements, however, Herbert asks rhetorical questions that imply his disgust with the tired aggrandizement of Petrarchan love poems: "Who says that exaggeration is the only way to praise?" and "Is there nothing beautiful in truth?" While it is always dangerous to ask genuine questions in poetry since the reader may supply the wrong answer, Herbert is the consistent master of this locution. He entices us to say to ourselves, "of course the simple truth is the most beautiful." Here, Herbert seems to dismiss the overwrought Petrarchan discourse; by the end of "Jordan (I)," however, he also dismisses the logical alternative to that discourse, the plain Puritan style of writing. When we try to make sense of these opposing claims in "Jordan (I)," we see that Herbert actually has retained rather than purged the Petrarchan "winding stair," and exaggerated metaphor even while he claims to purge it. We must go around the block to cross the street in the poem, unwinding all the rhetoric to discover that Herbert does not want to be forced to use Puritan poetics (language exclusive to praising God, as he describes it) to write poetry. Like Shakespeare, Herbert only seems to reject Petrarchism, while retaining the essence of its strategy.

Given the complexity of Herbert's rhetorical scheme in "Jordan (I)," it seems possible that Traherne takes Herbert at his word, at least his word at the outset of the poem, and builds upon his anti-Petrarchan claim in his work. Or perhaps Traherne understands the seeming contradiction in the poem—Herbert's rhetorical rejection both of Petrarchan and of Puritan styles—as an attempt to compromise, or to develop a new kind of poetry. Either way, Traherne's reading of Herbert yields a pledge that neither Herbert, nor any representative anti-Petrarchan poet, has made. While Herbert initially argues for the plain truth to bring subject and object close together, and while Shakespeare claims to compare his mistress' eyes not to the faraway sun, but to themselves, Traherne argues for metaphor with literally no distance between subject and comparison. "Things" simply appear in his poems, he argues, in non-referential language. Although each poet's assertions about his use of metaphor are somewhat inaccurate, nonetheless the underlying claims are perspicacious in their recognition of the problems inherent in Petrarchan metaphor. Traherne pushes these claims to an extreme.

Petrarch, Thomas Greene explains, took metaphor in a direction radically different from its use in Classical and Medieval poetry, initiating a new way of reading (and writing) poetry in the early modern period, which Greene calls "the activity of subreading." Petrarch's method in effect invents a poetry that is about bridging space and time, rather than adhering to hermeneutic methods.[17] Petrarch's new method concerns the poet's emphasis upon his subject position. Greene explains:

> The older [medieval hermeneutic] method presupposed a fullness
> of knowledge awaiting the successful interpreter—knowledge

that is whole and entire because it can be unlocked by a single operation of the appropriate intellectual key. This method aligned author and reader in a single universe of discourse wherein no cultural distance could exist because, with the sole exception of the Christian revelation, historical change was virtually unknown. The new "archeological" hermeneutic, on the other hand, presupposed a considerable distance and withheld a single all-divulging key. Instead of a relation between "veil" and "Truth" that, once discovered, is easily grasped and formulated, there emerges an interplay of entities that resists total description because it operates in the elusive domain of style. Style by definition cannot be described perfectly even if it can be categorized. And the poetic substance enmeshed in, or half-buried beneath, the verbal surface is now perceived as teaching the reader from far off, from a remote and prestigious world radically unlike his own.[18]

Greene's breakthrough here is two-fold: Unlike Medieval writers who wrote to add to texts and prevailing truths, and lacked a causal understanding of history, Petrarch discovers history and in so doing, also establishes a kind of subjectivity. Once Petrarch discovers the "ancient" aspect of historical texts, then he begins a process of imitating, rather than of adding to these texts. The subtle difference between imitation and addition gives us a Petrarchan text that is layered, rather than linear, in its use of influence. Thus the surface—the "style" of the Petrarchan text—emphasizes the individual writer, while the text taken as a whole alludes to an ancient precursor as it also highlights the individual imitator of that precursor. The nature of writing, according to Petrarch, is imitation, not addition: "A proper imitator should take care that what he writes resemble the original without reproducing it."[19] Through this process of imitation, Petrarch self-consciously distances himself from the historical text, and thus establishes a unique concept of subject and object position.[20] The writer imitating an ancient text buries that text as an object beneath his own subjective style. Reading Petrarch requires that the reader identify Petrarch's subjectivity, through his style, as well as the existence of an historical object, the ancient text, beneath that style.

In clarifying Petrarch's achievements, Greene advances our understanding of Traherne, though he does not consider him directly. The contrast that Greene points out between subjective style in Petrarch's text and the objectivity of the texts that Petrarch imitates (objectivity still available to readers if they "sub-read" Petrarch's text) carries implications for all aspects of reading post-Petrarchan texts, most profoundly for the conception and use of metaphor. The essence of metaphor is comparison, and the more a comparison is infused with the writer's subjectivity, the greater the distance between the

objects compared, as well as between the reader and the writer, both in experience and imagination. Before Petrarch, metaphors were not personal; after
Petrarch, the only way to read poetry with precision and certainty is to be the
poet. All other readers are disjoined from the writer's individual experience.
Traherne, more than any other anti-Petrarchan poet, reacts against the polarities inherent in Petrarchan subjectivity; in fact, he tries to move poetry back
to a pre-Petrarchan innocence.

For pre-Romantic writers, subjectivity holds a dual identity. Placement
of the individual *vis-à-vis* the object of his writing (or for the reader, placement *vis-à-vis* both the writer and the object of the writing) remains primary.
After Romanticism, this aspect of subjectivity collapses into its secondary
identity, that of personal emotions and feelings, so for modern readers, subjectivity indicates primarily the feelings of the writer about the material he
addresses. For pre-Romantics, however, feelings were not necessarily thought
to be "sincere;" rather, emotions simply added an intriguing and witty texture
to the work. As he attempts to return the subjective to a state closer to objectivity, Traherne remains the pre-Romantic and concentrates on the placement of the writer and reader in relationship to the object of focus.

### The Subject of Linear Perspective Is Subjectivity

In his attempt to reform the subjectivity he finds in Petrarchan metaphor,
Traherne replaces the rhetoric of anti-Petrarchism that he alludes to in the
introduction to his *Poems of Felicity* with the linguistic network of linear
perspective and its subset, the trope of the mirror. Despite the striking anti-
Petrarchan language of the preface, the *Poems of Felicity* do not themselves
employ this language. The preface poem seems, rather, to be the strategy
with which Traherne introduces us to his primary concern, but due to the
excessive baggage of anti-Petrarchan poetry, he moves to another language
and another strategy not only within this unfinished manuscript, but also
within all of his work. Traherne's subject—the issue of subjective placement—dominates the conversation concerning the development of linear
perspective in fifteenth-century Italy, while it is only one of a complement
of issues that Petrarchan language engages. Perspectival language thus
brings to poetry fewer complications and associations than the Petrarchan.
In all of his work, Traherne shapes perspectival language into the arena in
which he engages with the troubling issues that he finds inherent both in
subjective post-Petrarchan metaphor, and the subjective language describing linear perspective.

The invention of "linear" or "single-point" perspective in fifteenth-
century Florence narrowed the way that viewers looked at painting; a series
of mathematically placed orthogonal lines gives the illusion that the painting recedes into a single "vanishing point," thereby offering only one spot,

the centrist point, from which an individual viewer may see the painting in perfect three-dimensional perspective. Perspective, in its simplest terms, is about the relationship of one object to another in space. Once vision becomes concentrated upon the relationship among objects, as perspective forces it to do, the emphasis falls upon the individual viewer who sees and organizes those relationships. The individual visual subject, when viewing a scene in perspective, can and must move around, to find the correct viewing position, the centrist point. By emphasizing the relationship between objects and this movement of the viewing subject searching for the "correct" view, perspectival painting lays bare the question of subjective placement. This subjective orientation is a product of specific cultural forces. In *The Conquest of America* (trans., Richard Howard [New York: Harper Perennial, 1992]), Tzvetan Todorov points out how linear perspective informs the cultural narrative of subjectivity. Discussing the difference between European perspective and that of Aztec sculpture, he writes:

> The Aztec sculptures are worked on all sides, including the base, even if they weigh several tons; this is because the object's observer is as little individual as its executant; representation gives us essence and is not concerned with the impressions of any one man. European linear perspective may not have originated from the concern to validate a single and individual viewpoint, but it becomes its symbol, adding itself to the individuality of the objects represented. It may seem bold to link the introduction of perspective to the discovery and conquest of America, yet the relation is there, not because Toscanelli, inspirer of Columbus, was the friend of Brunelleschi and Alberti, pioneers of perspective (or because Piero della Francesca, another founder of perspective, died on October 12, 1492), but by reason of the transformation that both facts simultaneously reveal and produce in human consciousness.[21]

The invention of linear perspective stresses the shift from the seeming invisible objectivity of both artist and viewer. Todorov reminds us that the origin of perspective "validate[s] a single and individual viewpoint," and as such informs the cultural narrative that equates subjectivity with objectivity. Like linear perspective, as I have discussed, Petrarchism also authorizes such singularity of vision, and as such both Petrarchism and perspective engage in a discourse concerning subjectivity.

Like Petrarchism and perspective in painting, the clear glass mirror also is a part of the cultural narrative of subjectivity. The language of the mirror is a subset of perspectival language, because mirrors are intimately linked to the development of linear perspective. In his theoretical treatise *On Painting*

(1435–1436), the Florentine humanist Leon Battista Alberti notes the use of the accurate glass mirror to show defects in a painting: "A mirror will be an excellent guide [to judging relief-effect]. I do not know how it is that paintings that are without fault look beautiful in a mirror; and it is remarkable how every defect in a picture appears more unsightly in a mirror. So the things that are taken from Nature should be emended with the advice of the mirror."[22] The invention of accurate glass mirrors, notably this ability of the mirror to expose faults in relief, enabled Alberti and his contemporary Brunelleschi in their invention of linear perspective.[23]

Brunelleschi's 1425 vignette of the Baptistery of Florence, though now lost, is recognized as the work generating linear perspective. On this panel, Brunelleschi painted a view of the baptistery from a representation that he had traced on and over its mirror reflection. After determining the centric ray and the vanishing point, Brunelleschi drilled a hole in his panel at that exact spot.[24] The viewer was to peer through the hole from the backside of the panel into a mirror, which reversed the image again, reflecting the view in the correct direction. The viewer could slide the mirror, which reflected the real sky, with moving clouds, to change the scale.[25] In effect, the mirror proved that the artist's rendering of scale and proportion was accurate.[26] By establishing the accuracy of scale and proportion, the mirror seemed to prove that a painting in linear perspective was also "true" and real. This important slippage from "accurate" to "true" could lead the individual viewer to assume that the painter had captured general—objective—experience, rather than subjectively reconstructed an imitation of such experience. Such a slippage could lead the viewer to imagine and even assume that his point of view when observing the painting could be objective. But in fact, the accuracy of perspectival paintings is available only to one person at any given time (hence, its importance to notions of the individual as a coherent and unified entity), since there is only a single viewing spot, designated by the individual painter, that reveals the correct scale and proportion of the painting. Assuming the objectivity of the experience when viewing a perspectival painting effectively masks the subjectivity intrinsic to the construction of linear perspective.

Until the seventeenth century, English artists and patrons could experience the illusion of perspectival painting only by travelling to the Continent or seeing the few perspectival paintings imported to England from the Continent. Likewise, the English did not begin to mass-produce glass mirrors until the beginning of the seventeenth century, well after their widespread use in Italy.[27] Both Nicholas Hilliard, the English miniaturist, and poet Philip Sidney traveled to the Continent, but each came away with different ideas about perspectival reproduction. Hilliard eschews precise, mathematical perspectival painting in his treatise (ca. 1600), *The Arte of Limning* (Great Britain: Mid Northumberland Arts Group in association with Carcanet New

Press, 1981).[28] He argues that perspective is actually an "effect or judgment of the eye" which has the purpose of "deceiv[ing] both the understanding and the eye" (71).[29] As Hilliard understands it, perspectival painting is misleadingly "real," offering a restrictive though seductive view of the natural world that takes the viewer away from experiencing nature objectively. Hilliard's dismissal of perspective raises issues parallel to the Puritan Stephen Gossen's attack on poetry in *School of Abuse* as "the mother of lies" that represents a copy of nature falsely as the truth. In response to this argument, Philip Sidney writes, famously, "Nature never set forth the earth in so rich tapestry as divers [sic] poets have done; neither with so pleasant rivers, fruitful trees, sweet-smelling flowers, nor whatsoever else may make the too much loved earth more lovely. Her world is brazen, the poets only deliver a golden."[30] Sidney argues here that the poet does not conform to a mimesis or copy of nature as the Puritan polemicist would have it, but rather adheres to a mimesis of nature's internal virtues, to which he had access because of his own internal virtues. Nature's visible world is flawed, compared with its internal perfection. While Sidney attempts to argue for virtue within the self that gives the self contact with the objective virtues, this conception remains a sticking point in discussions such as Hilliard's about representation.[31]

Unlike Sidney's rebuttal of Gossen that emphasizes the subject's ability to transmit objective virtues, Hilliard's treatise argues the opposite. He determines that by employing the technique of linear perspective to construct subjectivity, his art (painting) would "deceive" and mislead the viewer because the subjective point of view could only seem objective, and not actually be objective, as Sidney contends. Hilliard, Sidney, and Gossen's arguments anticipate the problematic issues of subjectivity inherent both in Petrarchan poetry and in perspectival painting. In spite of objections and holdouts by esteemed English painters such as Hilliard, perspective becomes the mode of painting in seventeenth-century England, enough so that Traherne's technical knowledge of the method matches his understanding of the argument about subjectivity that lies beneath the practice.

## Perspective in Traherne

Compared to anti-Petrarchan rhetoric, perspectival language offers Traherne the relative isolation of his subject of subjectivity. Anti-Petrarchan rhetoric, as I have discussed, does not erase Petrarchan subjectivity; rather by employing the subjectivity of Petrarchan language in a more subtle form, anti-Petrarchan rhetoric heightens the importance of the individual. In order to attempt his project of moving poetic language to its seeming pre-Petrarchan objectivity, Traherne must move away from anti-Petrarchan language. Perspectival language provides Traherne with a cache of unique linguistic visual cues with which to make his claims about objectivity. Paradoxically, though the linguistic network of perspective is visual, it does not offer pictorial evidence for a poet to imitate in language in the manner of metaphoric writing; rather, it provides visual references that are not strictly imagistic in the sense that the metaphor itself is usually thought of as being imagistic. The language of linear perspective concerns the way that a painter establishes object relationships, not the specific objects themselves, and the mirror, of course, is merely reflective. Symbolically, there is no there, there. In using these two perspectival stores of language, Traherne must write about how they work and what they accomplish, rather than representing them imagistically as something only viewable by an individual subject. Thus with perspectival language Traherne may isolate subjectivity in order to attempt to erase, or at least reform, subjective assumptions.

Having noted that the subject of perspective is subjectivity, I seem to be arguing against myself when I say that perspectival language enables Traherne's claims about objectivity. The perspectival and mirroring networks do in one sense exhibit in their performance the subjectivity that is their subject: a poet can use perspectival language to describe the actions and results generated by his particular—subjective—point of view. However, because perspectival language removes the need to depict actions metaphorically or imagistically, techniques that revert to subjectivity, the poet can over-ballast his subjective position with non-metaphoric language that can function objectively. However, while perspective and the mirror each have no visual antecedent, unlike individual subjective points of view, they are not indeterminate; their function is always uniform and technical. In this sense, both perspectival and mirroring categories are objective. By using the language of these networks, Traherne attempts to maintain a patina of the complexity and materiality of Petrarchan subjectivity, while he also strives to give his text the objectivity, stability, and inclusivity lost when subjectivity is constructed by the text. In a sense, then, Traherne agrees with Sidney's contentions, that a poet can show an objective—golden and prelapsarian—world. Yet, in order to achieve Sidney's purpose, Traherne negates Sidney's Petrarchan and anti-Petrarchan metaphors with his claims and with his language.

The following passage of poetry from *Commentaries of Heaven* offers an overview of Traherne's use of the perspectival network, showing not only the language of perspective at the center of the passage (which I underscore) but also Traherne's attempt to use the network to locate his poetry away from the subjectivity of the single viewer and of Petrarchan metaphor, and toward the objectivity that seems to disappear with Petrarchan emphasis on the individual.

> But he that would enjoy the true Delight
> Of all . . . must all unite.

For Beauty is the Soul, that Life inspires
Into the Faith, which evry Soul admires
<u>Beauty's a Thing resulting (as we see)</u>
<u>From many Parts in their full Unitie.</u>
<u>Broken in Pieces, they disorderd lie</u>
<u>Tho they are more exposed to the Ey:</u>
<u>Relation and Proportion is the Thing</u>
<u>From whence all Lovely Symmetry doth spring:</u>
And one united fabrick when intire
Makes men the Beauty of it more admire
<u>The Parts do justify each other, to</u>
<u>The Ey of him, that all at once doth view.</u>
Searchd from the Bottom to the Top throughout
With in, in all its Intregues, round about,
<u>Before, Behind, and evry where, Faith is,</u>
<u>Or sees, the very Masterpiece of Bliss.</u>
All Its Materials are a Living Tomb
Of *Glory*, striking the <u>Spectator</u> dumb
And there our GOD <u>is seen in Perspective</u>
As if he were a BODY and alive.

("Article," lines 15–36)[32]

As with his claims about metaphor, Traherne's concern here is with division
of subject and object, in which subjective vision stands in for objectivity.
Making an assertion parallel to that about metaphor, Traherne nevertheless
shifts from anti-Petrarchan language—"no curling metaphors to gild the
sense"—to the language of linear perspective. Rather than description or
metaphor, Traherne gives us the abstract language of the activity of seeing:
"relation," "proportion," "symmetry," "justify," "viewing eye." Unless vision
organizes objects in the unified whole, "many parts in their full unity," then
vision is "broken," and consequently, so is the soul and life. Faithless human
vision, Traherne argues, is subjective and "broken;" yet perniciously, and as
with perspectival painting, that subjectivity can seem objective. Traherne
places God as a viewer of the universe who can choose to see from an infinite
number of positions, similiar to Todorov's viewers of Aztec sculpture, moving
around the object. Yet, while this kind of non-perspectival seeing does not
mistake the objective for the subjective, it remains "broken," with no sense of
unity. To see "all," however, the viewer must be where he can see in "Relation and Proportion," in other words, in the perspectival "centrist" position.
Remarkably, Traherne's God both moves beyond the piecemeal vision of pre-
perspectival vision and beyond the subjectivity of linear perspective as well:
"The Parts do justify each other, to / The Ey of him, that all at once doth

view." Traherne's God has the best of both kinds of seeing, a synchronicity of the partial vision of perspectival vision, with the intimacy and seeming objectivity of pre-perspectival vision. This combination of methods of seeing gives God perfect vision, seeing a "united Fabrick when intire," as well as a universe "Searchd from the Bottom to the Top throughout / With in, in all its Intregues, round about, / Before, Behind, and evry where."

Yet, Traherne does not leave us with a God that has perfect vision and a faithless human constituency who can see only bits and pieces. "Faith" is the vehicle by which individuals achieve this impossible combination of viewing positions, simultaneously allowing the viewer to see from the centrist position (symmetry and proportion) and from all possible angles (the whole). The faithful Christian gets the ultimate reward in Traherne's universe: with his newly-constructed vision, he sees God and is struck "dumb" when "GOD is seen in Perspective / As if he were a BODY and alive." Traherne insists that faith in an objective God overcomes the limitations of human vision; faith reforms the subjectivity of linear perspective by giving Christians perspectival views of God from a truly objective point of view.

Traherne also voices the perspectival relationship with God through his "every Christian" speaker in the third meditation from his *Centuries of Meditation*. Here the speaker finds himself in the wrong viewing position, and expands upon this condition to draw out the comparison between perspective and faith. Like the speaker of the lyrics, the speaker in *The Centuries* compares his misguided spiritual condition to one of spatial imbalance and disorder. He himself is a piece "out of frame," out of proportion, which he must place back into proper perspective. He must occupy the place of central perspective and simultaneously must sit on the throne with God, in order to enjoy the spectacle both of God and his creation from the proper vantage point, where "all things [are] well in their proper places."

> This spectacle once seen, will never be forgotten. It is a Great part of the Beatifick Vision. A Sight of Happiness is Happiness. It transforms the Soul and makes it Heavenly, it powerfully calls us to Communion with God, and weans us from the Customs of this World[.] It puts a lustre upon GOD and all His Creatures and makes us to see them in a Divine and Eternal Light. I no sooner discerned this but I was (as Plato saith, In summâ Rationis Arce Quies habitat) seated in a Throne of repose and perfect rest. All things were well in their Proper Places, I alone was out of frame and had need to be Mended. For all things were Gods treasures in their proper places, and I was to be restored to Gods Image. Whereupon you will not believ, how I was withdrawn from all Endeavors of altering and Mending Outward Things. They lay so

well methoughts, they could not be mended: but I must be Mended
to Enjoy them. (*C* 3. 60)

As in the previous passage, there are few specific objects here—the speaker
sees only "things" for example—but while this passage is barren of description and of concrete and compressed images (Eliot's "telescoping" images),
the network of perspectival language again functions as a substructure
shaping and formalizing the speaker's relationship to God. Also consistent with the previous passage is Traherne's stress upon the simultaneity
of viewing positions that faith allows; as an antidote to subjectivity, the
speaker envisions himself as occupying the perfect viewing position on the
throne with God, as well as remaining on earth, "mended" and enjoying
the physical world in its proper perspective. Unlike the previous passage,
this one is quite explicit here in its reference to Traherne's theory of metaphor. "A Sight of Happiness is Happiness," he writes, insisting as he does
in his "Author to the Critical Peruser" that the faithful Christian will find
no linguistic barriers of false subjectivity. Here, the language is visual,
consistent with the perspectival structure of the passage; yet, he insists
upon calling attention to his non-metaphorical use of visual language:
happiness is happiness, it is not "like" any object whatsoever. Further, he
attempts within this framework to objectify experience. Happiness here is
not an individual state; rather it is something objective, for all to see and
simultaneously to absorb. What may seem tautological—happiness being
happiness—epitomizes Traherne's use of perspectival language: to attempt
to move from the subjective and to the objective.

In these two passages showing Traherne's use of linear perspective, we
see also his understanding of the limitations that the centrist viewing position
imposes on viewers. The isolation of the self offers a destablizingly singular
and fragmented view of the world, a view that Traherne associates with the
individual who must be "mended" within through faith in God. Once faithful,
the individual can then envision from God's point of view and, simultaneously, envision God. Not limited by the rules of linear perspective, this view
also offers a picture of the world with the best characteristics of a perspectival
painting, as if the vision were "reall."

### "At Once the Mirror and the Object Be"

While Traherne employs three-dimensional perspective in the passages
above in his attempt to remove the flaws inherent in subjective representation, he suggests only in the vague phrase "beatifick Vision" how faith
allows the believer to experience this reformed vision, or where he may see
"our GOD . . . In Perspective / As if he were a BODY and alive." At this
juncture, Traherne's transition from the visual may seem simply mystical,

something only available in familiar non-material "visions." Certainly, this aspect of his attempt to create a non-visual visual language represents the most fraught and most demanding articulation of Traherne's project. To solve the puzzle of how one reaches this situation, he draws on the trope of the mirror. As with linear perspective, viewers of a reflection in a mirror can believe that they see something real, and as with viewers of perspectival painting, their experience is singular, particularly when viewing their own reflections. No individual can see another's reflection from the same point of view; this is an impossibly subjective experience. In the case of this clear mirror, as with the linear perspective that it enabled, one of the important results of technological development, then, is an emphasis upon subjectivity, rather than upon the objectivity that it comes to represent. In addition to its fundamental use in perspectival painting, the mirror may seem an especially fitting source for Traherne, for it has a long pedigree as an image for the Christian soul, rooted in the well-known passage from the book of Corinthians: "For now we see through a glass, darkly; but then face to face: now I know in part; but then shall I know even as also I am known" (1 Corinthians 12:13).[33] The image of the soul as a mirror of eternity is well developed in patristic literature, most notably in Augustine.[34] Indeed, readers associating Traherne's work with theological treatises have assumed that when Traherne writes of the soul as "The Mirror of an endless Life" ("Fulness," line 5), he merely reiterates early Christian writers. I argue, however, that while Traherne certainly draws upon previous uses of the mirror trope in Christian texts, he departs from traditional uses of this trope at critical points. Both the technical development of the mirror and its use to confirm drawings to scale require these departures.

In significant ways, Traherne's mirror trope remains congruous with early Christian definitions. For example, Traherne defines the reflections in the mirroring soul very strictly: they are "Ideas from the Skie." God is in the sky, and ideas emanate from him. This patristic formulation had its beginnings in classical philosophy. Plato argues that *ideas* represent objective standards, outlining what is real more accurately than does the physical world. Drawing upon Platonic thought, Augustine argues that *ideas* are actually God's objective pattern and as such exist in God's mind. These *ideas* appear in the mirror of the soul.[35] In the first stanza of "The Circulation," Traherne both articulates the attributes of the soul as a mirror, and sets out the identity of the reflections in that mirroring soul:

As fair Ideas from the Skie,
Or Images of Things,
Unto a Spotless Mirror flie,
On unperceived Wings;

And lodging there affect the Sence,
As if at first they came from thence;
While being there, they richly Beautifie
The Place they fill, and yet communicat
Themselves, reflecting to the Seers Ey,
Just such is our Estate.
No Prais can we return again,
No Glory in our selves possess,
But what derived from without we gain,
From all the Mysteries of Blessedness.

("The Circulation," lines 1–14)

The first two lines balance "fair Ideas" and "Images of Things" on either side of the equation; both "Ideas" and "Images of Things" may "Unto a Spotless Mirror flie." Further, both, when they "lodge" in the mirror, "affect the Sence." "Images of Things," it seems, would naturally affect the sense of sight, but it is less clear what "Sence" the "Ideas" affect, unless we take into account the history of the soul represented as a mirror, with ideas as objects reflected in the soul. The "Sence" that "Ideas" affect is the reflective "Sence" of the soul.[36]

Building upon Neo-platonic conceptions of the soul, Descartes explains this "sence" of the soul in his *Opticks:* "We know for certain it is the soul which has sensory perceptions, and not the body" (René Descartes, *Discourse on Method, Optics, Geometry, and Meteorology,* trans., Paul J. Olscamp [Indianapolis: Bobbs-Merrill, 1965], 164).[37] Descartes bases this conception upon the Platonic notion that ideas are more real than "things": Descartes' "soul" has a substance that is more "real" than the body. Traherne expresses a Neo-platonic view similar to Descartes' formulation, giving the soul substance and sensory perceptions. His analogy of the soul with the physical body offers the soul by association physical (mechanical) attributes:

[God] Can make the soul by Sense to feel and see,
And with her Joy the Senses wrap'd to be.
Yea while the Flesh of Body subject lies
To those Affections which in Souls arise;
All holy Glories from the Soul redound,
And in the Body by the Soul abound,
Are felt within, and ravish ev'ry Sense,
With all the Godhead's glorious Excellence:
Who found the way himself to dwell within,
As if even Flesh were nigh to him of kin.

("Thanksgivings for the Body II," lines 21–30)

This particular "Thanksgiving," though it is dedicated to the body, saves its most eloquent praise for the soul, which takes on body-like senses when the divine is present: "[God] Can make the soul by Sense to feel and see." Traherne here works from the commonplace that man is created in the image of God. He stretches this commonplace by placing God's image within man, then stretches it again even further; God's image in the soul has a particular form. The images in the soul, we recall, are ideas, or as Traherne designates them, "thoughts:"

> Thoughts are a kind of Strange Celestial Creature,
> That when they're Good, they're such in evry Feature,
> They bear the Image of their father's face,
> And Beautifie even all his Dwelling Place:
>                                      ("Thoughts." III., lines 29–33)

Each good "thought" is a "creature" bearing the image of God. Traherne emphasizes that these "thoughts" are "things" in their own right, and not representations. By exploiting the Augustinian tradition of the mirror to represent the soul containing ideas, or "thoughts," Traherne strategically advances his quest for non-metaphoric visual language. Consistent with Descartes, Traherne argues that the soul's images are more real than physical images. Unlike early uses of the mirroring soul, however, Traherne's version of the reflective Christian soul must take into account the use of the glass mirror to verify the accuracy of perspectival paintings. The mirror evolved from a crude antique steel instrument that reflected a shadowy, ill-defined figure, to the silver-backed glass with a reflection that seems to duplicate objects. This technology renders the Pauline construction of the dark glass at best obsolete. The clarity of Traherne's mirroring soul reflects images sharply, not darkly, and thus these images are available to the faithful Christian at the moment he looks into his soul.

Turning what could be a heresy—a living Christian's seeing God—into an advantage, Traherne underscores the accuracy of the mirroring soul. Because of their clarity, reflections are, Traherne argues, more real than the physical things of the world. Yet crucial to Traherne's project, unlike material things, reflections have not been tainted by description or metaphoric comparison. Thus, Traherne emphasizes that reflections in the Christian soul are a meta-reality. By emphasizing the Cartesian notion that "ideas," or "thoughts" are more real than "things," Traherne creates another important place in which he can reform poetic language in describing these "things." He advances his meta-reality in his series of four "Thoughts" poems.[38] In the first of these poems, Traherne shows how he will use language non-metaphorically to give us "things" greater than those previously represented in language:

Ye brisk Divine and Living things,
Ye Great Exemplars, and ye Heavenly Springs,
Which I within me see;
Ye Machines Great,
Which in my Spirit God did Seat,
Ye Engines of Felicitie;
Ye Wondrous Fabricks of his Hands,
Who all possesseth that he understands;
That ye are pent within my Brest,
Yet rove at large from East to West,
And are Invisible, yet Infinite;
Is my Transcendent, and my Best Delight.

. . . .

Ye Inward, and ye Living Things!
The Thought, or Joy Conceived is
The inward Fabrick of my Standing Bliss.
It is the substance of my Mind
Transformed, and with its Objects lind.

("Thoughts. I." lines 1–12; 54–58)

Thoughts are "Machines," "Engines," "Fabricks," "Objects," all material and substantive entities, yet non-specific and abstract. No matter that the "images" in the mirroring soul are "thoughts." Traherne continues to use the Cartesian understanding of "thoughts" as having material characteristics. Yet he makes a point neither to describe nor to compare "thoughts;" rather he asserts their existence and tells us how they function. With this important move, Traherne extends the non-visual, visual language he develops from the language of perspective. The Christian trope of the mirroring soul gives Traherne a further means to give the "reall" and "naked truth" in language, without giving objects or images specific, subjective identity. Thoughts, coming from God, are available to all, and simply are—Traherne refuses to subjectify these images through metaphoric or specific comparison.

Traherne's best-known poem, "Shadows in the Water," shows his most comprehensive thinking about reflection and subjectivity. Without the context of the mirror as a touchstone of accuracy, "Shadows in the Water" can be read as yet another version of the Narcissus tale, though one with a happier ending. A young boy peers into a pool, confused by the reflection or "Shadows" that he sees there. "In unexperienc'd Infancy," he believes that reflections in the pool show "Another World," beneath the pool. "Another World," "Another Sun," "other Worlds," "Another face," and so on; the repetition of "other" takes these various forms throughout the poem. The resolution of his "sweet mistake" occurs in stanza eight:

> O ye that stand upon the Brink,
> Whom I so near me, throu the Chink,
> With Wonder see: What Faces there,
> Whose Feet, whose Bodies, do ye wear?
> I my companions see
> In You, another Me.
> They seemed Others, but are We;
> Our second Selvs those Shadows be.

(lines 57–64)

The boy seems to realize that figures in the reflection are not inhabitants of "A new *Antipodes*," but are one and the same with the self. However, he seems to nullify his recognition at the end of the poem, and this seeming reversal clarifies the emphatic realization that the reflections are not "other." The speaker recognizes these reflections in the water as Heaven, and the beings there the better selves that he and his friends will meet/ become in heaven:

> . . . below the purling Stream
> som unknown Joys there be
> Laid up in Store for me;
> To which I shall, when that thin Skin
> Is broken, be admitted in.

(lines 76–80)

The problem that Traherne addresses here is the problem that the technically advanced mirror presents to Paul's "Now through a glass darkly; then face to face." Here, though looking in a pool, the speaker still sees clearly what is reflected there. Yet rather than the simple reflection of himself, which would show the speaker trapped in subjective vision, he sees rather a view of God's objective vision: he sees how his life will look in heaven. The barrier of darkness or "shadow" that separates the "now" and the Christian hereafter simply does not exist for this speaker; all that separates him from "then" is the surface of the pool, "that thin Skin." Traherne replaces the question of vision with one of meaning: yes, we can see clearly into the other world, the "then" of eternity, but what transpires there—the "joys"—remain "unknown." The Christian can see what awaits his reunion with God, but he cannot experience it. The fundamental aspect of that experience is suggested by the boy's view into the pool: the reflection seems to suggest to the individual what "being seen" is like. Yet, this is the supreme temptation offered by the mirror and its illusion of objectivity. The individual's view of himself is hopelessly subjective; the right view is the objective view, and one which only God with his truly perspectival and objective vision can obtain. "Shadows in the Water" proposes a replacement for the Pauline now/then—dark/clear construction, offering a vision of then, now, but one that remains subjective, as one's view of one's reflection is subjective. Traherne insists, however, that the Christian sees in his soul accurate images of his life in eternity; he simply must not mistake the felicity of those visions with the end itself.

The speaker in "The Odour," at the mid-point of the *Poems of Felicity*, suggests an organic unity between self and world as another means of envisioning the self as God objectively sees human beings:

> Like amber fair thy Fingers grow;
> With fragrant Honey-sucks thy Head is crown'd;
> Like Stars, thine eys; thy Cheeks like Roses shew:
> All are Delights profound.
> Talk with thy self; thy self enjoy and see:
> At once the Mirror and the object be.
>
> (lines 55–60)

While this passage is often discussed in terms of Lacanian mirror/object separation, within the context of Traherne's perspectival language, this construction serves as an important segue to the final move in his resolution to the problem of partial and subjective vision. A few lines before the above stanza, Traherne indicates the direction of the poem: "But he that cannot like an Angel see, / In Heven its self shall dwell in Misery" (lines 40–41). Ultimately, of course, his solution is metaphoric: in order to "see aright," we must see ourselves as God and the angels view creation. Because he is doing his utmost to write non- or pre-metaphorically, Traherne invents this Arcimbaldo-like technique of transforming the self into the world. Thus when one looks at the self, one sees both the human self, and the self as seen from heaven's perspective. This attempt at showing the limits of subjectivity without losing subjectivity does present a rather mind-boggling stretch of the visual imagination, yet this is the kind of mental stretching that Traherne expects of readers. Nothing naive or childlike here, but rather an attempt to solve the most vexing of cognitive problems: how do we perceive how we are perceived? How can a subject see objectively?

Traherne adopts in his *oeuvre* an elaborate theater combining seers, seeing, and reflections as he presents the penultimate move in his strategy to address this philosophical issue and "mend" the subjectivity of human perception. Trying to move beyond even the submerged metaphor of "seeing as seen" Traherne invents a scheme in which God is a "seer" as well as an image, who can see his image in its various forms in the soul of the believer.

"Thoughts" imprinted with God's image are reflected back to God, the prime viewer. "While being there [in the mirroring soul], they richly Beautifie / The Place they fill, and yet communicat / Themselvs, reflecting to the Seers ey" ("The Circulation," lines 7–9). Though the poem also asserts that "Only tis GOD above, / That from, and in himself doth live" (lines 72–73), as we read in a subsequent poem, God the "Seer" is also God the reflector: "[God's] bosom is the Glass, / Wherein we all things Everlasting See" ("The Anticipation," lines 24–25).[39] Like the human soul, God's soul is also a clear mirror. Each soul both reflects and comprehends the other's mirroring soul. Seeing the self as a part of the world external to the self allows a contiguous relationship with the external. The mirror in our souls allows God to see himself in his creation. And the mirror of God allows us to see ourselves in him. Thus for Traherne's speaker, the creation is no longer "other," nor does the speaker need to rely solely upon the strategy of seeing his limbs as those of a tree. The universe lies within the speaker, just as he simultaneously resides within God and his creation.

The "Circulation" in the title of the above lyric refers to the circulation of imagistic ideas between the mirroring souls of the Christian and God. The reflection of images between these reflecting souls elides into movement in subsequent poems. "The Vision," animates the mirroring soul: a "fountain"—a moving pool—becomes the "glass."[40] The fountain, not surprisingly, lies somewhere between a mirror and a stream; it both moves and reflects, always leading back to its own beginning, or "Caus":

To see the *Fountain* is a Blessed Thing;
It is to see the King
Of Glory face to face: But yet the End,
The Glorious Wondrous End, is more;
And yet the Fountain there we Comprehend,
The Spring we there adore:
For in the End the Fountain best is Shewn,
As by Effects the Caus is Known.
                                    ("The Vision," lines 41–48)

Traherne again addresses the potential heterodoxy that his hypothesis introduces: rather than seeing a dark and suggestive image in the mirroring soul—Paul's "through a glass, darkly"—the clear mirror yields a clear image of the divine. Similar to the relationship between clear vision and the hereafter in "Shadows in the Water," his transformation of the mirroring souls of God and man into a flowing fountain addresses both the subjectivity of the mirror, and the problem of seeing God's being. Even with his complex and elaborate uses of non-visual visual language, of course, Traherne cannot solve the problem he sets for himself. He must acknowledge that while Christians on earth have the ability "to see the King / Of Glory face to face"; purely objective vision cannot exist: "But yet the End, / The Glorious Wondrous End, is more." Even if we follow the steps of his invention, we are only ensured that "we also comprehend" that the "end is more." The image in the soul, while it is clear and accurate, is within a larger range of concomitant images that we "comprehend," but cannot freeze or possess. Faith, alas, remains the ineffable piece of the philosophical puzzle.

The problems inherent in our thinking in terms of subjectivity and objectivity continue to plague philosophers today. Traherne prophetically engages this important issue, though his solutions may seem both antique and untenable, and his cause, retrograde. Yet we marvel at the boldness of his enterprise: he attempts to undo 400 years of Petrarchan poetic practice, quite a risky undertaking in itself, but to do so he goes further out on a limb and employs the divisive technology of linear perspective. Combining the technology of the mirror as the enabling device for the development of perspective with the Christian symbolism of the mirroring soul, Traherne claims a metamorphosis of perspectival subjectivity into divine objectivity. This extraordinary amalgamation of elements reveals that Traherne himself embodies a rare alliance of attributes: conservative in his philosophical instincts, revolutionary in his use of poetic language and form, sagacious and forward thinking in his choice of means to achieve his end.

## Notes

1. The "Book of Private Devotions" is also called the "Churches' Yearbook." (Bodleian MS. Eng. Th. e. 51).

2. Margoliouth details the familiar story of Traherne's discovery in the introduction to his two-volume edition of Traherne (*Centuries, Poems, and Thanksgivings*, ed. H. M. Margoliouth, 2 vols. [Oxford: Clarendon Press, 1958]). In the winter of 1896–1897, W. T. Brooke bought the manuscripts of *The Centuries of Meditation* and the so-called Dobell folio of Traherne's lyrics. He paid a few pence for them at a London bookstall. These unidentified manuscripts fell into the hands of Alexander Grosart, who was working on an edition of Vaughan's poems. Grosart mistakenly attributed the manuscripts to Vaughan. Grosart died before his new edition of Vaughan could be produced, thus the Traherne poems were not published as Vaughan's (though the two poets have become linked in many discussions). The Traherne manuscripts fell into the hands of Bertram Dobell who ascribed the poems and *Centuries* to Traherne. He put out the first edition of the poems in 1903 (*The Poetical Works of Thomas Traherne*, ed., Bertram Dobell [London: P. J. & A. E. Dobell, 1903], 2nd ed. 1906) as well as an edition of the *Centuries of Meditations* (*Centuries of Meditations*, ed. Bertram Dobell [London: P. J. & A. E. Dobell, 1908. rep 1927]; in 1934 and 1948 without Dobell's introduction). For detailed descriptions of this scholarly detective work, see also Richard Altick, *The Scholar Adventurers* (New York: Macmillan, 1950).

3. *Listener* 3 (1930): 590–591, 590. See, as well, T. S. Eliot's essay "The Metaphysical Poets" in *Seventeenth-Century English Poetry*, ed., William R. Keast (New York: Oxford University Press, 1962), 23–31, 24. Because of Eliot's strong rhetoric, most readers attribute to Traherne the disinterested approach to the physical world of the *via negativa* mystic. Studies in the early years agree with Eliot's negative assessment of Traherne's poetry, offering instead discussion of his mysticism. See T. O. Beachcroft, "Traherne, and the Doctrine of Felicity," *Criterion*, 9 (1930): 291–307; Helen C. White, *The Metaphysical Poets: A Study in Religious Experience* (New York: Macmillan, 1936); K. W. Salter, *Thomas Traherne: Mystic and Poet* (New York: Barnes & Noble, 1964). Until the sixties, most readers follow Eliot and White when applying mystical readings to Traherne's poetry, and, less frequently, to his prose; they find discussing his mysticism more intriguing than analyzing his literary achievement. (See also Walter Lock, "An English Mystic," *The Constructive Quarterly*, 1 [1913]: 826–836; Alison J. Sherrington, *Mystical Symbolism in the Poetry of Thomas Traherne* (St. Lucia, Australia: University of Queensland Press, 1970). In the late 1960s, A. L. Clements in *The Mystical Poetry of Thomas Traherne* (Cambridge, Mass.: Harvard University Press, 1969) attempts a rereading of Traherne on the grounds that "discussions of Traherne's mysticism are general, superficial, and disappointing" (500) and do not address "the relation of content to form and style" in the poetry. Clements, however, still argues for Traherne's mystical quest for unity with God (500). Like Clements, Stanley Stewart in *The Expanded Voice: The Art of Thomas Traherne* (San Marino, Calif.: Huntington Library, 1970), believes Traherne to have been slighted by critics (those still under the influence of Eliot's judgments) who use invalid criteria such as "organic unity" and "concrete diction" in evaluating his poetry. Stewart asserts that Traherne "make[s] language do the impossible" (198) by using his particular style to render his irrational experiences "transparent;" because such experiences defy rational categories, Traherne's writing lies outside of logical progression as it dissolves or ignores all boundaries on an endless journey into the infinite. For Stewart, this quest for unity, coupled with a dual twisting of language—one that forces words to be both transparent and illogical—places Traherne in the category of the mystical poet. While both critics attempt to move Traherne beyond Eliot's poetic yardstick, both Clements and Stewart maintain the traditional understanding of mystical literature as the *via negativa*, detailing a journey ending in a state of union with the divine. In *Thomas Traherne: The Growth of a Mystic's Mind: A Study of the Evolution and the Phenomenology of Traherne's Mystical Consciousness* (Salzburg: Institut für Anglistik und Amerikanistik Universität Salzburg, 1982), Franz Wöhrer endeavors to correct these past "controversial" and "speculative" studies (7); he employs "an empirically substantiated 'psychology of mysticism'" (5). Wöhrer's attempt to shift the critical apparatus in Traherne scholarship incorporates the material aspects of phenomenological criticism. In doing so, he aspires to look at the way that Traherne discusses his world, rather than the fact that he denies his world. Wöhrer's combination of psychology and phenomenology at times takes away from a discussion of Traherne's language.

4. A long political poem at the Folger Library, and a three-part theological treatise at Lambeth Palace. See Julia Smith and Laetitia Yeadle, "Felicity Disguised in Fiery Words: Genesis and Exodus in a Newly Discovered Poem by Thomas Traherne," *Times Literary Supplement* 4936 (Nov. 7, 1997): 17, and D. Inge and

C. Macfarlane, "'Seeds of Eternity': A New Traherne Manuscript (Lambeth Palace Library Manuscript 1360)," *Times Literary Supplement* 5070 (June 2, 2000): 14.

5. Gladys I. Wade, *Thomas Traherne* (Princeton: Princeton University Press, 1944), 3.

6. In the Folger Shakespeare library in Washington, D.C. See Yeadle and Smith, "Felicity Disguised."

7. See N. I. Matur, "The Political Views of Thomas Traherne," *Huntington Library Quarterly* 57, no. 3 (1994): 241–253 and J. Smith, "Attitudes toward Conformity and Nonconformity in Thomas Traherne," *Bunyan Studies* 1, no. 1 (1988): 26–35. Critics also have attempted to place Traherne's language within theological movements such as Cambridge Platonism, and to read him through various critical lenses. Most recently in his *Traherne in Dialogue: Heidegger, Lacan, and Derrida* (Durham, N.C.: Duke University Press, 1988), A. Leigh DeNeef brings Traherne "into dialogue" with Heidegger, Lacan, and Derrida "to try to reveal the thinking that validates and authorizes his poetry" (20). DeNeef argues that Traherne's "imagination, continually returning to either a Heideggerian lack or a Lacanian want, must obsessively attempt to fill such abysses with [Derridian] 'more'" (21). His criticism of Traherne criticism is similar to my observations about the failures of biographical and historical criticism.

8. Traherne in *The Centuries of Meditation,* 132. All quotations from the *Centuries* are from the Margoliouth edition, *Centuries, Poems, and Thanksgivings,* ed. H. M. Margoliouth, 2 vols. (Oxford: Clarendon Press, 1958), and will be noted by *Century* number in the text. For discussion of Traherne's studies, see Carol L. Marks, "Thomas Traherne's Early Studies," *PBSA,* 62 (1968): 511–536. There is a body of criticism on Traherne and science, beginning with Rosalie Colie's unpublished master's thesis, "Cosmic Response of Thomas Traherne: A Study of Traherne against the Scientific Background of His Day," Columbia University, 1946. See also Marjorie Hope Nicolson, *The Breaking of the Circle: Studies in the Effect of the "New Science" upon Seventeenth-Century Poetry* (Evanston, 1950, Rev. ed. New York: Columbia University Press, 1960) and Robert Ellrodt, "Scientific Curiosity and Metaphysical Poetry in the Seventeenth Century," *MP* 61 (1964): 180–197.

9. See Barbara K. Lewalski, "Thomas Traherne: Naked Truth, Transparent Words, and The Renunciation of Metaphor." In *Protestant Poetics and the Seventeenth-Century Religious Lyric* (Princeton: Princeton University Press, 1979), 352–387 and Stewart, *The Expanded Voice,* for discussions of Traherne's metaphors as "naked" or "transparent." My argument, while benefiting from theirs, shifts the term from "transparent" to "non-visual," and I believe that Traherne attempts to write non-metaphorically for reasons that I shall elaborate.

10. For general discussion of perspective and poetry, see Myer H. Abrams, *The Mirror and the Lamp: Romantic Theory and the Critical Tradition* (New York: Oxford University Press, 1953); Lucy Gent, *Picture and Poetry, 1560–1620: Relations between Literature and the Visual Arts in the English Renaissance* (Leamington Spa: James Hall, 1981); Ernest B. Gilman, *The Curious Perspective: Literary and Pictorial Wit in the Seventeenth Century* (New Haven: Yale University Press, 1978); Claudio Guillen, "On the Concept of Metaphor of Perspective," in *Comparatists at Work,* ed., Stephen G. Nichols, Jr. and Richard Vowles (Waltham, Mass.: Blaisdell Publishing Company, 1968), 28–90; and Clark Hulse, *The Rule of Art: Literature and Painting in the Renaissance* (Chicago: University of Chicago Press, 1990).

11. Throughout this essay, I shall use Traherne's poems, and in one case, his prose poems, in an order that reflects his development of the idea, rather than in any predetermined order or group. Traherne's work survives only in manuscript and in a collection *(Poems of Felicity)* that he seems to have begun, but not completed. Thus, the order of poems as he intended does not exist.

12. "Gild" in its alchemical use means to infuse or to "impregnate" a body of matter with gold. One of the tenets of heraldry dictates that a metal must not be charged onto another metal. All quotations from *The Poems of Felicity* and from other Traherne poems are from the Margoliouth edition, *Centuries, Poems, and Thanksgivings,* ed., H. M. Margoliouth, 2 vols. (Oxford: Clarendon Press, 1958), and will be noted by line numbers in the text.

13. In *Echoes of Desire: English Petrarchism and Its Counterdiscourses* (Ithaca: Cornell University Press, 1995), Heather Dubrow discusses the "layering of anti-Petrarchan and Petrarchan sentiments within the same sequence" (74 ff.).

14. Dubrow, *Echoes,* summarizes the critical discussion about gender and power in Petrarchism (3 ff.).

15. Anti-Petrarchan poets reacted strongly against these lesser poems, such as this by the anonymous author of *Zepheria* (1594), who perhaps provides Shakespeare, in his "My mistress' eyes are nothing like the sun" with this muddle of Petrarchan metaphors to spurn:

> Thy coral-colored lips, how should I portray
> Unto the unmatchable pattern of their sweet?
> A draught of blessedness I stole away
> From them when last I Kiss'd. I taste it yet;
> So did that sug'ry touch my lips ensucket.
> On them, Minerva's honey birds do hive
> Mellifluous words, when so thou please to frame
> Thy speech to entertainment.

> Herschel Baker and Hyder E. Rollins, eds.,
> *The Renaissance in England: Non-dramatic Prose and Verse of the Sixteenth Century* [Lexington, Mass.: 1954], 503, lines 1–8).

The (presumably) unintended high comedy of these metaphors peaks with Minerva's "honey birds" building hives on the beloved's lips, though the real fun comes with imagining the lover kissing such an elaborate sticky mess.

16. In his "Church's Yearbook" (Bodleian MS. Eng. Th. e. 51) Traherne quotes Herbert's poem "To All Angels and Saints" in its entirety. As Clements (213) and others have noted, echoes of Herbert's poems appear throughout Traherne's work.

17. Thomas Greene, *The Light in Troy* (New Haven: Yale University Press, 1982), 94.

18. *Ibid.,* 94–95.

19. *Ibid.,* 95.

20. While discussions of autobiographical texts normally identify Augustine as the first writer to recognize subjectivity, Greene argues that Augustine practices a Medieval mode of rhetoric as imitation; thus he remains connected to the historical text. Further, as John Freccero has argued, Petrarch's use of the laurel tree compared to Augustine's use of the fig tree shows Petrarch's creation of an "autonomous

universe of autoreflexive signs without reference to an anterior Logos," while Augustine's fig is an allegorical sign which "stands for a referential series of anterior texts grounded in the Logos." Augustine may have written personal episodes, but because his are "Christian revelations," he does not attempt the kind of disconnect from what has come before that Petrarch attempts in his metaphoric punning on Laura. Thus Petrarch's is a true subjectivity, in that it consciously attempts to sever connection with a prior object, or world (Freccero in Greene, 114–115).

21. Tzvetan Todorov, *The Conquest of America*, trans. Richard Howard (New York: Harper Perennial, 1992), 121.

22. Alberti, *On Painting and On Sculpture: The Latin Texts of De Pictura and De Statua*, in Cecil Grayson, trans., ed., Martin Kemp (New York: Penguin, 1991), 83.

23. As a letter from 1413 verifies, Brunelleschi devised or "rediscovered" the mathematical theory for rendering three-dimensional space on a two-dimensional plane. See G. Tanturli, "Rapporti del Brunelleschi con gli ambienti letterai [sic]." In *Filippo Brunelleschi. Le sua opere e il suo tempo*. 2 vols. (Florence, 1980). Alberti elaborates upon and modifies this theory and its many aesthetical implications in his *On Painting* (1435–1436), which he first wrote in Latin, then translated into the vernacular. The interpretive works on the development of perspective and the life of Brunelleschi include G. C. Argan, "The Architecture of Brunelleschi and the Origins of Perspective Theory in the Fifteenth Century," *JWCI* 9 (1946): 96–121; Samuel Y. Edgerton, *The Renaissance Rediscovery of Linear Perspective* (New York: Harper & Row, 1975); William M. Ivins, Jr., *On the Rationalization of Sight* (New York: Da Capo Press, 1973); Mark Jarzombek, *On Leon Baptista Alberti: His Literary and Aesthetic Theories* (Cambridge, Mass.: MIT Press, 1989); Martin Kemp, *The Science of Art: Optical Themes in Western Art from Brunelleschi to Seurat* (New Haven: Yale University Press, 1990); David Lindberg, *Theories of Vision from Al-Kindi to Kepler* (Chicago: University of Chicago Press, 1976); A. Manetti, *The Life of Brunelleschi*, ed., H. Saalman, Trans. C. Engass (University Park, Pa.: Pennsylvania State University Press, 1970); M. H. Pirenne, *Optics, Painting, and Photography* (London: Cambridge University Press, 1969); Carroll W. Westfall, "Painting and the Liberal Arts: Alberti's View." *JHI*, Vol. 30 (1969): 487–506; and John White, *The Birth and Rebirth of Pictorial Space*, 3rd ed. (Cambridge: Belknap Press, 1987) and "Developments in Renaissance Perspectives," *JWCI* 12 (1949): 58–79.

24. To make these determinations, Brunelleschi used the principles of Ptolemy, who had shown how corresponding points could be traced on a mirror and had explained how to find intersecting points on a plane.

25. See D. Gioseffi, "Perspective." In *Encyclopedia of World Art*, Vol. 11 (New York: McGraw-Hill, 1966), 183–221. Renaissance manuals on perspective include: Daniele Barbaro, *Pratica della prospettiva* (Venice, 1569); Jean Dubreuil, *La Perspective Practique*, Trans. Robert Pricke (London: H. Lloyd, 1672); Richard Haydocke, *Preface to a Tracte Containing the Artes of Curious Painting Carvinge & Buildinge* (Oxford: 1598), his trans. of Lomazzo's *Trattato dell'arte della pittura* (Milan: 1584); Joseph Moxon, *Practical Perspective* (London: 1670); Andrea Pozzo, *Perspectiva pictorum et architectorum* (Rome: 1693), English edition (London: 1707); John Shute, *The First and Chief Groundes of Architecture* (London: 1563); Vitruvius, *The Ten Books of Architecture*, trans. Morris Hicky Morgan (New York: Dover, 1960); Witelo, *Book V of Witelo's Perspectiva*, ed. and trans., A. Mark Smith (Warsaw: 1983); Sir Henry Wotton, *The Elements of Architecture* (London: 1624).

26. For Brunelleschi to produce a three-dimensional image on a flat surface, two elements were necessary: the clear, accurate crystal mirror and the mathematical calculations that allowed proportional dimensions to be rendered on a plane.

27. See R. W. Symonds, "English Looking-Glass Plates and Their Manufacture." *Connoisseur* 97 (1936): 243–248 and Geoffrey Wills, *English Looking-glasses* (South Brunswick, N.J.: A. S. Barnes, 1965). While in this essay I concentrate upon two primary aspects of the mirror as a material object and a metaphor, the mirror has a long and rich history as a symbolic image in literature. See Herbert Grabes, *The Mutable Glass: Mirror-Imagery in Titles and Texts of the Middle Ages and English Renaissance*, trans., Gordon Collier (Cambridge: Cambridge University Press, 1982), for elaboration upon these traditional uses of the mirror. For more specific information, see Leroy Appleton and Stephen Bridges, *Symbolism in Liturgical Art* (New York: Scribner, 1959); Jurgis Baltrusaitis, *Le Miroir* (Paris, 1978); Morton W. Bloomfield, *The Seven Deadly Sins: An Introduction to the History of a Religious Concept* (East Lansing, Mich.: Michigan State College Press, 1967); Sister Ritamary Bradley, "Backgrounds of the Title *Speculum* in Medieval Literature," *Speculum* 24 (1954): 100–115; A. E. Crawley, "Mirror," *Encyclopaedia of Religion and Ethics*, ed., James Hastings. Vol. 8 (Edinburgh: T & T Clark, 1908–1926); James L. Miller, "The Mirrors of Dante's Paradiso," *UTQ* 46 (1977): 263–279; Heinrich Schwarz, "The Mirror in Art," *Art Quarterly* 15, no. 2 (1952): 96–118 and "The Mirror of the Artist and the Mirror of the Devout," *Studies in the History of Art for the Samuel H. Kress Foundation* (New York, 1959); James Williams, "Mirror and Speculum in Book Titles," *Law Magazine and Review* 26 (London: 1901): 157–163; Wolfgang M. Zucker, "Reflections on Reflections," *JAAC* 20 (1962): 239–250.

28. Nicholas Hilliard, *The Arte of Limning* (Great Britain: Mid-Northumberland Arts Group in association with Carcanet New Press, 1981). There were no practitioners of linear perspective in England during most of the sixteenth century other than Holbein, during his brief residence in the court of Henry VIII. (Holbein left Switzerland in the early sixteenth century because of the Iconoclasm associated with Calvinism.) Theoretical texts describing perspective only began appearing in English in 1598 with Richard Haydocke's translation and adaptation of *Preface to A Tracte,* Lomazzo's treatise on painting and carving. This text, as well as others, had previously been available in Latin. Haydocke's reason for translating Lomazzo, he says, was "the increase of the knowledge of the Arte, which . . . never attained to any great perfection among us (save in some feawe of late)." The Humanist movement in England assured that educated men would want to school themselves in the art of painting, and would bring continental notions about perspective into dominance by the mid-seventeenth century. In 1606, Henry Peacham (author of *The Complete Gentleman*) wrote *The Art of Drawing with the Pen,* and *Limning in Water Colours* (London, 1606) hoping to create in England a knowledgeable group of art collectors among his former students and friends. Most important, the philosophical, Humanist underpinnings of perspectival theory were available to a variety of readers, not just painters, and these ideas rapidly became a part of the gentleman's university curriculum. Robert Burton reflects this kind of education in *The Anatomy of Melancholy,* ed., Holbrook Jackson, 3 vols. (New York, 1932): "To most kind of men it is an extraordinary delight to study. For what a world of books offers itself, in all subjects, arts, and sciences, to the sweet content and capacity of the reader! In arithmetic, geometry, perspective, optics, astronomy, architecture, sculptura, pictura, of which so many and such elaborate treatises

are of late written" (88). The Earl of Arundel, listed as a patron in Peacham's *Art of Drawing*, collected Italian painting and sculpture; John Donne apparently owned a small number of paintings. Prince Charles acquired a taste for Titian, Rubens, and Velàsquez while visiting Spain in 1623; he later bought the private art holdings of the Duke of Mantua. During Charles's reign, Van Dyck, Rubens, and Gentileschi were a few of many artists who spent considerable time in England (See Gilman, Curious *Perspective* 53 and Eric Mercer, *English Art: 1553–1625* [Oxford: Clarendon Press, 1962]). As Roy Strong details, Prince Henry was a great lover of painting and a student of the famous French perspectivist, Salomon de Caus, who designed anamorphic gardens in England. See Roy Strong's *Henry Prince of Wales and England's Lost Renaissance* (New York: Thames & Hudson, 1986).

29. Roy Strong (*The English Renaissance Miniature* [New York: Thames and Hudson, 1983] asserts that Hilliard's miniature of Christopher Hatton "establishes [Hilliard's] total ignorance of the laws of perspective" (97). However, Hilliard's treatise proves that he is not ignorant of these laws; he chooses deliberately not to practice them.

30. "The Defense of Poesy," in *Critical Theory Since Plato*, ed. Hazard Adams (New York: Harcourt Brace Jovanovich, 1971): 155–177, 157.

31. Sidney and Hilliard were acquainted; Hilliard recounts a conversation with Sidney in his *The Art of Limning* (83) in which Sidney seems to be goading Hilliard for not using the rules of perspective. Presumably, Sidney's argument works better for poetry than for painting, which is, like nature, spatial. Leon Battisa Alberti's treatise on painting, *De pictura*, makes similar mimetic claims for painting that Sidney makes for poetry. Both claims are essentially Platonic. Sidney traveled widely on the continent and spent enough time in Venice to sit for Veronese. (See Hulse, *Rule of Art*, 117–119 for a discussion of Sidney and Hilliard's continental travels.. During his visit to Venice in 1574, Sidney could have read the Latin version of Alberti, translated by Lodovico Domenichi ([Venice, Giolito, 1547]; thanks to Melinda Schlitt for this information). There is an extensive literature on Alberti; the best place to start is with Cecil Grayson's introduction to his translation of the treatise. See also Argan; Jarzombek; Kemp, 1990; Joel Snyder, "Picturing Vision," *The Language of Images*, ed., W. J. T. Mitchell (Chicago: University of Chicago Press, 1980), 219–246; and Westfall.

32. *Commentaries of Heaven: The Poems*, ed., D. D. C. Chambers, Salzburg, Austria Studies in English Literature: Elizabethan & Renaissance Studies (Salzburg: Institut für Anglistik und Amerikanistik, 1989), 82.

33. From the *Authorized Version*. For commentary on the "glass" in Paul's writing, see George Arthur Buttrick, et al., eds., *The Interpreter's Bible*. Vol. 12 (New York: Abingdon-Cokesbury Press, 1953).

34. Traherne strikes a balance between Platonic (somewhat modified by Augustine) and Neo-platonic uses of ocular metaphors. In general, Renaissance humanists lump together in their mirror images Homer and Augustine, Plotinus, and Thomas Traherne, securely in the Florentine Neo-platonic tradition, also draws upon Cambridge Neo-platonic philosophy, as well as upon Augustinian mirror imagery. See Carol L. Marks, "Thomas Traherne and Cambridge Platonism," *PMLA* 81 (1966): 118–131 and C. A. Patrides, ed., *The Cambridge Platonists* (Cambridge: Cambridge University Press, 1969) for discussion of Traherne and Cambridge Neo-Platonism.

35. In Augustine, *De trinitate*, trans. Stephen McKenna (Washington, D.C.: Catholic University Press, 1970). See A. B. Acton, "Idealism," in *The Encyclopedia of Philosophy*, ed., Paul Edwards, Vol. 4 (New York: Macmillan, 1967), 110–118; Robert McRae, "'Idea' as a Philosophical Term in the Seventeenth Century," *JHI* 26 (1965): 175–190; and Erwin Panofsky, *Idea: A Concept in Art History*, trans., Joseph J. S. Peake (Columbia, S.C.: University of South Carolina Press, 1968) for explications of this term.

36. Several readers have noted the Lacanian implications in this poem. DeNeef, *Traherne in Dialogue*, addresses this issue.

37. René Descartes, *Discourse on Method, Optics, Geometry, and Meteorology*, trans. Paul J. Olscamp (Indianapolis: Bobbs-Merrill, 1965), 164. For Descartes, knowledge of the material world is not derived from the senses, except indirectly. Comprehension of the extended (material) world is rational and intellectual and cannot be represented in images. For further discussion of Descartes, see Richard Popkin, *The History of Skepticism from Erasmus to Descartes* (New York: The Humanities Press, 1964); Norman Kemp Smith, *New Studies in the Philosophy of Descartes* (New York: Russell & Russell, 1963); Bernard Williams, "René Descartes," in *The Encyclopedia of Philosophy*, ed., Paul Edwards, Vol. 2 (New York: Macmillan, 1967), 344–354.

38. These poems are the penultimate sequence in the "Dobell Manuscript." Had Traherne lived to finish the *Poems of Felicity*, the direction of his approach indicates that these poems would assume this position there, as well.

39. These two poems appear in the Dobell manuscript (Bodleian MSS. Eng. Poet. C. 42), which is written in Traherne's hand, with small emendations in another hand. The Burney manuscript (British Museum MS. Burney 392), the *Poems of Felicity*, contains many poems also in Dobell, though written in the hand of Philip, Traherne's brother. Traherne's intent in terms of ordering and organizing his lyrics can only be surmised through his numbered sequences (the "Thoughts" poems, for example) or with poems such as "The Circulation" and "The Anticipation," which form a sequence by virtue of content.

40. Augustine first used the image of the mirroring soul as a reflective pool.

ROBERT WHALEN

# George Herbert's Sacramental Puritanism

George Herbert (1593–1633) has been identified as among the earliest of divines "to proclaim the new Anglo-centric orthodoxy" of the English church (Milton, 528). Whereas for earlier conformists the Church of England was a champion of true religion against anti-Christian Rome, the later Jacobean and Caroline ecclesiastical establishment sought to extricate itself from the confessional struggles of European Protestantism. This middle road, it is crucial to note, was based not on the ideal moderation it eventually came to signify in later historiography, but rather on a complex mixture of nationalism, the need to establish a greater sense of contiguity with tradition, and the growing inclination to jettison an earlier Protestant identity. Distinct from foreign Calvinism, the English middle way in the 1620s and 1630s yielded increasingly to an emphasis on sacrament and ceremony to support the inclusivist policies of a state institution. Though most mainstream bishops and ministers sought to combine the ceremonial and doctrinal elements of English Christianity, long-standing conflict over the church's confessional identity intensified and threatened seriously to erode relations among the establishment clergy. With its strained fusion of Reform doctrine and Roman Catholic ecclesiology, the English *via media* was compromised whenever sacrament and ceremony on the one hand conflicted on the other with a religious practice more devotional, scriptural and homiletic in orientation.[1]

*Renaissance Quarterly*, Volume 54, Number 4, Part 1 (Winter 2001): pp. 1273–1307.

An elaboration of C. A. Patrides's observation that the Eucharist is "the marrow of Herbert's sensibility" (Herbert, 1988, 17), this paper elucidates a sacramental poetics through which the poet sought to reconcile the potentially contrary imperatives of public ceremony and private religious devotion. There is in *The Temple* a marked ambivalence toward the relationship between these modes of piety, particularly as they converge on Herbert's treatment of sacrament. The two are brought together successfully, but this success consists precisely in the drama resulting from the ideological conflict the poems trace. Unmistakably inward in focus, Herbert's devotional enthusiasm is cultivated nonetheless through a fully sacramental apparatus. Similarly, while in certain respects exemplary of what Peter Lake has described as "avant-garde conformity"—the aggressive promotion of a predominantly sacerdotal and ceremonial vision of the church (1991, 113–114)—Herbert's verse also typifies the "internal religious experience" Anthony Milton identifies as a distinctive feature of both moderate and more radical Puritan divinity (12).

Critical proponents of a coherent Stuart *via media* discern in Herbert a balance of Protestant doctrine and reverence for traditional ceremonial forms. In recent scholarship, however, the middle road tends often to veer in a decidedly Genevan direction. In *Love Known,* a sophisticated development of the Protestant poetics first advanced by William Halewood and Barbara Lewalski, Richard Strier avers that eucharistic terminology in *The Temple* is for the most part metaphorical (47).[2] Gene Veith, similarly, while allowing external forms "to have been closest to Herbert's experience," emphasizes the poet's discussion of the sacraments "in the more guarded terms of Reformed, Calvinist theology" (218; see also Clarke, 13). Christopher Hodgkins is more emphatic in identifying Herbert's *via media* as "very nearly Calvinist. Very, very nearly" (20). Hodgkins, like Veith, rightly points out the significant role sacrament and ceremony played in Reform theology and ecclesiology, and his analysis of *The Temple* persuasively challenges Louis Martz's influential view of Herbert as exemplary Anglo-Catholic. In his discussion of the church's and Herbert's indebtedness to Reform theology for their sacramental views, Hodgkins thus compares key passages from the *Institutes of the Christian Religion,* the Elizabethan Articles, and selected lines from several *Temple* lyrics (24–31). Perhaps the foremost champion of a Calvinist Herbert, Daniel Doerksen concurs with Hodgkins by seeing in the Jacobean and early Caroline church a middle road that runs directly *through* Geneva—between not Rome and Calvin's Swiss church, but rather Rome and the more radical separatists or "those considered heterodox in theology" (21). But this only restates rather than answers the question of the church's confessional identity: considered by whom? Indeed, what is the standard by which anyone in the pre-Civil War religious establishment is to be identified as heterodox, particularly with respect to sacraments and their role in the spiritual life of the church? Doerksen tells us that the eucharistic element in Herbert's poetry is "overrated" by those who neglect to notice that even the most sacramental of the lyrics are about the speaker's heart (97). His observation that Herbert's religion (and Donne's) is "personal and biblical rather than institutional" (139), however, is based on a false dichotomy, as though the focus on inwardness and scripture were not compatible with the contemporary religious hegemony. Indeed, Doerksen's study itself characterizes the conformist mainstream of the early Stuart church as predominantly and therefore *institutionally* Calvinist.

R. V. Young is the most recent and a very formidable critic of the Protestant poetics that has predominated in Herbert studies during the past several decades. His observation that such work "fails to do justice to either Catholic or Protestant, forcing both parties into narrow ideological categories," is long overdue. Particularly relevant to the present study is Young's recognition of the relevance of sacrament for meditational practices. "[T]he most intimate and withdrawn of *private* devotions," he writes, "involves the urge to escape the self" so that "solitude is only the means to a profounder communion" (88–89). Young does not consider, however, the extent to which the relationship between sacrament and devotional solitude could be one of conflict rather than cooperation, a conflict rooted in the confessional struggles of the English church. Critical of the "new-historicist inclination [to] try to explain devotional and doctrinal motifs in *The Temple* in terms of the socio-political imperatives of Jacobean and Caroline culture," he is concerned that "unless the poetry is, at some point, considered in its own right as poetry, then there is, finally, no point in studying it at all" (122). The detailed close readings provided here should allay such concern. But Young's insistence that Herbert "was not bound to any of the particular party platforms current in his day" (122) too hastily dismisses the considerable body of Church of England historiography produced in recent years and its relevance for our understanding of the period's literature. Herbert's doctrinal elusiveness, I suggest, is itself a political strategy—irenic in intent and pastoral in motivation, to be sure—but deeply aware of the controversies it navigates. Reading *The Temple* in light of church politics is neither "reductive" nor does it "threaten" Herbert's "poetic vitality" (122–123). On the contrary, that very vitality is evident in his subtle and often dazzling engagement with the socio-religious turbulence of the period. Herbert's heavenly verse in this respect is firmly on the ground, however exalting our definition of poetry "as poetry."

The relationship between doctrine and discipline—between, that is, formal theological belief and outward matters including church governance, polity, and ceremonial practice[3]—is important for our understanding of Herbert's sacramental poetics. Simply put, theories of eucharistic presence emphasizing its material aspects tended to support a sacerdotal style of divinity in which priest, ceremony and outward conformity are key features. Belief in the centrality of inward spiritual life, on the other hand, was reinforced by a theology in which the external elements are less effectual instruments than mere signs of a strictly invisible grace. These binarisms, of course, are problematic, but like all such polarities they are useful if understood as framing the ideological continuum traversed by early Stuart divines in their struggles over the church's confessional identity. Such labels, then, are less precise confessional categories than ideological tendencies, so that while there certainly were divines whose theological itineraries suggest a stable middle road embracing both Puritan and ceremonialist inclinations, such "Anglo-Catholics" or Puritan moderates or Calvinist conformists were not immune to the controversies that occupied their more openly polemical contemporaries. This critical flexibility is necessary in considering Herbert, who clearly valued both external and internal dimensions of religious piety. Achsah Guibbory demonstrates such sensitivity in suggesting that when Herbert's lyrics are personal and introspective they tend to "spiritualise the church festivals and ceremonies . . . in a way that deemphasises the material, ceremonial, and outward aspects of worship" (55). Another way of looking at this, however, is to see sacrament and ceremony as penetrating the inner devotional realm and claiming its otherwise insular space as contiguous with the trappings that are its institutional surface. In Elizabeth Clarke's attractive formulation, Herbert's poems externalize "the inward spiritual holiness which is the essence of Reformed piety" (115–116). Internal and external components of religious experience converge in *The Temple* on eucharistic topoi, devotional and ceremonial pieties vying for the identity of Christian grace and the location of its authority, just as competing sacramental theories focus on the manner in which the eucharistic elements communicate their holy referents. A style of divinity emphasizing religious experience as integral with ceremonial forms and ritual tends toward more sensualist eucharistic formulae. Obversely, the extent to which the Eucharist was thought to contain or otherwise effectually to communicate grace is an index of its sacerdotal status and role in promoting the church's social and confessional cohesion. The Pauline admonition to examine oneself when receiving the Eucharist was important for early Stuart divines of all stripes, whether moderate Puritan, conforming Calvinist, or avant-garde ceremonialist. But just as Jesus's words of institution were the site of exegetical conflict, so were the relative emphases placed on private devotion and ceremony potentially divisive. Sacramental topoi in *The Temple* manifest these competing claims to the identity and character of religious experience.[4]

* * *

The controversy over sacraments and other ceremonial forms that was to flare again during the Laudian archbishopric long had been a feature of the English church's struggle to establish a definitive confessional identity. Indeed, sixteenth-century views of the role and nature of sacraments were, at best, ambiguous. In the 1549 Prayer Book—Thomas Cranmer's supreme contribution to Edwardine reform, particularly as regards the Eucharist—the elevation of the Host at the sacring bell, the pax and holy bread were all removed from the official Church of England liturgy. Now absent from the calendar were most of the traditional feast days, and eliminated also were the very popular and widespread Jesus Masses (Duffy, 465). And yet as tenacious a traditionalist as the Bishop of Winchester, Stephen Gardiner, could find in the Prayer Book the teaching of the Mass to which he was accustomed, despite the obvious abrogation in its pages of essential features of English religious tradition (Ibid., 470). But if the Edwardine Prayer Book was largely an adaptation of the Roman Missal, that of 1552 constitutes dramatic Protestant revision, evident especially in the notorious Black Rubric, hastily added in response to the influential presbyterian John Knox and his disdain for popish ceremonies. It is perhaps one of the chief reasons the staunchly Roman Catholic Mary Tudor repealed the book upon her accession in 1553, for in addition to refusing the notion that kneeling in any way implies adoration, the Black Rubric was boldly Calvinist in its denial of "any real and essential presence there being of Christ's natural flesh and blood. For as concerning the sacramental bread and wine, they remain still in their very natural substances . . . And as concerning the natural body and blood of Our Saviour Christ, they are in heaven and not here" (Cressy and Ferrell, 48). To the elimination of the elevation of the Host in the 1549 version, the new book added the removal of the prayer of consecration at Communion and eliminated as well the signing of the cross over the elements and the stone altar, the latter to be replaced by a simple table in the body of the church (Duffy, 474). Under Mary, of course, the religious centrality of sacrament and ceremony was restored. Though advocating a balance of scriptural and ceremonial emphases, Cardinal Reginald Pole stressed that "the observatyon of ceremonyes, for obedyence sake, wyll gyve more light than all the readynge of Scrypture can doe." Though "the thynge that gyveth us the veraye light, ys none of them both," neither ceremonies nor scripture, yet "they are most apte to receyve light, that are more obeyent to follow ceremonyes, than to reade" (Ibid., 531). Marian primers did go some way to restore the pre-Reformation character totally absent from the Edwardine primer of 1553. Indeed, later editions include a didactic treatise on the Mass that explicates and defends that crucial doctrine of Roman Catholic piety, the Real Presence and Sacrifice. However, elaborate affective prayers on the Virgin Mary, the saints and the Blessed Sacrament, staples of the conservative books, were now almost entirely absent (Ibid., 540–542).

When the Book of Common Prayer was restored under Elizabeth in 1559, the controversial Black Rubric was removed, never to reappear. The final version is a hybrid of the relatively conservative Edwardine book of 1549 and the more radically Protestant version of 1552. It allows communicants to "eat of the flesh of thy dear Son Jesus Christ, and to drink his blood, that our sinful bodies may be made clean by his body, and our souls washed through his most precious blood." That both "body and soul" are fed is repeated in the minister's prayer of thanksgiving, but the added phrase insisting that all is done "in thy heart by faith, with thanksgiving" (Cressy and Ferrell, 47) severely attenuates any suggestion of a physiological reception. In 1559 the Act of Uniformity made adherence to the ceremonies of the Church of England legally binding. But the ambiguities already apparent in the wording of the Prayer Book took on even greater significance with the closing words of the Act:

> if there shall happen any contempt or irreverence to be used in the ceremonies or rites of the church by the misusing of the orders appointed in [the Prayer Book], the queen's majesty may, by the like advice of the said commissioners or metropolitan, ordain and publish such further ceremonies or rites as may be most for the advancement of God's glory, the edifying of his church, and the due reverence of Christ's holy mysteries and sacraments.
>
> (Cressy and Ferrell, 59)

If "contempt" and "irreverence" target anti-sacramental disdain, the same phrase might be said to refer to an excessive or popish regard (as opposed to the "due reverence" of the passage's final clause) and thereby offer consolation to those churchmen hopeful of further reform.

Neither were the Thirty Nine Articles (1571), doctrinal counterpart to the liturgy, without ambiguity. According to Article 28, the sacrament is "not only a sign"; the reception of the bread and wine, rather, is a "partaking" of the body and blood of Christ for those "such as rightly, worthily, and with faith, receive the same." "Transubstantiation" is "repugnant to the plain words of scripture, overthroweth the nature of a sacrament, and hath given occasion to many superstitions." Nevertheless, the "body of Christ is given, taken, and eaten," though again, "only after an heavenly and spiritual manner," while "the mean whereby the body of Christ is received and eaten in the supper is faith" (Cressy and Ferrell, 67). This careful balance affirming the physical act while subordinating it to spiritual mystery recalls Calvin's own reluctance to stress externals anymore than is absolutely necessary. Article 29, moreover, recalls Calvin's characterization of the wicked (*pace* Augustine) as he who "presses with the teeth" rather than "eats with the heart" (4.14.15). The Article states that those "void of a lively faith, although they do carnally and visibly press with their teeth (as St. Augustine saith) the sacrament of the body and blood of Christ, yet in no wise are they partakers of Christ: but rather, to their condemnation, do eat and drink the sign or sacrament of so great a thing" (Cressy and Ferrell, 67). That the Articles' most sensual language is applied to the wicked is perhaps a deliberate irony, but there is also the suggestion that the faithless, because they receive only in a carnal manner, do not attain to the edification of either soul or body, whereas for those who receive "worthily" and by "faith" the sacrament is of both spiritual and bodily benefit, what Article 25 describes as "a wholesome effect or operation" (Cressy and Ferrell, 66).

Despite echoes of Reform theology, however, both liturgical and doctrinal ambiguities contributed to continuing dissatisfaction among those for whom the Elizabethan settlement was decidedly less than sufficient. Conrad Russell points out that the Prayer Book and Settlement were constructed prior to the naming of bishops who thus bitterly complained of not being consulted. Formation of the Articles, however, because doctrinal in focus, had to wait until the first Protestant convocation in 1562–1563. The church's discipline and doctrine "came out of different minds, and therefore represented ideals of the church which were at least potentially divergent" (87). Those divines eager for further reform set their sights not only on the Prayer Book, however, but on the Articles as well. The "View of Popish Abuses" appended to the Puritan *Admonition to the Parliament,* itself following hot on the heels of the Articles in 1572, recognized both there and in the liturgy remnants of such popish practices as idolatrous kneeling and "breadengod" worship. This latter is described further as a "half communion, which is yet appointed like to the commemoration of the mass" (Cressy and Ferrell, 84). That such outrage was provoked by sacramental passages in the Articles is evidence against Christopher Hodgkins's claim that they are unambiguously Calvinist and that Rome, from a doctrinal perspective, "is off the map—dismissed with the kind of stinging language [Cardinal] Newman was to find so intractable" (27). If Elizabethan Catholics smarted under the language of the Articles, their enemies apparently thought papists had no small cause for celebration.

Though the intense debates over doctrinal Calvinism which plagued the final decades of the Elizabethan era abated somewhat with the Stuart succession, Reform theology was to have lasting impact on the church and especially on its handling of ceremonies. That Calvinism was thought by some to threaten the integrity of sacramental ministry is evident during the decade prior to the publication of Herbert's poems. Supporting the Arminian John Buckeridge's dispute with Thomas Morton over the doctrinal legitimacy of the largely Calvinist Dortrecht articles of 1618, Dean Frances White of Carlisle asked whether predestinarians in Holy Communion could "say to all communicants whatsoever, 'The Body of Our Lord which was given for thee,' as we are bound to say? Let the opinion of the Dortists be admitted, and the tenth person in the Church shall not have been redeemed" (Tyacke, 1995, 65). According to then Archbishop James Ussher, Samuel Ward had complained that some of the English delegates to the Synod of Dort were accused of being "half Remonstrants for extending the oblation made to the father to all and for holding sundry effects thereof offered *serio* and some really communicated to the reprobate" (Lake, 1987, 59). As Peter Lake has demonstrated, it is highly instructive to compare Ward's comments here with the irenic advice offered some ten years later to friend and fellow Dort delegate John Davenant. Ward advises Davenant to refrain from asserting that grace is conferred by Baptism, fearing "this time when the Arminians cleave so close one to another" (Ibid., 66). Once indignant at the accusation that he was a "half Remonstrant" for opposing the Calvinist doctrine of limited atonement, Ward now finds it necessary to protect his other half, so to speak. This caution against adding fuel to the fire is indicative of the subtlety of theological opinion among establishment divines during the decade following the 1618 Synod. Ward's advice was offered in 1629, the advent of Charles's personal rule—a period that would see a long-standing moderate, episcopalian and Calvinist unity yield to an Arminian/Puritan schism, each faction radicalizing the other. It was some sixteen years earlier, however, that the ex-chaplain and imminent Roman convert Benjamin Carier advised James I that Calvinist predestination renders the sacraments meaningless and thus undermines episcopacy (Tyacke, 1987, 5–6). White's and Ward's remarks only reinforce what Carier so presciently realized—that doctrinal issues arc of profound significance for the sacramental life of the church, the relationship between doctrine and ceremony crucial to the struggle over its confessional identity.

Essentially an alternative to the second-generation Calvinism of Theodore Beza, the views of Jacobus Arminius are distinct from Calvin's own in one important way. While he shared Calvin's conviction that Christ died for all even if not everyone is saved in the end, Arminius maintained a much greater degree of human autonomy.[5] Whereas the Remonstrant controversy on the continent was concerned almost exclusively with doctrine, English Arminianism included an emphasis on sacramental ministry as the external mark of its distinctive character. Not having experienced the same degree of ecclesiastical reform as its continental Protestant counterparts, the English religious establishment had retained not only episcopacy but also a liturgy which, in its inception at least, retained the spirit if not the letter of its Roman Catholic model. In rejecting the arbitrary grace of a predestinarian decree impervious to human will, English Arminians advanced the universalist doctrine of a grace freely offered in the sacraments and available to anyone who chose to receive them. Lake has located the origins of this English Arminianism in Richard Hooker, who was among the first of Protestants to emphasize the importance of ritual and ceremony as integral aspects of Christian communal experience rather than as matters to be regarded with indifference or, worse yet, merely tolerated (1988, 155–157). Hooker's "vision of the sacrament really offering Christ's body and blood to all who received it in good faith" (Lake, 1987, 42), moreover, dispensed with the tendency to distinguish between the godly and ungodly as suggested by a style of divinity more explicitly predestinarian in emphasis. But as Lake also points out, Hooker nowhere in the *Polity* explicitly attacks Calvinist thought, even if the doctrinal implications of his episcopalian and ceremonialist biases conflicted with Reform orthodoxy (Ibid.). Indeed, Lake might have observed in Hooker a more positive rather than merely tacit endorsement of such theology. If the eucharistic elements, for example, are not to be taken merely "for bare resemblances or memorials of things absent, neither for naked signs and testimonies assuring us of grace received before, but (as they are indeed and in verity) for means effectual," it is also true that "all receive not the grace of God which receive the sacraments of his grace" (2:236). This conflict between the visible and invisible communication of grace is not exclusive to Hooker, of course, but it does become for him an issue connected with his erastian tendencies: "It must be confessed that of Christ, working as a Creator, and a Governor of the world by providence, all are partakers; not all partakers of that grace whereby he inhabiteth whom he saveth" (2:232). If Calvinism was, in Patrick Collinson's phrase, "the theological cement" of the early Stuart church (1982, 82), some careful nuancing was required to reconcile its predestinarian and sacramental elements.[6]

The confessional broils of the English Reformation thus derived from a complex ecclesiastical history of which a crucial feature was debate over sacramental theories and practices, a debate comprised of two distinct though related issues: the material extent of divinity in the eucharistic species, and the role of religious subjectivity in the communication of grace. Though presumably the frail in faith might have doubted divine presence in the Eucharist as equally as the internal presence of the spirit, the availability of an external means of grace—whatever the individual vicissitudes of mood and psychological make-up—would have been reinforced by a doctrine which insisted not only on the efficacy of those means, but on the divine character of the instruments themselves. The reasons why Reformation *religieux* were so deeply divided over whether sacrament was more an internal than external matter is beyond the scope of this paper. A simple answer is that the notions *sola fidei* and *sola scriptura* displaced the ceremonial from its previously central position in Christian worship. Anxiety about the carnal dimension of the rite, however, was as much a feature of pre-scholastic and medieval theologies as of polemical battles in the sixteenth and seventeenth centuries.[7] Indeed, it is a problem that troubled not only the church fathers but at least one gospel writer for whom Jesus's disciples, shocked at his insisting that unless they eat of his flesh and drink of his blood they have no life, are perplexed yet again at the caveat that only the spirit gives life while the flesh profits nothing (Jn. 6.53–66). With scriptural authority so deeply vexing, it is not surprising that exegetes and other ecclesiastes subsequently struggled as fiercely as they did.

## Modus

Herbert was among those English divines whose reluctance to identify explicitly the modus of sacramental presence—an irenic agnosticism C. W. Dugmore has identified as the "mysterium tremendurn" approach to the Eucharist (61 n. 3)—did not prevent them from revering the material aspects of the ritual. These churchmen made some effort to distinguish, as did Hooker before them, between simply corporeal and more mystical understandings of presence. But if they were wary of the scholastic accretions attached to the Tridentine doctrine of transubstantiation, particularly the Aristotelian categories of substance and accident, English divines in the 1620s began to entertain similar if alternative interpretations.[8] The *Concilii Tridentini Acta* (7.187) determined that in the Eucharist is a "unique changing of the whole substance of bread into the body and of the whole substance of wine into the blood, while the species of bread and wine nonetheless remain, which change the Catholic Church very suitably calls transubstantiation" (Schilicbeeckx, 38). According to Dugmore, the Thomist doctrine actually denied presence *in loco*, allowing the body and blood a reality only *per modum substantiae* (26–27).[9] While it is not surprising that many saw in the Tridentine formula a too carnal and therefore idolatrous rendering, schooled divines would have recognized that the subtleties of the doctrine did not make such an interpretation necessary. This may help to explain why such clergy as Richard Montagu, Richard Neile, John Cosin, and William Laud advanced a sacramental vision of the ministry bordering on "popery," while maintaining, if sometimes disingenuously, a hostile stance toward the Roman church in general.[10] It is safe to speculate that one of the causes why avant-garde and Laudian divines were accused of popery by their opponents is the spectre of transubstantiation raised by this emphasis on ceremony and the sacramental dimension of the ministry. Such fears were not entirely unwarranted. Cosin, for example, endorsed the Jesuit Maldonatus's moderate views on eucharistic sacrifice and went so far as to advocate a rapprochement with Rome on the issue of real presence. Cosin's contemporary, William Forbes, denied the heretical status of transubstantiation and consubstantiation. Perhaps most disturbing about such "popish" flirtations were the implicit suggestion that the Tridentine canons on the Eucharist or even the Roman Missal itself could be interpreted in a manner harmonious with English doctrine, and that Roman divines such as Maldonatus or Sancta Clara were willing to offer such interpretations. Cosin, Forbes and others may have identified transubstantiation with simplified, vulgar interpretations of Roman doctrine common among both moderate and nonconforming Puritans, or they simply may have recognized the futility of encouraging tolerance for a formula whose complexity precluded popular access, in which case their occasional anti-Roman outbursts were less doctrinal in motivation than politically expedient. In any event, it is clear these divines sought not only to promote sacraments as essential means of grace, but on occasion appeared to advance sacramental formulae indistinguishable from that of their supposed Roman foes, and thus inadvertently exacerbated fears of crypto-popery.[11]

Like other establishment divines, Herbert more often than not sought to avoid controversy while maintaining both a sacerdotal and sacramental vision of the church. Richard Hooker provided Herbert and others with a model of behavior suitable for approaching Holy Communion:

> what moveth us to argue of the manner how life should come by bread, our duty being here but to take what is offered, and most assuredly to rest persuaded of this, that can we but eat we are safe? . . . Let it therefore be sufficient for me presenting my selfe at the Lords table to know what there I receive from him, without searching or inquiring of the maner how Christ performeth his promise.
>
> (2:330)

Herbert essentially agrees, even if his approach to such mystery is far from Hooker's measured rationality. The Country Parson,

> being to administer the Sacraments, is at a stand with himself, how or what behaviour to assume for so holy things. Especially at Communion times he is in a great confusion, as being not only to receive God, but to break, and administer him. Neither finds he any issue in this, but to throw himself down at the throne of grace, saying, Lord, thou knowest what thou didst, when thou apointedst it to be done thus; therefore doe thou fulfill what thou didst appoint; for thou art not only the feast, but the way to it.[12]

Poetic endorsement of this mysterium tremendum approach is apparent in "Divinitie," where theological curiosity is as presumptuous as the new philosophy's obsession with astronomical inquiry. Among the objects cut and carved "with the edge of wit" (line 7) is the Eucharist, which, Herbert implies, should be regarded as a simple matter and exempt from controversy:

> But he doth bid us take his bloud for wine.
>> Bid what he please; yet I am sure,
> To take and taste what he doth there designe,
>> Is all that saves, and not obscure. (21–24)

It may be, however, that the sacrament is not the least of "Gordian knots" (line 20) after all. The first line of this stanza certainly *does* obscure, grammatically allowing both the innocuous analogy "blood *as* wine" and the literal substitution "blood *in place of* wine," the equivocation exacerbated in the third line by "what," which invites the gloss "whatever."[13] The obscurity does not so much evade doctrinal commitment as deliberately avoid controversy and what can only amount to an absurd probing of that which finally is mysterious. "Yet," however, suggests no little reluctance to rest content with the mysterious words of institution. It is as if Herbert either understands the scripture to be saying one thing and proceeds to assert another, or, more likely, is frustrated by an obscurity inherent in the institution itself and, though allowing the ambiguity in his own assessment, has in mind a certain preference nonetheless. It may be recalled that whereas Christ says "take and eat," Herbert writes "take and taste," which, while not alone conclusive proof, does suggest the need for as carnal an apprehension of God's "designe" as is possible.

Sensory vividness is evident in an earlier stanza, where the proximity of "broacht" species to pierced side nevertheless is accompanied by a warning against excessive curiosity:

> Could not that Wisdome, which first broacht the wine,
>> Have thicken'd it with definitions?
> And jagg'd his seamlesse coat, had that been fine,
>> With curious questions and divisions?
>
>>>>>>> (9–12)

"Wisdome" indeed eventually did thicken the wine offered his disciples but with blood, not definitions—which only advances further the notion that the cup received in remembrance is somehow that which it signifies. It would appear on this account that the overly curious "edge of wit" does not pertain to any particular doctrinal formula; the poem condemns scholastic rationalism for applying precise formulae to what must remain a mystery, and thus for mocking that for which Herbert would retain the utmost dignity and reverence.

In the final stanza we find that "Faith needs no staffe of flesh, but stoutly can / To heav'n alone both go, and leade" (lines 27–28). Only faith, which, like "Divinities transcendent skie" is beyond material limitation, can provide the impetus truly to "take and taste," to believe that in so doing one receives that which is "all that saves" (24). Rather than advance theological formulae which render sacramental efficacy rationally palatable, Herbert advocates believing in the means of grace regardless. By instructing the "foolish man" to burn his "Epicycles" and "Break all thy spheres" (25–26) he figuratively attacks Ptolemaic apologists desperate to defend their waning cosmology with sophisticated and ultimately misguided models. Trans- and consubstantiation, Calvinist virtualism—these are as inadequate as their scholastic predecessors in addressing the mystery behind Jesus's words of institution. To persist in such scrutiny is tantamount to crucifying him anew, this time with "curious questions and divisions."

But perhaps simply to "take and taste" grace without trying to understand how grace is imparted in the sacrament is as difficult, finally, as retaining for the universe an Aristotelian hierarchy while dismissing the models which render it intelligible. Ignoring his own advice, Herbert left a record of "curious questions" about the Eucharist by way of two very different versions of "The H. Communion." In B and the *editio princeps* of 1633,[14] he avoids explicit mention of the various doctrinal formulae evident in the earlier Williams MS. He begins by rejecting the notion that God might be conveyed "in" such ceremonial trappings as "rich furniture ... fine aray" and "wedge of gold" (lines 1–4). It is important to note, however, that even if many of his contemporaries would have recognized these as the trappings of the Roman Mass, Herbert does not dismiss the use of such external finery *per se*.[15] His objection, rather, pertains specifically to the idea that externals might themselves effectually conjure or somehow contain their divine referents. For if they did, the sacrament's primarily internal and non-corporeal application would be compromised: "thou should'st without me still have been, / Leaving within me sinne" (5–6). But if the first stanza leads one to expect a moderate regard for the elements of bread and wine, the second describes a sacramental efficacy every bit as carnal as the Roman Catholic doctrine of transubstantiation:

> But by the way of nourishment and strength
>     Thou creep'st into my breast;
>     Making thy way my rest,
> And thy small quantities my length;
> Which spread their forces into every part,
>     Meeting sinnes force and art.
>
>         (7–12)

This essentially physiological description, while seeking to avoid the problem of determining how or at which point in the process the species become involved in conveying the sacrificial body and blood, nevertheless suggests

their instrumental and not merely representational status. Sacramental controversy resides in the silence between the first and second stanzas, between
awkwardness over the precise role of ceremonial trappings and scrutiny of
a mysterious process. Herbert deftly avoids such controversy by focusing on
the elements' internal operation, maintaining their carnality while accommodating a Reform emphasis on individuals' souls as the collective and
primary site of sacramental presence.

The separation of "souls and fleshy hearts" (line 15) in the following
stanzas nevertheless continues to suggest the need for a physical explanation of sacramental grace. God's "small quantities" cannot overcome the wall
which restrains mere "rebel-flesh" (17). Indeed, the "souls most subtile rooms"
are penetrable only by "grace," which, however, "with these elements comes,"
and which, having entered the soul, sends "Dispatches" to the sentinels or
"spirits refin'd" (19–24) guarding the way. They in turn distribute medicinal
sacramental benefits throughout the body. The process, figuratively, is a military coup: external finery accompanies but does not directly communicate
grace, which, nevertheless, is somehow connected with the elements, but only
after they are ingested. The masticated and divinely invigorated species then
"spread their forces into every part"; but it is grace, the commander-in-chief,
that breaches the stronghold and secures both the soul's terrain and a hitherto
"rebel-flesh."

It may be that what I have described as bordering on a Roman Catholic sacramental position is but the poetic description of what in fact is not a
physical process after all. This would be in keeping with Calvin's point that
God uses material means to communicate a more rarefied grace. The idea
that presence is conveyed "with" or alongside, rather than "in" the elements
is thoroughly consistent with Reform theology. The sacrament, rather than
an accident veiling an inward substance or, as for Luther, a consubstantial
manifestation of the hypostatic union, is instead an Augustinian seal ratify-
ing a sacramental reality solely in the heart or soul of the communicant. It is,
writes Calvin, "an outward sign by which the Lord seals on our consciences
the promises of his good will toward us" (4.14.1). The material elements are
important insofar as they are the means by which God chooses to indicate
or point toward his gifts, thus mitigating our inability to comprehend spiritual truths without material aids: our "small capacity" and the "dullest minds"
(4.17.1) are led by "a sort of analogy" from physical to spiritual things (4.17.3).
It is a Satanic error, however, to believe "that Christ's body, enclosed in the
bread, is transmitted by the mouth of the body into the stomach" (4.17.15).[16]
Young insists that "with these elements comes" excludes a Calvinist reading.
But the poem does not say that either God or grace is, as in Young's gloss,
"present in the eucharistic species" (138). Young cites Calvin's view that sacraments "do not bestow any grace of themselves, but announce and tell us" that

grace has been conferred (Calvin, 4.14.17; Young, 138). The key phrase here is "not . . . of themselves"—not, that is, *ex opere operato*. "With" in Herbert's poem upholds rather than excludes Calvin's "announce and tell." Nevertheless, the poem's physiological terminology would appear to invite Calvin's condemnation in suggesting that heaven's king might go a progress through the guts of a beggarly sinner—that the elements indeed are changed at the moment of ingestion. Just as the idea of the individual soul as site of a cosmic struggle would not have seemed odd to the early modern Christian, so did Herbert regard the personal drama of redemption as a very real rather than merely figurative battle—the arena corporeal, the conflict immanent. Whatever the extent of that war's reality, the forensic and equivocal "Not," "But," "Yet," and "Only" introducing each stanza are symptomatic less of a clear and stable *via media* than the irenic disposition of the Country Parson, who would that he were content to know that God is "not only the feast, but the way to it."[17]

The B version of "H. Communion" is sensitive to ecclesiastical controversy over the importance of ceremony and discipline relative to preaching and doctrine.[18] This becomes even more evident when it is compared with the earlier version of the Williams MS, where Herbert's theological sympathies are more clearly discernible.[19] The first stanza suggests two competing theories which recall early Reformation controversy. Roman trans- and Lutheran consubstantiation offer a choice between the notion that the bread's substance is wholly transformed and a doctrine of ubiquity wherein God's substantial presence does not exclude that of the bread. The choice, in hindsight, is of little importance, for in the following stanza Herbert dismisses the issue of the bread's status. What really matters is that his "gratious Lord" (line 1) and "all thy traine" (10) are present in the rite: how this comes about, suggests Herbert, is not nearly as important as simply recognizing that it does. In the third stanza, however, this adiaphoric stance yields to a more specifically Calvinist position: divine presence is asserted, but is confined to the communicant's soul; it is indicated, but not embodied, by the species of bread and wine. Explicit here, it is this doctrine that silently connects the first and second stanzas of the later version of the poem; and yet there "nourishment and strength" suggest a physiological grace.

The first stanza's suggestion that Luther was as mistaken as his Roman foes when it comes to sacramental theology is reiterated at the center of the poem where "Impanation" (line 25), the Lutheran view of sacramental presence based on the hypostatic union of the Incarnation, is explicitly rejected. Rather than bread becoming God, according to Luther, the divine substance becomes united with that of bread, just as the Word becomes flesh at its human birth (38:306–307). That God's nature takes on man's is, for this poem, doctrinally sound; but the notion that nature is united with mere bread is simply intolerable. Herbert here is willing to allow a significant role for the species, but he is wary, as was Calvin, of compromising the divine nature. Rather, it is "My flesh, & fleshly villany" that "made thee dead" (lines 29–30). If there is a sacrificial element in Holy Communion it is in God's gracious identification with the communicant's "rebel-flesh," the later poem's version of "fleshly villany. " And yet this new focus on the Incarnation abandons entirely the poem's earlier ecumenism by doubting whether the elements are at all involved in the flesh they supposedly declare: "That fflesh is there, mine eyes deny: / And what should flesh but flesh discry, / The noblest sence of five?" (31–32). The species point to rather than embody a process that occurs on a strictly spiritual level. As with the later poem, the W "H. Communion" registers a gap between flesh and soul, though here the absence of any physiological explanation only exacerbates the absence of Calvin's radically transcendent God:

> Into my soule this cannot pass;
> fflesh (though exalted) keeps his grass
>     And cannot turn to soule.
> Bodyes & Minds are different Spheres,
> Nor can they change their bounds & meres,
>     But keep a constant Pole.
>
>                                         (37–42)

Yet in the final stanza the "gift of all gifts," unlike flesh, can indeed "pass." This gift, of course, is none other than grace, explicitly identified in the later poem where, by dispatching sacramental and physiological "spirits refin'd," it overcomes "the wall that parts / Our souls and fleshy hearts."

In the earlier "H. Communion," then, Herbert allows little if any interpenetration of flesh and soul, maintaining instead a vision of sacramental grace as predominantly non-corporeal. The later B poem, conversely, is irenic in tone, accommodating a more integrated, amorphous relationship among body, soul, grace, and the material means of grace. Michael C. Schoenfeldt, in his examination of the eating trope in the poem, gets it right when he remarks that "the entry of God into his mortal subject . . . delineates the border between matter and spirit that it proceeds benevolently to transgress" (98). These poems, as Robert Ellrodt has suggested, thus frame a linear development in Herbert's sacramental thought (1960, 324–341). The time between their respective compositions parallels a period in Stuart church history, from the 1618 Synod of Dort to the advent of the Laudian archbishopric, in which sacrament and ceremony became increasingly central to the character of mainstream English divinity. Herbert's fondness for ceremony, then, may have coincided with the impatience of some for what they perceived to be an immoderate emphasis on preaching, doctrine and more private enthusiasms. Whether the change is a reflection of his spiritual development or a response to political realities is difficult to determine; such things, of course, are impossible to separate. For while there is no doubt that Herbert shared with other establishment divines a concern that the Eucharist somehow communicate divine presence, the *modus* of communication as variously expressed in the poetry suggests he would have been far from embracing wholeheartedly the Laudian ceremonial programme first implemented in 1633, the year of his death. Whatever his theological itinerary, the two versions of "H. Communion" document the array of sacramental theories available to Herbert's contemporaries and indicate that the English *via media* was less a harmonization of competing ecclesiastical and doctrinal ideologies than a way lacking both clarity and certainty.

If wary of an overly carnal or potentially idolatrous attitude toward sacraments, Herbert does not appear to have had much sympathy for those who regarded the elements merely as commemorative signs. In "Love Unknown" he implies that the "many" who "drunk bare wine" suffer considerable disadvantage relative to the speaker for whom "A friend did steal into my cup for good" (lines 42–43).[20] Herbert is far from reluctant to indulge a sensual vision of sacramental grace. And yet what is most striking is the passage's (albeit soft) predestinarian tone, Herbert allowing, as did Calvin, that the godly might worship alongside the wicked. The logic of coupling his own considerable commitment to the sacramental dimension of Christian worship with predestinarian doctrine resulted for Calvin in the caveat that the Eucharist "is turned into a deadly poison for all those whose faith it does not nourish and strengthen, and whom it does not arouse to thanksgiving and to love" (4.17.40).[21] That the sacrament may or may not nourish and arouse depends not simply on whether one is faithful, thankful, and loving; rather, one is faithful, thankful, and loving to the extent one is in fact nourished and aroused. Herbert's subtle manoeuvre in "Love Unknown" similarly maintains both a carnal emphasis and the broad-based vision of church membership sacraments support, while at the same time allowing for the possibility that some who drink and eat are not among the spiritually regenerated.[22] It would appear that predestinarian Calvinism for the speaker of "Love Unknown" is compatible with an avant-garde fondness for ceremony. The passage is thus an exception to Peter Lake's alignment of sacramental enthusiasm with anti-Calvinism (1987, 74–75). Herbert does not seem to have shared the concern of those who, like Benjamin Carier, worried that predestination compromises the sacramental dimension of Christian ministry and the social cohesion it supports.

In "The Water-course," more famously, Herbert allows that God

gives to man, as he sees fit, {          Salvation.

                                                   Damnation.

                                                                     (10)

In this uncharacteristically controversial lyric Herbert is perhaps deliberately playful, never clarifying the pronoun's correspondent—God or
man? R. V. Young calls Herbert's position here Thomist, one that sustains
both free will and predestination (35). But if this is meant to distance
Herbert from Calvin, it does not suffice, for surely Calvin maintained
that his position retains human free will, at least with respect to sin,
insisting, for example, that the reprobate are "justly charged against the
malice and depravity of their hearts," even though "given over" thereto
(3.24.14). Whatever the logical contradictions involved in such assertions,
Calvin was as concerned as Aquinas and the church fathers both to make
sin a strictly human responsibility and grace an unmerited gift. Differences—and they are significant—arise only in working out the technical
details involved in reconciling such claims with free will. A more general
difference is the extent to which Calvin was willing logically to go in
support of these cornerstone truths. By raising the issue of predestination
so explicitly in "The Water-course," Herbert thus reveals his affinity with
Calvin's own willingness to force consideration of the issue even while
demurring from stating clearly his own place within the English Calvinist tradition. As David Como has argued, the "hegemonic force of the
predestinarian consensus" among English Calvinists "was strongest when
it was tacit, assumed and unquestioned" (66). His reluctance to divulge
anything like a firm doctrinal position, however, did not prevent Herbert
from expressing his confidence in God's mercy, for it is the overwhelming
presence of sacramental grace, joined to the communicant's willingness to
receive it, that permeates both poem and title: "turn the pipe and waters
course / To serve thy sinnes, and furnish thee with store / Of sov'raigne
tears, springing from true remorse" (lines 6–8).

  Whatever the extent of his Calvinism and views on the controversial
issue of limited atonement, Herbert maintains a concern for the material integrity of sacramental grace. Eucharistic topoi for him indicated not
only necessary and effectual means, but also the conceptual and psychological framework within which to think the application of grace to the
human heart. "The Agonie," for example, renders the Atonement personal,
intimate, and visceral, Christ's sacrifice and the benefits it affords communicated via the sacrament: "Sinne is that presse and vice, which forceth
pain / To hunt his cruell food through ev'ry vein" and "Love is that liquor
sweet and most divine, / Which my God feels as bloud; but I, as wine"
(lines 11–12, 17–18). The juxtaposition of these two couplets is startling.
The Christ who in Pauline terms becomes sin (1 Pet. 2.24; 2 Cor. 5.21) is
filled here with sin's poison, which displaces the divine blood that in turn
becomes that of the communicant, who, presumably, was filled hitherto

with the sin now coursing through his saviour's veins. The final line may suggest a moderate sacramental position; indeed, Hutchinson called it "an inversion of the doctrine of transubstantiation" (Herbert, 1941, 488). But "feels" is at best ambiguous, allowing that the speaker's phenomenal experience of wine may intimate what in fact is a bloody affair, the two levels, appearance and veiled reality, evoking the Aristotelian categories of substance and accident implicit in the Tridentine canons on the Eucharist. Herbert, however, stops short of identifying explicitly the modus whereby sacramental grace is actualized. R. V. Young's assertion that in "The Agonie" Christ "is in some way present *under the form of*" the elements thus seems to me unwarranted, for nowhere in the poem is Herbert this specific. He indeed may "not have been happy" (Young, 121) with the 1552 BOCP, particularly the presence-denying Black Rubric; but the 1559 and subsequent versions of the Prayer Book no more provided Herbert with a rationale for specifying the mode of sacramental presence than the poem allows Young's reading. And yet the communicant's experience of wine rather than blood may be seen as compatible with transubstantiation after all, his senses apprehending as wine (accident) what is actually blood (substance). By this "liquor sweet" the benefits obtained by Christ's surrogate sufferings under the winepress of just wrath are transferred—or transfused—minus the sufferings themselves. Recourse "Unto Mount Olivet" for the speaker is purely imaginative, even if excruciating: "A man so wrung with pains, that all his hair, / His skinne, his garments bloudie be" (lines 9–10) suggests a meditative sharing in Christ's sufferings, but poetic artifice renders sweet that which for another was truly agonizing, just as the accidental species of a Roman sacrament veil even as they embody their substantial counterpart.

Less ambiguous is "The Invitation." Whereas Jesus said simply "drink" and "this is my blood," Herbert here introduces a rather provocative modification: "drink this, / Which *before* ye drink is bloud" (lines 11–12, my emphasis). It is possible that Herbert means only to distinguish between what is taken in the sacrament and what flowed at Golgotha; but it is at least as likely that he addresses the issue so carefully avoided in the 1633 "H. Communion," namely, the question of the spatial and temporal occurrence of body and blood—of when and where, exactly, the "friend" of "Love Unknown" steals into the speaker's cup. Whereas the blank space between the first and second stanzas of the later "H. Communion" allow him to avoid dealing too specifically with the manner of sacramental presence, here Herbert appears to advocate a change in the species prior to ingestion, thus going considerably beyond the moderate or Calvinist position which allows only a spiritual presence among the souls of the elect.

## SACRAMENTUM SACERDOTALIS

Undoubtedly a keen proponent of the church's sacramental policies and practices, Herbert nonetheless cautioned against too enthusiastic a regard for ceremonial trappings. At issue is conflict between, on the one hand, the sacerdotal vision of a church whose collective good consists in public, ceremonial conformity under episcopal discipline, and, on the other, a Puritan enthusiasm which locates true religious piety in the private and rarefied communion of God and individual. Controversy over the material extent and modus of divine presence in the Eucharist, then, is of no little consequence for the perceived role of institutional media in the dissemination of God's gifts. *The Temple*, however, is powerful evidence that these ideological poles were far from mutually exclusive, for Herbert's celebration of ceremonial forms not only complements but indeed is an integral feature of the devotional subjectivity he cultivates.

In "The Priesthood" Herbert stands in awe of the priestly office, especially the administering of sacraments. His profound respect for ritual is anticipated by subtle comparison of the Eucharist with the potter's art, which fits earth by "fire and trade . . . for the boards of those / Who make the bravest shows" (lines 16–18). In the next stanza we find that the inferior art is but earth delighting in earth, "both feeder, dish, and meat" having "one beginning and one finall summe" (21–22), and in the following stanza the sacramental pun on "boards" is confirmed:

> But th' holy men of God such vessels are,
> As serve him up, who all the world commands:
> When God vouchsafeth to become our fare,
> Their hands convey him, who conveys their hands.
> O what pure things, most pure must those things be,
>     Who bring my God to me!
>
> (25–30)

Perplexity results finally in a hyperbolic display of submission, the poet and aspiring priest recognizing his status as "lowly matter," the master potter's day thrown "at his [God's] feet" (35–36). Such prostration, however, represents more than admiration of and fear for the sacramental office. The Ark of the Covenant he hesitates to grasp, no doubt mindful of Uzzah's fate (2 Sam. 6.6), is typologically the sacrament, the vessel of the new covenant (Heb. 9.4), which here seems to "shake / Through th' old sinnes; and new doctrines of our land" (32–33). It is difficult to determine precisely what is meant by "new doctrines." The poem's title and reverent tone suggest Herbert's target is Puritan disregard for holy things. For R. V. Young, "new doctrines . . . can only be an attack upon Puritanism" (115). Indeed, it may

be that Herbert was responding to excessive fear of the church's increasingly sacramental orientation. On the other hand, Uzzah's presumptuous
approach to the presence housed in the Ark suggests Herbert may just as
likely condemn a too familiar, curious and thus potentially idolatrous regard
for sacraments, a charge often laid against the scholastic dissection of the
Eucharist associated with the Roman Catholic tradition. The latitude
allowed by "new doctrines" is perhaps deliberately ambiguous, referring to
any and all attitudes which threaten an ideal balance of pious restraint and
due reverence.

Sacerdotal and sacramental imperatives become mutually reinforcing
toward the poem's close, where, following the penultimate stanza's "I throw
me at his feet" (line 36), Herbert imagines himself an empty vessel not unlike
the eucharistic species, presented and now humbly awaiting divine invigora-
tion: "There will I lie, untill my Maker seek / For some mean stuffe whereon
to show his skill: / Then is my time" (37–39). Quiet anticipation of miraculous
transformation, whether of bread and wine or ministerial office, allows Herbert to indulge a celebration of his vocation, tempered by humility and short
of endorsing the *iure divino* episcopacy advocated by the more zealous of
his avant-garde peers.[23] Though considerably enamoured of the special privileges such office affords, and relishing the idea of his own hands being such
"pure things" as "bring my God to me," Herbert is self-effacing sufficiently as
to recognize the importance of sober and due submission, "Lest good come
short of ill / In praising might" (40–41).

Ceremonial caution and priestly reverence yield to a more relaxed wonder and awe in "The Invitation," where poetic structure mirrors the paradox
of the Word become flesh, made explicit, as we have seen, by the poem's
claim that the sacramental wine is blood "before ye drink" (line 12). Here
Herbert's dual vocation as priest and poet is most apparent, for "The Invitation" is not only about Holy Communion: the poem's subtle conflation of
profane and sacred experiences reflects the incarnational scandal even as it
exemplifies Herbert's metaphysical wit. The humble Parson extends gener-
ous welcome and mild admonition to those approaching the Lord's table,
compared to which all previous meals have failed to satisfy vain appetites:
"taste" is "waste" (1–2) and wine is "drunk amisse" (10) if not of "the feast,
/ God, in whom all dainties are" (5–6). And yet the most exquisite of human experiences is surpassed only by a joy which nevertheless resembles that
which it putatively transcends:

> Come ye hither All, whose love
>   Is your dove,
> And exalts you to the skie:
> Here is love, which having breath

> Ev'n in death,
> After death can never die.
>
> (25–30)

The balanced antithesis of Herbert's stanza lends formal support to the comparison. Secular love is neither dull nor sublunary. Nor does the love embodied in the Eucharist escape the death implicitly associated with sexual fulfilment, the familiar *petite mort* (more typical of Donne or Crashaw, unusual in Herbert) suggesting eucharistic sacrifice. Indeed, the paradox that lovers' orgasm signals the obsolescence of their efforts is analogous to the theological commonplace of the final line. This mirroring in the stanza's second half of qualities associated with the love celebrated by the first is reciprocated, "dove" evoking the Holy Spirit which descended both on Jesus to inaugurate his ministry, and on the Virgin Mary at his miraculous conception.[24] This in turn suggests for "breath" an association with the risen Christ's gift of the third member of the Trinity breathed on the apostles just prior to the Ascension (Jn. 20.22). In hindsight, then, the "All" of this penultimate stanza anticipates the identification of "All" and "All" in the final line, extends the invitation, "Come ye hither," to God, and thus advances the interpenetration of love and Love.

The hierarchical order evoked by a vertical structural arrangement (the fifth stanza's "All," "dove" and "skie" followed by "breath" and "death") is dissolved from within when we discover that both the exalting terms and those concerned with more earthly matters are performing double duty. Similarly complementary or imbricate pairs inform other stanzas: profane "fare" and heavenly "feast" in the first (lines 3, 5), "pain" and "cheer" in the third (13, 17), and, above all, "wine" and "bloud" in the second (7, 12). Both thematically and formally, then, the poem is incarnational in its treatment of sacramental ritual, the careful arrangement of antitheses and their instability reflecting the paradox that the Eucharist embodies. Finally, as if to render explicit the poem's thematic design, Herbert offers the theological assertion already discussed—"drink this, / Which before ye drink is bloud"—which appeals to while going beyond messianic authority, thus abandoning irenic caution for a decidedly corporeal vision of sacramental presence. Poetic ingenuity is a prominent feature of "The Invitation." But Herbert is sure to include amid the dazzle a plain, and not obscure, statement of that which is the source of all the fuss. Perhaps in no other *Temple* poem is the Renaissance notion of poet as quasi-divine maker more evident: priestly and poetic authorities combine to assert the Word become flesh offered to all who would receive it.

## DEVOTIO SACRAMENTALIS

Herbert's respect for ceremony and ritual is not confined to the institutional context they support and perpetuate; sacramental attitudes, rather, are comprehensive of a faith whose quotidian realities persist beyond religious ritual and observance. This is most evident in "Sunday," which recognizes an integral relationship between the Sabbath and other less celebrated days of the week. Sacraments are a key feature of Sunday's worship, here a divine signature or seal conferring on the day a promissory status:

> O Day most calm, most bright,
> The fruit of this, the next worlds bud,
> Th'indorsement of supreme delight,
> Writ by a friend, and with his bloud.
>
> (1–4)

The fruit of the vine is the seed of graces yet to come, a taste of the marriage supper of the Lamb to be celebrated at the end of history—as in "Love (III)," which also happens to be the final poem in *The Temple*. Such fruit is the harvest rest crowning man's toil, Sundays the "face" and "brow" which knock "at heaven" while "The worky-daies are the back-part" (lines 9–11). Human labour finds purpose here in relation to the ceremonial rest that is the Sabbath which parts the "ranks and orders" of the "fruitfull beds and borders / In Gods rich garden" (26–28). The wine consumed in the Eucharist, while anticipating essential joys, also addresses the effects of Adam's curse, man's share in the sufferings which the second Adam experiences in full. St. Augustine's assertion that the church is united with the sacrificial mystery on the altar in the Eucharist (Sermon 272, cited in Chauvet, 291–292) is relevant for a garden whose fruit is both delineated by human labour and a source of ease "for those / Who want herbs for their wound" (lines 41–42). The cyclical aspect of such ritual is no Blakean same dull round: seen as part of a succession "Thredded together on times string" (30), each Sunday performs an eschatological function, is

> a day of mirth:
> And where the week-dayes trail on ground,
> Thy flight is higher, as thy birth.
> O let me take thee at the bound,
> Leaping with thee from sev'n to sev'n,
> Till that we both, being toss'd from earth,
>     Flie hand in hand to heav'n!
>
> (57–63)

As the eucharistic species combine the fruit of human and divine labours in a healing balm and rest for the weary pilgrim, so is the back-breaking toil of "worky-daies" joined with the Sabbath to form a devotional pilgrimage almost giddy with its own momentum.

It is this combination of reverence for things divine and homely sympathy for the human condition in Herbert's poetry that allows official observances to reverberate beyond the church's sacred walls. A careful balance of respect and light-hearted familiarity or "domestic simplicity" (H. Davies, 287) integrates stylized ritual with the rhythms of Christian existence. Herbert's awareness of the incarnational paradox proclaimed in the Eucharist, its insistence on the Word become flesh, is the institutional basis for recognizing sacramental significance in daily human life and labour.

The contiguity of ritual and quotidian in "Sunday" is typical of *The Temple* as a whole. Like the speakers of Donne's divine poems, Herbert's devout finds in the institutional media of sacrament and ceremony relief from the oppressive guilt and sense of personal depravity which haunt the isolated devotional psyche. Herbert's crushing realizations of spiritual inadequacy, however, are often accompanied by a measured confidence rarely seen in Holy Sonnets. In "Conscience," for example, the relationship between devotional and sacramental pieties and its significance for penitential despair is particularly evident in the alternating voices of confident judge and guilty supplicant, where the violence of the Crucifixion is directed against the sorrow-dogging "pratler" (line 1) and his "chatting fears" (5). The speaker's only recourse is to go to

> My Saviours bloud: when ever at his board
> I do but taste it, straight it cleanseth me,
>    And leaves thee not a word;
> No, not a tooth or nail to scratch,
> And at my actions carp or catch.
>
>                                          (14–18)

Notable here is the association of "word" with the accusing Conscience while the silencing of this "pratler" is explicitly a matter of sacramental grace. This sacrament versus word/Conscience opposition is clarified and the tables turned when in the final stanza the cleansing "bloudie crosse" becomes the speaker's "sword," a weapon of "Some wood and nails to make a staff or bill / For those that trouble me" (21–24). Internal reflection and sacramental relief conflict violently within the devotional psyche itself. The speaker would escape Conscience's psychological tortures, finding in sacramental blood and the cross it stains the instruments of his liberation into an external *mythos*.[25] Herbert's poem appropriates the symbols of Christian ritual paradoxically to eradicate the accuser Conscience from whatever might then remain of the speaker's divided self. This sacramentalization of the religious psyche culminates in a devotional version of man-as-microcosm, where inward agony melts into the surrounding heavens: "My thoughts must work, but like a noiseless sphere" (8). It is perhaps strange that the target of eucharistic grace also happens to be a vital component of the Christian psyche, the censor who convicts of sin. Certain sweet dishes presumably are sour, certain fair looks foul. Yet Herbert apparently is concerned more with combating Conscience than those fleshly desires which threaten devotional integrity. It is as though music howls at all only because Conscience chides and clouds the ear, which otherwise might hear the "Harmonious peace" (9) of "noiselesse" thoughts and the Pythagorean song they whisper.

In "Love Unknown," Herbert sustains simultaneous recognition of both the penitent's moral depravity and the depth of God's love. His is a devotional psyche reluctantly assuaged by the assurances of sacramental grace. At the first attempt to appease his Lord the speaker's heart is "seis'd" and placed in a font

> wherein did fall
> A stream of bloud, which issu'd from the side
> Of a great rock: I well remember all,
> And have good cause: there it was dipt and dy'd,
> And washt, and wrung: the very wringing yet
> Enforceth tears.
>
> (13–18)

Herbert expands the traditional typology connecting the rock which fed the Israelites with Christ, Baptism and a spiritual food and drink (Ex. 17.6; 1 Cor. 10.1–4) to include more explicitly the blood of the Atonement. The qualification "yet," moreover, implies the heart's need of continual sacramental renewal and thus anticipates the eucharistic heart of the poem. At each painful discovery of the insufficiency of his sacrifices, the speaker acknowledges his friend's disappointments—*"Your heart was foul . . . hard . . . dull"* (lines 18, 37, 56)—and follows each with a brief confession. The second of these celebrates a remedy that also exemplifies the caution characteristic of Jacobean and Caroline divines' approach to sacramental doctrine:

> I found a callous matter
> Begin to spread and to expatiate there:
> But with a richer drug then scalding water
> I bath'd it often, ev'n with holy bloud,
> Which at a board, while many drunk bare wine,
> A friend did steal into my cup for good,
> Ev'n taken inwardly, and most divine
> To supple hardnesses.
>
> (38–45)

As we have seen, Herbert clearly regards as disadvantaged those whose views lean toward a merely commemorative ritual, "bare wine" evoking a disenchanted, ineffective means of grace. He is careful, however, to attenuate this assertion of carnal presence with "Ev'n taken inwardly," thus connecting any substantial transformation of the elements with the act of ingestion. This combination of effectual species and an emphasis on reception rather than the externals of ritual marks the threshold between the worlds of matter and spirit Herbert would fuse. He knows that sin is primarily a spiritual ailment and requires a penetrating, spiritual cure. But his is an undeniably material and somatic characterization of sin: "hardnesses" in need of "suppl[ing]," or, in "The Agonie," a "presse and vice, which forceth pain / To hunt his cruell food through ev'ry vein" (lines 11–12), both suggesting an overwhelmingly physiological need. Whereas for Calvin the material means are but God's concession to the fleshly limitations of his creatures, Herbert is much more reluctant to divest spiritual experience of its sublunary component.

The first and third confessions of "Love Unknown," in which the speaker comprehends his failure to merit salvation, are compensated by divine reassurance. Preoccupied with his many faults, the penitent "still askt pardon, and was not deni'd" (line 21), for his sins, as it turns out, are "by another paid, / Who took the debt upon him" (60–61). It is in between, following the second confession (38–39), that the sacramental grace cited above intervenes to assuage his anxieties. Just as Herbert's poetic and prayerful offerings are a sacrifice acceptable only when recognized as divinely initiated and sustained, so Christ's presence among the "rich furniture and fine array" of ceremony imbues what is otherwise meaningless ritual with true sacramental significance. Carnal indulgence is softened both by the homely image of Christ as a mischievous friend stealing his way into the cup, and by an emphasis on communal use—"Ev'n taken inwardly." This latter allows the potentially controversial problem of *modus* to be avoided, even if the evocative imagery and diction—"bath'd," "bloud," "drunk," "supple"—complicate such doctrinal evasion. On the one hand, Herbert is reluctant to allow his transcendent Lord to be subjected to the material limitations of carnal being; yet he also maintains the scandal of the Word become flesh, the need for a Christ actually present among both the means and "suppling" effects of God's gift. If some divines worried that overly carnal notions of sacramental presence compromise divine autonomy and transcendence, Herbert insists that such presence is but the divinely instituted and necessary expression of the Incarnation, a Will paradoxically stripped of power and subjected to history, a body and death.

But does Herbert finally rest secure in a primarily sacramental grace? "Love Unknown" is a psychological dramatization, gesturing only momentarily toward the soteriological efficacy of sacraments and the escape they provide from inner turmoil and doubt. The poem in this respect exemplifies a devotional tendency in Herbert which Achsah Guibbory has described as focusing "on the individual believer rather than the corporate religious community" (45).[26] The external remedy may provide a means of grace independent of psychological disposition, but as significant as it may be, the Eucharist nevertheless is overwhelmed, "Ev'n taken inwardly"—swallowed, as it were, by the speaker's ever vigilant Conscience. Even the communion with his crucified saviour which the ritual allows is compromised by an anxiety apparently impervious to sacramental persuasion, for immediately following the eucharistic encounter, the still unconvinced penitent hesitates:

> But when I thought to sleep out all these faults
>     (I sigh to speak)
> I found that some had stuff'd the bed with thoughts,
> I would say *thorns.*
>
> (49–52)

More than a *meditatio Christi,* the metaphor transfers the crown of thorns to the speaker's psyche and allows his ephemeral tortures the dignified status of messianic sacrifice. Though the focus here is inward, it forms part of what Elizabeth Clarke calls a process of "mortification-vivification" wherein Herbert's self-abnegation is a priestly sharing in the far superior priesthood of Christ. The inward focus, then, is paradoxically an effort to eliminate the self so that it might be more fully realized as integral with the greater body to which it belongs. Just as resurrection follows death, so does self-affirmation follow self-denial, a resurrection of self Clarke perceptively associates with the externals of ceremonial worship (193–194). If Herbert's sacramental vision suggests Roman sensualism and a fondness for ritual, however, these serve primarily to ceremonialize otherwise inward deliberations. And yet this fusion of inside and outside may not have the desired effect, for while ceremony provides escape from existential isolation, it may be that Herbert's distinctive self permeates rather than becomes lost in its institutional context. There is perhaps no rest for one who knows that even his prayers are inseparable from ritual, reverberating as they do between ceremonial and devotional, institutional and private spheres: "Though my lips went, my heart did stay behinde" (line 59). The crucial question is whether or not he can accept finally that his friend's suppling "holy bloud" will indeed render the heart *"new, tender, quick"* (70).

The liminal frontier between ceremony and devotion, the site of a psychological drama animated and reified by sacrament, is important for our understanding of Herbert's verse and its ostensibly inward focus. Inwardness in Herbert does not result in the desacramentalization of Christian worship identified long ago by Malcolm Ross as a central (and regrettable) feature of seventeenth-century religious poetry.[27] Eucharist and ritual, rather, are inseparable from the *The Temple*'s interiority, the latter an extension of its public, ceremonial context. The result is nothing less than a sacramental Puritanism, the integration of institutional and private aspects of religious experience, as in "Sinne (I)," where God's "fine nets and strategems to catch us in" include not only "laws," "Pulpits and Sundayes," but also "sorrow dogging sinne" and "anguish of all sizes" (lines 3–7); together, these are "Without, our shame; within, our consciences; / Angels and grace, eternall hopes and fears" (11–12). Woven into the fabric of his devotional experience, sacramental topoi for Herbert alleviate a self-absorbed psychomachia. The external means of grace provide a healing balm for "sorrow dogging sinne," sacraments penetrating the private psyche and materializing the otherwise ephemeral processes of Christian salvation. Herbert's sacramental Puritanism thus exemplifies what Ramie Targoff has described as "the direct correspondence between outward behavior and inward thought" in early modern subjectivity (50–51).

In addition to addressing the theological controversies of his era, sacrament in *The Temple* advances the Christian paradox of the Incarnation as central to Herbert's interrogation of the relationship between spiritual and material aspects of religious experience. The integration of internal and external modes is essential to both sacramental worship and devotional versification, for the Christian *mythos* attending ceremonial forms encompasses also the communicant's private reflections, whether at "board," prayer, or quill and "little book."[28] Herbert's poetry addresses matters of concern to the members of a faith community even as it portrays one individual working out his salvation in fear and trembling. Central to this integration of communal context and private devotional space, sacramental topoi establish the individual penitent's *rôle* in a larger scheme, both his or her performative ritual duty and status with respect to the register or book of life to which all hopeful souls aspire. The sober yet energetic creativity discernible in Herbert's verse is a result of his efforts to find in sacrament the mediation of a grace whose reality the most sincere and constant of devotional psyches is unable otherwise to sustain. It is only through continual return to its institutional and carnal status as sacrament that Herbert can think the Word become flesh and the supreme gift it declares.

## NOTES

*Versions of this paper were presented at the 1999 Sixteenth-Century Studies Conference in St. Louis and at the 2000 International Congress on Medieval Studies in Kalamazoo. I am grateful to the anonymous reviewers at *Renaissance Quarterly* for their thoughtful suggestions. For a computer-assisted statistical analysis of sacramental and devotional topoi in *The Temple* see Whalen.

1. Milton, 527–528, 470–475; J. Davies, 18–45; Lake, 1991, 113–133.

2. Halewood maintains a rigid opposition between sacramental formalism and the internalised spirituality symptomatic of Puritan doctrine and practice (65–73). According to Lewalski, the void left by this suspicion of sacramental divinity is filled by a word-centred piety that urges the sermon as a preparation for meditation (155–156). In keeping with current historiography the term "Reform" here refers to Calvinist theology (Milton, 8 and n. 14; see also J. Davies, 298).

3. For a recent and concise overview of these issues see Lake and Questier, ix–xx.

4. Even Martz, the influential champion of Anglo-Catholic poetics, recognized that although meditative practices had always had a strong psychological component, it was "the inward surge of Puritanism," combined with older techniques, that produced the distinctive religious devotion of the seventeenth century (9). It is "the weapon of mental communion" in Herbert "which makes the sacraments flow from Christ's side" (299). Martz even went so far as to suggest for one continental meditative a "Catholic Puritanism," but insists it was "free of predestination" (127–128).

5. For a nuanced discussion of English Arminianism see Kendall, 141–150. See also Lake, 1987, 39–40.

6. Collinson and others (Milton, 395–407, Sommerville, 208) agree that while there often was vehement disagreement over matters of church government and the externals of ceremonial worship, doctrinal Calvinism provided, for a time, a confessional identity of sorts. Tyacke finds that "Puritan" as a derogatory label did not become associated specifically with doctrinal Calvinism and predestinarian thought until the 1620s when the rise of Arminianism eventually rendered heterodox what hitherto had been the Reform core of English religious orthodoxy. Prior to this time, conformist and non-conformist alike shared a doctrinally Calvinist heritage, so that the majority of conformist divines, whether inclining to a sacrament-centred ministry or one which emphasized preaching and a private lay piety, may be called "Calvinist episcopalians" (1995, 68). Lake observes that while an anti-Calvinist element had always existed, the question is one of "Calvinist hegemony." Distaste for Reform orthodoxy did not prevent participation in Jacobean ecclesiastical life, nor, for that matter, opportunity for preferment. The relative silence of such individuals, however, is "evidence of the extent to which Calvinism had established itself in control of the crucial cultural media of the day" (1987, 34).

7. See Rubin, 17–34.

8. In addition to Dugmore see H. Davies, 288–291.

9. St. Thomas was influenced by his understanding of the Aristotelian philosophy of matter in which it is held that bodies consist of matter and form, form being an extension of matter governing its particular appearance. The substance or essence of a body inheres in both aspects or principles—both its matter and form. For Aquinas, it was possible that the matter or substance of Christ's body be present under the form of bread even while still in heaven. The conversion of the bread, then, is not a formal or accidental but rather substantial one only. The body of Christ, moreover, is present not as a "body in place," but in a "special way that is proper to this sacrament [sed quodum speciali modo, qui est proprius huic sacramento]" (3:75.1). It is present not locally, as an extended body is, but rather as

"purely and simply substance" (3:76.5). Just as the substance of bread is never present as an extended body, neither is the substance of the body of Christ. The doctrine of transubstantiation thus developed the idea that while the substance of the elements is wholly changed, the accidents or the elements' appearance remains, a view which was to persist through to and beyond later Tridentine reform.

10. Milton cites a speech given before the 1629 Parliament in which Neile goes so far as to dismiss not only the Church of Rome, but also the Mass and transubstantiation (86). It is important to emphasize however, that such vehemence among Laudians may have been less a statement of confessional loyalty than the expedient deflection of charges of Roman sympathy (84–91).

11. Ibid., 202–205, 63–72.

12. Herbert, 1941, 259. Unless otherwise indicated, Herbert citations are from this edition; 1633, B, and W refer to, respectively, the first edition printed by Thomas Buck at Cambridge, Buck's MS source transcribed by the Ferrars at Little Gidding (the Bodleian Library's Tanner 307) and supposedly based on Herbert's "little book" (now lost), and the earlier MS Jones 28.169 now in the Williams library. For a discussion of the dating of this latter and its autograph status see Charles, 78–87.

13. Strier insists that eucharistic readings of "Divinitie" are erroneous insofar as they neglect the non-conducive order of the words "bloud" and "wine" (47).

14. I do not include as part of "The H. Communion" what in B and 1633 apparently is the poem's second half and what in the earlier W is the separate poem, "Prayer (II)." For an account of possible editorial error see Huntley, 65–76. Allowing the two-part version authority, Clarke discerns a dual motion of outward form toward inward spirituality and the subsequent movement of the grace-inspired soul toward heaven (161). This outward-inward motion is apparent, it seems to me, in the poem's "first half" alone.

15. Russell notes that whereas the Prayer Book and Act of Uniformity both called for "common bread," the Queen's Injunction stipulated wafers (Herbert's "wedge of gold"?). "Everyone who took communion," writes Russell, in effect "had to disobey one of these requirements" (86).

16. To maintain significance for the elements as set apart from ordinary wine and bread while avoiding earthly contamination of the resurrected Christ, Calvin settled on what sometimes is referred to as virtualism, his singular contribution to sacramental theology. Christ's flesh, though "separated from us by such great distance," nevertheless "penetrates to us, so that it becomes our food"; the Spirit "truly unites things separated in space." Though the breaking of bread is a "symbol" and not "the thing itself," nevertheless, "by the showing of the symbol the thing itself is also shown" (4.17.10). Elsewhere Calvin writes, "Christ is not visibly present, and is not beheld with our eyes, as the symbols are which excite our remembrance by representing him. In short, in order that he may be present to us, he does not change his place, but communicates to us from heaven the virtue of his flesh as though it were present" (*Corpus Reformatorum*, 49.489, cited in McDonnell, 231). For Calvin, Augustine and "seal" see McDonnell, 286.

17. Ellrodt avers that Herbert's sacramental doctrine as expressed in the later "H. Communion" was "truly original" because it advanced simultaneously "two realities, sensible and spiritual, at once distinct and conjoined" (2000, 210–211). Whereas for Calvin the physical aspect of the Eucharist was only metaphorically parallel to an essentially spiritual operation, for Herbert the communication of

grace included a very real physical dimension. But this two-fold sacramentality nonetheless is clearly hierarchical: "Onely thy grace" (line 19), writes Herbert, can open "the souls most subtile rooms" (22). Neither is Herbert's more-than-merely-metaphorical parallel between matter and spirit without precedent in English Protestantism. Ridley, for example, held that "even as the mortal body is nourished by that visible bread, so is the internal soul fed with the heavenly food of Christ's body" (274), while Hooker could write that in receiving the sacrament "we arc dyed red both within and without, our hunger is satisfied and our thirst for ever quenched" (2:331). Anderson persuasively demonstrates that the early English reformers, anxious to maintain a real if non-corporeal presence in the sacrament, devised formulae in which sacramental signs derive substantive power from their referents without actually embodying them. If ostensibly metaphorical and symbolic, such understandings of sacramental presence were neither simply nor merely so (27–47).

18. Milton describes Laudian reform as "the desire to transform English Protestants' perception of the relative importance of discipline vis-à-vis doctrine, and of sacraments vis-à-vis preaching" (447).

19. That the W version was finally excluded from *The Temple* may be evidence of Herbert's increasingly irenic attitude (Summers, 24; McGill, 21–22; Stewart, 54).

20. This may be an indictment of the view tithe Swiss reformer Huldreich Zwingli, who sharply distinguished between Christ's two natures and insisted, as Calvin later would, that the ascended Christ is the divine Christ to which alone the sacrament refers. To "feed on Christ's body," he writes, is simply "to believe in him" (198).

21. Collinson (1989, 31) notes a similar position in Hooker (2:236), a position compatible with the Polity's tendency to condemn Puritan efforts to distinguish between the godly and ungodly in the visible church (see, for example, 2:342–343).

22. The poem recalls Donne's playful treatment of the sacramental-predestinarian connection in "Loves diet" where the mistress's tears and favours, her "drink" and "meate," must for some be "counterfeit," for "eyes which rowle towards all, weepe not, but sweat" (lines 17–18).

23. Though episcopacy by divine right was initially advanced by the more rigidly Calvinist conformists as a way of asserting their autonomy against the crown's own *jure divino* claims, Puritan reservation increased proportional to the doctrine's association with the sacerdotal policies and practices of the more avant-garde divines (Milton, 454–456).

24. This latter is a traditional feature of medieval and Renaissance iconography. See, for example, Timoteo Viti's *Annunciation*, where the infant Christ descends on a dove over the praying Virgin (D'Ancona, 38 and fig. 21).

25. Frye defined mythos variously as imitation of "generic and recurrent action or ritual" and of "the total conceivable action of an omnipotent god or human society" (366–367).

26. Shuger, similarly, argues that the "confessional intimacy of the divine-human encounter in Herbert fulfils the need for a relationship not available in society" (104).

27. In an early study of sacramental literature, Ross finds that eucharistic imagery in Herbert is but "Catholic rhetoric" as opposed to true "Catholic dogma," the former mere ornamental veneer, the latter absent altogether (179–180).

28. According to Walton, "little book" was Herbert's name for the volume of poems sent from his death-bed to Nicholas Ferrar (286). The editors of the B facsimile also use the phrase to describe the no longer extant MS likely received by Ferrar at Little Gidding (Herbert, 1984, xii). Amy Charles reminds us, however, that Walton knew Herbert's poems only as published and that "any of the seventeenth-century editions was, indeed, a little book" (182 n12).

## Works Cited

Anderson, Judith H. 2001. "Language and History in the Reformation: Cranmer, Gardiner, and the Words of Institution." *Renaissance Quarterly* 54.1: 20–51.

Aquinas, St. Thomas. 1964–1976. *Summa Theologiae*. 60 vols. London.

Calvin, John. 1960. *Institutes of the Christian Religion*. 2 vols. Ed. John T. McNeill. Trans. Ford Lewis Battles. Philadelphia.

Charles, Amy. 1987. *A Life of George Herbert*. Ithaca.

Chauvet, Louis-Marie. 1995. *Symbol and Sacrament: A Sacramental Reinterpretation of Christian Existence*. Trans. S. J. Patrick Madigan and Madeleine Beaumont. Collegeville, MN.

Clarke, Elizabeth. 1987. *Theory and Theology in George Herbert's Poetry: Divinitie, and Poesie, Met*. Oxford.

Collinson, Patrick. 1982. *The Religion of Protestants: The Church in English Society 1559–1625*. Oxford.

———. 1989. *The Puritan Character: Polemics and Polarities in Early Seventeenth-Century Culture*. Los Angeles.

Como, David. 2000. "Puritans, Predestination and the Construction of Orthodoxy in Early Seventeenth-Century England." In *Conformity and Orthodoxy in the English Church, c.1560–1660*, eds. Peter Lake and Michael Questier, 64–87. Woodbridge, Suffolk.

Cressy, David and Lori Anne Ferrell, eds. 1996. *Religion and Society in Early Modern England: A Sourcebook*. London.

Croken, Robert C., S. J. 1990. *Luther's First Font: The Eucharist as Sacrifice*. Ottawa.

Davies, Horton. 1975. *Worship and Theology in England: From Andrewes to Baxter and Fox, 1603–1690*. Vol. 2. Princeton.

Davies, Julian. 1992. *The Caroline Captivity of the Church: Charles I and the Remoulding of Anglicanism 1625–1641*. Oxford.

D'Ancona, Mirella Levi. 1957. *The Iconography of the Immaculate Conception in the Middle Ages and the Early Renaissance*. New York.

Doerksen, Daniel W, 1997. *Conforming to the Word: Herbert, Donne, and the English Church Before Laud*. Lewisburg, PA.

Donne, John. 1989. *The Complete English Poems of John Donne*. Ed. C. A. Patrides. London.

———. 1953–1962. *The Sermons of John Donne*. 10 vols. Eds. Evelyn M. Simpson and George R. Potter. Berkeley.

Duffy, Eamon. 1992. *The Stripping of the Altars: Traditional Religion in England c.1400–c.1580*. London.

Dugmore, C. W. 1942. *Eucharistic Doctrine in England from Hooker to Waterland: being the Norrisian prize essay in the University of Cambridge for the year 1940*. London.

Ellrodt, Robert. 1960. *Les Poètes Métaphysiques Anglais: John Donne et les poètes de la tradition chrétienne*. Vol. 1. Paris.

———. 2000. *Seven Metaphysical Poets. A Structural Study of the Unchanging Self*. Oxford.

Fish, Stanley. 1972. *Self-Consuming Artifacts: The Experience of Seventeenth-Century Literature*. Los Angeles.

Frye, Northrop. 1966. *Anatomy of Criticism*. 1957. Reprint, New York.

Guibbory, Achsah. 1998. *Ceremony and Community from Herbert to Milton: Literature, religion, and cultural conflict in seventeenth-century England*. Cambridge.

Halewood, W. H. 1970. *The Poetry of Grace: Reformation Themes and Structures in Seventeenth-Century Poetry*. New Haven.

Hall, Basil. 1979. "The Early Rise and Gradual Decline of Lutheranism in England (1520–1600)." In *Reform and Reformation: England and the Continent c. 1500–c. 1750*, ed. Derek Baker, 103–131. Oxford.

Herbert, George. 1941. *The Works of George Herbert*. Ed. F. E. Hutchinson. Oxford.

———. 1968. *George Herbert:* The Temple. *Sacred Poems and Private Ejaculations*. 1633. Facs. reprint, Yorkshire.

———. 1977. *The Williams Manuscript of George Herbert's Poems*. Ed. Amy M. Charles. Delmar, NY.

———. 1984. *The Bodleian Manuscript of George Herbert's Poems: A Facsimile of Tanner 307*. Eds. Amy M. Charles and Mario A. Di Cesare. New York.

———. 1988. *The English Poems of George Herbert*. Ed. C. A. Patrides. London.

Hodgkins, Christopher. 1993. *Authority, Church, and Society in George Herbert: Return to the Middle Way*. Columbia.

Hooker, Richard. 1963. *Of the Laws of Ecclesiastical Polity*. 2 vols. Ed. Christopher Morris. London.

Hunter, Jeanne Clayton. 1982. "'With Wings of Faith': Herbert's Communion Poems." *Journal of Religion* 62.1: 57–71.

Huntley, Frank L. 1981. "What Happened to Two of Herbert's Poems?" In *Essays in Persuasion: On Seventeenth-Century Literature*, ed. Frank L. Huntley, 65–76. Chicago.

Kendall, R. T. 1979. *Calvin and English Calvinism to 1649*. Oxford.

Lake, Peter. 1987. "Calvinism and the English Church." *Past and Present* 114: 32–76.

———. 1988. *Anglicans and Puritans? Presbyterian and English Conformist Thought from Whitgift to Hooker*. London.

———. 1991. "Lancelot Andrewes, John Buckeridge and avant-garde conformity at the court of James I." In *The Mental World of the Jacobean Court*, ed. L. Levy Peck, 113–133. Cambridge.

Lake, Peter, and Michael Questier, eds. 2000. *Conformity and Orthodoxy in the English Church, c.1560–1660*. Woodbridge, Suffolk: Boydell Press.

Lewalski, Barbara K. 1979. *Protestant Poetics and the Seventeenth-Century Religious Lyric*. Princeton.

Luther, Martin. 1971. *Luther's Works*. 55 vols. Gen. ed. Helmut T. Lehmann. Philadelphia.

Martz, Louis L. 1954. *The Poetry of Meditation: A Study in English Religious Literature of the Seventeenth Century*. New Haven.

McDonnell, Kilian. 1967. *John Calvin, the Church, and the Eucharist*. Princeton.

McGill, William J., Jr. 1966. "George Herbert's View of the Eucharist." *Lock Haven Review* 8: 16–24.

Milton, Anthony. 1995. *Catholic and Reformed: The Roman and Protestant Churches in English Protestant Thought*. Cambridge.

Ridley, Nicholas. 1841. *The Works of Nicholas Ridley*. Ed. Henry Christmas. Cambridge.

Ross, Malcolm Mackenzie. 1954. *Poetry and Dogma. The Transfiguration of Eucharistic Symbols in Seventeenth-Century English Poetry*. New Brunswick, NJ.

Rubin, Miri. 1991. *Corpus Christi: The Eucharist in Late Medieval Culture*. Cambridge.

Russell, Conrad. 1990. *The Causes of the English Civil War*. Oxford.

Schillebeeckx, E. 1968. *The Eucharist*. Trans. N. D. Smith. New York.

Schoenfeldt, Michael C. 1999. *Bodies and Selves in Early Modern England: Physiology and Inwardness in Spenser, Shakespeare, Herbert, and Milton.* Cambridge.

Shuger, Debora K. 1990. *Habits of Thought in the English Renaissance: Religion, Politics, and the Dominant Culture.* Los Angeles.

Sommerville, J. R 1986. *Politics and Ideology in England, 1603–1640.* London: Longman.

Stewart, Stanley. 1986. *George Herbert.* Boston.

Strier, Richard. 1983. *Love Known: Theology and Experience in George Herbert's Poetry.* Chicago.

Summers, Joseph H. 1993. "George Herbert and Anglican Traditions." *George Herbert Journal* 16.1: 21–39.

Targoff, Ramie. 1997. "The Performance of Prayer: Sincerity and Theatricality in Early Modern England." *Representations* 60: 49–69.

Tyacke, Nicholas. 1987. *Anti-Calvinists: The Rise of English Arminianism c.1590–1640.* Oxford.

———. 1995. "Puritanism, Arminianism and Counter-Revolution." In *Reformation to Revolution: Polities and Religion in Early Modern England,* ed. Margot Todd, 53–70. 1973. London.

Veith, Gene Edward, Jr. 1985. *Reformation Spirituality: The Religion of George Herbert.* Lewisburg.

Walton, Isaak. 1982. "The Life of Mr. George Herbert." *Seventeenth Century Prose and Poetry,* eds. A. M. Witherspoon and E J. Warnke, 2nd. ed. 271–288. Orlando.

Whalen, Robert. 2000. "'How shall I measure out thy bloud?' or 'Weening is not measure': TACT, Herbert and Sacramental Devotion in the Electronic Temple." *Early Modern Literary Studies* 5.3: 7.1–37. Jointly published in a special edition of *Text Technology* 9.3 (1999): 27–65.

Young, R. V. 2000. *Doctrine and Devotion in Seventeenth-Century Poetry: Studies in Donne, Herbert, Crashaw, and Vaughan.* Suffolk.

Zwingli, Huldreich. 1953. On the Lord's Supper. In *Zwingli and Bullinger.* Trans. G. W. Bromiley, 185–347. London.

MAUREEN SABINE

# Crashaw and Abjection:
# Reading the Unthinkable in His Devotional Verse

There looms, within abjection, one of those violent, dark revolts of
being, directed against a threat that seems to emanate from an exorbitant
outside or inside, ejected beyond the scope of the possible, the tolerable,
the thinkable.

—Julia Kristeva, *Powers of Horror*

What Julia Kristeva has to say about abjection at the outset of *Powers of Horror* (1980) offers a compelling theoretical framework for a study of the seventeenth-century baroque poet Richard Crashaw (1613–1649). Critics of varying persuasions have regularly resorted to epithets such as shocking, perverse, grotesque, neurotic, and queer to condemn, and occasionally to praise, Crashaw's devotional verse.[1] It is only an apparent paradox to add that Crashaw himself has since his own time been regarded as unworldly and ascetic—in short, a man who became a eunuch for the kingdom of heaven.

Kristeva describes abjection as a shudder in which the subject is assailed by a premonitory fear of the "loathsome," the "not me," a "weight of meaninglessness . . . on the edge of non-existence and hallucination . . . that, if I acknowledge it, annihilates me" (1980, 2). Abjection marks a breach in the first line of psychic defense against the ultimate horror of death, and it manifests itself as the uncanny awareness of a "collapse of the border between inside and outside" (53), what is within and beyond the control of the body.

*American Imago*, Volume 63, Number 4 (Winter 2006): pp. 423–443. Copyright © 2007 Johns Hopkins University Press.

According to Kristeva, three principal types of experience transgress the porous boundary between the "me" and the "not me." The first is any edible substance that brings to mind detritus, such as "skin on the surface of milk," the mucus of rotting vegetables, or the pong of decaying meat. The nausea provoked by ingesting such loathsome food is at once an expression of abjection and a doomed attempt to cleanse the body of pollution. As Kristeva says, "'I' expel it. But since the food is not an 'other' for 'me,' . . . I expel *myself*, I spit *myself* out, I abject *myself* within the same motion through which 'I' claim to establish *myself*" (2–3). The second expression of the abject is the horror arising from spectacles of disease, violence, and death. A wounded body oozes blood: when infected, it is filled with pus and the smell of putrefaction. A still-warm corpse erases the borderline between life and death. Kristeva comments that "these bodily fluids, this defilement, this shit are what life withstands . . . with difficulty, on the part of death" (3). Finally, Kristeva contends that the preoedipal child's fantasy of the "phallic" mother who begins life, as death will end it, generates archaic and outlandish expressions of abjection. The child seeks to separate himself from the mother and become self-sufficient, to achieve control over his body, and to neutralize "the horrors of maternal bowels" (53) that have thrust him out and threaten to suck him back in again. Menstruating, pregnant, and lactating women reawaken this dread and provoke "violent, dark revolts of being" (1), particularly in men indoctrinated by misogyny. Those who do not turn away in horror must sustain a dual fantasy of attraction and repulsion "for the desirable and terrifying, nourishing and murderous, fascinating and abject inside of the maternal body" (54).

Like Kristeva, Crashaw was fascinated by abjection, and he reconfigured its fantasies in his poetry with the dexterity of a tightrope walker without a safety net. Both the body of Christ and those of his female suppliants are shown to possess mouths, eyes, breasts, wombs, and wounds, and to emit milk, blood, tears, saliva, and feces. In "Dies Irae," a poem on the Last Judgment, Crashaw pleads that the "soft bowells" of Christ may "discharge that day" (Williams 1970, 191, st. 12)—that is, ransom his soul through a process of evacuation. In "The Weeper," Mary Magdalene's tears rise "Upwards" to thicken into the "Creame" of the "milky rivers" (Williams 1970, 124, st. 4) of Heaven. According to two epigrams on the Holy Innocents, they die while being nursed in a flood of dissolution that blends "Mothers Milk" with "Childrens blood" (Williams 1970, 10). Elsewhere Crashaw says of Mary Magdalene, "Her eyes flood lickes his feets faire staine" (Williams 1970, 13), with the "feet" of Christ alluding to the lowness of his genitalia, but then "Her haires flame lickes up that againe," with her red-gold tresses being symbolic not only of carnality but also of the refining fire of the Passion.[2]

Mary Magdalene replicates this rite of abjection, pollution, and puri-
fication in Crashaw's verse, "On the wounds of our crucified Lord," where
Christ's stigmata are voluptuous, bloody, and weeping mouths that become
the blood-shot eyes of inconsolable grief: "Lo! a mouth, whose full-bloom'd
lips / At too deare a rate are roses. / Lo! a blood-shot eye! that weepes / And
many a cruell teare discloses" (Williams 1970, 24–25, ll. 5–8). The Magdalene presses her lips passionately against the open wounds of Christ's feet, as
though giving mouth-to-mouth resuscitation: "This foot hath got a Mouth
and lippes, / To pay the sweet summe of thy kisses" (ll. 13–14). The abject
thrives on transgression of taboos and prohibitions, though it is a historical
irony that only after the early church banned women from handling the Eucharist did they begin to receive communion on the tongue, and consequently
to imagine mouth-to-mouth union with Christ (Bynum 1987, 56, 273).

Christian iconography sees the crucifixion as a fulfillment of the pre-
figuring promise made by Christ to his Father during the circumcision. As
Crashaw writes of the wound inflicted on Christ's penis as an infant in "Our
Lord in his Circumcision to his Father," "These purple buds of blooming
death may bee, / Erst the full stature of a fatall tree" (Williams 1970, 9–10,
ll. 15–16). In another divine epigram, "On our crucified Lord Naked, and
bloody" (Williams 1970, 24), Crashaw visualizes the spectacle that Mary
Magdalene cannot see in her self-abasement before Christ's minor wounds.
Christ's body hangs on the Cross, clothed only in a cloak of blood: "Th' have
left thee naked Lord, O that they had; / This Garment too I would they had
deny'd. / Thee with thy selfe they have too richly clad" (ll. 1–3). Paradoxically,
the "naked Lord" wears a "Garment" produced from the "purple wardrobe"
(l. 4) opened by the major wound in his side. As Kristeva (1980) aptly remarks, "one of the insights of Christianity . . . is to have gathered in a single
move perversion and beauty as the lining and the cloth of one and the same
economy" (125).

Both Crashaw and Kristeva draw inspiration from the ascetic practices
of late medieval women mystics and the men who wrote of their divine encounters. Their piety is replete with rituals that modern readers are likely to
find as morbid as anything in Crashaw's devotional verse. These women did
not refrain from putting their mouths to putrefying sores or sucking suppu-
rating breasts, drinking pus and the scabby water with which lepers had been
washed, eating lice, and using their effluvia as holy water to cleanse and heal
others (Bynum 1987, 114, 126, 144–145, 172). The ecstatic pleasure they derived from these practices suggests that they indeed cultivated what Kristeva
calls an "erotic cult of the abject" (1980, 55).

Kristeva's focus on mystical Christianity in *Powers of Horror* (1980),
including such holy women as Angela of Foligno and Elizabeth of Hun-
gary, extends her interest in the preoedipal bond of mother and child, their

polymorphous body language, and the *jouissance* they derive from this intimate bond.[3] Although Kristeva has had a vexed relationship to feminism, her research on sacred subjects has furthered the recovery of what Elizabeth Petroff (1979) has called "the underground history of holy women in Christianity" (i), and her chosen examples are featured also in the revisionist work of both Petroff and Caroline Walker Bynum.

Crashaw's own interest in feminine piety reflects the complex and unorthodox history probed by Kristeva, Petroff, and Bynum. He positions himself as a pupil, acolyte, confidant, and spiritual counselor of exemplary holy women in major poems on Mary Magdalene, the Virgin Mary, St. Teresa of Avila, and the Countess of Denbigh. The imagery of breast, milk, nest, womb, tears, and bleeding hearts saturating his poetry corresponds with Kristeva's designation of the maternal semiotic.[4] Crashaw's renown, in the words of Thomas Car's elegiac tribute, "Crashawe, the Anagramme," as "chaplaine of the virgine myld" (Williams 1970, 653, l. 38) brought him into conflict with the reforming wing of the English Church. While still an Anglican priest at Peterhouse, Cambridge, Crashaw was visited in 1641 in his curacy at Little St. Mary's by Puritan investigators scandalized by his "popish" and "superstitious" rituals, most notably his worship of the Virgin Mary.[5] The fact that his father, William Crashaw, had made his reputation as a denouncer of Roman Catholicism and Mariolatry added incense to injury. After his flight into exile on the continent in 1644 and his conversion to Catholicism, Richard Crashaw was introduced to the Pope as "the learned son of a famous Heretic" (Martin 1957, xxxv*n*4), though Puritans doubtless saw him as the heretical son of a learned Reformer.

It is now generally believed that no two men could have had less in common than William Crashaw and his son. In a 1966 essay in *American Imago*, Richard Geha argued that Richard Crashaw "committed himself to everything that his father most hated and feared" (158), that he fell "into the arms of that Catholic mother who unfailingly intercedes for the son and prevents the wrath of the father" (163), and that "the Counter-Reformation is the ego's painful walk around the father" (168). In 1983, Vera Camden went on to underline the oedipal struggle between father and son by suggesting that William Crashaw's Puritan zeal on behalf of God the Father led to Richard's flight "from the harsh strictures of his father's faith to the Mother Church in Rome" (259). Camden read Crashaw's imagery of bleeding wounds as a sign of his fear of castration at the hands of a wrathful father. To be sure, William Crashaw was a forceful opponent of popery, but he was not the implacable tyrant depicted in the analyses of both Geha and Camden.

Ruth Wallerstein (1935) is one of the few early critics to have perceived "a sympathetic communion of mind between father and son" (19). Both had passionate sensibilities, but where the father was fiery and vehement, the son was gentle and extravagant. Both were charismatic preachers, William with his thundering polemics and Richard with "thronged Sermons . . . that ravished more like Poems . . . scattering not so much Sentences [as] Extasies" (Martin 1957, 416). Even one of William Crashaw's Jesuit adversaries commented on "the sweetness of his [first] marriage" at the same time that he lamented the inability of William's wife to "mitigate the bitterness of his tongue" (Floyd 1612, 5). The 1620 funeral sermon by James Ussher, Bishop of Armagh, for William's second wife, Elizabeth Skinner Crashaw, remarked upon "her extraordinary love and almost strange affection" for a husband who was "twice her own age" (Henderson and McManus 1985, 346) and far from wealthy.[6] No less praiseworthy was "her singular motherly affection to the child of her predecessor: a rare virtue . . . in stepmothers at this day" (346). Throughout his life, Richard evoked devotion in others. On Crashaw's death in 1649, Thomas Car, the editor of his *Carmen Deo Nostro,* eulogized his friend as one "Who was belov'd by all; dispraysed by none" (Williams 1970, 652, l. 14).

Although William Crashaw was able to give Richard little financial and less emotional security—both his first and second wives having died before his son was seven—the father provided him with one legacy of enduring importance—an education. L. C. Martin (1957) notes that, as a Puritan controversialist, William put together "one of the finest private theological libraries of the time" (xvi). Book collecting was a rich man's avocation, though William's obsession with ferreting out proofs of Papist corruption consumed much of his "patrimonye" (xviii). William was forced to dispose of several thousand volumes prior to his death in 1626, but Richard had access to his father's library during his precocious childhood. According to Austin Warren (1939, 210–11n2), the works he is likely to have seen include St. Bernard of Clairvaux's *Sermons on the Song of Songs,* the life of Catherine of Siena, the *Revelations* of St. Bridget, and the writings of Richard Rolle.[7]

The texts assembled by William Crashaw foreshadow both the themes and sensibility of Richard Crashaw's devotional verse. Like Crashaw, Bernard of Clairvaux and Richard Rolle employed a "feminine" style of mysticism that appealed to pious women. They brought home the emotional reality of Christ's suffering by representing him as a nursing mother, and his crucifixion as a bloody birth that cost him his life—as childbirth probably claimed the life of Crashaw's own mother and was certainly responsible for the death of his stepmother and the baby Ussher termed her "dear-bought son" (Henderson and McManus 1985, 345), who would have been Crashaw's half-brother. Bernard's *Sermons on the Song of Songs* describe the ecstasy of eating God and being consumed by him. In medieval art illustrating the "Double Intercession," in which Bernard himself appears as a subject, Mary's maternal sacrifice as childbearer and breastfeeder is connected to Christ's offering of his body and blood on the Cross. In his vision of lactation, Bernard nurses

from the milk-laden breast of Mary in preference to the bleeding wound
of Christ (Bynum 1987, 25–26, 105–106, 270–272, 288; 1991, 93, 106–107,
124, 157–158, 190–191).

In his polemical treatise, *The Jesuit Gospel* (1610), William Crashaw
condemned as heretical any suggestion that "the Mother is compared to the
Sonne, not as being a childe, or a man, but as the Saviour and mediator: and
the pappes of a Woman equalled with the wounds of our Lord, and her milke
with his bloud" (32). His son, however, would later take this Catholic doctrine
of the double intercession and play ingeniously with its gender and familial
politics. By suggesting that the worshiper is not forced to choose between
Mother and Son, and that maternal succor does not undermine paternal authority, Crashaw sought through his poetry to keep faith with both his father
and his mother.

William Crashaw's (1610) fulmination against Catholics, "who in their
liturgies and daily prayers, call a creature the mother of mercy, and mother of
grace, oftener than either God the father, or Christ the redeemer" (88), illustrates not only the reaction of Reformers against late medieval Mariology and
feminine religiosity but also their fear that disturbing somatic undercurrents
would take hold of the imagination. Nowhere are the "tantalizing perversions" (Bertonasco 1964, 14) of late medieval mysticism more evident than in
the life of Catherine of Siena.[8] Indeed, Catherine described the Incarnation
as the mystery in which God hid his divinity within "the wretched dung heap
of Adam" (qtd. in Bynum 1987, 377*n*136). As her revulsion toward her body
and the food that nourished its health and beauty grew, so too did her hunger
for the filth produced by the bodies of the sick and dying. The only other food
she could tolerate was the Eucharist, but even that left a lingering taste of the
discharge of wounds or menstruation in her mouth. Bynum (1991) resists the
tendency to pathologize this abjection, and reads such relish for the festering
body as "a horrible yet delicious elevation" (182), akin to the transubstantiation, in which base human matter encounters the divine.

It is clear that female mystics such as Catherine of Siena anticipated
Crashaw's Baroque belief that "in my flesh shall I see God in His flesh" (Warren 1939, 151). But their ascetic zeal led them to exorbitance as they strove to
dissolve the boundaries separating the pure bodies of Christ and his Mother
from the unclean bodies of sinning and suffering humanity. Kristeva (1980)
is thus right to argue that Christianity makes self-abasement "the ultimate
proof of humility before God" (5) and that "the mystic's familiarity with abjection is a fount of infinite jouissance" (127). Catherine sealed her mystical
marriage to Christ in a vision with a ring made from the foreskin removed
at his circumcision. On another occasion, she stood beneath the scaffold to
receive the decapitated head of a political prisoner and was bathed in the
blood spurting from his arteries (Bynum 1987, 171–178). In both incidents,

the horror of abjection is intensified by a symbolic representation of the castration of the male genitals.

The death of Crashaw's father in 1626 must have left a void in Crashaw's life, especially as he appears to have had no other surviving kin. In his last will and testament, William Crashaw expressed his conviction that the tenets of Roman Catholicism polluted Christianity like diarrhoea coursing through the body of Christ and discharged into a running sewer: "I accounte Poperie . . . the heape and chaos of all heresies and the channell whereinto the fowlest impieties & heresies yt have byne in the christian Worlde have runn and closelye emptied themselues" (Martin 1957, xviii–xix). Melanie Klein, whom Kristeva (1980, 60) commends for having probed abjection's indistinct borders between inside and outside, provides a basis for surmising that William Crashaw's scatological attack can be read as a fantasied onslaught on the mother's body as an extension of her breast. The excrement hurled at the Church of Rome and the Blessed Virgin are, to extrapolate from Klein (1946), a means by which "the bad parts of the self" can be "expelled and projected" (8) into the hated other. Yet not only the bad but the good parts of the self are thus expelled, so excrement can also take on "the significance of gifts."

At the Charterhouse where Richard Crashaw was schooled, the headmaster, Robert Brook, laid the groundwork of his "Divine fancy" by requiring pupils to write Greek and Latin verses "on the Epistles and Gospels" (Martin 1957, xx, 415). Crashaw continued to compose sacred epigrams on Scripture as an undergraduate scholar at Pembroke College, Cambridge, from 1631 to 1635 (Sabine 1992, 111–145). As George Walton Williams (1970, 258–259) has noted, in these early epigrams assembled in the *Epigrammatum Sacrorum Liber* Crashaw perfected the subjects and themes that became central to his mature poetry.

Christ challenged his followers to confront abjection by recognizing that there is no difference between the clean and the unclean, the self and the loathed other:

Hear, and understand: Not that which goeth into the mouth defileth a man; but that which cometh out of the mouth, this defileth a man. . . . Do not ye understand, that whatsoever entereth in at the mouth goeth into the belly, and is cast out into the draught? But those things which proceed out of the mouth come forth from the heart; and they defile the man. (Matt. 15:10–18)

Christ turned primitive codes of pollution inside out by insisting that a man be judged by his heart and its intentions, not by what he expels from the body or does outwardly. He put his healing fingers into the ears of a deaf and dumb man and touched his tongue with spit. He cured a blind man by applying a paste of dirt and saliva to his eyes. He drank water from the jar of a Samaritan woman.[9] He ate with unwashed hands. He wrote in the dirt with his finger as he defended a woman caught in adultery. He washed the feet of the apostles. He cried over Jerusalem, sweated blood and tears in the Garden of Gethsemane, and shed his blood on the Cross. After his Resurrection, he invited Thomas to put his hand into the wound in his side.

In *Powers of Horror,* Kristeva (1980, 115) draws attention to Matthew 15:22–28, the same passage that inspired Crashaw's three Latin epigrams on Jesus's encounter with the woman of Canaan.[10] Medieval ascetics had previously cited this woman who groveled before Christ when they wished to emphasize the spiritual value of self-abasement (Bynum 1987, 107, 284). Initially, Jesus ignores her pleas to exorcize her daughter. When he eventually answers her, he appears to uphold traditional prohibitions by underlining her status as an outsider and a Gentile: "I am not sent but unto the lost sheep of the House of Israel" (Matt. 15:24). When the woman redoubles her entreaties, Jesus tests her to the limit by replying: "It is not meet to take the children's bread, and to cast it to dogs" (15:26). Unperturbed by being thus compared to an animal, the Canaanite woman shows that disarming mixture of servility and audacity characteristic of later female mystics: "Truth, Lord: yet the dogs eat of the crumbs which fall from their masters' table" (Matt. 15:27). Christ's final answer, "O woman, great is thy faith: be it unto thee as thou wilt" (15:28), reflects his amazement and approval. Like Mary Magdalene, the woman of Canaan is not demeaned but uplifted by her abjection at the feet of Christ, which enables her to overcome her ostracism and command his undivided attention (Petroff 1979, 13).

Crashaw's three Latin epigrams on this scriptural passage, written while still an apprentice poet, develop the idea that Christ does his sacred work through abjection. In *"Christus mulieri Canaaneae difficilior"* ("Christ rather obstinate toward the woman of Canaan"), he suggests that the harder the woman begs, the more obdurately Christ seems to withhold his help. However, *"In mulierem Canaanaeam"* ("On the woman of Canaan contending with the Master") opens with the woman wearing Christ down with her entreaties. "See, he is yielding. Now at this moment he will give in" (Williams 1970, 334). In this epigram, abjection is less a proof of humility before God than a source of power as the poet describes Christ conceding defeat: "he feels the strength in you and he loves it" (334). In his final epigram, *"Mulier Canaanitis"* ("The woman of Canaan"), Crashaw puts Christ's words of astonishment into his own mouth: "A woman, and of such strong faith? now I believe that faith is / more than grammatically of the *feminine gender*" (334; italics in original). As a mature poet, Crashaw continued to draw inspiration from these words written in schoolboy Latin to please learned

men such as his father. He increasingly allowed his own imagination to take
flight in forms that were "more than grammatically of the *feminine gender*" as
he contemplated the invincible faith that women exemplified through their
seeming weakness.

Perhaps the poem that best epitomizes Crashaw's preoccupation with
abjection is a divine epigram that he wrote in Latin and translated into
English verse. It was first published in his *Epigrammatum Sacrorum Liber*
of 1634 as *"Beatus venter & ubera"* ("Blessed is the womb and the paps"),
and is placed immediately after *"Christus mulieri Canaaneae difficilior"* (Martin 1957, 40). The English version, "Blessed be the paps which Thou hast
sucked," appeared in his 1646 volume of sacred poems, *Steps to the Temple*
(Martin 1957, 94). In only four lines, it recapitulates Crashaw's psychic odyssey from a motherless childhood and early adolescence, when his father's
influence was strong, to young adulthood, when he moved away from Puritanism toward faith of the *"feminine gender,"* which, ironically, he may have
first imbibed in his father's library:

> Suppose he had been Tabled at thy Teates,
>     Thy hunger feels not what he eates:
> Hee'l have his Teat e're long (a bloody one)
>     The Mother then must suck the Son.
>
>                                         (Williams 1970, 14)

The Latin epigram from which this poem is derived, *"Beatus venter &
ubera,"* is about as exciting as Gerber baby food: "And what if Jesus should
indeed drink from your breast? / what does it do to your thirst because he
drinks? / And soon He will lay bare his breast—alas, not milky!— / from
her son then the *mother* will drink" (Williams 1970, 324–325).

The Latin epigram is based on a passage in Luke where a woman inter-
rupts Jesus's preaching by crying aloud: "Blessed is the womb that bare thee,
and the paps which thou hast sucked" (11:27–28). His English version is not a
mere translation but a new and provocative creation. Crashaw takes the words
from the mouth of the woman and makes them into the title of the poem. In
so doing, he forces readers to confront the elusive boundary between sexuality
and religion (Warren 1939, 202; Shell 1999, 100). For the wholesome "drink"
*(bibit)*, he substitutes "suck." This verb is rooted in the flesh and, through its
alliterative link with "Son," it provides the punch in the final line. The use of
"suck" is closer to scripture than is "drink," even though it departs from the
Latin epigram Crashaw wrote as an undergraduate. The unidentified woman
responds euphorically to Christ's magnetism as a preacher with a fantasy in
which she lifts her voice in praise and envy of the maternal body privileged
to bear and suckle him. However, Christ corrects her: "Yea rather, blessed are

they that hear the word of God, and keep it" (Luke 11:29). He exhorts her to imbibe his holy words rather than extol the good breast. He invites all who heed his words to consider themselves more privileged than his mother.

"Blessed be the paps" would have made William Crashaw roll over in his grave. In *The Jesuit Gospel* (1610), he had vented his spleen against Catholic veneration of the *Virgo Lactans* and any suggestion that, as *deipara* or divine childbearer, Mary should be regarded as having the power to intercede with her Son, let alone the authority to overrule him by reminding Christ he was once her little boy. Crashaw's Jesuit disputant John Floyd (1612) argued that "M. Crashaw . . . doth forget himselfe saying, that no extraordinary blessednesse doth belong to the wombe of the Virgin, none to her breasts in this regard only, that they did breed, and feed the Sonne of God, that she whome we do so exalt, is no more than another holy woman" (28). On a psychological level, William Crashaw was laying down the law of the father in demanding that Christians renounce their attachment to the personal motherhood of Mary. But on a theological level, he was simply echoing Christ who had discouraged idealization of his mother as a woman of singular sanctity.

Richard Crashaw, however, fervently embraced the Laudian revival of Marian devotion at Peterhouse. As we have seen, his evolution into the "chaplaine of the virgine myld" is usually read as a return to the phallic mother of early infancy and a rejection of the father (Geha 1966, 158–163; Camden 1983, 259, 277). Yet "Blessed be the paps" demonstrates Crashaw's fidelity to his father by transforming into poetry William Crashaw's clinching argument in *The Jesuit Gospel* (1610) that Mary "was more blessed by conceiving Christ in her heart then in her wombe and by beleeving in him then by bearing him" (16). William hoped that by promoting Mary's spiritual motherhood, he would stamp out the last remnants of devotion to the ancient cult of the *Virgo Lactans*. In effect, he was saying that it was high time Christians were weaned.

Crashaw's line, "Suppose he had been Tabled at thy Teates," cultivates the detachment required by his father by exhorting his readers to "suppose" that they themselves have replaced the *Virgo Lactans* as wet nurses to Jesus. They are asked to identify with the archetypal woman in Luke 11 who saw Mary as supremely blessed by her physical bond with Christ. Christ responded by distancing himself from his natural mother and inviting this woman to become his mother in spirit. William Crashaw (1610), too, insisted that Mary's "spirituall bearing of Christ was happier than her carnall" (15). The poet, however, refuses to minimize the role of the "carnall" body in becoming a spiritual mother to Christ. He insists that the reader put herself in the place of the woman from Luke and imagine what it must have been like to suckle Christ in infancy.

By drawing the reader into a sympathetic identification that extends from the woman in Luke to the maternal body that inspired her praise, Crashaw was able to honor the will of his father without disavowing the nursing mother. Yet it has proved difficult for readers to contemplate this composite figure. To do so, one must visualize prolonged and nonexclusive breastfeeding of Christ. Above all, the closing injunction that, after the crucifixion, the mother "must suck the Son" has proved an insuperable stumbling block.[11] As adoration of the nursing Virgin fell into disrepute in Protestant countries during the sixteenth and seventeenth centuries, English women of the middle and upper classes increasingly farmed their infants out to wet nurses. That Crashaw may have owed his own survival to wet nursing gives emotional conviction to his image of Christ as a maternal savior. But the breast bared for nursing was increasingly becoming a sight that gave rise to feelings of abjection. In the words of Sir John Acton, "a sucking child makes a most dreadful spectacle" (qtd. in McLaren 1985, 28; see also Warner 1976, 203). Indeed, William Crashaw's (1610) description of the "pretty Childe that playeth in thy mothers armes, and hangeth at her brests" (62) leads John Floyd (1612) to accuse him of a "grosse and carnall imagination" in presuming vicariously to fondle the Virgin's breasts and "touch them by imagination" (54–55).

Readers of Crashaw's epigram should bear in mind Elizabeth Petroff's (1979) caveat that "asceticism is of course, extremely sensual . . . and may even be dangerously erotic, for the attempt to deny the body through certain bodily practices turns the smallest act of physical gratification . . . into a stunning sensual experience" (34). Crashaw's first line reactivates that tumult of sensual and tender feelings associated with the mother's breast as the first love object. But such feelings, as Klein (1937) points out, are "closely linked up with aggressive impulses and phantasies, with guilt and the fear of the death" of the loved person (326–327). These anxieties augment the intimation that death lies in wait from the moment of birth. Crashaw excited these feelings in order to provoke a psychic upheaval in which the defenses against abjection give way and the boundaries separating subject and object, self and other, the somatic and the sacred are lowered. The polymorphously perverse body—with a history extending back to infancy—is no longer a sight to be expunged from devotion. "Suppose" says yes to the unthinkable.

No sooner does Crashaw let down the barriers than the imagination runs up against the stony verb "Tabled." While the word refers principally to the Eucharistic altar, William Empson (1930) has suggested that "Tabled" may also allude to the Judaic law and the tablets on which Moses inscribed God's ten commandments (221). "Tabled" is thus a reminder not only of the mother's body as what Klein calls the "land flowing with milk and honey" (1937, 334), but also of the law of the father. None of this explains away the oddity in Crashaw's play on words and syntax.[12] "Tabled" creates an object of veneration—the stony altar made by a mother's soft breasts—that, like abjection itself, is built on antithesis. "Tabled" also evokes Psalm 23, where David proclaims to the Lord, "Thou preparest a table before me in the presence of mine enemies" (5).

The paps of the woman in Luke now repay this divine hospitality, but the image obtrudes of Christ feeding off them with disturbing gusto. In "O Gloriosa Domina," Crashaw suggests that Christ is so happy with this arrangement that he takes up permanent room and board at Mary's breast:

> The whole world's host would be thy guest
> And board himself at thy rich BREST.
> O boundless Hospitality!
> The FEAST of all things feeds on thee.
>                                   (Williams 1970, 195, ll. 7–10)

In the epigram, "Tabled" suggests the simultaneous love and hate that the mother inspires in the infant, who attempts to manage this conflict by splitting his image of her into good and bad breasts. Klein (1936) describes the intense pleasure the infant derives from the mouth as it "is stimulated by sucking at his mother's breast. This gratification is an essential part of the child's sexuality, and is indeed its initial expression. Pleasure is experienced also when the warm stream of milk runs down the throat and fills the stomach" (290). In his youthful paraphrase of Psalm 23, Crashaw articulated the satiety the infant achieves through rhythmic sucking at the good breast: "Pleasure sings my soule to rest, / Plenty weares me at her brest" (Williams 1970, 5, ll. 9–10). However, when the breast is withheld, the infant feels a destructive impulse to bite, tear up, and devour the libidinal object. These cannibalistic fantasies are linked with the growing capacity to hurt the mother. Teething presages weaning, the separation from the breast that, in Klein's view, heralds the early stages of the Oedipus conflict. Thus, the hunger of the suckling is suffused with trauma and the sorrow of loss.

The surprise of the second line, "Thy hunger feels not what he eats," lies in the way that Crashaw shifts from the hunger of the suckling child to that of the woman who nurses him. As Bynum (1987) has shown, during the later Middle Ages female mystics felt they came in touch with God through the mouth that licked, sucked, consumed, and even regurgitated food. According to Ana-Maria Rizzuto (1979), this grand desire has "a humble beginning" (45) in the young child's curiosity about the bodily functions of both the parents and God. Klein (1937, 325) argues that it is imperative for the infant to find ways of replacing the breast milk by other foods that satisfy the desires for pleasure, love, and safety. As we have seen, the ascetics who starved themselves in order to induce mystical visions ate chiefly the Eucharist and the abject leftovers of the body. Crashaw coaxes ordinary mothers to acknowledge their pleasure in oral stimulation during breastfeeding and then to redirect this hunger to the vision of the crucifixion that gave mystics not only spiritual sustenance but orgasmic bliss.

The final half of the line dwells on the mystery of the Incarnation: that Christ is a man who knows what it is to crave food and feel all the hungers of the body. Indeed, it is his empathy with the human condition that enables him to satisfy the "hunger" of his worshipers. Yet it is hard for anyone except a mystic to share his hunger because he is also the God who expiates all human defilement on the Cross. Crashaw epitomizes redemption as a recycling of the bodily fluids of abjection. Christ sucks milk, which, according to traditional physiology, was produced from the refined blood of the mother. In turn, he sheds blood that was seen as analogous to breast milk, the flow of menstruation, and even the emission of semen (Bynum 1991, 100, 109, 114, 142, 214–215, 220).

The first line of the final couplet, "Hee'l have his Teat e're long (a bloody one)," turns from the benign image of nursing to what many readers regard as the tasteless and perverse (Sabine 1992, 185–187). Crucified, Christ becomes an exhibition of what the Incarnation and his Virgin Mother's parthenogenesis make him—a freak of nature. Empson (1930) is one of the few critics to share Crashaw's enjoyment of the tableau of the crucified Christ. Kristeva (1980, 9) maintains that jouissance goes hand in hand with abjection; and Empson's critique of the third and fourth lines bears this out:

> A wide variety of sexual perversions can be included in the notion of sucking a long bloody teat which is also a deep wound. The sacrificial idea is aligned with incest, the infantile pleasures, and cannibalism; we contemplate the god with a sort of savage chuckle; he is made to flower, a monstrous hermaphrodite deity. (1930, 221)

Empson captures the wonderment of a pierced and protuberant God who has the life sucked out of him on the Cross. In his edition of Crashaw, Williams (1970) dismisses Empson's description of the faithful "sucking a long bloody teat which is also a deep wound" as pure invention (14). But Empson astutely sees that Crashaw puts "long" in close proximity to "Teat" not only to pun on the fact that Longinus's spear caused the wound in Christ's side but also to play on the sense that this bloody pap is also phallic. Empson's description of "a long bloody teat" returns us to the sexual amorphousness of early infancy. It also captures the spirit of mystics who crossed the boundaries between male and female, parent and child, sacred and profane love, and sometimes passed the point of no return.

The turning point of the epigram occurs when Crashaw shifts his focus from the mother's breast to the father's penis. He was heir not only to William Crashaw's library of devotional literature but also to his father's anti-Catholic tracts. Crashaw now draws on his "carnall imagination" to generate a compensating fantasy in which his father's phallus—bequeathed to him as writer—no longer rhetorically destroys but saves "the Mother" through the act of reparation on the Cross. While Klein argues that the imago of the mother's breast is the first to be established in the psyche, as it is first projected in the poem, it is succeeded by the imago of the father's penis, which Crashaw will now recuperate by identifying with both "the Mother" who sucks and "the Son" who offers up his phallus as sacrifice in the final line of the poem. By eucharistically receiving, in Klein's words, "the mother's loving and giving breast and the father's creative penis" (1937, 336), and taking them into himself, the poet has internalized the kindness, generosity, and wisdom both of the parental couple and of God.

The interchangeability of roles in this epigram is a poetic strategy that allows Crashaw daringly to realign the characters of the family romance. But the final line, "The Mother then must suck the Son," has proved an insuperable stumbling block to many readers because it fuses two powerful fantasies. The first reverses the early parent-child relationship and restores the mother and father as the child wanted them to be, or as he wished to have behaved in his relation to them. This fantasy is conflated with the mystical vision of Christ as a mother who feeds the soul with the blood pouring from his teat-wound. In these visions the mystic not only voluptuously sucked the blood of the crucified Christ but was sucked, panting for more, into his side (Petroff 1979, 67–75; Bynum 1987, 154–157, 246–249; 1991, 129–130, 190–192). But did the poet intend his conflation of this mystical vision of a union with Christ with the fantasy of reversing the child-parent relationship to give rise to depictions of incest, fellatio, and sodomy?[13]

We can maintain that these sexual intimations were inadvertent only if we agree with Bynum (1991) that later medieval "theologians did not discuss Christ as a sexual male" (82) and that the people of that time "saw Christ's penis not primarily as a sexual organ but as the object of circumcision and therefore as . . . wounded, bleeding flesh" (86). There is no denying that the wound, the penis, and the breast signified Christ's suffering on the Cross, and they do so in "Blessed be the paps." But as a seventeenth-century Baroque poet, Crashaw was familiar with female mysticism, which by Bynum's own admission is replete with erotic imagery, and he was writing after John Donne had already deployed metaphysical wit to compare erection to resurrection in "The Canonization": "Wee dye and rise the same, and prove / Mysterious by this love" (Grierson 1912, 15, ll. 26–27). Similarly, Crashaw did not wish to represent Christ on the Cross as a neutered figure who confirms anxieties of castration, but as one whose resurrection would give new dignity and hope to *homo erectus.*

In the divine epigram that precedes "Blessed be the paps" in *Steps to the Temple,* "On the Blessed Virgins bashfulnesse," Crashaw envisions a nativity scene in which the mother gazes in adoration at the infant in her lap: "She can see heaven, and ne're lift up her eyes: / ... / 'Twas once *looke up,* 'tis now *looke downe* to Heaven" (Williams 1970, 9, ll. 6, 8). Yet the Virgin's eyes point the reader to a God who has taken his seat below her waist and who, as Julian of Norwich insisted, "comes down to us to the lowest part of our need; for he has no contempt of what he has made" (Pelphrey 1989, 173). In "Blessed be the paps," Crashaw looks up from the Virgin's lap to her breast. But he concludes his epigram by again "looking down to heaven." He depicts the breast and the penis in Kleinian fashion as the primary objects of oral and sexual desire. As Empson (1930) points out, this breast-penis is first and foremost a bleeding wound, a wound that in other poems Crashaw likens to an eye and mouth. The Christ he honored in his poetry overturned conventional codes of propriety by insisting that "not that which goeth into the mouth defileth a man." Female saints imitated Christ by lapping up what was unclean, while mystics united with him in fantasy in every conceivable form and position. To the "wide variety of sexual perversions" found in Crashaw's epigram we should add cunnilingus. For the image of the breast-penis is inseparable from the tongue-penis that sucks the teat or that can be inserted into the "unclean" mouth of the vulva-anus (Kristeva 1980, 108–114; Fischer 1983, 185–189; Geha 1966, 167).

Ultimately, the integrity of "Blessed be the paps" derives from the recognition that sexuality cannot be kept separate from spirituality, and that bodily feelings enter powerfully into the religious experience. Crashaw acknowledged the incestuous origin of the romance even of the holiest family and the ways in which mothers and fathers are recreated in the love relationships of later life. Above all, he used his "carnall imagination" to embrace those traditionally stigmatized as abject, especially on account of "unclean" or deviant sexual practices. For Crashaw, no expression of human love is beyond the reach of salvation through Christ.

## NOTES

1. William Empson (1930) was one of the first to point out how Crashaw uses horror to "excite adoration" (221). More recently, the queer theorist Richard Rambuss (1998) has observed that "perhaps even more than is the case with Donne, reading Crashaw has been critically constituted as something of a dirty pleasure" (141n11). Concurring with Rambuss in highlighting Crashaw's "explicit eroticism" and "disputing the tendency to allegorical interpretation that would de-sexualize the imagery," Elizabeth Clarke (2000) remarks that "many critics are uncomfortable

with . . . his 'indecorous' rhetoric" (416–417). For a broad range of commentary, see further Low (1978, 116–117, 156–157); Roberts and Roberts (1990); Cunnar (1994, 237–238); Shell (1999, 102–103); Punter (2001, 53–54); and Rambuss (1998, 32–35, 145–146).

2. On the "feet" as symbolic substitutes for the genital organs as the lowest part of Christ's body, see Steinberg (1996, 149–151). Haskins (1993, 247–248) notes that from the fourteenth century Mary Magdalene's hair was depicted as either red or golden.

3. See Elizabeth Grosz's summary (1992) of Kristeva's thought in *Feminism and Psychoanalysis.*

4. Crashaw's devotion to the Mother and Child, especially in her role as *Virgo Lactans,* led Leah Marcus (1978) to conclude that he retreated "into the phantasmagoric world of baroque Catholic spirituality and the poetic role of infant" (139).

5. See Allan Pritchard's account (1964) of the Puritan report that Crashaw allegedly turned to a picture of the Virgin Mary in the college chapel at Peterhouse and prayed *hanc adoramus.* Roman Catholics distinguish their veneration of Mary from the adoration reserved only for God.

6. In *Half Humankind,* Henderson and McManus (1985, 344–350) have reprinted the seventeenth-century equivalent of a bullet point summary of Ussher's funeral sermon, from which I have taken my quotations.

7. Warren has an informative note on the literary career of William Crashaw. Although we cannot be sure exactly which books Richard Crashaw read, Warren acknowledges that "Richard could scarcely have escaped some acquaintance with his father's library, rich in the literature of Popery," and this "may well have introduced the poet to Catholic authors and the Catholic spirit" (1939, 19).

8. Marc F. Bertonasco's dissertation precedes Bynum's better-known exposition (1991) of the view that "the Reformation both continued and rejected the female piety of the late Middle Ages" (78).

9. Jewish law perpetuated the myth of Samaritan women's uncleanliness by deeming them "menstruants from their cradle" (Haskins 1993, 406n57). Among other ways that Christ embraced outcasts, he cured lepers and a man suffering from a skin-disease by his touch. He healed an epileptic who foamed at the mouth and exorcised those afflicted by evil spirits. He invited tax collectors to eat with him. He healed a woman who suffered from a hemorrhage for twelve years and had been condemned as untouchable. He let a woman of ill repute touch his feet with her mouth and clean them with her tears and hair.

10. Kristeva (1980) interprets Christ's overthrow of the religious and social taboos regulating pollution as merely a shift from exterior to interior abjection. In contrast to her pessimistic conclusion that abjection "endures through the subjection to God of a speaking being who is innerly divided and, precisely through speech, does not cease purging himself of it" (113), I see a transformation from outward sanctimoniousness to inner moral integrity.

11. Thomas Healy argues that "the exaggerated quality of Christ's teat" makes it "difficult to compose a visual emblem of the scene, as suggested by the epigram" (1990, 52). Eugene Cunnar agrees that "it is difficult to visualize what are commonly thought to be perverse or grotesque images, even on a psychological level" (1994, 238). Steinberg, too, maintains (1996, 377–378) that Christ's teat is

impossible to visualize. Crashaw's epigram is a direct challenge to these masculine expressions of disbelief.

12. See again Healy, who argues that "the Child could not be 'tabled' at [Mary's] breasts, since the word indicates sacramental food available only from Christ" (1990, 55), and Cunnar's citation (1990) of a follower of Bernard of Clairvaux that there are "two altars, one in the breast, the other in the body of Christ" (104). The latter opinion would have made William Crashaw apoplectic.

13. Rambuss (1998) has read Crashaw's poems on the Passion as love songs to a homoeroticized Christ who is penetrated on the Cross (13–19, 26–49, 61–63). What he suggests is consistent with the medieval mystics who made "the 'rape' of Christ on the cross become the ecstatic 'raptus' of the visionary" (Petroff 1979, 73).

## WORKS CITED

Bertonasco, Marc F. 1964. *The Intellectual Element in the Imagery of Richard Crashaw*. Ann Arbor: University Microfilms.

Bynum, Caroline Walker. 1987. *Holy Feast and Holy Fast: The Religious Significance of Food to Medieval Women*. Berkeley: University of California Press.

———. 1991. *Fragmentation and Redemption: Essays on Gender and the Human Body in Medieval Religion*. New York: Zone Books.

Camden, Vera J. 1983. Richard Crashaw's Poetry: The Imagery of Bleeding Wounds. *American Imago*, 40:257–279.

Clarke, Elizabeth. 2000. Religious Verse. In Michael Hattaway, ed., *A Companion to English Renaissance Literature and Culture*. Oxford: Blackwell, pp. 404–418.

Crashaw, William. 1610. *The Jesuit Gospel*. London: E. A. for Leonard Becket.

Cunnar, Eugene R. 1990. Crashaw's "Sancta Maria Dolorum": Controversy and Coherence. In Roberts 1990, pp. 99–126.

———. 1994. Opening the Religious Lyric: Crashaw's Ritual, Liminal, and Visual Wounds. In John R. Roberts, ed., *New Perspectives on the Seventeenth-Century English Religious Lyric*. Columbia: University of Missouri Press, pp. 237–267.

Empson, William. 1930. *Seven Types of Ambiguity*. New York: New Directions, 1966.

Fischer, Sandra K. 1983. Crashaw, St. Teresa, and the Icon of Mystical Ravishment. *Journal of Evolutional Psychology*, 4:182–192.

Floyd, John. 1612. *The Overthrow of the Protestants Pulpit-Babels, Confuting W. Crashawe's Sermon at the Crosse*. London.

Geha, Richard, Jr. 1966. Richard Crashaw: The Ego's Soft Fall. *American Imago*, 23:158–168.

Grierson, Herbert J. C., ed. 1912. *The Poems of John Donne*. Vol. 1. Oxford: Oxford University Press, 1968.

Grosz, Elizabeth. 1992. Julia Kristeva. In Elizabeth Wright, ed., *Feminism and Psychoanalysis: A Critical Dictionary*. Oxford: Blackwell, pp. 194–200.

Haskins, Susan. 1993. *Mary Magdalen: Myth and Metaphor*. London: Harper Collins.

Healy, Thomas F. 1990. Crashaw and the Sense of History. In Roberts 1990, pp. 49–65.

Henderson, Katherine Usher, and Barbara F. McManus, eds. 1985. *Half Humankind: Contexts and Texts of the Controversy about Women in England, 1540–1640*. Chicago: University of Illinois Press.

Klein, Melanie. 1936. Weaning. In Klein 1975, pp. 290–305.

———. 1937. Love, Guilt and Reparation. In Klein 1975, pp. 306–343.

———— . 1946. Notes on Some Schizoid Mechanisms. In *Envy and Gratitude and Other Works, 1946–1963*. Ed. Roger Money-Kyrle et al. New York: Free Press, pp. 1–24.

———— . 1975. *Love, Guilt and Reparation and Other Works, 1921–1945*. Ed. Roger Money-Kyrle et al. New York: Free Press.

Kristeva, Julia. 1980. *Powers of Horror: An Essay on Abjection*. Trans. Leon S. Roudiez. New York: Columbia University Press, 1980.

Low, Anthony. 1978. *Love's Architecture: Devotional Modes in Seventeenth-Century English Poetry*. New York: New York University Press.

Marcus, Leah Sinanoglou. 1978. *Childhood and Cultural Despair: A Theme and Variations in Seventeenth-Century Literature*. Pittsburgh: University of Pittsburgh Press.

Martin, L. C., ed. 1957. *The Poems of Richard Crashaw, English, Latin and Greek*. 2nd ed. Oxford: Clarendon Press.

McLaren, Dorothy. 1985. Marital Fertility and Lactation, 1570–1720. In Mary Prior, ed., *Women in English Society, 1500–1800*. London: Methuen, pp. 22–53.

Pelphrey, Brant. 1989. *Christ Our Mother: Julian of Norwich*. London: Darton, Longman and Todd.

Petroff, Elizabeth. 1979. *Consolation of the Blessed*. New York: Alta Gaia Society.

Pritchard, Allan. 1964. Puritan Charges against Crashaw and Beaumont. *Times Literary Supplment*, July 2, p. 578.

Punter, David. 2001. *Writing the Passions*. Harlow, England: Longman.

Rambuss, Richard. 1998. *Closet Devotions*. Durham: Duke University Press.

Rizzuto, Ana-Maria. 1979. *The Birth of the Living God: A Psychoanalytic Study*. Chicago: University of Chicago Press.

Roberts, John R., ed. 1990. *New Perspectives on the Life and Art of Richard Crashaw*. Columbia: University of Missouri Press.

Roberts, Lorraine M., and John R. Roberts. 1990. Crashavian Criticism: A Brief Interpretative History. In Roberts 1990, pp. 1–29.

Sabine, Maureen. 1992. *Feminine Engendered Faith: The Poetry of John Donne and Richard Crashaw*. London: Macmillan.

Shell, Alison. 1999. *Catholicism, Controversy and the English Literary Imagination, 1558–1660*. Cambridge: Cambridge University Press.

Steinberg, Leo. 1996. *The Sexuality of Christ in Renaissance Art and in Modern Oblivion*. 2nd ed. Chicago: University of Chicago Press.

Wallerstein, Ruth. 1935. *Richard Crashaw: A Study in Style and Poetic Development*. Madison: University of Wisconsin Press, 1962.

Warner, Marina. 1976. *Alone of All Her Sex: The Myth and Cult of the Virgin Mary*. London: Picador, 1985.

Warren, Austin. 1939. *Richard Crashaw: A Study in Baroque Sensibility*. London: Faber and Faber.

Williams, George Walton, ed. 1970. *The Complete Poetry of Richard Crashaw*. New York: Norton, 1974.

ANNE-MARIE MILLER BLAISE

# George Herbert's Distemper:
## An Honest Shepherd's Remedy for Melancholy

What a striking change there is in tone when one compares George Herbert's 1619 letter to his step-father and his advice to Arthur Woodnoth in continuing his living with the same Sir John Danvers twelve years later. The younger Herbert seems both flattered by his forthcoming Cambridge oratorship and eager to benefit from the prestige and sense of power of such employment:

> The Orators place . . . is the finest place in the University, though not the gainfullest; yet that will be about 30 *l. per an.* but the commodiousness is beyond the Revenue; for the Orator writes all the University Letters, makes all the Orations, be it to King, Prince . . . , he takes place next the Doctors . . . and sits above the Proctors.[1]

The mature priest of Bemerton, on the other hand, gives serene words of encouragement to a friend who doubts his usefulness in fighting against the extravagance of John Danvers in his second marriage and to whom Herbert had earlier boasted the merits of becoming public orator: "Though you want all success either in inclining or restraining, To desire good & endeavour it when we can doe no more, is to doe it" (p. 381). Commentators

*George Herbert Journal*, Volume 30, Numbers 1–2 (Fall 2006/Spring 2007): pp. 59–82.
Copyright © 2007 *George Herbert Journal*.

and biographers of Herbert have often wondered at such a transformation. The turning point in Herbert's life occurred in those years for which we have the least information. How can one account for Herbert's letting go of court hopes and committing himself not only to the Church but to the small parish of Bemerton? Had he simply lost all his patrons? Was it illness, as he himself claimed, that made him "unable to perform those Offices for which I came into the World"?[2] Did the death of loved ones—especially that of his mother in 1627—lead him to further relinquish worldly honors? Or was it all a matter of personal piety?

Lynette Muir, who looks at George Herbert's life from a historical viewpoint, alongside that of his Cambridge days friend, Nicholas Ferrar, dismisses the third hypothesis, the most attractive in building up Herbert's saintliness. Muir's answer to both men's simultaneous withdrawal from public life is political: they sought disengagement and a commitment to Christian separation as part of a reaction not against monarchy itself but Charles's monarchical absolutism. One may notice how such an interpretation substitutes political idealism—the Church becoming "a new satisfactory institutional identity"—for pureness of faith.[3] Even Izaak Walton implicitly stated that Herbert's taking orders was to be linked to the loss of his patrons:

> God . . . in a short time put an end to the lives of two of his most obliging and most powerful friends, Lodowick, Duke of Richmond, and James, Marquess of Hamilton; and not long after him King James died also, and with them all Mr Herbert's Court hopes. So that presently he betook himself to a retreat from London, to a friend in Kent. . . . In this time of retirement he had many conflicts with himself, whether he should return to the painted pleasures of a life or betake himself to a study of Divinity, and enter into the Sacred Orders?[4]

Of course, suggesting that Herbert may have chosen "the painted pleasures of a Court life" had he wished to do so, enhances the final decision of "Holy Mr Herbert."

Cristina Malcolmson's biography of George Herbert reads as a serious challenge to traditional interpretations of those relatively mysterious years from 1624 to 1630 during which the poet abandoned his seat at Parliament and took up holy orders, accepting a modest church position and resigning his Cambridge oratorship in the process. She argues that the period emerges neither as a moment of disinterested retirement from public life, nor as deliberate disengagement, but rather as a time of continued "frustration at lack of preferment," whether in the Church or more worldly positions.[5] While I am greatly indebted to Malcolmson in what follows, I would like to suggest yet another reading of these years which shows that apparently conflicting interpretations are not in fact mutually exclusive. Looking through the lens of early seventeenth-century thought, Herbert's sense of a frustrated career, his fragile health, his grief at the death of his mother, his silent retreat from the world, but also his supposed mythical pious retirement all relate to the early modern definition of melancholy. All of these states and preoccupations either function as symptoms, causes, or remedies to what has been called "the Elizabethan Malady."[6]

Indeed, in his *Anatomy of Melancholy*, first published in 1621 and augmented for the first two times in 1624 and 1628, Robert Burton names, beyond one's natural and physical disposition, loss of office, lack of employment, and death of friends as possible causes for melancholy.[7] Though isolation can also function as a cause, Burton chiefly analyzes it as a symptom. The descriptions he gives of solitariness quite strikingly resemble the information Herbert provides on his own state in *Memoriae Matris Sacrum,* the collection of Latin and Greek poems he wrote on the occasion of his mother's death in 1627. Herbert's final years in Bemerton show him energetically carrying out so many of the occupations which Burton recommends as cures to melancholy: active employment—however modest be the trade—music, regular exercise, special diets, use of herbs, and prayer.

Interpreting Herbert's life in the late 1620s and early 1630s in the light of "melancholy" does not constitute a psychoanalytical or a strictly historicist view. This approach seeks rather to draw upon a "category," readily available in the Elizabethan and Stuart episteme, which stands at the crossroads of the dietary and medical, the theological, and the literary all of which were of prime importance to George Herbert. Though the initial hypothesis is biographical in nature, I will mostly be looking at the literary, expression and resolution of the problem of melancholy. Reading over *Memoriae Matris Sacrum* in particular helps to understand, by way of contrast, Herbert's theological and literary struggle to "temper" melancholy—but without dismissing passions—which is found in other works, such as *The Temple, The Country Parson,* and even his English translation of Luigi Cornaro's *Treatise of Temperance.* Such a survey also elucidates the poet's particular relationship to pastoral literary conventions in his chief work, *The Temple,* given the intimate link that binds together melancholy and pastoral retreat.

### Melancholy Herbert

The term "melancholy" is seldom associated with George Herbert and he himself never uses it in his English verse and pastoral manual. Perhaps this failure to recognize the expression of melancholy in Herbert's poetry is due to a misconception on the part of later readers of early modern emotion codes. Richard Strier has shown how Herbert's move towards temperance is often mistakenly interpreted as a Stoic attempt to control passion by submitting it to the powers of reason.[8] However, it has been noted that William Cowper for one, during a bout of extreme dejection in the 1750s when still a student at the Inns of Court, "gave himself over to Herbert's poetry in the hopes that the piety contained within *The Temple* might cure him of his melancholy."[9] Herbert may have envisioned himself as potentially suffering from the same malady and may attributed to his writing a similar curative property. In the case of Cowper, who identified with and delighted in Herbert's "Affliction" series, it seems that the remedy had little effect: "At length I was advised by a very near and dear relation to lay him aside, for he thought such an author was more likely to nourish my melancholy than to remove it."[10] The ineffectiveness of the Herbertian remedy on Cowper might demonstrate that the eighteenth century poet already stood on the other side of the divide in terms of emotional codes, expecting the metaphysical poet to overcome the distresses of body and mind which are in fact part of the healing process for the latter.

Whether Herbert was able to cure himself or not, at least he showed concern for the subject of melancholy and its remedies. Sharing an interest in dietary issues with his friends Nicholas Ferrar and Francis Bacon, he translated Luigi Cornaro's *Treatise of Temperance* at approximately the same time as he was writing a *Priest to the Temple*.[11] In her biography of Herbert, Malcolmson notes in passing that the treatise is interesting "for [Herbert's] concerns about diet and the lifestyle of the landed elite."[12] However, it also addresses the question of dietary treatments of melancholy. Cornaro, a noble Venetian who lived to be over ninety, advocated dietary temperance partly as a means to overcome his own temporary mid-age illness but also as a way to fight long-standing infirmities ("a most cold & moist stomack" in his case, [p. 291]), preserving humoral balance, and living a long life. According to Herbert's translation of Cornaro's *Trattato de la vita sobria:*

> from the time that I was made whole, I never since departed from
> my settled course of *Sobrietie,* whose admirable power causeth that
> the meat and drink that is taken in fit measure, gives true strength
> to the bodie, all superfluities passing away without difficultie, and
> no ill humours being ingendred in the body. (p. 293)

One of Cornaro's greatest "victories" is to have grown insensitive to "discommodities of the bodie, and troubles of the minde" thanks to his diet:

> For when my brother and others of my kindred saw some great
> powerfull men pick quarrels against me, fearing lest I should be
> overthrown, they were possessed with a deep Melancholie (a thing

usuall to disorderly lives) which increased so much in them, that it brought them to a sudden end. But I, whom that matter ought to have affected most, received no inconvenience thereby. (p. 294)

From Walton's biographical account, Herbert is known to have sought to cure his own severe "ague," especially in 1626 when sojourning in Woodford, Essex, through the same type of lean diet as advocated by Cornaro.[13] As Cornaro, he may have conceived of "proportion of meat and drink" as a way to "preserv[e] [himself] also, as much as [he] could, from hatred, and melancholie, and, other perturbations of the minde" (p. 293).

In chapter 26, "The Parson's eye, analyzing gluttony, one of those "vices whose natures, at least in the beginning, are dark and obscure," Herbert warns that people should be aware of "what [they] can well digest" in order not to "disable themselves from a fit discharging either of their Divine duties, or duties of their calling" (pp. 264–267). More remarkable yet is his digression in chapter 10 on the proper diet of those living within the parson's house. After insisting on the need and modes of "observing fasting days," he gives special attention to those whose condition "breaks these obligations" (p. 242). It is tempting to read the following passage, in which Herbert qualifies his position on the duty of fasting, as an autobiographical comment:

> To conclude, the Parson, if he be in full health, keeps the three obligations, eating fish, or roots, and that for quantity little, for quality unpleasant. If his body be weak and obstructed, as most Students are, he cannot keep the last obligation, nor suffer others in his house that are so, to keep it; but only the two former, which also in diseases of exinaniation (as consumptions) must be broken: For meat was made for man, not man for meat. To all this may be added, not for emboldening the unruly, but to comfort the weak, that not onely sicknesse breaks these obligations of fasting, but sicklinesse also. For it is as unnatural to do any thing, that leads me to a sicknesse, to which I am inclined, as not to get out of that sicknesse, when I am in it, by any diet. One thing is evident, that an English body, and a Students body, are two great obstructed vessels, and there is nothing that is food, and not phisick, which doth lesse obstruct, then flesh moderately taken; as being immoderately taken, it is exceeding obstructive. And obstructions are the cause of most diseases. (pp. 242–243)

Contrary to what happens in most chapters of *The Country Parson*, this one, supposedly dedicated to the private dwelling of the Pastor, does not finish with a neat alignment of the factual with the metaphorical and the biblical. The concluding lines of "The Parson's eye" which deal with gluttony contrast with those cited above:

> As when the people hungred and thirsted after our Saviours Doctrine, and tarryed so long at it, that they would have fainted, had they returned empty, He suffered it not; but rather made food miraculously, than suffered so good desires to miscarry (p. 267).

In chapter 10, however, Herbert's final considerations are purely "medical." In many ways, they recall Burton's subsections on remedies to melancholy, "Diet Rectified in Quantity" and "Retention, and Evacuation Rectified."[14] The transition from the third person to the first person ("that leads *me* to a sicknesse, to which *I* am inclined") and the parallelism which is drawn between the parson and the student are quite revealing: they seem to bespeak the personal experience of George Herbert the man, the erstwhile student, now turned country parson, but still predisposed to the same symptoms—"exinaniation," "sicklinesse," "obstruction." The Cambridge scholar and his dashed hopes still lie not far under the surface. In his contemporary comprehensive study of melancholy, Burton assigns a special place to just that scholar who is unable to find a position equal to his training.[15]

Giving up both his political career and his position as the university's orator, Herbert's destiny from 1624 on strangely resembles that of the "miseries of scholars" as described by Burton, prone more than others to melancholy because of their constant meditations:

> No labour in the world is like unto study. It may bee, their temperature will not endure it, but striving to be excellent to knowe all, they loose health, wealth, wit, life and all. Let him yet happily escape all these hazards, *aeneis intestines*, with a body of brasse, and now consummate and ripe, hee hath profited in his studies, and proceeded with all applause: after many expenses, he is fit for preferment, where shall he have it? He is as farre to seek it as he was (after twenty yeares standing) at the first day of his coming to the *University*. For what course shall he take, being now capable and ready? The most parable and easie, and about which many are imployed is to teach a Schoole, turne Lecturer or Curat, and for that he shall have Faulkners wages, 10 pounds *per annum*, and his diet, or some small stipend, so long as he can please his Patron or the parish; if they approve him not (for usually they doe but a yeare or two) as inconstant, as they that cryed *Hosanna* one day, and *crucifie* him the other; serving-man like, he must goe looke for a new master: if they doe what is his reward?" (Part. 1, Sect; 2, Memb. 3, Subs. 15, vol. I, p. 308)

Burton's quote acquires deep resonance in the case of George Herbert, who, along with his own "Patron," William Herbert, the Earl of Pembroke, seems to have fallen quite out of Caroline favor even though he had long occupied "the finest place the University" and whose best hopes may now have been to choose God as new master. Whether it was his "ill health" or an oration perceived as offensive by Prince Charles and Buckingham that barred Herbert's way to advancement or whether his bodily afflictions were only a wishful explanation to justify in his own eyes his inability to occupy "those offices" for which he felt destined, it seems likely that Herbert could have recognized himself in the figure of the miserable sickly scholar.[16] Malcolmson very interestingly notes that Herbert probably identified with another great scholar's illness and exclusion from public office, those of Bacon.[17] She draws attention to the particular use of the same Latin term, "tabidus," which means "wasting away," to describe the state of Bacon in the elegy Herbert wrote on the occasion of his friend's death in 1626, and to describe his own state after his mother's death in the seventh poem of *Memoriae Matris Sacrum* in 1627.[18] The dietary interests manifested in Herbert's translating of Cornaro as well as in certain passages of his own *Country Parson* seem to have been only one of the means used to fight an evil which had afflicted the student and which, in later years, was still afflicting the scholar-turned-priest. As the death of Magdalene Danvers furnished an extra occasion for what Burton calls "transitory Melancholy," the melancholy habit of Herbert, expressed in his illness and already enhanced by loss of preferment, can be seen reaching its peak in 1627, at least in terms of its literary expression.[19]

### Melancholy Pastoral Retreat in Memoriae Matris Sacrum

Herbert's sense of unemployment coalesces with the sorrow of mourning. In another passage by Burton, which this time describes the melancholy of those who have lost loved ones, we can once more read a near portrait of Herbert in 1627:

If parting of friends, absence alone can worke such violent effects, what shall death doe, when they must eternally be separated, never in the world to meet againe? This is so grievous a torment for the time, that it takes away their appetite, desire of life, extinguisheth all delights, it causeth deepe sighes and groanes, teares, exclamations . . . howling, roaring, many bitter pangs, *(lamentis gemituque & faemino ululate Tecta fremunt)* and by frequent meditation extend so farre sometimes, *they thinke they see their dead friends continually in their eyes, observantes imagines,* as *Conciliator* confesseth he saw his mothers ghost, presenting her selfe still before him. (Part I, Sect. 2, Memb. 4, Subs. 7, vol. 1, pp. 356–357).

In *Memoriae Matris Sacrum*, Herbert depicts himself as this kind of melancholy mourner. At the end of the first poem of the series, through a pun on *Mater* and *Metra*, Herbert clearly indicates that his project, as would be expected in a funeral elegy, is to transform the grief of having lost his mother into poetry: "Tantùm istaec scribo gratus, ne tu mihi tantùm / Mater: & ista Dolar nunc tibi Metra parit" (p. 422) ["With thanks I write these things alone— / You my Mother, mine alone: mourning / Now creates these poems for you."][20] However, the repetition of "tantùm" ("only" or "alone") in the penultimate line already points to the poet's excessive delight in tears and solitude in the following pieces. Herbert tends to describe himself as the only true heir to his mother, the only one who grieves enough, isolating himself in turn from his family and from his nation as a whole. In poem 9 he implicitly refers to Buckingham's expedition of one hundred ships and 6,000 men for the relief of La Rochelle, opposing it to his solitary verse of grief. Herbert offers a "sacred parody" of the *topos* of the melancholy lover who has abandoned the role of a glorious warrior as he dreams of other matters.[21] Throughout *Memoriae Matris Sacrum* Herbert works at conferring upon himself the traditional dignity of melancholy retreat. Yet the account of his torments mostly shows him as a delirious idolater of his deceased mother. As in Burton's description of melancholy mourners, the poet has lost the "desire of life," repeatedly wishing for his own death:

> Per te nascor in hunc globum
> Exemplóque tuo nascor in alterum. (IV, 13–14)

> [ . . . It was
> By you I came into the world; with you
> To follow, I come into the next.]

> Non tibi nunc soli filum abrupere sorores,
> Dissitus videor funere & ipse tuo. (XI, 11–12)

> [The Fates haven't cut your thread alone now,
> But by your death I am unraveled too.]

The last line of poem 15 also expresses the same fascination with death: "Sure that death is better than a life in vain."[22]

Symptoms culminate in poem 7 when the speaker's disturbed imagination presents him, as in Burton's example of Conciliator's hallucination, with the vision of his mother's monstrous ghost. His reaction is to escape the fearful apparition by conjuring up another more pleasing fantasy as he imagines himself reuniting with his mother, whom he names "Astrea," the last of the gods to have left the earth at the end of the Golden Age. The setting for the reunion is pastoral: it takes place in a small house in the country surrounded by a garden of flowers which itself recalls the bed of spices of the Song of Songs. This fragrant nest ("nidis odorum") is a *topos* in Christian pastoral literature which one can find, for example in Crashaw's later poem "In the Holy Nativity as sung by the shepherds." The *locus amoenus* becomes the place of transfigured grief as the speaker shuns the pallid ghost to welcome instead the true face of his mother.[23] But the end of the poem enhances the fragility of the process of sublimation:

> . . . tantùm verum indue vultum
> Affetûsque mei similem; nec languida misce
> Ora meae memori menti: ne dispare cultu
> Pugnaces, teneros florum tubemus odores,
> Atque inter reliquos horti crescentia foetus
> Nostra etiam paribus marcescant gaudia fatis. (VII, 29–34)

> [Only assume your true expression, similar in feeling to mine, and don't confuse this faint face with the one I remember, lest we, at odds because of different situations, confound the tender odors of the flowers, and lest, among the other fruits of the garden, our growing joys (the flowers) begin to droop because of fates like ours.][24]

Greg Miller has convincingly shown how Herbert is writing in the tradition of Theocritus's first Idyll in these funeral elegies, likening himself to Thyrsis and designating his mother as the dead Daphnis.[25] Herbert's mother, alternatively taking on the shape of Astrea or Daphnis and occupying the bed of spices, which in the Christian reading of the classics is the space of Christ, emerges almost as a substitute goddess or as an idol. Poem 3 is strangely evocative of "The Pearl" and "Mattens" in *The Temple,* two poems found in the Williams Manuscript and therefore almost certainly written before the funeral elegies. In "The Pearl," Christ, the sole mediator, is compared to a "silk twist let down from heav'n to me [i.e., the poet]" which "Did both conduct and teach me, how / To climbe to thee [i.e., God]" (ll. 38–40). The speaker of "Mattens" too, seeks to "climbe to thee" thanks to a "sunne-beam" and a "new light, which now I see" (ll. 18, 20). In the third poem of *Memoriae Matris Sacrum,* however, the motherly figure, who stands with the sun, becomes: the source of the sun rays coming down from heaven which can lead the speaker back up to her.[26]

According to Miller, the use of the classical pastoral tradition enables Herbert to make a statement on grief directed against self-controlling

Stoicism as a means to heal. In poem 6, the speaker takes a stance against the vanity of Galenic humoralism, apostrophizing Galen directly and denying the effectiveness of any balm or medicine for his sickness of the mind ("aegroto mentis" [l. 5]). Instead, he claims that what Galen "believe[s] to be a fever / is healthful and for the soul what alone is healing."[27] However, should one take this statement at face value? Is the stubborn delight in grief not in itself a typical symptom of melancholy? Is not the speaker wishfully transforming the degrading abnormality of the body evidenced by Galen into a dignified state in which suffering becomes the sign of a spiritual experience and of the artistic ability of the poet? Poem 8, which certain critics have identified as a turning point in the series, opens up the way for another interpretation:

> Paruam piámque dum lubenter semitam
>     Grandi reaéque praefero,
> Carpsit malignum sydus hanc modestiam
>     Vinúmque felle miscuit.
> Hinc fremere totus & minari gestio
>     Ipsis seuerus orbibus; Tandem prehensâ comiter lacernulâ
> Susurrat aure quispiam. Haec fuerat olim potio Domini tui.
>     Gusto probóque Dolium. (VIII)

> [While I prefer with pleasure the small and holy pathway to the grand and guilty highway, a malignant star has destroyed this moderation, and mixed bile with my wine. From this time all my being burns with rage and bluster: I lower against the very heavens. At length someone takes me by the cloak in a friendly way and whispers in my ear: "this once was your Lord's bitter draught." I taste and approve the vintage.][28]

In this poem, whose ending in dialogue form recalls that of "The Collar," the bile ("felle") which is mixed in with the wine could be the yellow bile of choler or the black bile of melancholy. It could refer to the rage and frustration of someone who has lost the ways of honor and preferment, but who is also overcome with pathological grief. The friendly voice that whispers to the raging speaker reminds him, however, that all the grief was Christ's. By drinking again and participating in the Eucharist, self-centered melancholy is surpassed and transcended, not by the moderating powers of reason, of course, but by the Passion. Beatrice Grove, studying the meaning of the title of one of Herbert's English poems, "Temperance," underlines that, though this meaning is not recorded by the *OED*, the verb "temper" had a specialized meaning of adding water to the communion wine just before the consecration.[29] Herbert is probably also alluding to this commixture of the chalice in poem 8. Christ's sacrifice, during which he sheds water as well as blood, and the Eucharist, both offer a tempering and passionate remedy for the distempered mind of the speaker. Where pastoral retreat and song have failed in the end to cure the speaker, the participation in the commemorating rite of the Church may succeed.

*Memoriae Matris Sacrum* concludes with a poem in which the speaker explains that he was compelled by the Muse to write these poems of grief:

> Excussos manibus calamos, falcémque resumptam
>     Rare, sibi dixit Musa fuisse probro
> Aggreditur Matrem (conductis carmine Parcis)
>     Funeréque hoc cultum vindicat aegra suum.
>
> Non potui non ire acri stimulante flagello:
>     Quin Matris superans carmina poscit honos.
> Eia, agedum scribo : vicisti, Musa . . . (XIX, 1–7)

> [Had the reeds been knocked from hands and scythes taken up again
> In the fields, said the Muse, it would have been shameful.
> She goes to Mother (the Fates having been bribed with song),
> Weakened by her death, to claim her own just reverence.
> I was in no way able at all to resist, driven by the cruel scourge:
> Mother's distinctive excellence requires songs.
> Well, you moved me to write, you have won, Muse, . . . ][30]

As the end of the poem shows, however, it is now time to silence the plaintive song: "sed audi [,] / Stulta: semel scribo, perpetuo vt sileam" (XIX, 7–8) ["But hear me, I write these foolish things once in order to remain silent."][31] According to Greg Miller, critics have mistakenly interpreted "Stulta" as a vocative feminine, following Hutchinson who found it necessary to add a colon to the original edition. Miller argues in favour of a plural neuter accusative, thus translating "foolish things" (i.e., Herbert's funeral elegies) instead of "vain one" (i.e., the Muse).[32] He thus defends the idea that the poet admits "he cannot truly recuperate [his mother's] presence in the pastoral world of reeds and scythes" rather than that he rejects the process of writing these elegies.[33] Yet, "reeds" and "scythes" should be read in opposition to each other. Whether it is the muse who is foolish, or Herbert's own poetical lament, it is time to put down the reeds of pastoral retreat and grief in order to endorse a new life with the scythe of the georgic which we can associate, in 1627, with Herbert's still fairly recent taking of orders and his forthcoming priesthood. On the literary level, Herbert puts aside his self-representation as a melancholy mourner whose grief, though sublimated at times through the pleasant reification of his mother, has not been remedied by classical pastoral conventions. He chooses instead to add poems to his *Temple* spoken by a priestly persona on his pastoral employment and to write a pastoral manual which in many ways draws on the georgic.[34]

### The Honest Poet/Pastor's Remedy

The use of classical pastoral conventions and their ultimate discarding in *Memoriae Matris Sacrum* may help us to read *The Temple* afresh. They may elucidate in particular the relationship Herbert establishes to the pastoral literary tradition in the poem, "Jordan" (I), which the title of this essay draws upon. Whereas Herbert's early sonnet to his mother (1610) clearly demonstrates the young poet's wish to write sacred verse rather than Petrarchan love poetry, "Jordan" (I) evaluates his poetic project in relationship to the well-established tradition of pastoral poetry in England. "Jordan" (I) accounts for the way in which these pastoral conventions are most often relegated to the margins of Herbert's English poetical work. While rejecting the illusions of a world in which the shepherds are but courtiers in disguise—its "enchanted groves" (l. 6), "purling streams" (l. 7), and "nightingale[s]" (l. 13), immutable "spring" (l. 13)—Herbert retains true "Shepherds," those "honest people" (l. 11) who are invited to sing their simple song of godly praise. As for the poet, he hopes he will not be "punished with loss of rhyme" (l. 14) as he follows the example of the honest shepherds in "plainly" singing *"My God, my King"* (l. 15). One could assume that Herbert is advocating Christian joy and devotion in lieu of the self-centered, illusory melancholy of the pastoral pause. However *"My God, my King,"* printed in italics at the end of the poem, is to be read as a citation. Herbert is repeating the song of David in the Psalms, a song in which calling out the name of God is alternatively an expression of joy and an expression of dejection. What matters is the plain style of the outcry and its honesty. Herbert carries out this idea in accord with both Luther and Calvin, for whom a "man groaning for grace" is the essential picture of piety.[35]

Just like Burton, Herbert is fully aware that two of the best remedies to melancholy are employment and music. It is no surprise if the poem which directly follows "Jordan" (I) is entitled 'Employment" (I) and testifies to the poet's urgent desire that God give him a "reed," that is, the same poetical gift as David. But becoming like David does not suffice to cure melancholy. It only substitutes for other forms of melancholy that which is termed "religious" by Burton in the last part of his *Anatomy*. Burton begins this last part of his book by arguing that he is the first to attempt a systematic definition of "religious" melancholy. He identifies two major types of religious melancholy: the excessively zealous attitude of believers who despise any but their own

sect on the one hand, and the "defect" of love of God of the "Epicures" and
"Atheists" on the other hand. But there is a third type of religious melancholy,
namely "desperation." Burton's subsections on despair clearly reveal that all
believers are subject to "this mischief." The psalmist stands as the epitome of
the melancholy believer who, doubting at times his own election, is close to
the desperate reprobate. Donne's Holy Sonnets illustrate particularly well the
fine line between despair and reprobation, their speaker constantly expressing
melancholy words of fear.

Though in *The Temple,* Herbert alludes to some of the same forms of
melancholy as those he deals with in *Memoriae Matris Sacrum,* he seems intent primarily on exploring the temporary religious melancholy, which can
also be termed despair. Herbert's religious affliction seems less specifically focused on the fear of reprobation than that at work in Donne's Holy Sonnets.
In "Conscience," the speaker resists the process of self-examination which is
viewed positively in the more Puritan fringe of the Church of England but
which appears to him as the sickening work of a "pratler":

> Peace pratler, do not lowre:
> Not a fair look, but thou dost call foul:
> Not a sweet dish, but thou, dost call it sowre:
> Musick to thee doth howl.
> By listening to thy chatting fears
> I have both lost mine eyes and eares.
> . . . . . . . . . .
> If thou persistest, I will tell thee,
> That I have physick to expel thee. (ll. 1–6, 11–12)

Sidney Gottlieb argues that "we need to take more seriously the extent to
which Herbert personifies conscience as a non-conforming, radical Protestant, a danger not only to one's peace of mind but also to one's Church and
society."[36] Herbert's argument here is evocative of Burton's conception of
religious melancholy resulting from excess of zeal. He too holds prattling
ministers responsible for the disease:

> 'Tis familiar with our Papists to terrify mens soules with purgatory,
> tales, visions, apparitions. . . . Our indiscreet Pastors many of them
> come not farre behinde, whilest in their ordinary sermons they
> speake so much of election, predestination, reprobation ab aeterno
> . . . with such scrupulous points, they still aggravate sinne, thunder
> out Gods judgement without respect, intempestively raile at and
> pronounce them damned, in all auditories, for giving so much to
> sports and honest recreations, making every small fault and thing

indifferent, an irremissible offence, they so rent, teare and wound mens consciences, that they are almost mad, and at their wits ends. (Part. 3, Sect. 4, Memb. 2, Subs. 3, vol. 3, p. 415)

Though Herbert's adherence to a true *via media* leads him along with Burton to dispel the melancholy methods of such ministers, the constant spiritual crisis the speaker experiences is, nevertheless, conveyed in terms of melancholy. These are not simple metaphors but testify to the way in which spiritual dejection was truly conceived of as a form of malady. The "sighs," "groanes," "teares," and "griefs" that repetitively punctuate *The Temple* reveal the distress of a soul in a body already predisposed to melancholy. The doubts of the poet appear as the symptoms of a cold disease in which the body is gradually turned to "bones" ("Death," l. 2) or "dust" ("Sighs and. Grones," l. 17) and the "hard heart" ("The Altar," l. 10), "cemented with tears" (l. 2), is constantly made to become "such a stone" (l. 6) under the effect of excessive grief.

"Affliction" (I), commonly read as the most autobiographical poem of the collection, surveys the different sorrows of the speaker—ill health, loss of friends, "ling'ring" studies—before he gives himself up to God, signalled by the phrase "Now I am here." The symptoms he describes in stanza 5 are typically those of a melancholy body and mind:

> My flesh began unto my soul in pain,
>     Sicknesses cleave my bones;
> Consuming agues dwell in ev'ry vein,
>     And tune my breath to grones.
> Sorrow was all my soul. (ll. 25–29)

Yet, even though it is the speaker's "grief" that "[tells him] roundly, that [he] live[s]," giving himself up to God does not cure all forms of affliction. In the penultimate stanza, which echoes Psalm 84 and the psalmist's desire to enter the House of God, the speaker is still yearning for God and fruition: "I read, and sigh, and wish I were a tree; / For sure then I should grow / To fruit or shade: at least some bird would trust / Her household to me, and I should be just" (ll. 57–60). The poem finishes with a simultaneous sense of unworthiness and desire to be chosen by God: "Let me not love thee, if I love thee not." "Employment" (II) is very similar to "Affliction" (I). Once more, the speaker desires to leave the habit of the student which suits "cold complexions"—melancholy is a cold and dry disease according to humoralism—and find true employment instead. In the second to last stanza, the speaker again wishes he were a busy tree: "Oh that I were an Orange-tree, / That busie plant!" (ll. 21–22). However, he is confronted at the very end with the natural melancholy of humanity which leads him towards the coldness and dryness of death: "So we freeze on, / Untill the grave increase our cold" (ll. 29–30). In both poems, the pastoral image of the tree only serves to express the speaker's unsatisfied desire for true employment and his acknowledgement of the unworthiness of humankind.

The remedy for melancholy appears more clearly in the later poems, those of the Bodleian Manuscript, which are more likely to have been written after Herbert had actually taken orders. They illustrate how pastoral song does not heal on its own the strife of the poet and how it is only through pastoral employment, in the other sense of pastoral, that relief can finally be found. A great sense of unworthiness still prevails in a poem such as "Dialogue." The speaker despairs because of the lack of control he has over his own salvation, manifesting the prime symptom of the melancholy of the zealous. Cristina Malcolmson has rightly argued that this sense of unworthiness is similar to a sense of personal merit in that "they both obscure the significance of the crucifixion."[37] The speaker's outcry asking God to silence that voice which breaks his heart is to be interpreted positively. Indeed, through Christ's crucifixion and the memory thereof, God is able to break man's heart, that heart which has nearly been choked by the black bile of melancholy. God's method, as it is described in "The Crosse," is quite "a strange and uncouth thing." The speaker, looking back on his life, summarizes the surprising process, "To make me sigh, and seek, and faint, and die, / Untill I had some place, where I might sing, / And serve thee" (ll. 2–4). It is only through God's "cross actions" (l. 32), "taking [him] up" and "throwing [him] downe" (l. 22) that the speaker becomes truly alive. God "cut[s] [his] heart" (l. 33), freeing it through passion from the numbing effects of self-centered melancholy. He is the only one who can move the speaker's heart, make it bleed, before nourishing it again with the new regenerating blood of Christ. As in the eighth poem of *Memoriae Matris Sacrum,* the poet praises his Lord who tempers bile with the blood of the Passion: "Then let wrath remove; / Love will do the deed: / For with love / Stony hearts will bleed" ("Discipline," ll. 17–20).

Part of the realization that appears in the later poems of *The Temple* is that, even though the speaker may not recover from his own disease, he can still participate in God's remedial design. The revived "busie heart" of the poet is able to "spin" a song of praise "all [his] dayes," even if this means "wring[ing] it with a sigh or a grone" from time to time ("Praise" [III], ll. 3–5). His very defects are what found his new ministry: "Yet since my heart, / Though press'd, runnes thin; / O that I might some other hearts convert, / and so take up at use good store" ("Praise" [III], ll. 37–40). "The Priesthood," which relates to Herbert's awaiting a divine call, as Christopher Hodgkins has shown, states that delay in the speaker's sense of calling rested at first in his "slender compositions" which could refer to his weakness of mind as well as of body, and his feeling "unfit."[38] It is only once he comes to terms with the idea that God can choose to make "vessels" of "lowly matter," as in the Eucharist, that he "throw[s] [himself] at his feet" (ll. 34–36). Not only does he have to see beyond the grief of social frustration and mourning, but he also has to remember, through the Eucharist, itself a communal reenactment of the crucifixion, that grief is not his. Grief belongs to God. Grief's remedy also belongs to God, as the speaker's sense of utter unworthiness is transcended by God's appointment. And thus, the sickly "obstructed vessel" of chapter 10 in *The Country Parson* is transformed, through God's grace, into one of those "other vessels" which in "Sighs and Grones" act as a "Cordiall," soothing the poet's own "bitter box":

> O do not fill me
> With the turn'd viall of thy bitter wrath!
> For thou has other vessels full of bloud,
> A part whereof my Saviour empti'd hath,
> Ev'n unto death: since he di'd for my good. (ll. 19–23)

The calling of the priest is to distribute of the life-giving divine blood of Christ. In chapter 15 of *The Country Parson*, the pastor's best means of comforting "when any of his cure is sick, or afflicted with losse of friend, or estate, or any ways distressed" is to administer the "holy Sacrament" which, as in "Conscience," is a form of "physick": "how comfortable, and Soveraigne a Medicine it is to all sin-sick souls" (p. 250). In some of the last poems of the Bodleian manuscript of *The Temple*, the poet's invitation to experience the same subduing "sweetnesse" of the Eucharist ("The Banquet") similarly extends to "All, whom Pain / Doth arraigne" ("The Invitation," ll. 13–14).

Herbert seems to have thoroughly listened to Burton's final injunction: "Be not solitary, be not idle." Having wept the death of his mother and his lack of preferment, he let go of the reed of traditional pastoral complaint and decided to truly lead, as the honest shepherd of his flock, others in the rites which commemorate the sacrifice of the King of Sorrows. He also seems to have listened to Burton's reminder to all those troubled by their sins or their fundamental human unworthiness that they should not doubt God's mercy:

> these men must knowe there is no sin so haynous which is not pardonable in its selfe, no crime so great, but by Gods mercy it may be forgiven. . . . His Mercy is a panacea, a balsom for an afflicted soule, a Sovereign medicine. (Part. 3, Sect. 4, Memb. 2, Subs. 6, vol. 3. p. 427)[39]

Pastoral song which only attempts to sublimate solitary grief cannot heal the "perturbations" of the poet's mind and body. However, by weaving affliction into his verse, accepting his weaknesses, and seeking employment in the life of his community, the melancholy frustrated scholar can nevertheless become God's honest shepherd in testifying that God has a remedy for fallen humankind. It is no surprise, then, if Herbert chose to keep "Love" (III), as a conclusion to "The Church." The unworthy believer is asked to sit down and rejoice in a feast. Whereas earlier poems in the series dwell upon the sweetness of the wine of the Eucharist, the ultimate poem is an invitation to "eat" (l. 18). The speaker is no longer under the threat of gluttony. Just as Luigi Cornaro's body had become insensitive to occasional excesses thanks to a sober life and lean diet, the speaker's soul can in no way be harmed, for it has been forever tempered by Christ's own blood and bile.

## NOTES

1. "To Sir John Danvers," in *The Works of George Herbert*, ed. F. E. Hutchinson (Oxford: Clarendon Press, 1941), pp. 369–370. All further quotations from Herbert's works, unless otherwise specified, are taken from this edition. They are referred to by title and line number for the poetry and by page number for the prose.

2. The quotation comes from a letter Herbert sent to his mother during her illness in 1622. What Herbert means by "offices" here is probably church ministry. However, the allusion to the notion of birth provides evidence that he probably did not have in mind, at this stage, priesthood in a modest, rural setting. Hutchinson suggests a parallel between this statement and "The Crosse."

3. Lynette R. Muir and John A. White, ed., *Materials for the Life of Nicholas Ferrar* (Leeds: The Leeds Philosophical and Literary Society, 1996), p. 29.

4. Izaak Walton, *The Life of Mr George Herbert*, in John Tobin, ed., *George Herbert, The Complete English Poems* (London: Penguin, 1991), p. 281.

5. See Cristina Malcolmson, *George Herbert, A Literary Life* (New York: Palgrave Macmillan, 2004).

6. See Lawrence Babb, *The Elizabethan Malady: A Study of Melancholia in English Literature from 1580 to 1642* (East Lansing: Michigan State College Press, 1951).

7. "There is another sorrow, which ariseth from the losse of temporall goods and fortunes, which equally afflicteth, and may goe hand in hand with the precedent; losse of time, losse of honour, office, of good name, of labour, frustrate hopes, will much torment; but in my judgement, there is not torture like unto it, or that sooner procureth this malady and, mischiefe: *Ploratur lachrymis amissa pecunia veris:* it wrings true teares from our eyes, many sighes, much sorrow from our hearts, and often causeth habituall melancholy it selfe." Robert Burton, *The Anatomy of Melancholy*, ed. Thomas C. Faulkner, Nicolas K. Kiessling, and Rhonda, L. Blair (Oxford.: Clarendon Press, 1989–2000), Part I, Sect. 2, Memb. 4, Subs. 7, vol. I, pp. 359–360. All subsequent quotes of Burton will be taken from this edition. Herbert, alternately student in divinity, teacher, and Orator at Cambridge, could well have read or heard of *The Anatomy of Melancholy* when the Oxford theologian first published his work in 1621 or when he augmented it for the first and second times in 1624 and 1628.

8. See Richard Strier, "Against the Rule of Reason: Praise of Passion from Petrarch to Luther to Shakespeare to Herbert," in *Reading the Early Modern Passions,* ed. Gail Paster, Katherine Rowe, and Mary Floyd-Wilson (Philadelphia: University of Pennsylvania Press, 2004), pp. 23–42.

9. See A. W. Barnes, "Editing George Herbert's Ejaculations," *Textual Cultures* 1, no. 2 (2006): 90–113, 209, 211.

10. Barnes, "Editing George Herbert's Ejaculations," p. 106.

11. Hutchinson shows that there is conflict of evidence as to who asked Herbert to translate Cornaro. Both hypotheses—Nicholas Ferrar and Francis Bacon—somehow corroborate the idea of Herbert's melancholy. Herbert's translation of *Trattato de la vita sobria* was appended to a translation of Leonard Lessius's treatise *Hygiasticon* published in Cambridge in 1634. The preface to the English *Hygiasticon* mentions that some "Noble Personage" asked Herbert to translate Cornaro's work into English. Either this personage was Ferrar who, having travelled in Italy and having been ill there, would have brought the treatise back with him, or Francis Bacon who, himself well acquainted with ill health, drew attention to "the Regiment and Diet which the *Venetian Cornarus used*" in his own *Historia Vitae et Mortis* (1623). For more details see Hutchinson's commentary; pp. 564–565. In her French edition and translation of Burton, Giséle Venet also reminds us that Bacon specifically used the language of humoral medicine to address the "distempers of learning" in *The Advancement of Learning.* See Giséle Venet, ed., *Robert Burton, Anatomie de la Mélancolie* (Paris: Gallimard, 2005). p. 402.

12. Malcolmson, *George Herbert,* p. 166n.

13. See Walton, *The Life,* in Tobin, ed., pp. 286–287: "About the year 1629 and the thirty-fourth of his age, Mr. Herbert was seized with a sharp quotidian ague, and thought to remove it by a change of air; to which end he went to Woodford in Essex, but thither more chiefly to enjoy the company of his beloved brother Henry Herbert and other friends then of that family. In his house he remained about twelve months, and there became his own physician, and cured himself of his ague by forbearing drink and not eating any meat, no not mutton, not hen, or pigeon, unless they were salted; and by such a constant diet he removed his ague but with inconveniences that were worse; for he brought upon himself a disposition to rheums, and other weaknesses, and a supposed consumption." Tobin notes that the date of "1629" is a printer's error and should be "1626." Herbert's age in the quotation (34) testifies to the fact that the date is indeed 1626.

14. See *The Anatomy,* Part. 2. Sect. 2, Memb. 1, Subs. 2 and Memb. 2, Subs. 1, vol. 2, pp. 24–33.

15. The quotation in the preceding note from Walton's *Life* also favors an autobiographical reading of the passage on food in chapter 10 of *The Country Parson.*

16. Malcolmson explains that Herbert's oration at Cambridge before Prince Charles and the Duke of Buckingham in 1623 may have been taken as an offence. The oration is in Hutchinson, pp. 444–455. Although Herbert defends civil obedience to the King above all, his opposition to the war against Spain may have displeased the Prince. Furthermore, he does not mention the Prince's favorite at all. Standing under Pembroke's patronage, Herbert would have been quite naturally rejected when the Buckingham/Pembroke antagonism developed in the following years. Finally, the church parsonage Herbert received from Archbishop Abbot

and Bishop Williams after 1623 set him in the camp of the "Calvinist enemies of Buckingham" (See Malcolmson, *George Herbert*, pp. 39–48 and 79–81).

17. Malcolmson, *George Herbert*, p. 86,

18. The original Latin elegy for Bacon reads:

> Dvm longi lentíque gemis sub pondere morbi
> Atque haeret dubio tabida vita pede,
> Quid voluit prudens Fatum, iam sentio tandem:
> Constat, *Aprile* vno te potuisse mori:
> Vt. *Flos* hinc lacrymis, illinc *Philomela* querelis,
> Deducant *linguae* funera sola tuae.
>
> > (*"In obitum incomparabilis Francisci*
> > *Vicecomitis Sancti Albani, Baronis Verulamij")*

The English translation reads:

> While you groan beneath the weight of long-
> Drawn-out illness, and with a tottering foot
> Life, wasting away, hangs on, I see at last
> What discreet destiny has willed: it is
> Certain there has never been a choice: April
> Has always been the month for you to die in, that here
> Flora with her tears, and Philomela there
> With her lamentations, may conduct
> Your idiom's lonely funeral cortege.

The translation is by Mark McCloskey and Paul R. Murphy, in *The Latin Poetry of George Herbert: A Bilingual Edition* (Athens: Ohio University Press, 1965). Scholars have drawn attention to the fact that their translations do not always closely follow the syntax and word choices of Herbert. In poem VII of *Memoriae Matris Sacrum*, the poet says of himself:

> Nec querar ingratos, studijs dum tabidus insto,
> Effluxisse dies, suffocatáme Mineruam,
> Aut spes productas, barbatáque somnia vertam
> In vicium mundo sterili, cui cedo cometas
> Ipse suos tanquam digno pallentiáque astra. (ll. 16–20)

Deborah Rubin's translation, quoted by Cristina Malcolmson in *George Herbert*, p. 89, reads:

> Nor will I bewail the thankless days, that have passed by as I, wasting away, pursued my studies—Minerva strangled—or hopes postponed, and my maturer dreams I'll cast off into the barren world of mutability, to which, for it deserves them, I leave its comets and pale stars.

19. At the beginning of his *Anatomy of Melancholy*, Burton distinguishes between melancholy "disposition" and. "habite," also respectively termed "transitory melancholy" and "chronicke" melancholy. The first type is that which "goes &

comes upon every small occasion of sorrow, need, sicknesse, trouble, feare, griefe, passion, or perturbation of the Minde." All men are subject, at times, to this form of melancholy. The second type, the one Burton is concerned with in his *Anatomy*, is a "setled humor . . . not errant but fixed, and as it was long increasing, so now being (pleasant or painefull) growne to an habit." (Part. 1, Sect. 1, Memb. 1, Subs. 5, vol. 1, pp. 136–139).

20. McCloskey and Murphy's translation.

21. See for example "See yonder melancholy gentleman" by Sir John Davies, "Having this day my horse" by Philip Sidney, or sonnet LII in Edmund Spenser's *Amoretti*.

22. Translations of the quotations from poems 4, 11, and 15 are all by McCloskey and Murphy. Poem 15 is originally in Greek.

23. For pastoral as sublimated grief see Paul Alpers's in-depth study, *What is Pastoral?* (London: University of Chicago Press, 1997).

24. Rubin's translation, quoted in Malcolmson, *George Herbert*, p. 89.

25. Greg Miller, "Self-Parody and Pastoral Praise: George Herbert's *Memoriae Matris Sacrum*," *George Herbert Journal* 26, nos. 1 & 2 (fall 2002/spring 2003): 15–34. For Magdalene as a dead Daphnis, see in particular, pp. 18–19.

26. The end of poem 3 reads:

> Verùm heus, si nequeas caelo demittere matrem,
> Sítque omnis motûs nescia tanta quies,
> Fac radios saltem ingemines, vt dextera tortos
> Implicet, & matrem, matre manente, petam. (III, 7–10)

McCloskey and Murphy's translation is as follows:

> . . . O yet if you my mother
> Cain't send down from heaven, if your
> Huge immobility no motion knows,
> Multiply your rays of light
> That I may wind and twist
> My hands in them, and, my mother staying
> Where she is, climb up to her.

McCloskey and Murphy's translation largely exaggerates similarities in wordings between "The Pearl" and the third poem in memory of Magdalene Danvers. Yet as both Hutchinson and Miller have noted, the image of Jacob's Ladder serves as a basis for Herbert's metaphors in both cases. See Hutchinson, p. 594 and Greg Miller, "Self-Parody and Pastoral Praise," p. 20. Miller also gives a closer translation of the last two lines of the poem: "Spread your rays, at least redoubled, so that with hands, / She might entwine, and, with Mother leading, I might seek my mother."

27. This is Greg Miller's translation in "Self-Parody and Pastoral Praise," p. 26. The end of the poem in Latin reads: "Quod tu febrem censes, salubre est / Atque animo medicatur vnum" (VI, 23–24).

28. Hilton Kelliher's translation, quoted in Malcolmson, *George Herbert*, p. 94.

29. Beatrice Graves, "'Temper'd with a Sinners Tears': Herbert and the Eucharistic Significance of the Word *Temper*," *Notes and Queries*, 49, no. 3 (2002): 329–330.

30. Miller's translation in "Self-Parody and Pastoral Praise," p. 17.

31. Miller's translation in "Self-Parody and Pastoral Praise," p. 17.

32. McCloskey and Murphy's translation follows Hutchinson's punctuation: "Muse, you win. But hear, / O vain one! This one time I write / To be forever still."

33. Greg Miller, "Self-Parody and Pastoral Praise," p. 17.

34. On the differences between pastoral and georgic seventeenth-century England, as well as the displacement of pastoral by georgic, see Alastair Fowler, "Georgic and Pastoral: Laws of Genre in the Seventeenth Century," in *Culture and Cultivation in Early Modern England*, ed. Michael Leslie and Timothy Raylor (London: Leicester University Press, 1992), pp. 81–88. Fowler notes that in georgic, though the setting is often the same as in pastoral, there is a didactical purpose and rustic voices are filtered through that of the poet. There is also a presence of calendar time.

35. See Richard Strier, "Against the Rule of Reason," p. 40.

36. Sidney Gottlieb, "Herbert's Case of 'Conscience': Public or Private Poem," *Studies in English Literature* 25 (1985): 114.

37. Cristina Malcolmson, *George Herbert*, p. 107.

38. See Christopher Hodgkins, *Authority, Church, and Society in George Herbert: Return to the Middle Way* (Columbia: University of Missouri Press, 1993).

39. Subsection 6, on the remedies to despair, was added by Burton in 1624.

HOLLY FAITH NELSON

# Historical Consciousness and the Politics of Translation in the Psalms of Henry Vaughan[1]

"No one can escape the substance of his time any more than he can jump out of his skin," wrote Georg Hegel, leading him to conclude that Bible commentaries "do not so much acquaint us with content of scripture as with the mode of thought of their age."[2] Gerald L. Bruns, reflecting on Hegelian hermeneutics, observes: "It is not enough to reproduce another's thought; it is necessary to think it as one's own. The dead letter must be reinvested with one's own spirit, meaning that one . . . appropriates it, not merely as a preserved artifact but as something internalized, that is, essential to one's self-reflection and self-identity."[3] The verse and prose translations of Henry Vaughan, a poet known for his "unusual reliance upon prior texts," reveal this very historicity or cultural embeddedness of language; for in these works, Vaughan responds to the philosophy and politics of the volatile world he inhabits.[4] His source texts are refracted through the prism of his life context and conceptual frame. Louise Imogen Guiney discerned this early last century when she recorded in an unpublished manuscript: "Whenever [Vaughan] falls to translating, it is time for the sympathetic reader to prick up his ears" as Vaughan "seeks often this oblique outlet for his inmost thought."[5]

Vaughan's nostalgic exaltation of the past through textual duplication has long been recognized, yet many of his verse translations, the most

*Studies in Philology*, Volume 104, Number 4 (Fall 2007): pp. 501–525. Copyright © 2007 University of North Carolina Press.

intertextual of his lyrics, have failed to garner sustained attention. In response to this critical gap, Robert Wilcher and Jonathan Nauman have recently explored the poetic and political significance of Vaughan's verse translations in *Poems* (1646) and *Olor Iscanus* (1651).[6] The three psalm translations in *Silex Scintillans*, however, have largely been dismissed as banal duplications of the biblical text or "quite undistinguished" poetic works, despite Jonathan Post's insight that they "certainly deserve more attention than the few glances so far given them by modern critics."[7] Although Vaughan encodes in these psalms his vision of the natural, social, and spiritual spheres, one rarely finds in discussions of *Silex Scintillans* more than a paragraph on any of his psalm translations, even in book-length studies dedicated to uses of scripture in his poetry.

Vaughan certainly engages in "sacramental imitation" in his translations of Psalms 65, 104 and 121: he "celebrates an enshrined primary text" by frequently repeating the linearized properties, or signs, of the pretexts.[8] Vaughan is, no doubt, more conservative than Sir Thomas Wyatt or Mary Sidney Herbert, Countess of Pembroke, in his attitude toward altering the substance of Scripture. Vaughan might well have said with Matthew Parker, the archbishop of Canterbury, who had translated the Psalms nearly a century earlier,

> Require not heere: great difference,
>     In wordes so ofte the same:
> Although to féele: great violence,
>     I might not chaunge the name.
> Conceyve in hart: no griefe to sore,
>     wordes olde so ofte to vewe:
> Thy gayne thereby: is wrought the more,
>     though wordes be never newe.[9]

As is evident in "To Mr M. L. Upon His Reduction of the Psalms into Method," Vaughan envisages a translator or paraphrast as one who imposes structure without modifying substance; for when he praises Mr. M. L., he remarks, "He [David] gave the *matter*, you the *form* did give."[10] Nevertheless, Vaughan's psalms do not merely repeat the master text. In fact, an examination of his textual modifications reveals in these biblical verse translations not only his "religious attitude and individual sensibility," as E. C. Pettet speculated, but in particular a royalist sensibility.[11] Specifically, the vocabularies of hiddenness, veiled divinity, cosmic sentience, military invasion, concealed resistance, duty and sovereignty, and finally order restored in "Psalm 65," "Psalm 104," and "Psalm 121" disclose the philosophy and politics of a poet whose worldview is grounded in a culture of royalist defeat and anticipated restoration.[12]

# I

It is no surprise that Vaughan would be drawn to the Psalms. It was, in the mid seventeenth century, not only viewed as a literary model and an anatomy of the soul but also as a politically charged biblical book. In *Psalm Culture and Early Modern English Literature,* Hannibal Hamlin maps out the "huge diversity of [psalm] translators, representing a startling range of aesthetic, doctrinal, ecclesiastical, and political positions," from "the Royalist adventurer George Sandys" to "the Parliamentarian populist George Wither."[13] *Eikon Basilike* (1649), presented to the public as the last work of Charles I, intensified interest in, and reinforced the polemical potential of, the Psalms, as the king assumes a Davidic voice in this volume when defending his political actions and concludes each chapter with a psalmic prayer. Translation of the Psalms, therefore, was an aesthetic, spiritual, and political act that strove to alter the human heart and the public sphere.

Eluned Brown claims that *Silex Scintillans* is greatly indebted to the Psalter, sensing that Vaughan shared John Donne's "spiritual appetite" for the "*Psalms* of David"; of Vaughan's devotional poetry, she remarks: "direct quotation from the Psalms possibly predominates in Vaughan over other biblical echoes."[14] This, in fact, is not the case as references to Genesis, Revelation, and Matthew outweigh those to the Psalms.[15] Vaughan does, however, often allude to the Psalms in *The Mount of Olives: or, Solitary Devotions,* a work of devotional prose. Here, the Psalms offer Vaughan both a situational parallel of religio-political persecution and a treasure chest of semantic responses, articulated in mantra-like fashion to ward off his enemies. A fragment of Psalm 84:2, *desire and longing for the Courts of the Lord,* for example, activates an analogous situation through which Vaughan expresses distress at his separation from the "reverend and sacred buildings (however now vilified and shut up)" just as David *"driuen forthe of his countrey . . . [d]esireth moste ardently to come again to the Tabernacle of the Lord & the assemblie of the Saints to praise God."*[16] A psychological exile, Vaughan longs, in *The Mount of Olives,* to enter into the courts of the most holy but must instead find comfort in the repeated invocations of the Psalmist. The supplicant's voice as expressed through Psalm 17:8, "So receive thou me under the shadow of thy wings" (AV), and in Psalm 70:1, *"Haste thee, O God, to deliver me, make haste to help me, O Lord"* (AV), is echoed with such urgency in *The Mount of Olives* that it seems somehow invested with a magical efficacy to purify and preserve (145, 153).

Vaughan conceives of the spiritual potency of the Psalms in *The Mount of Olives* within a particular setting—that of highly ritualized worship. The performative magic of the Psalmist's words is contained within a work structured much like the devotional manual of Bishop John Cosin, bound up with Matins and Evensong, with set prayers and the Eucharist, all of which clearly challenge the *"frequent* Extasies, *and raptures to third heaven"* of self-styled

Saints (140). Vaughan alludes to the Psalmist's plea in Psalm 51:10—"Create in me a clean heart, O God, and renew a right spirit within me" (AV)—to locate it within the ritualized sacrament of the Lord's Table, the "great Feast" in which he might "eate and drink salvation" (163). The words of the Psalmist become intricately connected with Laudian sacramentalism. Such verbal borrowings from the Psalter in *The Mount of Olives*, therefore, serve to authorize a politicized liturgical practice.

## II

Given the early modern habit of reading and rewriting the Psalms in a partisan fashion and in light of Vaughan's political construction of this biblical book in his devotional prose, one might expect to find in *Silex Scintillans* a more pronounced political dependence on the Psalms. However, Vaughan transparently alludes to the Psalter within the context of political turmoil in only three poems, excluding his psalm translations. In "The Constellation," the speaker re-imagines the ordered creation of Psalm 147:4, "He telleth the number of the stars: he calleth them all by *their* names," to contrast such order with the fragmenting brutality of schismatical "black self-will" that rends the "humble, holy nation" of England (231–232). In a similar vein, the speaker in "Jacob's Pillow, and Pillar" refers to Psalm 124:5, "Then the proud waters had gone ouer our soule" (AV) and Psalm 126:4, "Turne again our captiuitie, O Lord: as the streames in the South" (AV) to request of God that he no longer allow the bondage of the elect and political rule by "heathens" (296). In his final poem, "L'Envoy," Vaughan again relies on the voice of the Psalmist to produce an afflicted speaker confronted with the sword-like words of the political enemy. In the last biblical allusion of *Silex Scintillans* (1655), the speaker cries out in the voice of David (Psalm 126:4), "So shall we know in war and peace / Thy service to be our sole ease, / With prostrate souls adoring thee, / Who turned our sad captivity!" ("L'Envoy," 313).

Despite his ability to engage the polemical power of the Davidic voice in prose and verse, Vaughan does not elect to translate psalms typically associated with political debate. Psalms 65, 104, and 121 are neither monarchic psalms that extol kingship nor historical psalms that explicitly address Israelite suffering. And yet, in all three of Vaughan's psalm translations, themes emerge which reflect his response to a landscape not long before wounded by the fury of war. We need look no further than Vaughan's psalm translations to uncover the language of hiddenness and secrecy frequently found in royalist writings. We detect, as well, desperation to render the absent present (the invisible visible) and to restore the desecrated—features not unexpected in royalist Interregnum verse. These translations also give voice to the royalist rejection of a corrupt political environment—"a darksome intricate wood full of *Ambushes* and dangers" that offers little hope to one who will not, in Vaughan's opinion, sell his soul and breath to the Commonwealth of Cromwell (*Mount of Olives*, 146; "The Proffer," 250).

"Psalm 121" is the only biblical translation in the 1650 edition of *Silex Scintillans*. A song of ascent, Psalm 121 was presumably sung by pilgrims "who had journeyed from their homes . . . to Jerusalem for one or more of the great festivals of the year."[17] Psalm 121, as with the two other psalms translated by Vaughan, records the Hebraic longing for divine presence. It is generally believed that the speaker of Psalm 121 looks to the temple in the holy city of Sion, an interpretation accepted by Thomas Sternhold and John Hopkins who render the first verse, "I Lift mine ey[e]s to Sion hill, / From whence I do attend / That succour God me send," and by George Sandys, who translates verses one and two, "To the hills thine eyes erect, / Help from those alone expect. / He, Who heav'n and earth hath made, / Shall from Sion send thee aid."[18] However, the Septuagint does not mention Sion, referring simply to the mountains, and the Hebrew text, like the Authorized Version (1611), alludes only to the hills in their generic sense.[19]

Regardless of the specific object of the speaker's gaze (hill, mountain, Sion, or Creator), Vaughan's translation of the first two verses reveals a desire for divine presence:

> Up to those bright, and gladsome hills
>     Whence flows my weal, and mirth,
> I look, and sigh for him, who fills
>     (Unseen,) both heaven, and earth. (218)

In *Reflections on the Psalms*, C. S. Lewis has described such longing as an "appetite for God."[20] Vaughan may have identified the experience of the psychologically exiled royalist with the Jewish pilgrim as both craved divine presence in a temple often out of reach. And yet the speaker in "Psalm 121" transcends the Psalmist's expression of longing. The Psalmist looks to the hills for "helpe" (AV, v. 1) alone; he desires divine assistance in the face of danger. Vaughan augments the source text to create an atmosphere of potential delight in the presence of the Lord. The hills become "bright" and "gladsome" and offer "weal" and "mirth," emotions hardly connoted by the terms "helpe" in the Authorized Version, "succour" in Sternhold and Hopkins (92), or "reliefe," "aid," and "comfort" in Mary Sidney Herbert's translation.[21] This semantic alteration generates an atmosphere of potential joy and well-being not present in the source text. Unlike the Psalmist who envisions a distant Creator, the speaker of "Psalm 121" looks to an immanent God: "I look, and sigh for him, who fills / (Unseen,) both heaven, and earth" (218). We should pause to note Vaughan's semantic substitution of "fills / (Unseen)" for "made" (AV, v. 2). Coverdale's translation and George

Sandys's paraphrase of Psalm 121 retain the original word and Sidney-Herbert conveys the sense of God as maker: "O there, O there abides the worlds Creator" (294)[22] Vaughan, in contrast, deemphasizes God's transcendent role as Creator in order to foreground his immanence within the natural and supernatural realms, "both heaven, and earth" (218).

Despite His immanence, however, God remains for Vaughan "unseen," a word that appears thirteen times in *Silex Scintillans*.[23] Vaughan reads secrecy, a hiddenness, into the Psalmist's account of God and creation, a theme which reemerges throughout his work. It is expressed in "The Stone" where "God and his Creatures, though unseen" engage in a "busy commerce" (281) and in "The Star" as a sign of spiritual purity: "For where desire, celestial, pure desire / Hath taken root, and grows, and cloth not tire, / There God a commerce states, and sheds / His secret on their heads" (253).

Alan Rudrum locates this vision of a creation encoded with the hidden and the secret in hermeticism. For the hermetic philosopher, the secrets of the universe can only be discovered through a mystical search for the divine in nature. As Vaughan's brother Thomas explains in *Magia Adamica*, the hermetic arts allow a seeker to "attain . . . all the *Secrets* and *Mysteries* in Nature*," leading "directly to the *Knowledge* of the true *God*."[24] Henry Vaughan echoes this sentiment in *Hermetical Physick*, in which he describes the "most private and abstruse closets of nature" that only the Hermetic philosopher can open when he becomes *"the servant, not the Master of nature"* (549, 580). Vaughan's recourse to the language of secrecy in "Psalm 121," however, is also politically inspired. Lois Potter has demonstrated that royalists deploy the discourse of secrecy as a strategy of political defiance.[25] More specifically, Stevie Davies conceives of the unseen and hidden in Vaughan's poetry as royalist metaphors for "buried resistance" and "underground survival."[26] Perhaps such secrecy and hiddenness serve as a counterpart to the "loss and abandonment" characteristic of "the poetry of Anglican survivalism" as understood by Claude J. Summers.[27] Vaughan, that is, may imagine a secret or hidden force that awaits restoration in order to mitigate his despair about the absence of the true British church.

Longing for some indication of divine presence on earth is again expressed at the conclusion of "Psalm 121." While the Psalmist sings, "The Lord shall preserue thy going out, and thy comming in: from this time foorth, and euen for euermore" (AV, v. 8), the speaker in Vaughan's "Psalm 121" declares, "Whether abroad, amidst the crowd, / Or else within my door, / He is my Pillar, and my Cloud, / Now, and for evermore" (218). Vaughan clearly expands the source text in these lines, alluding to the pillars of cloud and fire in which God appears in Exodus, Numbers and Deuteronomy. These allusions establish the physical nature of divine presence. Nehemiah interprets the manifestation of the divine in the pillars as evidence of God's refusal to abandon His people: "Yet thou, in thy manifold mercies, forsookest them not in the wildernesses the pillar of the cloude departed not from them by day, to leade them in the way, neither the pillar of fire by night, to shew them light, and the way wherein they should goe" (9:19).

Vaughan's inclusion of "Pillar" and "Cloud" in his translation of this verse is not, however, unique. Both the Calvinist theologian Giovanni Diodati and the royalist biblical commentator Henry Hammond establish a connection between the pillars and Psalm 121. Of the words "by day" in Psalm 121:6, Diodati writes: "He hath a relation to the pillar of cloud by day, and of fire in the night, which God imployed in the bringing of the people forth of Egypt, and to defend them from the harmfull air that it might not hurt them: see *Isa.* 49.10. *Rev.* 7.16. And this may also be applyed to the return from Babylon under Gods protection."[28] We find similar intertextual referencing in Hammond's paraphrase of Psalm 121:5–6: "The omnipotent Lord of heaven and earth shall be present to thee, and overrule all his creatures, and keep thee from being mischieved by them; his protection, as the cloud to the Israelites, or as a faithfull second in a duel, shall defend thee from all approach of danger."[29] There is, therefore, an interpretive context within which Vaughan operates to reconstitute this psalm as one that envisions paradoxically a materialized yet veiled, immanent yet invisible, God. God for Vaughan both transcends and enters history.

Such a vision of divine immanence in history is extended into a context far more martial in nature in "Psalm 121" than the biblical pretext suggests. Vaughan's contemporaries generally agree that Psalm 121 treats God's providential protection of his church. The Geneva Bible introduces the Psalm as one that "teacheth that the faithful oght onely to loke for helpe at God . . . Who onely doeth mainteine, preserve and prosper his Church" (Geneva, 262). In its heading to this psalm, the Authorized Version directs the reader away from the ecclesiastical formation, attending to the security of the godly in general: it speaks of "The great safety of the godly, who put their trust in Gods protection." Though Hammond, following the Authorized Version, interprets this psalm as one of general assurance in the face of a physical or spiritual onslaught ("The hundred twenty first is a repose in God, and a confident expectation of succour and safety under his protection"), he also produces a finely tuned military interpretation of the psalm: "But for the immediate sense of them [the words], the scheme seems to be martial. The besieged person daily looks to the *hills*, to see if any relief be coming from any quarter, any signal by fire or the like, giving intelligence of succour approaching."[30]

The semantic changes in Vaughan's "Psalm 121" suggest that he too imagines this psalm within the context of the attempted enslavement of the godly perhaps by parliamentarian enemies. After all, his rendition of Psalm 121:6 and 7 thrusts the reader into a scene of military machinations and intrigue.

The biblical "[t]he sunne shall not smite thee by day; nor the moon by night" (AV) is transformed by Vaughan into the language of invasion:

> The glorious God is my sole stay,
>     He is my Sun, and shade,
> The cold by night, the heat by day,
>     Neither shall me invade.
>
>                                                    (218)

In the stanza that follows, we find an even more radical departure from the source text. While the Authorized Version describes the enemy in rather vague terms, "The Lord shall preserue thee from all euill: hee shall preserue thy soule" (121:7), Vaughan injects into his translation the image of scheming, vengeful enemies against whom he must be shielded:

> He keeps me from the spite of foes,
>     Doeth all their plots control,
> And is a shield (not reckoning those,)
>     Unto my very soul.
>
>                                                    (218)

In the fourth stanza of "Providence," Vaughan employs the word "plots" to register resistance to the temporal power of the Sequestration Committee established by Parliament:

> I will not fear what man,
> With all his plots and power can;
> Bags that wax old may plundered be,
> But none can sequester or let
> A state that with the sun doth set
> And comes next morning fresh as he.
>
>                                                    (271)

An intratextual reading of *Silex Scintillans* indicates, therefore, that the term "plot" carries political and martial connotations. The language of "plots" and "inva[sions]" is supplemented in Vaughan's "Psalm 121" by the threatening image of the crowd, which frequently surfaces in his lyrics to convey a sense of spiritual and physical peril. While Psalm 121:8 speaks of the Lord's preservation in "thy going out" (AV) Vaughan writes of entering the public world or community, of finding oneself "amidst the crowd" (218). In "Jacob's Pillow, and Pillar," Christ is "slain by the crowd"; it is the "multitude" that seeks to destroy the divine (218). By inserting the language of invasions, plots and crowds into his translation of Psalm 121, Vaughan makes more vivid the external forces, possibly military and coercive, that threaten to penetrate his body and soul.

Vaughan places the language of martial threat and invasion and that of hiddenness and secrecy within a contemporary context in "Psalm 121" by excising the reference to the God of Israel in the original text: "Behold, he that keepeth Israel; shall neither slumber nor sleepe" (AV, v. 4). Vaughan omits the descriptive phrase that points to God's national affiliation, "he that keepeth Israel," and instead directs the reader's attention to the recipient of God's unyielding protection, the "beloved": "His watchful Eye is ever ope, / And guardeth his beloved" (218). Gérard Genette labels this type of textual modification a "diegetic transposition" whose purpose "is a movement of proximization" that brings the source text "up to date and closer to its own audience (in temporal, geographic, or social terms)."[31] Vaughan appears unconcerned with the historical relationship between Jehovah and the Israelites, modifying the text to convey a proximate vision of God's protective powers.

Though Thomas Calhoun has described Vaughan's "Psalm 121" as a "relatively strict" rendering of the biblical psalm, it is evident that Vaughan's semantic modifications in his translation result, at the very least, in a thematic extension if not a transformation of the biblical text.[32] Vaughan invests his translation of Psalm 121 with the vision of the immanent but invisible God manifest in nature through which the divine and human interact. Such divine presence is established as the vehicle that enables the speaker to combat the coercive tactics of foes that threaten to invade his very being. This thematic transformation occurs because Vaughan's body of devotional verse is permeated with a sense of divine presence in the natural world that may result from the absence of a national church that Vaughan can enter to experience the presence of God. Christ (and king) must flee into the pastoral landscape of the Canticles while the ecclesiastical body is purged, and so Vaughan indubitably secretes the divine externally within the natural landscape or internally within the soul. Though we do not have here a detailed account of the subterranean subterfuge of a royalist rebel, Vaughan's vision of "a God-animated universe," in conjunction with the languages of secrecy invasion and social withdrawal, intimate a poetic response to Parliamentary rule.[33]

The Psalm translations in the 1655 edition of *Silex Scintillans* offer an even more expansive vision of a vital universe in which the dynamic "natural world retains an enjoyment of close relationship with God" even if the social, political, and ecclesiastical formations offer no such harmony.[34] There has been much agreement on the motivation behind Vaughan's selection of Psalm 104. Barbara Lewalski finds it typical of his "meditations on the creatures."[35] A hymn of creation and a call to praise, Psalm 104 presents a God who makes and preserves all living creatures; here we find "a vast cosmos, teeming with life and full of light, bounded by God's ordering power."[36] This theme of a dynamic, responsive, harmonious creation recurs through-out *Silex Scintillans,* and such biblical hymns of divine cosmic rule would have an immediate appeal for Vaughan. There is a long exegetical tradition which reads Psalm 104 as a hymn of cosmic harmony. The patristic writer Cassiodorus explains that therein "the prophet wishes to demonstrate that the state of the world shows forth the divine mysteries" and to "acknowledge that all things are truly in harmony with each other, created as they were by a single Maker."[37] During the Reformation, John Calvin found in this psalm a "lively image of his [God's] wisdom, power and goodness in the creation of the world, and in the order of nature."[38] It is, to use the recent typology of the theologian Walter Brueggemann, a psalm of orientation, in which "all is right with the world."[39]

Vaughan's contemporaries found in Psalm 104 not merely a song of orientation but also a celebration of humanity's central place in the ordered universe. Chana Bloch observes that in "Providence," a free paraphrase of Psalm 104, George Herbert's "purview is restricted to the world where man is comfortably the master."[40] In the second and third stanzas of "Providence," Herbert identifies humanity alone as the recipient of inspired language and divine knowledge:

> Of all the creatures both in sea and land
> Only to Man thou hast made known thy ways,
> And put the pen alone into his hand,
> And made him Secretary of thy praise.
>
> Beasts fain would sing; birds ditty to their notes;
> Trees would be tuning on their native lute
> To thy renown; but all their hands and throats
> Are brought to Man, while they are lame and mute.[41]

In his poetic rendering of Psalm 104, Herbert appears to insert the anthro-pocentric view of creation recorded in Psalm 8: "What *is* man, that thou art mindfull of him? and the sonne of man, that thou visitest him? For thou hast made him a little lower then the Angels; and hast crowned him with glory and honour. Thou madest him to haue dominion ouer the worker of thy hands; thou hast put all things vnder his feete" (AV, vv. 4–6). Thomas Tra-herne, in "Thanksgivings for the Glory of God's Works," unites elements of Psalm 104 and Psalm 8 to place humanity, the governing agent, at the locus of creation: "The heavens are the Lords, but the earth hath he given to the children of men"; "The woods, and trees, and fields, and valleys, hast thou subjected to the Government and work of our hands"; "All these / Hast thou given to our bodies, / Subjected the same to the use of our hands."[42] According to Mary Ann Radzinowicz, John Milton's treatment of Psalm 104 also focuses on the human; to Milton, Psalm 104 stands as a model of hymnody through which the poet prophet, the center of the created universe, can constitute an authorial identity in relation to his Maker.[43] This is not surprising, as Psalm 104 is a Whitsun Proper Psalm, White Sunday marking the vocal inspiration of the disciples on the descent of the Holy Spirit (Acts 2:1–4).[44]

Unlike Herbert, Traherne and Milton, who transform Psalm 104 into a hymn of orientation with humanity as the matrix, Vaughan augments the pre-text to expand his sense of God's cosmic, yet hidden, identity and to create a sense of retirement and secrecy in the natural landscape, changes consistent with those found in "Psalm 121." In "Psalm 104," Vaughan also points to the collective response of nonhuman creation and implicitly compares this to the selective union between God and particular human souls.

Vaughan's first significant modification of the biblical source can be found in the third and fourth lines of "Psalm 104" where he describes the Creator: "Honour and majesty have their abode / With thee, and crown thy brow." The Psalmist refers only to a God "clothed with honour and majesty" (AV, v. 1). Vaughan could have easily transformed this verse into royalist propaganda; Sidney-Herbert imagined a kinglike God in her version of the same verse: "To thee, to thee, all roiall pompes belonge, / Clothed art thou in state and glory bright:" (241). However, Vaughan is a little more ambiguous in his addition of the phrase "crown thy brow." On the one hand, Vaughan does produce an image of kingship with the interpolation of the word "crown" to describe the "majesty" of God. However, "crown thy brow" may also signal Vaughan's reading of Christ into the Jehovah of the Old Testament, as it could refer to the crown of triumph. If such an association is made, Christ is injected into a hymn of praise to Jehovah, a reading worthy of St. Paul who imagined such a Cosmic Christ in Colossians 1:16: "For by him [Christ] were all things created that are in heauen, and that are in earth, visible and inuisible, whether *they be* thrones, or dominions, or principalities, or powers: all things were created by him, and for him" (AV). Vaughan's reference, therefore, to crowning in "Psalm 104" inspires a vision of both monarchy and cosmology, king and Christ, as the locus of order in the universe.

Vaughan's "Psalm 104" not only calls attention to but also augments the Psalmist's rendition of this ordered cosmos. Where the Psalmist is content to describe God stretching out "the heauen like a curtain" (AV, v. 2), Vaughan specifies the nature of the "globe / Of Air, and Sea, and Land" (258). But as he did in Psalm 121, Vaughan discovers that this expansive globe is penetrated by the hidden and secret; the beams of God's "bright chambers" are laid "[i]n the deep waters, which no eye can find," the earth is hidden "[a]s with a veil," and the waters pass through the mountains "by secret ways" (258). Safety and retreat accompany such secrecy when Vaughan adds the language of play, retirement and healing to the biblical pretext. For the Psalmist, "the waters stood" (AV, v. 6), for Vaughan the "floods played" (258). For the Psalmist the waters haste away at the voice of thunder, the "conies" find "refuge" in the "rocker;' and the young lions lay "down in their dennes" (AV, vv. 7, 18, and 21–22), while for Vaughan, the waters "retired apace," the conies find a "retiring place" in the rocks, and the lions "[r]etire into their dens" (258–259). Finally, for the Psalmist, the earth is "satisfied" with the plentiful waters (AV, v. 13), but for Vaughan the parched hills are "[h]ealed by the showers from high" (259). Vaughan's desire to present nature as a sacred and secure landscape accounts for most of his modifications to Psalm 104 and may well point, on some level, to the politics of retirement characteristic of much Cavalier verse.

However, one should be wary of reading the language of retirement in "Psalm 104" and other lyrics as an expression of passive political withdrawal. Recent analysis of royalist verse has led to the conclusion that apparently "private codes" of defeated royalists are, in fact, a "means of illicit communication and subversion during the Civil War" and Interregnum.[45] Publishing poetry and prose on retirement is hardly Vaughan's act of withdrawal from the world; it is a political act. By comparison, in publicly fashioning himself an unworldly creature, content to reflect on the things of God, Vaughan designates those who wish to achieve power during the Civil Wars and Interregnum "worldly" creatures, destined for eternal punishment.

Into the tableau of secrecy, retirement, and healing of "Psalm 104," Vaughan injects two types of commerce, that between the nonhuman creature and God and that between God and holy souls. The Psalmist does not speak of nature's praise of its Creator in Psalm 104; no such view of nature can be found in its twenty-fourth verse: "O Lord, how manifold are thy workes! in wisedome hast thou made them all: the earth is full of thy riches" (AV). Vaughan, however, interpolates into his translation a vision of the natural world's response to God:

> O Lord my God, how many and how rare
> Are thy great works! In wisdom hast thou made
> Them all, and this the earth, and every blade
> Of grass, we tread, declare.
>
> (259)

Vaughan's conception of the semiotics of nature is scattered throughout his lyrics. The view of a communicative nature can be found in the Old Testament where the floods "clap their hands" and the hills, "joyful together," praise their Creator (AV, Psalm 98:8). In the Hebraic landscape of Isaiah 55:12, the "mountains and the hilles . . . breake forth . . . into singing, and al[l] the trees of the field . . . clap *their* hands" (AV) to signify God's mercy to the righteous ones, a verse Vaughan integrates into the "The Bird," which immediately follows "Psalm 104" to celebrate the silent consciousness of some natural elements:

> So hills and valleys into singing break,
> And though poor stones have neither speech nor tongue,
> While active winds and streams both run and speak,
> Yet stones are deep in admiration.
>
> (261)

The New Testament also offers Vaughan a vision of a sentient creation. In "Church-Service," Vaughan relies on Romans 8:26 to affirm the "sighs and groans" of nature, a sentiment expressed in "And do they so?" which glosses Romans 8:19 to reveal an animate and inspired nature.[46] Vaughan may well have been influenced directly by both Testaments in his production of a worshipping earth in "Psalm 104" and other lyrics. Alternatively, given his propensity to regard humanity as inferior to the rest of creation, Vaughan may also be espousing a "primitive appreciation of nature" much as Michel Montaigne celebrated the beast to "wound man's pride" and "reduce his arrogance."[47]

Rudrum's claim that Vaughan read the scriptures, including Psalm 104, through the filter of the Hermetica to derive a vision of a vital universe filled with sentient creatures is also convincing. In *Anthroposophia Theomagica*, Thomas Vaughan envisions "the *world*, which is *Gods building*" as "full of *Spirit, quick* and *living*" (52), a view espoused in *Libellus IV* and *VII* of the *Hermetica* where it is written: "The Kosmos also . . . has sense and thought; but its sense and thought are of a kind peculiar to itself, not like the sense and thought of man, not varying like his, but mightier and less diversified."[48] In her philosophical writings, Margaret Cavendish had come to even more radical conclusions about nonhuman creation without adopting a hermetic worldview; in the preface to *Philosophical Letters,* she concludes that "not on-ley Animals, but also Vegetables, Minerals and Elements, and what more is in Nature, are endued with this Life and Soul, Sense and Reason" as all of creation is "composed of the same matter."[49] However, Henry Vaughan was no adherent of newfangled theories that explained the universe simply in materialist terms. Instead, he shared with Lady Anne Conway a belief in "sacramental vitalism," recognizing, in accordance with Hermetic and Caba-listic thought, that the universe was composed of one basic vital, spiritual substance, vital in so far as matter is alive and "inherently endowed with force and activity."[50]

Vaughan's elevation of nature in his emphasis on the spiritual sentience
of all creation in "Psalm 104" and other lyrics, however, might also, once
again, hint at a political subtext. Potter has argued that "the royalist mode
in the mid-century is increasingly characterised" by a "sense of darkness and
confined spaces," many royalists finding an identity within the tavern and
prison.[51] To some extent, Vaughan associates his natural society with darkness and confinement, forging in it the language of hiddeness and secrecy.
His allusions to the garden of the Song of Songs, for example, often reflect a
sense of an idyllic enclosure, threatened from without by the "vulgar" popu-
lace. However, Vaughan's society of nature is also allied with open pastoral
space and the vast cosmos. "Psalm 104" conveys this paradoxical sense of
the cosmic society of which his lyric speakers are a part; they are, as it were,
hidden in full view.

The speaker of "Psalm 104," therefore, finds himself within a sentient
and vital natural landscape, a "society" in which humanity is not high priest.
However, humanity, or at least some of its members, shares in this communion with God. In Psalm 104:4, the Psalmist describes God as He who "ma-
keth his Angels spirits: his ministers a flaming fire" (AV). However, Vaughan
makes a substantial interpolation to this verse, radically departing from the
pre-text:

> In thy celestial, gladsome messages
>    Dispatched to holy souls, sick with desire
> And love of thee, each willing Angel is
>    Thy minister in fire.
>
>                                                          (258)

While the Psalmist only describes the nature of the angelic ministers
of God, Vaughan characterizes their actions and the recipients of that
action. Only those "holy souls, sick with desire / And love of thee" will
receive those "celestial, gladsome messages" dispatched by God. There
are Arminian overtones to this interpolation, as divine communion can
only come about, Vaughan intimates, with the desire of the believer.
More importantly, however, Vaughan's interpolation restricts the vision
of cosmic orientation in terms of human creation. The response of nature
seems an instinctual, collective act; "every blade / Of grass, we tread"
declares God's wisdom, while only "holy [human] souls" commune with
the divine. Unlike his contemporaries, therefore, Vaughan does not find
in Psalm 104 a vision of humanity at the center of the cosmos worshiping
the Creator and mastering creation. Rather some "holy souls" along with
nonhuman creatures come together as a spiritual society to worship their
Maker.

"Psalm 65," the final psalm translation in *Silex Scintillans*, is, like "Psalm 104," a hymn of worship that celebrates God's mercy to the elect and all creation. Psalm 65 observes God's presence in Zion, understood as the true church by reformation exegetes, and in the temple of nature.[52] It has been described as a hymn of confidence and a song of craving; that is, the Psalmist appreciates God's mercy as evidenced in creation and yearns to be fulfilled with the delights of the temple.[53] As with Psalms 121 and 104, Psalm 65 celebrates God's engagement with humanity (or at least the elect) and envisions God's presence within the created universe. And like Psalm 104, Psalm 65 presents a God of cosmic order. The speaker of Psalm 65, however, hopes to find a place for himself within the holy temple or church. Satisfaction within an ecclesiastical setting is only hinted at in Vaughan's "Psalm 121" in an oblique reference to the "hills" of Zion and is not addressed at all in "Psalm 104." In "Psalm 65," however, there is a desire to experience the divine within the boundaries of the temple, which signals a craving for spiritual and political restoration.

Though patristic, reformed, and early modern exegetes interpreted Psalm 65 as a hymn that prophesied the election of the Gentiles, this seems of little concern to Vaughan. No textual modifications are made by Vaughan to address election. The speaker in "Psalm 65" is far more concerned with God's presence within his temples, which he utters, once again, through the discourse of secrecy and sentience. In his account of God's attendance on nature, the speaker of "Psalm 65" declares,

> Thou water'st every ridge of land
> And settlest with thy secret hand
> The furrows of it; then thy warm
> And opening showers (restrained from harm)
> Soften the mould, while all unseen
> The blade grows up alive and green.
>
> (301)

In typical fashion, Vaughan finds in nature life and growth unseen and unveils the secret practices of the Creator. As expected, no such secrecy is recorded in the tenth verse of Psalm 65: "Thou waterest the ridges thereof abundantly: thou settlest the furrowes thereof: thou makest it soft with showres, thou blessest the springing thereof" (AV). Though Vaughan is more orthodox here in his vision of nature in service of humanity, "Thou visit'st the low earth, and then / Water'st it for the sons of men" (301), his lines are again infused with the hermetic and political language of unseen growth. So too does he choose to translate a psalm permeated by sentient and expressive nonhuman creatures:

> The fruitful flocks fill every dale,
> And purling corn doth clothe the vale;
> They shout for joy, and jointly sing,
> *Glory to thee eternal King!*
>
> (301)

Vaughan is drawn to psalms that imbue nature with a spirit of life, creating once again a society of nature of which humanity is but a part.

Though the speaker of "Psalm 65" celebrates the earth's richness, secret growth and sentience, he does not always express the confidence of the Psalmist. In the Authorized Version and the Geneva Bible, the Psalmist reassures himself about God's mercy toward, and purgation of, his personal iniquities and the nation's collective transgressions (v. 3). Some of Vaughan's contemporaries also incorporate this sense of assurance in their verse translations of Psalm 65:3. In *The Psalmes of David, from The New Translation of the Bible turned into Meter,* Henry King describes the sins of the Psalmist and his people as purged:

> My misdeeds (Lord) 'gainst me prevaile;
>     Thy mercies though nere faile:
> Who our transgressions from thy sight
>     Remov'st, and purgest quite.[54]

In contrast, Vaughan's speaker conveys a sense of urgency rather than cheerful assurance in his rendition of the verse,

> But sinful words and works still spread
> And over-run my heart and head;
> Transgressions make me foul each day,
> O purge them, purge them all away!
>
> (300)

Having personalized and internalized the misdeeds, the speaker utters an anxious plea for purgation and does not, like the Psalmist, highlight the cleansing of past sin; in this, he echoes the speakers of Sternhold and Hopkins's metrical psalms who cry out: "But Lord forgive our great misdeeds, / and purge us from our sin" (33). Sidney-Herbert does likewise in her translation of the same psalm, highlighting the shame of the speaker, while inscribing a more convincing sense of the incineration of sin: "There [Sion] thou my sines prevailing to my shame / Dost turne to smoake of sacrificing flame" (147).

Perhaps Vaughan's anxiety and guilt is grounded in a deeper sense of human degradation. Vaughan does, after all, augment Psalm 65:3 to amplify the account of sin; while the Authorized Version mentions "[i]niquities" that "preuaile against me" and "our transgressions," Vaughan's speaker recalls the "sinful words and works" that "spread" and "over-run" his "heart and head" rendering him "foul each day" (300). Sin infects both his wit and will, his cognition and volition. Despite Vaughan's Arminian leanings, in typical Calvinist fashion he negates the sense of human worthiness in the face of the divine when he modifies Psalm 65:4.[55] The biblical text reads, "Blessed *is the man whom* thou choosest and causest to approach *unto thee, that* hee may dwell in thy Courts: we shalbe satisfied with the goodnesse of thy house, *euen* of thy holy temple" (AV). In Vaughan's translation of these lines, he suppresses the biblical image of man approaching God (albeit at God's instigation) to enjoy the pleasures of His temple:

> Happy is he! whom thou wilt choose
> To serve thee in thy blessed house!
> Who in thy holy Temple dwells,
> And filled with joy, thy goodness tells!
>
> (300)

While the Psalmist speaks of God rousing the chosen one to draw near to and inhabit the temple, underscoring divine initiative and human response, Vaughan simply highlights human gratitude for admittance into the temple, where the chosen can joyfully "serve" the Creator.

Having identified his sinful nature and longing to experience divine presence in the temple, the speaker of "Psalm 65," like the Psalmist, attempts to define the nature of God, a process which leads to the politicization of his verse. In Psalm 65, David experiences God as a figure of order and provision. In Vaughan's "Psalm 65," the language of kingship is injected into the poem's fabric to fashion this stable, munificent God. In his rendering of the fifth verse, Vaughan engages in semantic substitution; "King of Salvation" (300) is substituted for the biblical "God of our saluation" (AV). In his translation of the final verse of Psalm 65, Vaughan extends the text for the same purpose. In Psalm 65:13, the Psalmist observes, "The pastures are cloathed with flockes; the valleis also are couered ouer with corn; they shout for ioy, they also sing" (AV); Vaughan expands this passage by inserting his account of the substance of nature's joyful hymn: "They shout for joy, and jointly sing, *Glory to thee eternal King!*" (301). The Coverdale, Geneva, and Authorized versions of Psalm 65 do not translate the Hebrew אלהים or Greek θεὸς "King."[56] Neither do we find God described as king in the metrical versions of Sternhold and Hopkins, Sandys, or Sidney-Herbert. Sandys, however, does envision

God in monarchic terms in his translation of Psalm 657 "*Which* stilleth the
noise of the seas; the noise of their waues, and the tumult of the people." For
this verse, Sandys conjures up a military scene and a regal God who employs
his "sceptre" to quash "the tumultuary jars / Of people breathing blood and
Wars" (2:181).

Vaughan's monarchic God is similarly associated with the restoration of
order. While Psalm 65:5 reads, "*By* terrible things in righteousnesse, wilt thou
answere vs, O God of our saluation" (AV), Vaughan writes, "King of Salvation!
by strange things / And terrible, thy Justice brings / Man to his duty" (300).
In these lines, Vaughan merges the language of sovereignty with the language
of duty. Stephen Collins has demonstrated that conservative politicians in
Renaissance England relied on similar discourses to promote their platform.
"Order" he writes, "meant fixity, constancy, immutability. Change was the
greatest of all enemies"; when king or subject forgot his duty, the cosmic
order was threatened.[57] Sir Robert Filmer, an apologist for Stuart absolutism,
wed the concepts of duty and sovereignty in *Patriarcha* and *The Free-holders
Grand Inquest*, frequently reminding his readers of their obligation to the
monarch: "every subject in particular, by duty and allegiance is bound to give
his best advice to his sovereign when he is thought worthy to have his counsel
asked."[58] He finds countless precedents for such a blending of concepts in the
common law, citing in *The Free-holders Grand Inquest* the following Tudor
Statute: "The king our sovereign lord, calling to his remembrance the duty of
allegiance of his subjects of this his realm, and that by reason of the same they
are bound to serve their prince and sovereign lord for the time being in his
wars, for the defence of him and the land against every rebellion, power and
might reared against him, and with him to enter and abide in service in battle,
if case so require."[59] Though we should be wary of reading a coherent royalist
platform into Vaughan's adoption of the language of sovereignty and duty in
Psalm 65, we can hardly ignore the political implications of such language in
a description of the ecclesiastical and natural temples. With the language of
monarchy and duty comes a vision of civil and natural harmony that would
be coincident with the royalist scheme.

Vaughan's attempt to frame this psalm within an apocalyptic context
of the restored Christ might also hint at a longing for the restoration of
the earthly king. Some reformation exegetes claimed that Psalm 65 referred
to the return of Christ, Calvin interpreting Psalm 65:2, "O thou that hear-
est prayer, vnto, thee shall all flesh come," as "a prediction of Christ's future
kingdom" (2:453). In *Silex Scintillans*, "Psalm 65" is inserted between "The
Day of Judgement [II]" and "The Throne," both of which address the Second
Coming and enthronement of Christ. Framed by two eschatological lyrics,
"Psalm 65" is placed within a context of future orientation. Such a reading
is encouraged by Vaughan's use of the future tense in his translation of the

first section of Psalm 65:4. While the biblical text reads "Blessed *is the man whom* thou choosest" (AV), Vaughan's speaker exclaims, "Happy is he! whom thou wilt choose" (300). Vaughan's substitution of "whom thou wilt choose" for "*whom* thou choosest" suggests that dwelling in the temple is an impending occurrence. This future orientation is linked to enthronement in the last line of "Psalm 65" and in the title, introductory epigraph, and first lines of "The Throne." "Psalm 65" concludes with the exclamation *"Glory to thee eternal King!"* and "The Throne" begins with a reference to Revelation 20:11, a verse that speaks of the ceremony of enthronement: "And I saw a great white throne, and him that sate on it, from whose face the earth and the heauen fled away, and there was found no place for them" (AV). Here is an idealized image of monarchy restored.

In "Psalm 65" and the lyrics framing that poem, therefore, Vaughan attempts to blend the language of monarchy, duty, enthronement, and restoration when depicting the return of Christ, but he is also, very possibly, envisioning the restoration of Charles II, as the enthronement of Christ and a Stuart monarch were not always seen as distinct entities. In his Latin lyric "Carolus *Primus,* Anglorum. *Rex*" ("Charles I. King of England"), Thomas Vaughan dissolves the border between the throne of Charles I and that of God, describing King Charles thus: "En, en Deorum *Magnes,* et tracti Numinis / Sub sole *Thronus.*" ("Behold, the magnet of the gods, and the throne of God who has been drawn down below the sun") (573, 749). Henry Vaughan, in much the same way, imports into "Psalm 65" the language of sovereignty and duty and surrounds that psalm with the vocabulary of enthronement and restoration because his political affiliations make this discourse inviting. Such vocabularies complement the royalist vision of dutiful man within a harmonious, ordered cosmos.

### III

Mikhail Bakhtin observes that "an utterance . . . even if it has only one word, can never be repeated: it is always a new utterance (even if it is a quotation)."[60] Though sacramental imitation often leads the writer away from aesthetic innovation given a fascination with the original source text, Vaughan does not only record "his development as a man and a writer" in his translations, as Wilcher perceptively remarks; he also inevitably writes his culture and his royalist sensibility into the scriptural text during the act of translation.[61] Translation is, by its very nature, a hermeneutic activity, and "the space of interpretation," as Bruns explains, "is always historical, always political and ethical as well as analytical."[62] Vaughan's translations, therefore, engage in a "hermeneutical conversation" with the biblical source text based on his *"historically effected consciousness."*[63] That is, Vaughan reads himself and his historical situation into his psalms in order to reform the self and to transform "the oncoming world of conduct and action" not merely to reconstitute "an original message or state of affairs."[64]

Certainly in "Psalm 65," "Psalm 104," and "Psalm 121," Vaughan does not transparently pen royalist resistance. As Potter has demonstrated, "Vaughan's parables . . . do not always make clear which is the plain text and which the coded one" because he writes in an age in which "a general point, a biblical reference or an allusion to contemporary events" often appear indistinguishable.[65] Nevertheless, we should note the political implications of Vaughan's textual modifications, particularly when these may be read within the broader context of his systematic subversion of the ideological state apparatus of the new regime. Translation, therefore, becomes a form of cultural capital and a means of political, and thus cognitive, defiance; in an age of biblicalism, Vaughan speaks through the authorized linguistic idiom of scripture to constitute a new vision of his world in the hope of transforming it in accordance with royalist interests.[66]

## Notes

1. Henry Vaughan's facility in Greek suggests that he could read the Septuagint and he may, like his twin brother Thomas, have been able to read the Old Testament in Hebrew. However, the semantics and syntax of his translations indicate that he took the Authorized Version as his primary source and model. Jonathan Post, in *Henry Vaughan: The Unfolding Vision* (Princeton: Princeton University Press, 1982), and Philip West, in *Henry Vaughan's "Silex Scintillans": Scripture Uses* (Oxford: Oxford University Press, 2001), refer to Vaughan's psalms as translations, likely using the term in its loosest sense, and I follow this practice here.

2. Georg Hegel, *Introduction to the Lectures on the History of Philosophy*, quoted in Gerald L. Bruns, *Hermeneutics: Ancient and Modern* (New Haven: Yale University Press, 1992), 151.

3. Bruns, *Hermeneutics: Ancient and Modern*, 150.

4. Thomas O. Calhoun, *Henry Vaughan: The Achievement of "Silex Scintillans"* (Newark: University of Delaware Press, 1981), 67.

5. Quoted in Jonathan Nauman's "Boethius and Henry Vaughan: The *Consolatio* Translations of *Olor Iscanus*," in *Of Paradise and Light: Essays on Henry Vaughan and John Milton in Honor of Alan Rudrum*, ed. Donald R. Dickson and Holly Faith Nelson (Newark: University of Delaware Press, 2004), 193. See also Nauman's "F. E. Hutchinson, Louise Gurney, and Henry Vaughan," *Scintilla* 6 (2002): 135–147.

6. Wilcher, "'Feathering some slower hours': Henry Vaughan's Verse Translations," *Scintilla* 4 (2000): 142–161; Nauman, "Boethius and Henry Vaughan."

7. E. C. Pettet, *Of Paradise and Light: A Study of Vaughan's "Silex Scintillans"* (Cambridge: Cambridge University Press, 1960), 47; Post, *Henry Vaughan*, 90.

8. Thomas M. Greene, *The Light in Troy: Imitation and Discovery in Renaissance Poetry* (New Haven: Yale University Press, 1982), 38.

9. Matthew Parker, "Of the vertue of Psalmes," in *The whole Psalter translated into English metre* (London, 1567).

10. *Henry Vaughan: The Complete Poems*, ed. Alan Rudrum (1976; repr., Harmondsworth: Penguin, 1995), 330. All subsequent quotations from Vaughan's poetry are from this edition and will be cited parenthetically within the text by page number.

11. Pettet, *Of Paradise and Light*, 47.

12. Some of these vocabularies have been identified and perceptively examined in Vaughan's poetry; but not in relation to his psalm translations. See, for example, Rudrum, *Henry Vaughan* (Cardiff: University of Wales Press, 1981), and Stevie Davies, *Henry Vaughan* (Bridgend, Mid Glamorgan: Seren, 1995). Vaughan's three psalm translations will be placed in quotation marks throughout this essay. Unless otherwise noted, all subsequent quotations from the Psalms and other biblical books will be taken from the Authorized Version, hereafter AV, and will be cited within the text by chapter and verse.

13. Hamlin, *Psalm Culture and Early Modern English Literature* (Cambridge: Cambridge University Press, 2004), 51. Though George Sandys's *A Paraphrase upon the Psalmes of David* (1636) was published prior to the civil wars, they lend themselves to a royalist vision.

14. Brown, "Henry Vaughan's Biblical Landscapes," *Essays and Studies* 1977 (London: John Murray, 1977), 53–54.

15 Here I address only Vaughan's reproduction of the linear textual features of the Psalms. In "Biblical Structures in *Silex Scintillans:* The Poetics and Politics of Intertextuality" (*Of Paradise and Light*, ed. Dickson and Nelson, 165–191), I consider his reliance on the formal or structural features of the Psalms.

16. *The Works of Henry Vaughan*, ed. L. C. Martin, 2nd ed. (Oxford: Clarendon Press, 1957) 147; all subsequent quotations from Henry Vaughan's prose are from this edition and will be cited parenthetically within the text. "Headnote to Psalm 84," in *The Geneva Bible: A Facsimile of the 1560 Edition* (Madison: University of Wisconsin Press, 1969), 253; all subsequent quotations from the *Geneva Bible* are from this edition and will be cited parenthetically within the text.

17. Mary Ellen Chase, *The Psalms for the Common Reader* (New York: W.W. Norton, 1962), 58.

18. Thomas Sternhold, John Hopkins, et al. *The Whole Book of Psalms: Collected into English Meetre* (London, 1671), 92; all subsequent quotations are from this edition and will be cited parenthetically within the text by page number. *The Poetical Works of George Sandys,* ed. Richard Hooper, 2 vols. (1872; repr., Hildesheim: Georg Olms, 1968), 2:280; all subsequent quotations are from this edition and will be cited parenthetically within the text by volume and page number.

19. *The Septuagint with Apocrypha: Greek and English*, ed. Lancelot C. L. Brenton (1851; repr, Grand Rapids, MI: Zondervan, 1982); *The Interlinear Hebrew Aramaic Old Testament,* ed. Jay P. Green, 2nd ed. (Peabody, MA: Hendrickson, 1986).

20. Lewis, *Reflections on the Psalms* (1958; repr., San Diego: Harcourt Brace Jovanovich, 1986), 51.

21. *The Psalms of Sir Philip Sidney and the Countess of Pembroke*, ed. J. C. A. Rathmell (New York: New York University Press, 1963), 294. All subsequent quotations are from this edition and will be cited parenthetically within the text by page number.

22. Sternhold and Hopkins replace "made" with "framed" (92).

23. Imilda Tuttle, *Concordance to Vaughan's "Silex Scintillans"* (University Park: Pennsylvania State University Press, 1969), 219.

24. Thomas Vaughan, *The Works of Thomas Vaughan*, ed. Alan Rudrum (Oxford: Clarendon Press, 1984), 166; all subsequent quotations from Thomas Vaughan's works are from this edition and will be cited parenthetically within the text.

25. Lois Potter, *Secret Rites and Secret Writing: Royalist Literature, 1641–1660* (Cambridge: Cambridge University Press, 1989).

26. Davies, *Henry Vaughan*, 157.

27. Claude J. Summers, "Herrick, Vaughan, and the Poetry of Anglican Survivalism," in *New Perspectives on the Seventeenth-Century English Religious Lyric*, ed. John R. Roberts (Columbia: University of Missouri Press, 1994), 49.

28. Giovanni Diodati, *Piovs Annotations Vpon the Holy Bible*, 3rd ed. (London, 1651).

29. Henry Hammond, *A Paraphrase and Annotations upon the Book of the Psalms* (London, 1659), 631.

30. Ibid., 632.

31. Genette, *Palimpsests: Literature in the Second Degree*, trans. Channa Newman and Claude Doubinsky (Lincoln: University of Nebraska Press, 1997), 304.

32. Calhoun, *Henry Vaughan*, 70.

33. Rudrum, *Henry Vaughan*, 65.

34. Ibid., 59.

35. Barbara Lewalski, *Protestant Poetics and the Seventeenth-Century Religious Lyric* (Princeton: Princeton University Press, 1979), 52.

36. S. E. Gillingham, *The Poems and Psalms of the Hebrew Bible* (Oxford: Oxford University Press, 1994), 102.

37. Cassiodorus, *Cassiodorus: Explanation of the Psalms*, trans. P. G. Walsh, 2 vols. (New York: Paulist Press, 199:1), 2:30.

38. John Calvin, *Commentary on the Book of Psalms by John Calvin*, trans. James Anderson, 5 vols. (Edinburgh, 1845–1849), 4:143; all subsequent quotations from Calvin are from this edition and will be cited parenthetically within the text by volume and page.

39. Walter Brueggemann, in *The Message of the Psalms* (Minneapolis: Augsburg, 1984), categorizes psalms as those of orientation, disorientation, and reorientation; see also Gillingham, *The Poems and Psalms of the Hebrew Bible*, 188–189.

40. Chang Bloch, *Spelling the Word: George Herbert and the Bible* (Berkeley: University of California Press, 1985), 254.

41. George Herbert, *George Herbert: The Complete English Works*, ed. Ann Pasternak Slater (New York: Alfred A. Knopf, 1995), 113.

42. Thomas Traherne, *A Serious and Pathetical Contemplation of the Mercies of God in Several Most Devout and Sublime Thanksgivings for the Same*, ed. R. Daniells (Toronto: University of Toronto Press, 1941), 43–45.

43. Radzinowicz, *Milton's Epics and the Book of Psalms* (Princeton: Princeton University Press, 1989), 208.

44. Bloch, *Spelling the Word*, 251.

45. Timothy Raylor, *Cavaliers, Clubs, and Literary Culture: Sir John Mennen, James Smith, and the Order of the Fancy* (Newark: University of Delaware Press, 1994), 182

46. See Rudrum's reading of "And do they so?" in "Henry Vaughan, the Liberation of the Creatures, and Seventeenth Century English Calvinism," *The Seventeenth Century* 4, no. 1 (1989): 33–54.

47. George Boas, *The Happy Beast in French Thought of the Seventeenth Century* (1933; repr., New York: Octagon, 1966), 56.

48. Hermes Trismegistus, *Hermetica: The Writings Attributed to Hermes Trismegistus,* trans. and ed. Walter Scott (Bath: Solos Press, 1992), 75.

49. Margaret Cavendish, "The Preface," *The Philosophical Letters* (London, 1664), 192.

50. Diane Kelsey McColley, "Water, Wood, and Stone: The Living Earth in Poems of Vaughan and Milton," in *Of Paradise and Light: Essays on Henry Vaughan and John Milton,* ed. Dickson and Nelson, 273; Allison P. Coudert and Taylor Corse, eds., *Anne Conway: The Principles of the Most Ancient and Modern Philosophy* (Cambridge: Cambridge University Press, 1996), xxxi.

51. Potter, *Secret Rites and Secret Writing,* 134.

52. For example, the headnote to Psalm 65 in the Geneva Bible interprets Zion as a figure of the invisible church (composed of committed believers): *"A praise and thanksgiuing unto God by the faithful, who are signified by Zion"* (248).

53. Gillingham, *The Poems and Psalms of the Hebrew Bible,* 225; Lewis, *Reflections on the Psalms,* 50–51.

54. King, preface to *The Psalmes of David, from The New Translation of the Bible turned into Meter* (London, 1654), 113.

55. Vaughan's Arminian doctrinal leanings were first introduced into Vaughan scholarship by Rudrum. Some aspects of Vaughan's Arminianism have been recently considered in my essay "'Make all things new! And without end!' The Eschatological Vision of Henry Vaughan," *Scintilla* 10 (2006): 222–235.

56. Though not discussing "Psalm 65" at any length, Rudrum points out that Vaughan's choice "to address God as *King* in translating a psalm, where the original gives no warrant for the word" has "implications" ("The Liberation of the Creatures," 34).

57. Stephen Collins, *From Divine Cosmos to Sovereign State: An Intellectual History of Consciousness and the Idea of Order in Renaissance England* (Oxford: Oxford University Press, 1989), 16, 19.

58. Sir Robert Filmer, *Sir Robert Filmer: "Patriarcha" and Other Writings,* ed. Johann P. Sommerville (Cambridge: Cambridge University Press, 1991), 87.

59. Ibid., 106.

60. Bakhtin, "The Problem of the Text in Linguistics, Philology, and the Human Sciences: An Experiment in Philosophical Analysis," in *Speech Genres and Other Late Essays,* ed. Caryl Emerson and Michael Holquist, trans. Vern W. McGee (Austin: University of Texas Press, :1986), 108.

61. Wilcher, "Feathering some slower hours," 142; Greene, *The Light in Troy,* 39.

62. Bruns, *Hermeneutics: Ancient and Modern,* 239.

63. Hans-Georg Gadamer, *Truth and Method,* trans. Joel Weinsheimer and Donald G. Marshall, 2nd rev. ed. (New York: Continuum, '1994), 387, 389.

64. Bruns, *Hermeneutics: Ancient and Modern,* 240.

65. Potter, *Secret Rites and Secret Writing*, 133.

66. In *Language and Symbolic Power*, Pierre Bourdieu explains that "political subversion presupposes cognitive subversion, a conversion of the vision of the world" (ed. John B. Thompson, trans. Gino Raymond and Matthew Adamson [Cambridge: Harvard University Press, 1994], 127–128).

PIERS BROWN

# "Hac ex consilio meo via progredieris": Courtly Reading and Secretarial Mediation in Donne's The Courtier's Library

## 1. Introduction

Sometime after the execution of the Earl of Essex in 1601, and probably before he joined the Drury household in 1610, John Donne (1572–1631) wrote a short Latin *jeu d'esprit*, the *Catalogus librorum aulicorum incomparabilium et non vendibilium*, now known as *The Courtier's Library*. First published in 1650 as an addition to posthumous editions of Donne's poetry, the *Catalogus* originally circulated in manuscript among a coterie audience.[1] Like Rabelais's (ca. 1494–1553) list of the books belonging to the Library of St. Victor in the seventh chapter of *Pantagruel*, *The Courtier's Library* uses the form of the library catalogue to make a series of jokes at the expense of learned culture.[2] However, where Rabelais satirizes the scholastic learning associated with monasteries, Donne takes aim at the humanist methods adapted by secretaries to produce knowledge for courtly display. The *Catalogus* provides a parodic image of the Republic of Letters seen from the contemporary English perspective. It lists imaginary books attributed to major Continental figures, such as *Martin Luther, On shortening the Lord's Prayer* and *On the Diametrical Current through the Center from Pole to Pole, Navigable without a Compass, by André Thevet;* alongside these are titles that satirize contemporary English figures and institutions, for example, *One*

*Renaissance Quarterly*, Volume 61, Number 3 (Fall 2008): pp. 833–866. Copyright © 2008 University of Chicago Press/Renaissance Society of America

*Book On False Knights, by Edward Prinne, Slightly Enlarged by Edward Chute*
and *On the Privileges of Parliament* by the famous clown Richard Tarleton.[3]
This list is prefaced by an introduction in which a fictive secretary or tutor
offers these books as a course of study, suggesting that its "incomparable and
unsaleable" books will provide courtiers with irrefutable authorities to support their assertions.[4] However, the *Catalogus* is not simply a conventional
attack upon courts and courtiers: while its jokes are often not particularly
subtle, they attest to the problematic displacement of the secretarial labor
that undergirded the courtly display of learning.

Despite the complex relation between knowledge production and courtly display in *The Courtier's Library,* it is one of the most neglected works by
Donne. Only two critics, Evelyn Simpson and Anne Lake Prescott, have engaged seriously with the text during the last century. Simpson identifies the
allusions in the individual items of the *Catalogus* and considers both dating
and general context.[5] Indeed, her exemplary thoroughness is probably one
reason for the work's subsequent neglect. Her emphasis on the identification
of the figures whom Donne satirizes has framed its reception: *The Courtier's
Library* has been consulted only occasionally, usually in a biographical context
in order to situate Donne's opinions on a variety of authors and fellow countrymen, rather than as a text in its own right.[6]

By focusing attention on the individual items of the *Catalogus,* such biographical readings ignore the importance of secretarial activity to the framing
of the text, which is striking given Simpson's dating of the *Catalogus* to the
first decade of the seventeenth century. These years—from 1601, when Donne
lost his place as secretary to Lord Keeper Sir Thomas Egerton (1540–1617)
as a result of his marriage to Ann More (1584–1617), until 1610, when he
gained a relatively secure position with Sir Robert Drury (1575–1615)—were
perhaps the most difficult of his life. For much of the decade, Donne and his
family lived in borrowed lodgings, first at Pyrford, the home of his cousin-in-
law Francis Wolley, then at Mitcham. Donne's letters from this period attest
to his desire for a stable and productive place in society where his abilities
would be put to use, as they had been during his employment with Egerton.
The context of *The Courtier's Library*'s composition thus suggests that it might
offer itself as a source for understanding Donne's perception of his time as
Egerton's secretary.[7]

Anne Prescott's perceptive treatment in *Imagining Rabelais in Renaissance England* suggests that the *Catalogus* is amenable to far more nuanced
readings than simply the biographical. Her consideration of *The Courtier's
Library* as a Rabelaisian paratext places Donne's work in the context of the
wider European culture of learning (albeit one that had changed significantly
since Rabelais was writing).[8] In this scholarly context, both Rabelais's account
of the Library of St. Victor and Donne's *Catalogus* are more important than

their relative brevity would suggest: not only do they draw attention to the activities of the Republic of Letters, but they do so in one of the forms by which scholarly learning was itself organized and mobilized.

Prescott concludes with a question that points to a lacuna in book history: "What is the material history of books with names but no bodies?"[9] Her question draws attention to the problematic relationship between this list of bodiless titles and the material practices—the acts of annotation, summary, and citation—used to organize and transmit them. Seen in this light, the imaginary works of the *Catalogus* are almost indistinguishable from the excerpts and summaries of real works that circulated separately from their original forms. Disembodied books offer the fantasy of knowledge without the labor of humanist learning, and thus implicitly draw attention to the neglected figure of the secretary, whose practices of reading, interpretation, and organization are displayed in the text.

*The Courtier's Library* offers a chance to reconsider the role of secretaries in the acquisition and display of learning in English courtly settings during the late sixteenth and early seventeenth centuries. This article examines the material history of disembodied knowledge and its interaction with the cultural matrix in which it was produced, distributed, and consumed, and considers the secretary's problematic relationship with both the material he mediated for his master and the social position he occupied. Taking Donne's secretarial career and his habits of reading, marginal annotation, and note-taking as an example, this article investigates the production of knowledge by secretaries for courtly display and considers Donne's difficult negotiation of his liminal and shifting positions in English gentle society—as courtier, as gentleman, and as secretary—and his struggle for preferment that might support his claim to any of these positions.

First, I focus on the preface to the *Catalogus* and its portrayal of courtly reading, considering the use of humanist learning as a stepping-stone to courtly advancement in the context of the classical binary of *otium* (leisure) and *negotium* (work). Then, I examine the secretarial mediation of learning for courtiers in the context of Donne's career and of the unstable politics of late Elizabethan and early Jacobean England. Finally, the argument turns to the *Catalogus* itself and to Donne's practices of humanist reading and note-taking. I examine the relationship between satire, knowledge-making, and authority that Donne constructs in the *Catalogus,* and the alternative to these reductive forms of knowledge that he proposes to the friends in his coterie circle.

## 2. Humanist Reading and Courtly Display

Though *The Courtier's Library* contains, to use Prescott's term, "nonbooks," the majority of the forty parodic titles are based on real books. I want to

begin by considering a real book whose material body suggests both the
argument and the method of *The Courtier's Library*. The first item in the
*Catalogus* is one of five items in the satire that critiques authors whose books
appear in Donne's extant library. The description of *Nicolas Hill, On Distinguishing the Sex and Hermaphroditism of Atoms; The same, On their Anatomy,
and How to Aid in their Births when they are buried* is a mocking reference
to Nicholas Hill's (1570–ca. 1610) *Philosophia Epicurea, Democritiana,
Theophrastica proposita simpliciter, non edocta*, a collection of excerpts from
the newly revived Skeptical writers, printed in Paris in 1601.[10] Hill's book,
with its simplified and fashionable atomism rendered in *sententiae*, presents
exactly the sort of inappropriate learning that Donne satirizes. Indeed,
skepticism, with its claim that one can know nothing, acts as a figure for
reductive knowledge in the *Catalogus*.[11]

Donne's copy of Hill's book, now in the library of the Middle Temple
in London, is ornately bound in tooled, gilt leather with the badge of Christ's
College, Cambridge in the middle of the front cover, and contains interleaved
blank pages for note-taking, which nevertheless remained unused.[12] Although
it is by no means unusual to discover an interleaved book with unused, blank
pages, the combination of expensive binding and interleaving distinguishes
the book in Donne's library as both conspicuously valuable and intended for
study.[13] The contrast between the ornamented exterior and the neglected interior is suggestive of the disjunction between the appearance and the reality of
learning that the *Catalogus* satirizes. The elaborate binding signals the value of
the book's contents and the status of the college to which it belonged, but the
complete absence of notes on the blank interleaved pages suggests, by contrast,
that its readers may have failed to transform that content into useful knowledge, a failure that is particularly noteworthy given the simple, unmethodized
form—*proposita simpliciter, non edocta*—that the title advertises. The disjunction between exterior embellishment and interior neglect mimics the critique
of the ignorant courtiers in the *Catalogus*, who are concerned with the appearance of learning rather than the real fruits of scholarship.

The marks of subsequent ownership in the book comment on this disjunction, attributing it in part to an inappropriate choice of reading matter.
The book bears the crossed-out motto of Ben Jonson (1572–1637) in the
top right-hand corner of the title page and, in the center, Jonson's name
underneath a pasted slip of paper with Donne's signature. The mocking inscription at the top of the verso of the title page, "non lectore tuis opus est,
sed Apolline libris" ("your books do not need a reader, but [rather] Apollo"),
when read in this context, seems to comment on the misused learning of
the book.[14] It suggests both the incomprehensibility of the contents to the
less-than-divine reader and the disjunction between the work for which
this book was prepared—the acts of reading and note-taking by a student,

possibly with the aid of a tutor—and the value of the knowledge it contains.[15] The prominent position of Hill's book in the *Catalogus* suggests that this copy was either an inspiration for Donne's list of books or a gift commemorating it. In this context, the author of the epigram suggests that the book is not valuable in itself, but only for the poetic uses to which it might be put: scholarly practice is thus transformed into literary material for use in courtly settings.

This literary transformation takes the form of a parodic courtly world portrayed in the *Catalogus*, in which the appearance of knowing rather than actual substantial knowledge is important. Donne begins with a claim about the task of reading in relation to the appearance of knowledge: "We are cast by chance into an age in which nothing is worse than to be openly ignorant, nothing more rare than to be fully learned. Just as everyone knows something of letters, no one knows everything. The middle, and therefore common, way to proceed in order to avoid both the shame of ignorance and the bother of reading, is to use one art in all things in order to seem to know all the rest."[16] By presenting ignorance as disgraceful, rather than as a defect, and reading as merely tedious, the introduction suggests the ignorance hidden under the veneer of knowledge displayed to the court.[17] Put in this way, the *Catalogus* seems to be a simple unmasking of courtly decadence. However, while the list includes references to actual satires of courtly corruption, such as Sir John Harington's *The Metamorphosis of Ajax*—whose joke about the need for "jakes" at court appears amplified as *Hercules, or Concerning the method of emptying the dung from Noah's Ark*—Donne's satire is not so onesided.[18] The highly competitive environment of the late Elizabethan and early Jacobean courts implicated everyone, courtiers and scholars alike, in a complex negotiation between depth of knowledge and the display of learning, both of which were important in different contexts.

Donne's satire is striking because, instead of offering a conventional satirical condemnation of excess, *The Courtier's Library* instead attacks the attempt to pursue a *via media*, or middle way, between ignorance and laborious study. In doing so, it suggests the failure of the conventional early modern divisions between scholarly and courtly activity, in particular the distinction between *otium* and *negotium*. These classical categories were mapped onto different cultural formations throughout the early modern period, in particular the secular *vita activa* and the religious *vita contemplativa*, the active life involved in the world, and the contemplative life separated from it. Donne's own motto—"Per Rachel ho servito & non per Lea" ("I served you for Rachel and not for Leah")—that appears on the title page of many of his books plays on this distinction. Drawn from Petrarch, it refers to Jacob's two wives, who in medieval allegory represented the different rewards gained by laboring in the *vita activa* and the *vita contemplativa:* the plain Leah substituted for her sister, and the beautiful, beloved Rachel only obtained after a further seven years' toil.[19]

These binaries came under increasing strain during the sixteenth century due to competing conceptions of scholarly work. Sir Francis Bacon's (ca. 1587–1657) essay "Of Studies" (1597) divides the uses of learning into three, rather than two, categories: "Studies serve for pastimes, for ornaments, and for abilities. Their chief use for pastimes is in privateness and retiring; for ornament is in discourse, and for ability is in judgment."[20] Bacon distinguishes between the leisurely, courtly, and instrumental purposes to which classical and humanist learning might be turned, and suggests the split in the conception of *otium* caused by the courtly appropriation of humanist work. This new use of the *studia humanitatis*, drawing on the classical tradition and on Cicero in particular, was significantly mediated for Renaissance England by Castiglione's *Book of the Courtier*. In describing learning as ornament, Bacon's formulation puts an emphasis on a display of knowledge linked with the conception of *sprezzatura* that Castiglione articulates: a seeming nonchalance and unstudied familiarity with the classics based upon intensive study and practice.[21]

The function of humanist learning as a marker of nobility and as an asset for the conduct of governmental business became well established in England during the course of the sixteenth century.[22] While Castiglione describes the duty of a courtier to advise the prince on affairs of state, the development of bureaucratic systems of government in England, staffed by men chosen for their ability, broke down the distinction between expert and learned advice by making scholarship applicable to the affairs of government.[23] In providing administrators for government, humanist education attempted to transform itself into a system of expert knowledge, and became divided around the laborious nature of humanist learning and the value of new forms of education. The contrast between the preferment available to those with a humanist education and the lack of learning associated with an earlier aristocratic model of upbringing—which valued leisurely noble activities such as hunting—led to attempts by the gentry and nobility to monopolize educational resources.[24] In response, humanist scholars developed a streak of competitive self-abnegation, in which acquisition of such specialized knowledge was portrayed as incompatible with the leisurely activities of the noble and gentleman. As humanist education became the norm for young men hoping to improve their position, gentle and aristocratic families attempted to differentiate themselves through the choice of tutors and increasingly sophisticated programs of study for their children.[25] The appropriation of humanist learning by the nobility established this knowledge as a marker of distinction in Pierre Bourdieu's sense: as a mutually supporting signal of taste and status. This increasingly successful system produced more and more young men whose studies suited them for government.[26] As a result, in the competitive world of Elizabethan and Jacobean prefer- ment, which demanded ceaseless application to business, literary activity had a problematic, peripheral place. While providing a route to advancement, its association with exile—voluntary or involuntary—made it antithetical to the business of government.

For English humanist scholars of this period, the appropriation of study as a pastime in the noble sense—as in some way interchangeable with hunting, dancing, and other frivolous activities—was inherently contradictory. Such an appropriation devalued the intense effort involved in acquiring a humanist education and was incompatible with the devotion to governmental busi- ness necessary to gain advancement. Officials who had risen because of their expertise, such as William Cecil, Lord Burleigh (1520/21–1598), appropri- ated humanism as an ornament for governmental business. Burleigh's habit of carrying a copy of Cicero's *De officiis* while conducting business functioned both as an admonition to attend to business and as a display of learning and diligence.[27] At the same time, courtly graces remained an equally important marker, without which the value of humanistic learning was limited, as Gabri- el Harvey's failed attempts to use scholarly methods to study courtly manners suggest. Harvey's embarrassing appearance as a courtier at Audley End, which Nashe derides in *Have With You to Saffron Walden* (1596), as well as his failures to gain advancement at university or at court, demonstrate the extent to which a lack of courtly refinement could lead to embarrassment.[28]

The *Catalogus* reveals this conflict between the use of courtly and schol- arly activity as markers of status in its description of courtiers' daily appear- ance at court: "And because the natural occupations of court, in which you spend your time, do not allow you the leisure for literature, because, after sleep, which by custom must not be shaken off until after ten in the morning; after you have dressed in the clothes appropriate to the day, place, and pas- sions; after having composed your face in the mirror, and worked out whom to receive with a jeer or with a frown; after banquets and amusements— how much time is left over in your life for reading and the improvement of your mind?"[29] Donne's choice of vocabulary and phrasing slyly conflates these preparations for court with the processes of rhetorical composition. The courtier's preparations mimic the rhetorical processes of *inventio, dispositio, elocutio, memoria,* and *actio* (or *pronuntiatio*), implying that the lazy activity of the courtier is both incompatible with diligent study and a replacement for it. Thus, the use of *excutiendum* suggests not only the burdensome necessity of shaking off sleep, but also the inventive practice of searching for material. The process of dressing ("vestes diei, loco, affectibus proprias indutas"), plays on the metaphorical equivalence of dressing for court and ordering words ac- cording to place, occasion, and effect. Then, the courtier "compos[es]" himself in front of the imitative surface of the mirror and makes a decision about the gestures he will make, before he proceeds to the "banquets and amusements" that are the site of rhetorical performance.

Donne's description of the courtier sleeping until ten is remarkably similar to Isaak Walton's (1593–1683) description of Donne's own habits of study during his youth, which involved a similar attempt to negotiate the demands of study and leisure: "Nor was his age onely so industrious, but in the most unsetled dayes of his youth, his bed was not able to detain him beyond the hour of four in a morning: and it was no common business that drew him out of his chamber till past ten. All which time was employed in study; though he took great liberty after it."[30] Donne's division of his day between a period of intensive study and the "great liberty" he allowed himself afterwards, while he was at the Inns of Court, provided a solution to these competing needs. By contrast, in a letter to his friend Sir Henry Goodyer (ca. 1571–1627), written while in rural exile, Donne is able to find no such compromise, owing to his desire to be usefully employed. Donne compares his situation to that of his friends Goodyer and Sir Henry Wotton (1568–1639), remarking that "the memory of friends (I meane onely for letters), neither enters ordinarily into busied men, because they are ever imployed within, nor into men of pleasure, because they are never at home. For these wishes therefore w[hi]ch you won out of your pleasure & recreation, you were as excusable to mee if you writ seldome as Sir H. Wootton is, under the opression of businesse, or the necessitie of seeming so: Or more than hee, because I hope you have both pleasure and businesse. Only to me, who have neither, this omission were sinne."[31] At the root of Donne's complaint is not only a lack of employment in service to the crown, but also the absence of income necessary to pursue a compensatory leisure: he is prevented from contributing to the commonwealth, and his fortune will not support his leisure. In these straitened circumstances, Donne could not display a taste for the conventional noble pleasures of either court or countryside that were available to his friend Goodyer, nor could he claim the distraction of business and its associated prospects for advancement.

Sir Francis Bacon, seeking preferment for himself in the dedication of his *Advancement of Learning* (1605), negotiates this dilemma differently, by reconstructing the categories of work and leisure to make them compatible. He claims: "And that learning should take up too much time or leasure: I answere, the most active or busie man that hath been or can bee, hath (no question) many vacant times of leasure while he expecteth the tides and returnes of businesse (except he be either tedious and of no dispatch, or lightly and unworthily ambitious, to meddle in thinges that may be better done by others), and then the question is, but how those spaces and times of leasure shall be filled and spent; whether in pleasures, or in studies."[32] Bacon's claim "that learning take up too much time or leasure" is not simply rhetorical amplification, but points to the mutually exclusive definitions of the *vita activa* and *vita contemplativa*. Bacon responds by making leisurely activity coexist with diligent application to duty. Indeed, he defines diligence, in his essay "Of Dispatch" (1625), as attention to the proper moment for different activities, a definition that allows the business of government to coexist with humanist learning.[33] Bacon, however, passes over the unnamed secretaries that supported his discovery of a middle way between *otium* and *negotium*. His depictions of courtly learning focus on display without considering the methods or individuals that mediated knowledge for use by courtiers. Much like Donne's description of preparing for court elides the aid of valets in the process of dressing, descriptions of courtly learning neglect the roles of these scholars. I will now turn to the secretaries, tutors, and professional readers who gathered knowledge and prepared their masters for courtly display.

### 3. Scholarly Learning and Secretarial Counsel in the Egerton Circle

Donne's marriage to Ann More and his subsequent dismissal from the service of Sir Thomas Egerton have conventionally been framed as a major turning point in his life, representing the moment when Donne lost his footing upon the ladder of advancement, and thus his opportunity for a career in service to the crown. However, there is a substantial continuity in the methods by which Donne sought advancement and the sorts of services he offered his patrons and employers, both while Egerton's secretary and in the years that followed.[34] While Egerton's positions as the Master of the Rolls and the Keeper of the Great Seal meant that his endeavors were overwhelmingly concerned with the legal system, Donne's work demonstrates the wide range of activities that a scholarly reader might provide. As well as legal work, both for the Lord Keeper and later for Robert Cotton, Donne wrote controversial and polemic works, as well as the poetic works for which he is more commonly known.[35] He acted as a secretary, or gentlemanly companion, not only for Egerton, but also for Sir Walter Chute and later for Sir Robert Drury. These struggles to turn secretarial work to productive ends frame our understanding of the *Catalogus* and reveal the extent to which secretarial culture in late Elizabethan England is implicated in this satire.

The introduction to *The Courtier's Library* portrays its contents as a plan for learning aimed at courtiers, prescribed by a secretary or tutor. Such scholarly advice was a *via* in two senses: it was not only intended as a course of study, but also as a path of advancement for both the courtier and his scholarly assistant. Lisa Jardine, Anthony Grafton, and William Sherman describe "knowledge transactions" and point to the importance of "scholarly services" in late sixteenth-century England that were provided by both those employed as secretaries and those working on a more informal basis.[36] They suggest that these professional readers mediated texts for their employers and patrons in a variety of ways, via accompanied readings, oral advice, and written arguments. They also emphasize the utility of "goaloriented reading," drawing attention to humanist activities beyond the rhetoricizing of material for persuasive purposes, activities that took the form of expert advice and methods for collecting, organizing, and mobilizing information.[37]

Walton's biography suggests that Donne was an extremely capable scholar and secretary. He claims that Egerton, when dismissing Donne, said that he "parted with a Friend, and such a Secretary as was fitter to serve a King, then a subject."[38] This testimony to Donne's ability as a secretary is undercut by its implication that there were problems of subjection, and thus subordination, in the relationship between Donne and Egerton. While Walton claims that Donne was Egerton's "Chief secretary," he was in fact only one of five secretaries in Egerton's household, serving with the more experienced legal secretaries, George Carew and Gregory Downhall, and alongside the secretaries who dealt with Egerton's private affairs, Henry Jones and John Panton.[39] However, the absence of any evidence of Donne's work or remuneration among Egerton's remaining papers makes it difficult to assess his position in the household, though Donne's secret marriage to Egerton's stepniece and its disastrous fallout hint at the apparent disjunction between Donne's evaluation of his position and his employer's conception of that position.[40] Egerton's secretariat, however, was only the core of a wider network of scholarly and legal activity that centered upon the Lord Keeper, ranging from those employed for particular tasks—such as Sir John Davies's work on a reform of the laws of Ireland or Donne's work on the project to reform lawyers' and courts' fees—to the wider circle of writers who dedicated books to Egerton.[41] Together, the whole circle of clients and retainers presented an image of their patron's nobility, learning, and wisdom.

This wider circle gathered not in the closet, but at the dinner table, which Walton explicitly connects with Donne's status in the household. According to him, Egerton "did alwayes use [Donne] with much courtesie, appointing him a place at his own Table, to which he esteemed his Company and Discourse to be a great Ornament."[42] Donne's dinner-table conversation thus becomes a reflection of Egerton's own learning and a means for the exchange of knowledge among the members of the extended household. Donne is dismissive of this sort of superficial learning, which he satirizes elsewhere as the product of "Tables, or fruit-trenchers," linking conversation at dinner with the use of table books and collections of *sententiae*.[43] In *The Courtier's Library*, he extends this critique to the table manners of other members of Egerton's circle, who are depicted as having inappropriate responses to the consumption and digestion of knowledge: thus his inclusion of *The Afternoon Belchings of Edward Hoby, or On Univocals* and *What not? or a confutation of all errors in*

*Theology as well as in the other sciences, and the mechanical arts, by all men, dead, living, and to be born, put together one night after supper, by Doctor Sutcliffe.*[44]

The diverse range of patronage that Egerton offered—gifts to authors for dedications, positions in his secretariat, other offices and benefices, and other advantages offered by his favor at court—bound these individuals together. As Paul Hammer's description of the contemporaneous activities of Essex's secretariat (in which Donne's close friend Sir Henry Wotton served) suggests, the differing divisions of labor, responsibility, and reward both within and outside of noble households were strongly related to social status. The anxiety and jealousy among those in Essex's service reinforced the marked distinctions among those seeking, but denied, the position of secretary, such as Edward Jones; those employed as secretaries, including Edward Reynoldes, William Temple, Henry Cuffe, and Henry Wotton; and those, like Anthony Bacon, who performed similar functions but were rewarded as equals, rather than as employees.[45] The differentiation of status among Essex's secretaries and other retainers, and between this group and the gentlemen in Essex's wider affinity who aided him, was reinforced by the methods by which these different scholarly readers were recompensed.[46]

*The Courtier's Library* suggests similar frictions within Egerton's circle: a number of individuals associated with the Lord Keeper appear in the *Catalogus*, including Sir Francis Bacon, William Barlow, Sir John Davies, Mathew Sutcliffe, and Richard Topcliffe; works by Bacon, Barlow, and Sutcliffe were also in Donne's own library.[47] Donne's satire of these figures suggests that Donne, like Wotton, saw his position as secretary only as a stepping-stone to the preferment that they both eventually achieved, despite the lapses in their careers.[48] As such, their cultivation of gentle learning outside of the context of their respective secretariats was aimed, in part, at establishing their status, sometimes at the expense of their competitors.

While the employers of these humanist intelligencers were not the ill-learned courtiers parodied in the *Catalogus*, but well-educated and serious members of Elizabethan government, their reliance on the work of others raised worries for both patron and scholar. As Richard Rambuss suggests, there is a potential inversion of authority implicit in the relationship between secretary and master.[49] Rather than the secretary appropriating the master's voice, however, here the worry is that the master has appropriated the voice of his servant. Donne attacks this sort of appropriation by depicting it as a failure of digestion in his *Satire 2*:

> hee is worst, who (beggarly) doth chaw,
> Others wits fruits, and in his ravenous maw
> Rankly digested, those things out-spue,
> As his owne things; and they are his owne, 'tis true,

For if one eate my meate, though it be known
The meate was mine, th'excrement is his owne.[50]

Rambuss notes that secrecy became vital because it obscured those moments
of appropriation, in which the secretary became the tutor and the master his
pupil. Thus, the policy arguments produced as a result of these consultations
depended on the secretary as a trusted and discreet mediator of texts—someone "to whom [the courtier] can safely confess [his] ignorance"—because the
secretary also potentially exposed the employer to mockery.[51] The implied
secretarial author of the *Catalogus* abuses this trust by slyly purveying non-
sensical books to his ignorant patron, suggesting the frustration experienced
by scholars who were condemned to subordinate positions despite their
superior learning. Read in this way, the *Catalogus* acts as a critique by the
providers of mediated learning, directed at the recipients of such learning.

Worries about the ventriloquization of knowledge went both ways. Not
only was there a concern on the scholar's part about the appropriation of his
words by his patron, but there was also a concomitant discomfort about the
value of the learning conveyed. Though written as an intervention in serious
debates concerning policy and later used as a source for directed readings,
John Dee's *General and Rare Memorials pertayning to the perfect Arte of Navi-
gation* (1577) is parodied in the *Catalogus* as *On the Navigability of the Waters
above the heavens, and whether Ships in the Firmament will land there or on our
shores on the Day of Judgment*.[52] The fictitious work ascribed to Dee suggests
the extent to which speculative policy advice could later be seen as slipping
free of its mooring to the realities of politics.[53]

These worries reach their extreme in the titles that comment on the
circumstances of the Essex revolt of 1601. Donne's position as a secretary
to Egerton, who was held captive during the revolt, allowed him to witness
the event at close hand.[54] Secretarial counsel was deeply implicated in the
aftermath, particularly in the case of Essex's secretary Henry Cuffe.[55] While
both Essex at his trial and official accounts written afterwards blamed Cuffe
for leading his master astray, the *Catalogus* suggests that two figures, William Barlow and Sir Francis Bacon, are guilty of disloyalty, hypocrisy, and
lack of discretion.

The *Catalogus* attributes to Barlow, who had given the encomium for
Essex after the Cadiz expedition in 1596 and had heard his last confession, a
book entitled *An Encomium of Doctor Shaw, Chaplain of Richard III*, presumably on the strength of Barlow's decision to announce the official explanation for Essex's execution from the St. Paul's Cross pulpit.[56] Bacon, one of
Egerton's clients who was closely connected to Essex's circle via his brother,
Anthony, comes off looking even worse. His contribution to the affair is com-
memorated by two consecutive entries, *The Brazen Head of Francis Bacon: On*

*Robert I, King of England* and *The Lawyers' Onion, or the Art of Weeping during trials*.[57] Donne's attribution of these books to Bacon is an accusation of disloyalty and hypocrisy that sharply contrasts Bacon's role as an advisor before Essex's plot with his role as prosecutor at his trial afterward.[58] These titles underline the importance of the secretary's role in political judgment by suggesting the very real harm that could result from inappropriate and disloyal secretarial advice. The mechanical methods of mediation may be the cause of this harm: by depicting an advisor who portrays himself as an oracular automaton or one who uses an onion to provoke false tears, *The Brazen Head* and *The Lawyers'Onion* transform the reliability of secretaries and the methodical nature of their products into a threat.[59]

### 4. Libraries, Satire, and the Mediation of Knowledge

Secretarial mediation relied not only on individuals, but on their practices of marginal annotation, note-taking, and summary. The books listed in the *Catalogus* display these problematic acts of mediation. However, while the entries that parody English figures usually critique societal failings, those directed toward Continental figures concentrate on defects of scholarship, whether religious or secular, such as *That the Chimera is a Sign of the Antichrist, by an anonymous member of the Sorbonne* and *A Handful of Oak Trees, or The Art of Getting Ahold of Transcendentals, Written by Raimond Sebond*.[60] *The Courtier's Library* is founded on the humanist tradition of organizing and mediating knowledge. Donne's use of the term *catalogus* connects his little work to the great book lists of the sixteenth-century compilers Abbot Trithemius and John Bale, as well as those of their successor Conrad Gesner. As Roger Chartier points out, both Trithemius and Bale call their lists of hypothetical libraries by the name *catalogus*, suggesting both a library and a list, and it was only after Gesner's *Bibliotheca Universalis* that the term *bibliotheca* came to displace it as the common term for such a production.[61] These formal, compendious book lists depend on and refer to methods of organizing books and ordering knowledge, whether the lists of cited authors appended to learned works as far back as Pliny or the more modest domestic library lists produced by secretaries, the latter private rehearsals of the sort of advice that Gabriel Naudé was to give in his *Advis pour dresser une bibliothèque* (1627).[62]

These idealized attempts at a comprehensive list of books bear the same sort of relation to the frivolous *The Courtier's Library* as the famous library of the Monastery of St. Victor does to Rabelais's parodic recounting of its contents. In parodying these methods of organizing knowledge, both satires depend upon an understanding of their function and social context. While Donne's and Rabelais's lists of imaginary books do not attempt to organize the material they contain, they resemble their real counterparts to the extent that they also attempt to survey and describe all knowledge, if only to satirize it. Rather than taking the methodical form of alphabetical lists or division by discipline, however, their ordering follows the associative logic of jokes: the satirical force of the two entries attributed to Sir Francis Bacon depend on the contrast between the activities described in the consecutive titles. While this ordering may seem arbitrary, it resembles that of Erasmus, who preferred methods of organization based upon "infinitely extensible chains of words connected by likenesses, affinities, and contraries," in order to promote rhetorical invention.[63]

Among Donne's other works, the nearest equivalent to the list of books in the *Catalogus* appears in the altogether more serious treatise on suicide, *Biathanatos* (1608). It is prefaced by a list of the authorities cited in that work that self-consciously mimics the list at the beginning of Pliny the Elder's *Historia Naturalis* written to refute charges of plagiarism.[64] Even more than Donne's other divine writings—*Pseudo-Martyr*, *Essays in Divinity*, the *Devotions*, or his *Sermons*—*Biathanatos* provides an example of his diligent scholarly activity, with its dependence on methodical note-taking practices, as Donne's note to his list of cited works suggests. He claims: "In citing these authors, for those which I produce only for ornament and illustration, I have trusted my own old notes, which, though I have no reason to suspect, yet I confess here my laziness, and that I did not refresh them with going to the original."[65] While the citations in both *Biathanatos* and *Pseudo-Martyr* testify to the original work of reading performed during their composition, they depend more fundamentally still on the accumulated scholarly work from Donne's wide reading, collected in his notes (further evidence of which can be seen in his library).

Donne's extant library provides much-neglected evidence for his reading methods, though his collection of books almost certainly underrepresents the ambit of his reading. The lending and borrowing of books played a significant part in the dissemination and circulation of knowledge in the period, and the books that have been officially associated with Donne—because his inscription is on the book's title page or because the book was bound with a book so inscribed—comprise only a part of the books he owned or read.[66] Donne's own letters testify to this fact: he writes to Sir Henry Goodyer, while in residence at Mitcham, of receiving "the Catalogue of your Books" and refers in a later letter to his "study, (which your books make a prety library)."[67] Similarly, Donne's closeness to his hosts at Pyrford, courtesy of his cousin-in-law, Sir Francis Wolley, is marked by the presence in his library of a copy of Robert Moor's *Diarium Historicopoeticum* inscribed to Sir Francis's father, Sir John Wolley, Queen Elizabeth's Latin secretary and the former owner of Pyrford (L126). This suggests that there existed a widespread tradition of borrowing, lending, and giving

books as gifts, in which Donne himself participated, as his own gifts suggest (L214–L218).

Equally significant is the evidence provided by Donne's marginalia.
Walton remarks on Donne's practices of note-taking and annotation and
describes his copy of Cardinal Bellarmine as "marked with many weighty
observations under his own hand."[68] This untraced annotation of Bellarmine
is, according to Walton's description, entirely different from Donne's other
books. Other than his title-page inscriptions, Donne's marginalia is primarily in pencil and, rather than consisting of "weighty observations," mark the
text with vertical and diagonal lines and brackets, and, very occasionally, NBs,
question marks, and underlining.

Donne's decision to gather and keep notes separate from books, rather
than to inscribe notes in them, is indicative not only of his lack of resources,
but also of the dependent situation in which he found himself as a secretary.
His use of pencil for his marginalia left him the option of removing the traces
of his work from books. The patterns of Donne's marginalia point to a hybrid method of note-taking and annotation with two modes: one in which
sections of interest are marked for later digestion into notes, and another, in
which the markings are confined to discrete sections, in which they indicate
working directly from books at hand. In both cases, the emphasis was on the
work that could be carried away from the book after reading.

In a letter to Walton, Henry King, Bishop of Chichester, writes that
Donne "gave me all his Sermon-Notes, and his other Papers, containing an
Extract of near Fifteen hundred Authors."[69] In Walton's own account, these
notes, which were later lost, shrink slightly, to "the resultance of 1400. Authors, most of them abridged and analyzed with his own hand," but they
are more than supplemented by the other notes Donne made: "Nor were
these onely found in his study; but all businesses that past of any publick
consequence, either in this, or any of our neighbor nations, he abbreviated
either in Latine, or in the Language of that Nation, and kept them by him
for useful memorials. So he did the copies of divers Letters and cases of
Conscience that had concerned his friends, with his observations and solutions of them; and, divers other businesses of importance; all particularly
and methodically digested by himself."[70] Here Donne's formal methods of
note-taking and commonplacing, acquired during his time at university and
at the Inns of Court, become mingled with secretarial methods used to digest
his master's business. One of Donne's own descriptions of his notes suggests
something of their form. He writes that, "It were no service to you, to send
you my notes upon the Book, because they are sandy, and incoherent ragges,
for my memory, not for your judgement; and to extend them to an easinesse,
and perspicuity, would make them a Pamphlet, not a Letter."[71] The notes were
compiled with a compression and haste suggested by both their raggedness

and their sandiness. Not only is the information reduced into torn pieces that need to be fitted back together, but Donne's description of the sandy papers suggests the semantic latitude of the verb *excutere* that Donne exploited in the passage on the sleeping courtiers. The gathered leaves had been neither searched through nor shaken out since the final stages of their composition, when they were sprinkled with sand to dry the ink.

These serious practices reappear through a comic lens in *The Courtier's Library*. Donne's satire sets itself apart from these supposedly diligent practices of scholarly collection and organization, at the same time that it depends upon them for its form. As a genre, satire simultaneously attends to and flattens out the qualities of its subjects, in much the same way that Donne's transformation of Cardano's 1550 *On the subtlety of things (De subtilitate)* into *On the nothingness of a fart* seizes upon his conception of subtlety only to transform it into a joke about the tenuous nature of farts.[72] This resort to the scatological recalls many of the books Rabelais includes in his library, and also suggests the limitations of the *Catalogus* as a medium of knowledge. Yet the *Catalogus* mediates knowledge by means of, rather than in spite of, its satirical form. For all its parodical distortions, satire is both a rehearsal and a display of knowledge. While in some cases this is topical rather than literary knowledge, the heterogeneous contents mimic the products of his note-making practices, in which Donne appears to have been an inveterate gatherer of diverse knowledge. Donne's parodies depend upon familiarity with the works and authors he describes, and his satire of the advice given to courtiers recalls the serious advice from which it was born. In the *Catalogus*, the knowledge contained in the original books is digested and reshaped to satirical ends. In the same way that early modern book titles function as summaries of their contents, Donne's titles not only satirize, but also epitomize, the works and authors that they parody. Moreover, like the grotesque figures prescribed in the *Ad Herennium*, they connect ideas with striking images, so that they might be more easily recalled. Associating Pico della Mirandola (1463–1494) with Kabbalistic numerology by ascribing to him a book titled *The Judeo-Christian Pythagorus, in which 99 and 66 are shown to be the same number if the page is turned upside down* may not be fair, but it is certainly memorable.[73]

Donne's preface to the list makes clear that satire is not only the genre of *The Courtier's Library*, but one of the methods of organizing knowledge that it criticizes: "The middle, and therefore common, way to proceed in order to avoid both the shame of ignorance and the bother of reading, is to use one art in all things in order to seem to know all the rest. Thus, others delight in epitomes, paradoxes, and the stings of extravagant wits, and hence place a high value upon Ramon Lull, Gemma Frisius, Raimond Sebond, Sextus Empiricus, the Abbot Trithemius, Henry Cornelius Agrippa, Erasmus, Peter Ramus, and the heretical writers."[74] Donne's grouping of writers seems eclectic: they do not appear to offer "one art" by which courtiers may "seem to know" all the rest, but rather a multiplicity of competing and contradictory strategies. Donne's list of the authors links synthesizers, organizers, and compilers of various sorts (Agrippa, Lull, Gemma Frisius, Trithemius, Erasmus, Ramus) with skeptics (Agrippa, Sextus Empiricus, Raymond Sebond), occultists (Lull, Trithemius, Agrippa), and satirists (Agrippa's *De Vanitate Scientarum*, Erasmus's *Encomium Morae*).[75] Indeed, the list itself mimics the sort of ragbag assortment of learning and approaches to knowledge that the *Catalogus* critiques.

All of these writers, however, offer strategies that mediate knowledge for consumption by the reader. Donne's description of these methods of summary and compression—"epitomes, paradoxes, and the stings of extravagant wits"—makes sense of the list that follows by associating the effects of these different genres. He suggests that the summary of knowledge provided by epitomes is similar to the startling juxtapositions of paradoxes, and that paradoxes are like the itchy sting of satirical writing. By equating epitomes, paradoxes, and satires, moreover, he points to what is lost in the mediation of knowledge in these forms. While the fragments of knowledge remain the same, the processes of summary remove them from their context, potentially distorting their comprehension. The epitome of a book may turn its argument into a paradox, and paradox teeters on the brink of satire. Donne's addition of the heretical writers at the end of his list punctuates his critique of misplaced authority, and points directly to the dangers inherent in reliance upon the authority of an interpreter. In a sense, all these methods—whether Trithemius's act of compendious listing, Ramus's reduction to dichotomies, or Empiricus's skeptical questioning of all knowledge—act as competing forms of false authority that substitute themselves for a well-grounded set of sources. These authors are implicitly contrasted with the authors that are strikingly absent from the *Catalogus:* classical authorities, who conventionally provided the foundations of early modern knowledge. Instead, they are deliberately dismissed in the preface: the courtiers are advised to leave "those authors that they call the Classics to academics and schoolmasters to wear out."[76]

Donne's library and marginalia suggest that this attack on mediated knowledge was not a simple rejection of the use of epitomes and collections of *sententiae*. For instance, in Donne's copy of the *Opera Omnia* of Aeneas Silvius Piccolomini (L176) the most intensive annotation is confined to the *gnomologia* that collects and organizes quotable sentences from throughout the book. Likewise, the marginal annotation of a work such as D'Averoltius's *Catechismus Historicus, sive Flores Exemplorum* (L60) shows Donne's willingness to make use of collections of *sententiae*, a practice common to both scholars and divines. Donne does, however, attend scrupulously to his citational habits, as his preface to *Biathantatos* makes clear: "Of those few which

I have not seen in the books themselves—for there are some such even of places cited for greatest strength—besides the integrity of my purpose, I have this safe defense against any quarreler: that what place so ever I cite from any Catholic author, if I have not considered the book itself, I cite him from another Catholic writer; and the like course I hold for the Reformers, so that I shall hardly be condemned of any false citation, except to make me accessory, they pronounce one of their own friends principal."[77] Though engaged in an argument against received authority on the topic of suicide, Donne attempts to assure his readers about his use of sources. He does so not on the basis of a claim concerning his own reliability, but by citing authorities who would, owing to their own partisan attachment, be likely to reproduce the quotations faithfully.

At issue here is the status of authority in a system of learning where knowledge is repeatedly mediated and remediated, summarized, digested, compressed, epitomized, and transmitted: a society suffering from information overload.[78] In the *Catalogus*, the novel solution to this problem is the provision of nonexistent books, promising that "your audience—who before seemed to know everything—may, with reverence for you, hear about new authors."[79] Following the advice of his secretarial advisor, the courtier will not "produce anything in conversations from generally known authorities," relying instead on irrefutable citation of the *Catalogus*, so that he "might suddenly spring forth, on almost all topics, if not more learned than others, at least as learned in a different way."[80]

## 5. Conclusion: Conversible Knowledge

The *Catalogus* advises a move from the use of summaries and collections that encapsulate knowledge to the mere citation of irrefutable authority, in the form of nonbooks that no one else can consult. This parodic suggestion is not just a critique of the secretarial mediation of knowledge but also of the baseless authority of those who rely on it. As a moralized lesson, the *Catalogus* suggests that learning as a marker of status is useless without a proper educational foundation. Moreover, by asserting that attempts to evade this problem will be convincing only to others with the same lack of learning, it seeks to reinscribe the cultural superiority of humanist learning at a moment when its value as a path of advancement seemed to be uncertain.

As a performance of learning, however, *The Courtier's Library* intervenes in the circulation and display of knowledge. Both the manuscript transmission and the contents of the *Catalogus* suggest that it was meant for a coterie audience; as a result, the bonds of friendship meant its critique of the disjunction between authority and learning would not apply. By cataloguing these authors in the form of satirical book titles, Donne makes the knowledge implicit in these parodies amenable to courtly taste. Although the imaginary books of *The Courtier's Library* are not useful to his putative audience of courtiers, they are useful to his readers, friends who share his learned background and desire for advancement, and who are thus able to benefit fully from Donne's mixture of the pleasing with the useful. As such, the nonbooks of the *Catalogus* function as a literal recapitulation of knowledge, a reordering of old material under new heads. Satirical reuse becomes, as in the literary games of the Inns of Court, a rehearsal of shared knowledge among a coterie of close friends, a practice that, Donne argues in a letter, is vital to its comprehension and retention: "much of the knowledge buried in Books perisheth, and becomes ineffectuall, if it be not applied, and refreshed by a companion, or friend. . . . For with how much desire we read the papers of any living now (especially friends), which we would scarce allow a boxe in our cabinet, or shelf in our Library, if they were dead? And we do justly in it, for the writings and words of men present, we may examine, controll, and expostulate, and receive satisfaction from the authors; but the other we must beleeve, or discredit; they present no mean."[81]

Donne's description of the advantages of living knowledge, which one "may examine, controll, and expostulate, and receive satisfaction from the author," emphasizes the importance of searching, sifting, and organizing knowledge as a conversation among equals, where the authority associated with authorship is set to one side. The discussion of material gathered from reading in letters, as in a dialogue, lies in the chewing over and proper digestion of the material. In contrast to the dyspeptic scenes associated with some of Egerton's circle, these playful exercises in virtuosity are opportunities to practice methods of invention, organization, and deployment, and to make the products of such work available to his correspondents. Donne's letters unearth the "knowledge buried in Books"—which "perisheth, and becomes ineffectuall, if not applied and refreshed by a companion, or friend"—and sends it abroad. These processes of exchange vivify knowledge. After receipt, the letters of friends are placed in "a boxe in our cabinet, or shelf in our Library" (whereas the letters of the dead are not), and become part both of the library and of the system by which knowledge is organized. Indeed, they become material that can be reused in subsequent exchanges.[82] The aim is to become conversant in the literal sense: to have mastered material sufficiently for the purposes of conversation in the social world of court.

Donne's idealistic description of learning as inhering in conversation or in the exchange of letters between friends allowed him to find a mean, a straight path between aristocratic and humanistic conceptions of *otium*. He transformed the scholarly matter of the *Catalogus* by mobilizing it in a palatable form. If elsewhere the materials gathered from books that Donne circulates among his coterie are serious, not flowers but the bitter "sallads and onions of Mitcham," the fruits that he purveys to his friends in the *Catalogus* are very much the outlandish "Melons and *Quelque-choses* of Court."[83]

## NOTES

1. Donne, 1930, 7–13 (Evelyn Simpson's "Introduction"). Simpson's dating is conjectural, but on balance the broad range she offers, as opposed to the tight date of 1604–1605, seems likely. As she points out, a number of the items in the list refer to the execution of Essex, and the publication dates of several books owned by Donne and alluded to in the list suggest 1603 as the *terminus a quo*. Her suggested latest date of 1611 is far less firm, but I am inclined to accept it, not, as Simpson suggests, because of Lady Drury's possible disapproval of items mocking her half-uncle Francis Bacon, but because of the mention of a "Catalogus Satyircorum" in the letter to Sir Henry Goodyer: Donne, 1635, 275–276; mentioned by Simpson in Donne, 1930, 4.

2. On the relationship between Donne's and Rabelais's lists of imaginary books, see Prescott, 173–175.

3. "M. Lutherus de abbreviatione orationis Dominicae"; "De Gurgite diametrali a Polo ad Polum, per centrum navigabili sine pyxide per Andr. Thevet"; "De militibus Apocryphis per Edw. Prinne lib. unus, per Edw. Chute paulo amplior factus"; "Tarltonus de privilegiis Parliamenti." For the original Latin and new translation of *The Courtier's Library*, see the Appendix below, pp. 858–863. All references in the text, unless otherwise noted, follow the new translation, with the Latin appearing in the accompanying notes. For comparison, I have also consulted Percy Simpson's translation in Donne, 1930, 27–38.

4. The 1930 edition was the first to adopt the title *The Courtier's Library*, based on the title of the Trinity manuscript, *Catalogus librorum aulicorum incomparabilium et non vendibilium*. In the four editions prior to the twentieth century (1650, 1654, 1669, and 1719), the introduction appears untitled, while the list of books is headed by the title *Catalogus Librorum*. See Donne, 1930, 79–89.

5. See Donne, 1930, 1–26; Simpson, 149–158.

6. See Bald, 34, 73–74 n. 3, 113–114, 145, 216, 223, 241, 259 n. 2; see also Marotti, 1986, 188–189; Knafla, 2003, 52, 55, 62–63.

7. For Donne's life during this period, see Bald, 128–199.

8. Prescott, 173–175.

9. Ibid., 175.

10. I list books from Donne's library by the numbering established in the standard bibliography: Keynes, 1973, 258–280 (L1–L218). See also Dubinskaya; Keynes, 1977 (L219–L228) and 1978 (L229–L240); Hobbs; Pearson; Woodhuysen. For Hill's book, see Keynes, 1973, 270–271, L102. The other books in Donne's library whose authors reappear in *The Courtier's Library* are: [Sir Francis Bacon], *A Declaration of the Practices & Treasons attempted and committed by Robert late Earle of Essex and complices*, London, 1601 (263, L3); William Barlow, *The Summe and Substance of the Conference in his Maiesties Privy-Chamber, at Hampton Court. Ianuary 14, 1603*, London, 1604 (264, L17); Edward Hoby, *A Letter to Mr. T[heoph.] H[iggons]*, London, 1609 (271, L103); Mathew Sutcliffe, *An Answere unto a certaine clumnious letter published by M. Job Throckmorton*, London, 1595 (276, L173);

Mathew Sutcliffe, *Subversion of Robert Parsons, his confused and worthlesse work, entituled a Treatise of Three Conversions of England*, London, 1606 (276, L174). For Donne and atomism, see Hirsch.

11. Donne, 1959, 260 (7.10) makes the following remarks in a sermon: "One Philosopher thinks he is dived to the bottome, when he sayes, he knows nothing but this, That he knows nothing; and yet another thinks, that he hath expressed more knowledge then he, saying That he knows not so much as that, That he knows nothing.

12. Philip Oldfield, personal communication, 29 November 2007.

13. While a complete provenance of the book is only conjectural, its presence among Donne's books at the Middle Temple library, which were probably acquired as a lot by its founder Robert Ashley after Donne's death in 1631, suggests that the book passed directly from Christ's College to Ben Jonson, to Donne, to Ashley, and then into the library upon its foundation in 1641. On Ashley's acquisition of Donne's books, see Keynes, 1973, 258.

14. See Keynes, 1973, 270–271, L102. Mark Bland, personal communication, 23 February 2008, suggests that the inscription might be in Jonson's hand, but is definitely not in Donne's.

15. Jonson also mentions Hill and Democritus disparagingly in Jonson, 1975, 86–92, lines 124–131 ("On the Famous Voyage"): "Here several ghosts did flit / About the shore, of farts, but late departed, / White, black, blue, green, and in more forms outsmarted, / That all those *atomi* ridiculous, / Whereof old Democrite, and Hill Nicolas, / One said, the other swore, the world consists. / These be the cause of those thick frequent mists / Arising from that place." See Donne, 1930, 55.

16. "Aevum sortiti sumus quo plane indoctis nihil turpius, plene doctis nihil rarius. Tam omnes in literis aliquid sciunt, tam nemo omnia. Media igitur plerumque itur via, et ad evitandam ignorantiae turpitudinem et legendi fastidium ars una est omnibus ut reliquas scire videri possint."

17. For Donne and courtliness, see Marotti, 1986, 34–37, 192–232; Wiggins, 1–20, 87–94. For the history of courtesy in the period generally, see Bryson. For courtesy and humanist education, see Hexter; Grafton and Jardine.

18. "Ioh. Harringtoni Hercules, sive de modo quo evacuabatur a faecibus Arca Noae."

19. Keynes, 1973, 260; Bald, 122–123.

20. Bacon, 1996, 81, quoting from the 1597 edition. The longer version of the essay in the 1625 edition substitutes "delight" for "pastimes": Bacon, 1985, 152.

21. For the descent of ideas of courtesy from Cicero, see Pincombe, 6–9, 15–36. For Castiglione as an interpreter of Ciceronian dialogue, see Richards, 43–64. For Cicero, Castiglione, and the performance of the self, see Posner, 9–16. See also Whigham, 88–93 ("The Fetish of Recreation"), 93–95 ("Sprezzatura").

22. For an overview of humanism in sixteenth-century England, see Elton; Boutcher, 1996; Woolfson.

23. On humanism and early modern schooling, see Bushnell; Grafton and Jardine, especially 122–157; Waquet, 7–40.

24. See Hexter; Crane, 116–135.

25. Boutcher, 2002, 248–251, provides a good account of this double movement.

26. Marotti, 1981, 210; Glimp, 30–36; Bourdieu, 11–96.

27. Crane, 118.

28. See Pincombe, 84–103; Wolfe, 125–160.

29. "Et quia per occupationes Aulae, qua degis, naturales, tibi vacare literis non licet (nam post somnum non nisi post decimam ex more excutiendum, post vestes diei, loco, affectibus proprias indutas, post faciem speculo compositam, et quo quis cachinno, superciliove excipiendus sit resolutionem, post epulas lususque, quota pars vitae literis, animoque excolendo relinquitur?)"

30. Walton, 61–62 ("The Life of Dr. John Donne"). Walton's portrayal of Donne's habits of work undermines the dichotomy between Jack Donne and Dr. John Donne that he constructs throughout the autobiography, reducing Jack Donne to an outward pretense supported by an underlying diligence. For a critique of Walton's account of Donne, see Flynn, 5–16.

31. Donne, 1635, 290.

32. Bacon, 2000, 13.

33. Bacon, 1985, 76–78.

34. For Donne as Egerton's secretary, see Knafla, 2003; Wiggins, 25–32.

35. Bald, 142–143.

36. See Jardine and Grafton; Jardine and Sherman; see also Stewart, 1997, 148–160.

37. Jardine and Grafton, 30.

38. Walton, 19 ("The Life of Dr. John Donne").

39. Knafla, 1983, 44, 51–52; Bald, 96–98.

40. For Donne and Egerton's circle, see Knafla, 2003, 62–63; Bald, 93–127; Flynn, 173–177. On Egerton and patronage more generally, see Knafla, 1983. For the lack of evidence concerning Donne's work as secretary, see Donne, 2005, 26, n. 15; for an evaluation of the circumstances surrounding Donne's marriage, see ibid., 10–32.

41. See Knafla, 2003, 48, 52–53; Knafla, 1983, esp. 104–115.

42. Walton, 17 ("The Life of Dr. John Donne").

43. Donne, 1968, 212–213, line 44. On the use of table books, see Stallybrass.

44. "Edw. Hobaei eructationes pomeridianae, sive de univocis, utpote de praerogativa Regum, et chimaeris, morbo Regio, et morbo Gallico, etc."; "Quid non? sive confutatio omnium errorum tam in Theologia quam in aliis scientiis, artibusque mechanicis, praeteritorum, praesentium et futurorum, omnium hominum mortuorum, superstitum, nascendorumque; una nocte post coenam confecta per D. Sutcliffe."

45. Hammer, 28–29, 34–35.

46. Ibid., 35; Jardine and Sherman, 107–112. Compare the secretariat of the Cecils in A. Smith, 1968.

47. For the *Catalogus* and Egerton's circle, see Knafla, 1983, 62–63; Bald, 113–114.

48. For contemporary accounts of both Donne and Wotton, see Walton ("The Life of Dr. John Donne," 1–88; "The Life of Sir Henry Wotton," 1–79). Ibid., 17, claims that Egerton appointed Donne secretary "supposing and intending it to be an Introduction to some more weighty Employment in the State; for which . . . he thought him very fit." For Wotton's biography, see L. P. Smith.

49. Rambuss, 38–48.

50. Donne, 1968, 18–22, lines 25–30.

51. Rambuss, 42. For secretaries and secrecy, see ibid., 5–9, 30–48; Goldberg, 231–278; Stewart, 1997, 161–168 (all of whom draw upon Angel Day's *English Secretorie* [1586]). See also Biow, 155–196.

52. "De navigabilitate aquarum supercoelestium et utrum ibi an apud nos navis in firmamento in judicio sit appulsura."

53. On Dee's *Navigations*, see Sherman, 152–171; Jardine and Sherman, 112.

54. See Bald, 103–114.

55. See Stewart, 2005.

56. "Encomium Doctoris Shaw Cappellini Richardi 3. per Doct. Barlow." On Barlow, see Knighton.

57. "Caput aeneum Fran. Baconi: de Roberto primo Angliae rege"; "Caepe advocatorum, sive ars plorani in Iudiciis, per eudem." The depiction of Bacon counseled by the "Brazen Head" also draws upon the link between his name and that of Roger Bacon, as depicted in Robert Greene's *Friar Bacon and Friar Bungay* (1594), as well as intimating a connection between the work of the two Bacons in natural philosophy.

58. Donne's accusation of Bacon's insincerity during the trial is confirmed by the paraphrase of Samuel 16:10 that Donne inscribed in his copy of Bacon's account of the trial (Keynes, 1973, 263, L3): *"Sinite eum maledicere, nos[ter] Dominus iusit & reg[it]"* ("Let him curse, our Lord has ordered and ruled it" ). See Bald, 113.

59. On mechanism in early modern Europe, see Wolfe, especially 88–124 on ambassadors as automata.

60. "Chimeram praedicari de Antichristo autore Sorbonista Anonymo"; "Manipulus quercuum, sive ars comprehendendi transcendentia. Autore Raim. Sebundo."

61. Chartier, 71–76.

62. On the Renaissance library and the organization of knowledge, see Chartier, 61–88; Grafton, 19–35; Blair, 1997, 153–79; Moss; Nelles. For the reconstruction of the contemporary library of Egerton's daughter-in-law and stepdaughter, see Hackel, 240–255, 260–281.

63. Moss, 44.

64. Donne, 1982, 7–10.

65. Ibid., 9.

66. See Sherman, 38–45.

67. Donne, 1977, 31, 60.

68. Walton, 15–16 ("The Life of Dr. John Donne").

69. Ibid., 2.

70. Ibid., 62–63.

71. Donne, 1977, 162–163.

72. "De nullibietate crepitus."

73. "Pythagoras Iudaeo-Christianus, Numerum 99 et 66 verso folio esse eundem, per super-seraphicum Io. Picum." The characterization is particularly ironic, given Walton's account of Donne's early gifts (Walton, 12–13, "The Life of Dr. John Donne" ): "in his tenth year was sent to the University of *Oxford*, having at

that time a good command both of the French and Latine Tongue. This and some other of his remarkable Abilities, made one give this censure of him, *That this age had brought forth another Picus Mirandula;* of whom Story sayes, *That he was rather born than made wise by study.*"

74. "Media igitur plerumuqe itur via, et ad evitandam ignorantiae turpitudienem et legendi fastidium ars una est omnibus ut reliquas scire videri possint. Inde Epitomis, paradoxis, et pruritibus exorbitantium ingeniorum delectantur. Hinc tam sunt in pretio, Lullius, Gemma, Sebundus, Empiricus, Trithemius, Agrippa, Erasmus, Ramus, et Haeretici."

75. Agrippa also appears as one of the additional authors in the Trinity Manuscript of the *Catalogus*, where he is mocked. See Donne, 1930, 53: *Agrippa, On the Vanity of the Sciences; and the Praise of the Ass by the same* (38: "Agrippa de vanitate Scientarum; et Encomium Asini per eundem"). The inclusion of the real *De Vanitate* in the *Catalogus* satirizes that work both by implying that it is as ridiculous as the imaginary works with which it is associated, and by joining it with the imaginary *Praise of the Ass*, a genre of paradoxical encomium with which is it usually associated: see Lehrich, 32–36. The implication is, of course, that Agrippa is the ass in question.

76. "Relictis Authoribus quos vocant Classicos Academicis et paedagogis terendis, enitere."

77. Donne, 1982, 9–10.

78. See Rosenberg; Blair, 2003.

79. "[N]ovos authores cum reverentia tui audiant illi, qui omnia anti visi sunt."

80. "Hunc ergo catalogum ad usum tuum exaravi, ut his paratis libris, in omni pene scientia, si non magis, saltem aliter doctus, quam caeteri, subito prosilias."

81. Donne, 1977, 106–107.

82. The circulation of literary material occurs, for example, in Sir Henry Goodyer's reuse of one of Donne's letters in a poem that commemorates Prince Charles's journey to Spain in 1623. See Considine.

83. Donne, 1977, 64.

## Works Cited

Bacon, Francis. *The Essayes or Counsels, Civill and Morall*. Ed. Michael Kiernan. Oxford, 1985.

———. *The Major Works*. Ed. Brian Vickers. Oxford, 1996.

———. *The Advancement of Learning*. Ed. Michael Kiernan. Oxford, 2000.

Bald, Robert Cecil. *John Donne: A Life*. London, 1970.

Biow, Douglas. *Doctors, Ambassadors, Secretaries: Humanism and Professions in Renaissance Italy*. Chicago, 2002.

Blair, Ann. *The Theatre of Nature: Jean Bodin and Renaissance Science*. Princeton, 1997.

———. "Reading Strategies for Coping with Information Overload ca. 1550-1700." *Journal of the History of Ideas* 64 (2003): 11–28.

Bourdieu, Pierre. *Distinction: A Social Critique of the Judgment of Taste*. Trans. Richard Nice. Cambridge, MA, 1984.

Boutcher, Warren. "Vernacular Humanism in the Sixteenth Century." In *The Cambridge Companion to Renaissance Humanism*, ed. Jill Kraye, 189-202. Cambridge, 1996.

————. "Humanism and Literature in Late Tudor England: Translation, the Continental Book and the Case of Montaigne's *Essais*." In *Reassessing Tudor Humanism* (2002), 243–268.

Bryson, Anna. *From Courtesy to Civility*. Oxford, 1998.

Bushnell, Rebecca W. *A Culture of Teaching: Early Modern Humanism in Theory and Practice*. Ithaca, 1996.

Chartier, Roger. *The Order of Books: Readers, Authors, and Libraries in Europe between the Fourteenth and Eighteenth Centuries*. Trans. Lydia G. Cochrane. Stanford, 1994.

Considine, John. "Goodere, Sir Henry (bap. 1571, d. 1627)." In *Oxford Dictionary of National Biography*. Oxford, 2004. Online edition: http://www.oxforddnb.com.myaccess. library.toronto.ca/view/article/1100, accessed 14 March 2008.

Crane, Mary Thomas. *Framing Authority: Sayings, Self, and Society in Sixteenth Century England*. Princeton, 1993.

Donne, John. *Poems*. London, 1635.

————. *Poems, by J. D. with Elegies on the Authors Death. To Which is added divers Copies under his own hand never before in print*. London, 1650.

————. *The Courtier's Library, or Catalogus Librorum Aulicorum Incomparabilium Et Non Vendibilium*. Trans. Percy Simpson. Ed. Evelyn Mary Simpson. London, 1930.

————. *The Sermons of John Donne*. Ed. George R. Potter and Evelyn M. Simpson. Berkeley, 1959.

————. *The Complete Poetry of John Donne*. Ed. John T. Shawcross. New York, 1968.

————. *Letters to Severall Persons of Honour*. Reprint, Delmar, NY, 1977.

————. *Biathanatos*. Ed. Micharil Rudick and M. Pabst Battin. New York, 1982.

————. *John Donne's Marriage Letters*. Ed. M. Thomas Hester, Robert Parker Sorlien, and Dennis Flynn. Washington, DC, 2005.

Dubinskaya, M. P. "A Book from John Donne's Library." *Kollektstii-knigiavtografy* 1 (1989): 95–102.

Elton, Geoffrey. "Humanism in England." In *The Impact of Humanism on Western Europe*, ed. Anthony Goodman and Angus MacKay, 259–278. London, 1990.

Flynn, Dennis. *John Donne and the Ancient Catholic Nobility*. Bloomington, 1995.

Glimp, David. *Increase and Multiply: Governing Cultural Reproduction in Early Modern England*. Minneapolis, 2003.

Goldberg, Jonathan. *Writing Matter: From the Hands of the English Renaissance*. Stanford, 1990.

Grafton, Anthony. *Commerce with the Classics*. Ann Arbor, 1997.

Grafton, Anthony, and Lisa Jardine. *From Humanism to the Humanities: Education and the Liberal Arts in Fifteenth- and Sixteenth-Century Europe*. London, 1986.

Hackel, Heidi Brayman. *Reading Material in Early Modern England: Print, Gender, and Literacy*. Cambridge, 2005.

Hammer, Paul E. J. "The Uses of Scholarship: The Secretariat of Robert Devereux, Second Earl of Essex, c. 1585–1601." *English Historical Review* 109 (1994): 26–51.

Hexter, Jack H. "The Education of the Aristocracy in the Renaissance." In Hexter, *Reappraisals in History*, 45–70. New York, 1961.

Hirsch, David A. "Donne's Atomies and Anatomies: Deconstructed Bodies and the Resurrection of Atomic Theory." *Studies in English Literature* 31 (1991): 69–94.

Hobbs, Mary. "Bibliographical Notes and Queries." *Book Collector* 29 (1980): 590–592.

Jardine, Lisa, and Anthony Grafton. "'Studied for Action': How Gabriel Harvey Read His Livy." *Past and Present* 129 (1990): 20–78.

Jardine, Lisa, and William Sherman. "Pragmatic Readers: Knowledge Transactions and Scholarly Services in Late Elizabethan England." In *Religion, Culture, and Society in Early Modern Britain: Essays in Honour of Patrick Collinson*, ed. Anthony Fletcher and Peter Roberts, 102–124. Cambridge, 1994.

Jonson, Ben. *Complete Poems*. Ed. George Parfitt. London, 1975.

Keynes, Geoffrey. *A Bibliography of Dr. John Donne*. 4th ed., Oxford, 1973.

———. "More Books from the Library of John Donne." *Book Collector* 26 (1977): 29–35.

———. "Bibliographical Notes and Queries." *Book Collector* 27 (1978): 570–572.

Knafla, Louis A. "The 'Country' Chancellor: The Patronage of Sir Thomas Egerton, Baron Ellesmere." In *Patronage in Late Renaissance England,* eds. French R. Fogle and Louis A. Knafla, 31–115. Los Angeles, 1983.

———. "Mr. Secretary Donne: The Years with Sir Thomas Egerton." In *John Donne's Professional Lives,* ed. David Colclough, 37–72. Cambridge, 2003.

Knighton, Charles S. "Barlow, William (d. 1613)." In *Oxford Dictionary of National Biography*. Oxford, 2004. Online edition: http://www.oxforddnb.com.myaccess.library.utoronto.ca/view/article/1443, accessed 3 March 2008.

Lehrich, Christopher I. *The Language of Demons and Angels: Cornelius Agrippa's Occult Philosophy*. Leiden, 2003.

Marotti, Arthur F. "John Donne and the Rewards of Patronage." In *Patronage in the Renaissance,* ed. Guy Fitch Lytle and Stephen Orgel, 207–234. Princeton, 1981.

———. *John Donne, Coterie Poet*. Madison, 1986.

Moss, Ann. "Locating Knowledge." In *Cognition and the Book: Typologies of Formal Organization of Knowledge in the Printed Book of the Early Modern Period,* ed. Karl A. E. Enenkel and Wolfgang Neuber, 35–49. Leiden, 2005.

Nelles, Paul. "The Library as an Instrument of Discovery: Gabriel Naudé and the Uses of History." In *History and the Disciplines: The Reclassification of Knowledge in Early Modern Europe,* ed. Donald R. Kelly, 41–57. Rochester, 1997.

Ong, Walter J. Ramus, *Method, and the Decay of Dialogue: From the Art of Discourse to the Art of Reason*. 1958. Reprint, Chicago, 2004.

Pearson, David. "An Unrecorded Book from the Library of John Donne." *Book Collector* 35 (1986): 246.

Pincombe, Mike. *Elizabethan Humanism: Literature and Learning in the Later Sixteenth Century*. Harlow, UK, 2001.

Posner, David Matthew. *The Performance of Nobility in Early Modern European Literature*. Cambridge, 1999.

Prescott, Anne Lake. *Imagining Rabelais in Renaissance England*. New Haven, 1998.

Puttenham, George. *The Arte of English Poesie*. 1589. Reprint, Menston, 1968.

Rambuss, Richard. *Spenser's Secret Career*. Cambridge, 1993.

*Reassessing Tudor Humanism*. Ed. Jonathan Woolfson. Basingstoke, 2002.

Richards, Jennifer. *Rhetoric and Courtliness in Early Modern Literature*. Cambridge, 2003.

Rosenberg, Daniel. "Early Modern Information Overload: Introduction." *Journal of the History of Ideas* 64 (2003): 1–9.

Scott-Warren, Jason. *Sir John Harington and the Book as Gift*. Oxford, 2001.

Serrai, Alfredo. *Conrad Gesner*. Rome, 1990.

Sherman, William. *John Dee: The Politics of Reading and Writing in the English Renaissance*. Amherst, 1995.

Simpson, Evelyn M. *A Study of the Prose Works of John Donne*. 2nd ed., Oxford, 1948.

Smith, Alan G. R. "The Secretariats of the Cecils, circa 1580–1612." *English Historical Review* 83 (1968): 481–504.

Smith, Logan Pearsall. *The Life and Letters of Sir Henry Wotton.* 2 vols. Oxford, 1907.

Stallybrass, Peter, Roger Chartier, J. Franklin Mowrey, and Heather Wolfe. "Hamlet's Tables and the Technologies of Writing in Renaissance England." *Shakespeare Quarterly* 55 (2004): 379–419.

Stewart, Alan. *Close Readers: Humanism and Sodomy in Early Modern England.* Princeton, 1997.

———. "Instigating Treason: The Life and Death of Henry Cuffe, Secretary." In *Literature, Politics and Law in Renaissance England,* eds. Erica Sheen and Lorna Hutson, 50–71. Basingstoke, 2005.

Walton, Isaak. *The Lives of Dr. John Donne, Sir Henry Wotton, Mr. Richard Hooker, Mr. George Herbert.* 1670. Reprint, Menston, 1969.

Waquet, Françoise. *Latin or the Empire of a Sign: From the Sixteenth to the Twentieth Centuries.* Trans. John Howe. London, 2001.

Weil, Judith. *Service and Dependency in Shakespeare's Plays.* Cambridge, 2005.

Whigham, Frank. *Ambition and Privilege: The Social Tropes of Elizabethan Courtesy Theory.* Berkeley, 1984.

Wiggins, Peter DeSa. *Donne, Castiglione, and the Poetry of Courtliness.* Bloomington, 2000.

Wolfe, Jessica. *Humanism, Machinery, and Renaissance Literature.* Cambridge, 2004.

Woodhuysen, Henry R. "Two More Books from the Library of John Donne." *Book Collector* 32 (1983): 349.

Woolfson, Jonathan. "Introduction." In *Reassessing Tudor Humanism* (2002), 1–21.

## ACKNOWLEDGEMENT

Versions of this essay were presented at the Centre for Reformation and Renaissance Studies at the University of Toronto, 7 October 2005, and at the Annual Meeting of The Renaissance Society of America in Miami, 22–24 March 2007. I wish to thank Mark Bland, David Galbraith, Elizabeth Harvey, Katie Larson, Arthur Marotti, Philip Oldfield, Jess Paehlke, Anne Lake Prescott, Renae Satterley, Flora Ward, and the anonymous reader for Renaissance Quarterly for their commentary, criticism, and aid.

## APPENDIX: THE TEXT OF THE COURTIER'S LIBRARY*

Aevum sortiti sumus quo plane indoctis nihil turpius, plene doctis nihil rarius. Tam omnes in literis aliquid sciunt, tam nemo omnia. Media igitur plerumque itur via, et ad evitandam ignorantiae turpitudinem et legendi fastidium ars una est omnibus ut reliquas scire videri possint. Inde Epitomis, paradoxis, et pruritibus exorbitantium ingeniorum delectantur. Hinc tam sunt in pretio, Lullius, Gemma, Sebundus, Empiricus, Trithemius, Agrippa, Erasmus, Ramus, et Haeretici. Satis enim sibi videntur scire ignava ingenia si aliorum scientiam imperfectam esse probabiliter possint demonstrare. Sed nimis invidiae subest, et se prodit aerea haec, procax et tuberosa scientia. Tibi generosior, celerior, candidior, et minus speculatoribus literarum obnoxia via subeunda est. Et quia per occupationes Aulae, qua degis, naturales, tibi vacare literis non licet (nam post somnum non nisi post decimam ex more excutiendum, post vestes diei, loco, affectibus proprias indutas, post faciem speculo compositam, et quo quis cachinno, superciliove excipiendus sit resolutionem, post epulas lususque, quota pars vitae literis, animoque excolendo relinquitur?) et tamen doctus videri non dedignaris, ut aliquando habeas quo eleganter et apposite canes Regios conservos tuos possis laudare, et quamvis scire quae alii sciunt non poteris, saltem scire valeas quae illi nesciunt; hac ex consilio meo via progredieris.

Relictis authoribus quos vocant Classicos Academicis et paedagogis terendis, enitere per omnes quibus ignorantiam fateri secure poteris, libros aliis inventu difficiles exquirere. Nec in colloquiis quid ex autoribus vulgo notis afferas, sed ex istis ut ita quae dicis aut tua videri possint, si nomina taceas, aut si minus digna sint, et authoritate egeant, novos authores cum reverentia tui audiant illi, qui omnia scire sibi ante visi sunt. Hunc ergo catalogum ad usum tuum exaravi, ut his paratis libris, in omni pene scientia, si non magis, saltem aliter doctus quam caeteri, subito prosilias.

We are cast by chance into an age in which nothing is worse than to be openly ignorant, nothing more rare than to be fully learned. Just as everyone knows something of letters, no one knows everything. The middle, and therefore common, way to proceed in order to avoid both the shame of ignorance and the bother of reading, is to use one art in all things in order to seem to know all the rest. Thus, others delight in epitomes, paradoxes, and the stings of extravagant wits, and hence place a high value upon Ramon Lull, Gemma Frisius, Raimond Sebond, Sextus Empiricus, the Abbot Trithemius, Henry Cornelius Aggrippa, Erasmus, Peter Ramus, and the heretical writers. It is enough for lazy wits to have the appearance of knowing, if they are able to plausibly show that others' knowledge is flawed. But envy underlies this attitude, and produces as a result this ungrounded, frivolous, and overblown knowledge. You must climb a nobler, swifter, and clearer path, and one less open to those who keep an eye on literature. And because the natural occupations of court, in which you spend your time, do not allow you the leisure for literature, because, after sleep, which by custom must not be shaken off until after ten in the morning; after you have dressed in the clothes appropriate to the day, place, and passions; after having composed your face in the mirror, and worked out whom to receive with a jeer or with a frown; after banquets and amusements—how much time is left over in your life for reading and the improvement of your mind? Yet you do not disdain to appear learned, that you sometimes might praise elegantly and suitably your companions, the royal hounds, and although you are not able to know those things that others know, at least you manage to know what they do not know; you will advance yourself along this path, by means of my advice.

Having abandoned those authors that they call the Classics to academics and schoolmasters to wear out, instead strive—with the help of those to whom you are safely able to admit ignorance—to seek out books difficult for others to locate. Nor should you produce anything in conversations from generally known authorities. Instead cite from these other authorities, such that your words either seem to be your own, if you leave the names unmentioned, or, if what you say is not dignified and is in need of authority, your audience—who before seemed to know everything—may, with reverence for you, hear about new authors. Therefore, I note down this list for your use, that having prepared these books, you might suddenly spring forth, on almost all topics, if not more learned than others, at least as learned in a different way.

*I follow the original published text in Donne, 1650, 371–375, with the emendations made by Evelyn Simpson from her collation of that text with the Trinity Manuscript: see "Textual Notes" in Donne, 1930, 79–93. For the identification of historical persons in the text, see "Explanatory Notes" in ibid., 54–78.

## CATALOGUS LIBRORUM

1. Nicolai Hill Angli, de sexu et Hermaphroditate dignoscenda in Atomis; Idem de eorum Anatomia, et obstetricatione in partubus humatis, cui annectitur ars conficiendorum ignis vasorum, et instrumentorum ad haec omnia propriorum, per conterraneum, et synchronon suum Magistrum Plat.

2. Aemulus Moysis. Ars conservandi vestimenta ultra quadraginta annos, autore Topcliffo Anglo. postillata per Iac. Stonehouse anglice, qui eodem idiomate edidit tractatum, *To keep clothes near the fashion.*

3. Ars exscribendi omnia ea quae vere ad idem dicuntur in Joanne Foxe in ambitu denarii, autore P. Bales.

4. Chimaeram praedicari de Antichristo autore Sorbonista Anonymo.

5. Galatinus, Judaeos ubiquitarios esse, quia nusquam sunt.

6. Librum Tobiae esse canonicum. Ubi ex Rabbinis et secretioribus Theologis numerantur pili caudae eius canis, ex quorum varia retortione, et invicem conjunctione conficiuntur literae, ex quibus mirifica verba consistunt. Autore Francisco Georgio Veneto.

7. Pax in Hierusalem, sive conciliatio flagrantissimi dissidii inter Rabbi Simeon Kimchi, et Onkelos, utrum caro humana ex carne suilla comesta (quod avertat deus) concreta in resurrectione removebitur, annihilabitur, aut purificabitur, per illuminatissimum Doctorem Reuchlinum.

8. Pythagoras Iudaeo-Christianus, Numerum 99 et 66 verso folio esse eundem, per superseraphicum Io. Picum.

9. Quidlibet ex quolibet; *Or the art of decyphering and finding some treason in any intercepted letter,* by Philips.

10. Ioh. Harringtoni Hercules, sive de modo quo evacuabatur a faecibus Arca Noae.

11. Crede quod habes et habes. Criterium Antiquitatum; lib. magnus de minimis a Walt. Copo dictatus, et ab uxore exscriptus, et ab amanuensi suo Iohan. Pory latinitate donatus.

12. Subsalvator; in quo illuminatus, sed parum illuminans, Hugo Broughton incredibiliter docet linguam Hebraicam esse de essentia salutis, et sua praecepta esse de essentia linguae.

13. M. Lutherus de abbreviatione orationis Dominicae.

14. Manipulus quercuum, sive ars comprehendendi transcendentia. Autore Raim. Sebundo.

15. Oceanus Aulicus, sive Pyramis, sive Colossus, sive Abyssus ingeniorum: ubi per 60000 literas a Milordis omnium nationum ad evitandam ostentationem vulgaribus semper linguis datas et acceptas, traditur quicquid tradi potest de Dentiscalpiis et unguium reduviis. Collectae sunt et in unum corpus reductae singulisque autoribus dedicatae per Io. Florio Italo-Anglum. Eorum quae in hoc

libro continentur capita habentur primis 70 paginis; Diplomata Regum cum eorum titulis et approbationes inquisitorum 107 sequentibus, poemata in laudem Autoris 97 libris proximis.

16. Iustitia Angliae. Vacationes Io. Davis de Arte Anagrammatum verisimiliter conficiendorum, et sententiolis annulis inscribendis.

17. Tractatuli aliquot adjectitii libris Pancirolli; libro de rebus perditis, additur de virtute, et de libertate populi; quod a Capellano quodam Io. Cadi inchoatum a Buchanano perfectum est, libro de rebus inventis, additur de morbo multinomino per Tho. Thorney Anglice, et post latine per Tho. Campianum, et de uxoratione post vota per Carolostadium.

18. Bonaventura de particula Non a decalogo adimenda, et Symbolo Apostolorum adiicienda.

19. De militibus Apocryphis per Edw. Prinne lib. unus, per Edw. Chute paulo amplior factus.

20. De navigabilitate aquarum supercoelestium, et utrum ibi an apud nos navis in firmamento in judicio sit appulsura, Io. Dee Autore.

21. Manuale justiciariorum, continens plurimas confessiones veneficarum Manwoodo judici exhibitas, et ab illo abstergendis postea natibus, et evacuationibus adhibitas; nunc a servulis suis redemptae, et in usum suum collectae sunt a Io. Helo.

22. Aequilibrium. Tom. 2. Sive ars acquiescendi in Controversiis. Primus modus dicitur simplex, quia data controversia (utpote estne transubstantiatio?) scribitur sic, et non, variis sed aequalibus chartulis, et trutinae imponuntur, et ponderosiori adhaerendum. Alius modus est compositus, quia data thesi ex una parte, datur etiam altera ex altera: ut Petrus sedet Romae, et Ioannes sedet Romae, et etiam si aequalibus literis scribuntur, etc. ponderosiori adhaerendum: autore Erasmo Roterod.

23. Cardanus de nullibietate crepitus.

24. Edw. Hobaei eructationes pomeridianae, sive de univocis, utpote de praerogativa Regum, et chimaeris, morbo Regio, et morbo Gallico etc.

25. Ars Spiritualis inescandi mulieres, sive conciones subcingulares Egertoni.

26. De Pessario animato, et omni morbo foeminis dando, per Magistrum Butler Cantabr.

27. Caput aeneum Fran. Baconi: de Roberto primo Angliae rege.

28. Caepe advocatorum, sive ars plorandi in Iudiciis, per eundem. Sesqui-barbarus, sive de medietate linguae.

29. De Gurgite diametrali a Polo ad Polum, per centrum navigabili sine pyxide per Andr. Thevet.

30. Quintessentia inferni; sive camera privata infernalis, ubi tractatur de loco quinto ab Homero, Virgilio, Dante, caeterisque papisticis praetermisso, ubi Reges praeter damni poenas, et sensus, recordatione praeteritorum cruciantur.

31. Encomium Doctoris Shaw Capellani Richardi 3. per Doct. Barlow.

32. Quid non? sive confutatio omnium errorum tam in Theologia quam in aliis scientiis, artibusque mechanicis, praeteritorum, praesentium et futurorum, omnium hominum mortuorum, superstitum, nascendorumque; una nocte post coenam confecta per D. Sutcliffe.

33. De Episcopabilitate Puritani. Dr. Robinson.

34. Tarltonus de privilegiis Parliamenti.

## The List of Books

1. Nicolas Hill, On Distinguishing the Sex and Hermaphroditism of Atoms; The same, On their Anatomy, and How to Aid in their Births when they are buried. To which is added The Art of Making Fire-Pots, and all the equipment necessary for that purpose, by his countryman and contemporary Master Plat.

2. The Imitator of Moses. The Art of Preserving Clothes beyond Forty years by the English Author Topcliffe, with a commentary in English by Jacob Stonehouse, who has put forth a treatise entitled *To keep clothes near the fashion,* in the same language.

3. The art of writing out, within the circumference of a penny, all true things in John Foxe that were related to him, written by Peter Bales.

4. That the Chimera is a Sign of the Antichrist, by an anonymous member of the Sorbonne.

5. Galatinus: That Jews are Ubiquitaries, because they belong nowhere.

6. That the book of Tobit is canonical. In which, drawing upon the Rabbis and other more obscure Theologians, the hairs on the tail of the dog are counted and from their differing turns and combinations letters are put together to create amazing words. By Francis George, the Venetian.

7. Peace in Jerusalem, or The Settlement of the most passionate disagreement between Rabbi Simeon Kimchi and Onkelos, On whether a human body composed (may God forbid) from the consumption of pig flesh will be put away, annihilated, or purified on the Ressurection, by the most enlighted Doctor Reuchlin.

8. The Judeo-Christian Pythagorus, in which 99 and 66 are shown to be the same number if the page is turned upside down, by the more than angelic Giovanni Pico Della Mirandola.

9. What you please out of what you please; *Or the art of decyphering and finding some treason in any intercepted letter,* by Philips.

10. The Hercules of John Harington, or Concerning the method of emptying the dung from Noah's Ark.

11. Believe you have something and you have it. A rule for antiquities: a great book on tiny things, dictated by Walter Cope, written down by his wife, and translated into Latin by his amanuensis John Pory.

12. The sub-savior: in which the enlightened, but barely enlightening, Hugh Broughton surprisingly teaches that the Hebrew language is the secret of health, and that his teachings are the secret of the language.

13. Martin Luther, On shortening the Lord's Prayer.

14. A Handful of Oak Trees, or The Art of Getting Ahold of Transcendentals. Written by Raimond Sebond.

15. The Princely Ocean, or The Pyramid, or The Colossus, or The Abyss of Wits: where by means of 60,000 letters to the Nobles of all nations (always sent and received in the common tongues, in order to avoid ostentation) are related everything that is able to be related concerning toothpicks and hangnails. They have been brought together and reduced into a single collection, dedicated to each individual patron by John Florio, the Italo-Englishman. On the first seventy pages are the headings of those things that this book contains; the Diplomas of the Kings with their titles and the approval of the inquisitors on the next 107; [and] poems in praise of the author in the next ninety-seven books.

16. The Justice of England. The holiday work of Sir John Davies, On the Making of Approximate Anagrams, and of Writing Little Mottoes in Rings.

17. Several little accounts added to the books of Panirolli; to the book on lost things is added On the virtue and liberty of the people; begun by the Chaplain to John Cade and perfected by Buchanan. To the book of things discovered, is added the Many-Named Disease in English by Thomas Thorney and afterwards in Latin by Thomas Campion, and On a desire for a wife after vows, by Carlstadt.

18. Bonaventura, On Removing the Word Not from the Ten Commandments, and adding it to the Apostles' Creed.

19. One Book On False Knights, by Edward Prinne, Slightly Enlarged by Edward Chute.

20. On the Navigability of the Waters above the heavens, and whether Ships in the Firmament will land there or on our shores on the Day of Judgment, by John Dee.

21. The Judges' Handbook, containing the many confessions of poisoners given to Justice Manwood, and used by him afterwards in wiping his buttocks, and in examining his evacuations; now recovered from his servants, and gathered together for his own use, by John Hele.

22. On Equilibrium, Two Volumes. Or The Art of Settling on a Position in Controversy. The First method is called simple, because given a controversy (such as, Is there such a thing as transubstantiation?) yes and no are written on different but equal pieces of paper, and placed on a pair of scales, and the heavier must be stuck to. The other method is compound, because given a proposition from one side, another is given from the other: such as Peter sits in Rome, and John sits in Rome, and even if they are written in letters of equal size, and so on, the heavier must be chosen: by Erasmus of Rotterdam.

23. Cardano, On the nothingness of a fart.

24. The Afternoon Belchings of Edward Hoby, or On Univocals, namely, On the Right of Kings, and On Chimeras, such as the King's Evil, the French Disease, and so on.

25. The Spiritual Art of Enticing Women, or Egerton's Sermons Beneath Undergarments.

26. On the Living Pessary, and the Means of Producing every Female Disease, by Master Butler of Cambridge.

27. The Brazen Head of Francis Bacon: On Robert I, King of England.

28. The Lawyers' Onion, or the Art of Weeping during trials, by the same. The More-than-Half Uncivilized, or On the Mid-Point of the Tongue.

29. On the Diametrical Current through the Center from Pole to Pole, Navigable without a Compass, by André Thevet.

30. The Quintessence of Hell; or the Private Chamber of the Infernal Regions, in which is discussed the fifth area overlooked by Homer, Virgil, Dante, and other papist writers, where Kings and their senses, in addition to the pain of damnation, are tortured by the recollection of the events of the past.

31. An Encomium of Doctor Shaw, Chaplain of Richard III, by Doctor Barlow.

32. What not? or a confutation of all errors in Theology as well as in the other sciences, and the mechanical arts, by all men, dead, living, and to be born, put together one night after supper, by Doctor Sutcliffe.

33. On the Suitability for a Bishopric of a Puritan, by Doctor Robinson.
34. Tarlton, On the Privileges of Parliament.

GARY KUCHAR

# Ecstatic Donne: Conscience, Sin, and
# Surprise in the Sermons and the Mitcham Letters

*Be you and I behind an arras then. Mark the encounter.*
                                            —Polonius, *Hamlet*

When John Donne describes the effects of a well-delivered sermon in a 1620 address at Lincoln's Inn, he exploits the way in which conscience is generally thought, in Reformation theology, to be an agency rather than an act. The rhetorical power of his description of a good sermon relies, that is, on the Protestant view that conscience is a voice of judgment that speaks to us, rather than a rational process that is conducted by us—as in most forms of scholastic thought.[1] According to Donne, "It is not the depth, nor the wit, nor the eloquence of the Preacher that pierces us, but his neareness; that hee speaks to my conscience, as though he had been behinde the hangings when I sinned, and as though he had read the book of the day of Judgement already" (*Sermons*, 3.5.142).[2] The rhetorical force and spiritual meaningfulness of Donne's nearness effect both rest on the Protestant view that conscience is as an agency of judgment within the soul that produces knowledge of one's actions, rather than being a name for such knowledge itself. Exploiting this Reformed view of conscience as a distinct power *(virtus)* of the soul, Donne says, in effect, that the preacher should speak in a voice that is intimate enough with me to know my most disavowed secrets, but other enough from me to shock me by revealing them: the preacher, that is,

*Criticism*, Volume 50, Number 4 (Fall 2008): pp. 631–654. Copyright © Wayne State University Press.

should pierce my conscience by speaking as though he were my conscience. For Donne, the power of fascination a preacher possesses is directly proportional to his ability to get auditors to feel as well as understand the shock of surprise attendant upon an encounter with one's conscience as God's witness within the soul.

By identifying how Donne shows rather than merely tells us about the nearness effect in his sermons and letters, we will see how he conveys conscience as an ecstatic phenomenon that is crucial to both Jacobean pulpit oratory and the early modern experience of Protestant faith more generally. In this context, *ecstatic* should not be understood as implying anything mystical in the sense we use the term in relation to contemplative or nonconformist traditions; rather, it refers to the way that conscience can feel other to me in the sense that it can speak to me even if I don't want it to, even if its speaking is not willed by me.[3] In the Reformation context of sin and conscience informing Donne's sermons, then, *ecstatic experiences* refer to phenomena that happen to me but feel as though they are somehow not proper to me as such. Because the ecstatic experience of hearing one's conscience against one's own intention is crucial to how Donne understands the role of a preacher and the experience of faith per se, it informs both the rhetorical structure and thematic itinerary of many individual sermons, as well as some of Donne's most compelling private letters.

### The Sermons

The scenario of the lurking preacher from the 1620 Lincoln's Inn address is a case in point. Donne's description of how a good sermon should affect us is an unusually evocative articulation of the general idea that preachers should "bind," "touch," "pierce," or "move" the conscience.[4] To express the sensation of having one's conscience bound, Donne presents the preacher's gaze both spatially, through the image of the witness behind the hangings, and temporally, through the perception that the preacher is privy to the Book of Judgment. By doing so, Donne expresses his hope that auditors will experience his voice according to three temporalities: one emanating from the disavowed moment of transgression in the past; one experienced in the shocking immediacy of the present—in the time of the sermon itself; and one looking back from the day of judgment in the eschatological future. In this way, the voice of the preacher is designed to produce the sort of guilt Martin Luther describes, in Michael Baylor's words, as "a claustrophobic kind of 'narrowness' that produces an urgent desire to escape."[5]

Yet, even as we are circumscribed temporally by the preacher's voice, we are also bound spatially through the image of the preacher hiding behind the arras: he sees us *now* as he saw us *then* and as we *shall* be seen. Through these images of circumscription, Donne conveys what it feels like to be pierced by conscience. He expresses what it is like to feel oneself being seen by the strange nearness of a personally omnivoyant conscience. According to Donne's description, we should feel the preacher gazing at us in the private space of sin, just as our conscience gazes at us within the innermost recesses of our soul. This parallel between preacher and conscience rests, in part, on Romans 2:15–16, which asserts that the conscience gives the appearance of having access to the Book of Judgment. By granting this eschatological insight to the preacher, Donne speaks to our conscience by speaking as though he were our conscience.[6]

In his 1596 work *Discourse of Conscience,* William Perkins theorizes the ecstatic nature of conscience that Donne's scenario of the lurking preacher dramatizes. Drawing extensively on Calvin's analysis of conscience in the *Institutes,*[7] Perkins contends that

> conscience is of a divine nature, and is a thing placed of God in the middest betweene him and man, as an arbitratour to give sentence & to pronounce either with man or against man unto God. For otherwhiles, it consents and speakes with God against the man in whom it is placed: otherwhiles againe it consents with him and speakes for him before the mind, and knowes what the mind thinks, so as if a man would goe about to hide his sinfull thoughts from God, his conscience as it were Lord *[sic].*

Like Perkins's conscience, Donne's lurking preacher "knows what the mind thinks." Donne's scenario of the preacher and auditor thus dramatizes how the mind and conscience constitute, as Perkins proceeds to explain in light of Calvin's analysis, two related but discrete entities:

> [H]ence comes one reason of the name of conscience. *Scire,* to know, is of one man alone by himself: and *conscire* is, when two at the least knowe some one secret thing; either of them knowing it togither with the other. Therefore the name . . . *conscientia,* Conscience, is that thing that combines two togither, and makes them partners in the knowledge of one and the same secret.[8]

For Perkins, the conscience is not part of man *qua* man. Rather, it is a faculty within us, which is not, strictly speaking, part of us, that knows, keeps, and judges our secrets.

By adopting this view, Perkins follows Calvin in asserting that, in Randall Zachman's formulation, "The knowing subject of *scientia* is the human being [while] the knowing subject of *conscientia* is God the judge."[9] Perkins thus reiterates Calvin's view of conscience over and against scholastic positions on the topic, as he indicates in the following:

> Againe I say that conscience . . . is not a bare knowledge or judgement of the understanding (as men comonly write) but a naturall power, facultie, or created qualitie from whence knowledge and judgement proceede as effects. This the Scriptures confirme, in that they ascribe sundrie workes and actions to conscience, as accusing, excusing, comforting, terrifying: which actions could not thence proceede, if conscience were no more but an action or acte of the minde. (5)

Although Perkins is less rigorous than Calvin in separating the conscience from the faculty of understanding, he shares Calvin's view, *pace* certain strains of scholasticism, that conscience is entirely distinct from the will *(voluntas)*.[10] This Reformed view results in formulations such as that by Jeremiah Dyke, who describes conscience "as Gods spy, and man's superior and overseer."[11] Because knowledge produced by the conscience is separate from the will, such knowledge cannot be wholly suppressed. As a result of being subject to the knowledge of the conscience, the Christian soul, according to Calvin, is repeatedly placed before the judgment of God, even when the will would desire otherwise.[12] This aspect of conscience is crucial to Donne's representation of the life of faith in the sermons. Indeed, although Donne arguably attributes greater authority to reason in the human psyche than does either Perkins or Calvin, he shares their Protestant view that the conscience is a divine witness within and of the soul.[13] Thus, by speaking to our conscience as though he were spying on us while we sinned, Donne's ideal preacher speaks as though he were our Pauline-Reformed conscience.

Insofar as this Reformed notion of conscience emphasizes its daimonic otherness to us as volitional agents, it has much greater potential to be experienced as alarmingly alien than medieval versions of conscience, especially those that place conscience within the faculty of the will.[14] Because Aquinas and other writers in both the *Via Antiqua* and the *Via Moderna* view conscience as an act of mind rather than an agency of judgment, they do not generally represent conscience as alien in the sense Luther, Calvin, and their followers tend to.[15] The perturbing qualities inherent in Reformed notions of conscience are powerfully evinced when Perkins addresses the question of "[h]ow long conscience beares witnes" of oneself:

> [I]t doth it continually; not for a minute, or a day, or a moneth, or a yeare, but for ever; when a man dies, conscience dieth not:

when the body is rotten in the grave, conscience liveth & is safe & sound: and when we shall rise againe, conscience shall come with us to the barre of Goddes judgement, either to accuse or excuse us before God, Rom. 2.15.16. *Their conscience bearing witnesse at the day when God shall judge the secrets of men.* (8)

The idea that there is an immanent and immortal power witnessing and testifying to one's actions is cause, Perkins argues, for at least five passions: shame, sorrow, feare, desperation, and perturbation (39). Donne seeks to provoke such perturbations of conscience when he asserts that the preacher's voice has access to your sins in a way that is analogous to God's witness in the soul. Indeed, the dramatic force of Donne's sermons often rests on his ability to both enact and inspire the kind of shock associated with the daimonic nearness of a conscience that is within us but is other to us as willful beings.

The specific modality of surprise attendant upon the nearness effect is best captured by the verb "deprehend," which Donne uses in several places to express the process of discovering something previously unknown or forgotten. A much richer word than "surprise," *deprehend* can mean "to seize, capture, arrest or apprehend" (*Oxford English Dictionary [OED]*, 1); "to catch or detect (a person) in the commission of some evil or secret deed; to take by surprise" (*OED*, 2); "to convict or prove guilty" (*OED*, 2b); or "to detect or discover (anything concealed or liable to escape notice)" (*OED*, 3).[16] Donne uses this term in a sermon that seems directed at an auditor who "longeth for the end of the Sermon, or the end of that point in the Sermon, which is a thorne to his conscience" in order to express the experience of spiritual awakening (4.8.212). Even a congregant who may appear to be listening, or a soul who may appear to be in search of God's light, sometimes is not and so "often may you surprise and deprehend a man, whom you thinke directly to look upon such an object, yet if you aske him the quality or colour of it, he will tell you, he saw it not?" (4.8.212). As this passage suggests, Donne generally uses deprehend to express distinctly spiritual forms of apprehension. As a result, he employs the term as a way of articulating acts of knowing that involve an element of surprise or, more interestingly, those that do not happen consciously. In a sermon on Romans 13:7, for example, Donne discusses the importance of remaining steadfast in matters of conscience, teaching that "God heares the very first motions of a mans heart, which, that man, till he proceed to a farther consideration, doth not heare, not feele, not deprehend in himselfe" (4.12.310). Most importantly, then, deprehension entails a mode of *knowing-with*, of rediscovering oneself by means of an encounter with another person, text, or, as in the case of the last quotation, the motions of one's heart as something that is not under the control of one's will and understanding and that is thus, from a phenomenological standpoint, other to oneself.

The shock attendant upon the experience of being deprehended is expressed in a sermon on Psalm 6.1, in which Donne explores some of the ways God uses the interrogative mode. Donne describes the process of being "deprehended" when he explains how God's questions work by confounding us, eliciting surprise, wonder, and renewed self-analysis: "If God surprize a Conscience with a sudden question, if God deprehend a man in the Act of his sin, and while he accomplishes and consummates that sin, say to his soul, Why dost thou this, upon which mine anger hangs? there God speaks to that sinner, but he confounds him with the question" (5.16.334). A sermon is successful when auditors are confounded by a preacher's words in the same way they are confounded by the voice of their own conscience. In the act of being deprehended, one is led to know-with one's conscience, which, in Perkins' formulations, is like a "Notarie, or a Register that hath alwaies the penne in his hand, to note & record whatsoever is said or done" (8).

From a phenomenological standpoint, the experience of being deprehended by one's conscience is uncanny in the sense David Krell defines the term. In an essay that draws together Heidegger's and Freud's theorizing on the topic, Krell defines the *uncanny* as a species of terror that arises in relation to "something long familiar, something experienced and known of old in a nonintellectual way, something both lost and found in the mists of time."[17] For Krell, the uncanny is best understood structurally, as an encounter with something that had been kept secret but reemerges unexpectedly. The process of this return, moreover, induces a crisis of propriety; it generates a newfound sense that the relation between what is me and what is not-me is neither simple nor under my control.[18]

If Perkins expresses the uncanny qualities of conscience by figuring it variously as a notary, a witness, and a judge, Donne figures such qualities by describing conscience as oracular. In a sermon on Genesis 32:10, Donne asserts, *pace* Plutarch, that the classical oracles did not cease but were internalized into Christian souls:

> God is not departed from thee; thou knowest by thy self, it is a vain complaint that *Plutarch* makes, *defectu oraculorum*, that oracles are ceased; there is no defect of oracles in thine own bosome . . . Here is no *defectus Oraculorum* no ceasing of Oracles . . . Every mans Diligence, and discretion is a God to himselfe . . . bring thine Actions . . . to the debatement of thy conscience rectified, and [thou] still shalt hear, *Jubentem Dominum* or *Dominum Revocantem*, God will bid thee stop, or God will bid Thee go forwards in that way. (1.7.282)

Christians have access to the divine, Donne claims, simply by listening to the oracular voice of their own guilt. The externality of classical oracles is thus internalized through the strangely interior-exterior modality of the Protestant conscience as an inward voice that is not directly one's own. So when Donne says that the preacher's voice should speak to our conscience as though he were present at the moment we sinned, he is saying, in effect, that it should pierce our soul with the force of an oracle who knows our secrets with greater clarity than we have wanted to know them ourselves. By figuring the preacher as one who knows and judges our secrets, Donne positions himself in the role of conscience as such. This externalization of conscience is similar to how conscience is actually experienced by the Christian soul.

The rhetorical power of Donne's externalization of conscience in the 1620 Lincoln's Inn sermon rests, in part, on its notably theatrical character. The image of the preacher behind the hangings at the primal scene of sin is consistent with accounts of the dramatic nature of Donne's sermons, as well as the fact that playgoers in the period were almost inevitably sermongoers, especially those at Lincoln's Inn.[19] Indeed, Donne's description of sacred rhetoric in this sermon seems to rely on his audience's awareness of early modern staging practices, something Donne would certainly have known from his relatively well-documented love of the early modern theater and from his time as Master of the Revels at the Inns of Court. In particular, his description of the preacher behind the hangings recalls how many early modern plays depict a sin being either witnessed or committed by someone hiding behind the curtains that were normally suspended in front of the tiring-house wall. Numerous early modern plays take advantage of this feature of the early modern stage, including Jonson's *Volpone* (1606) (which Donne praised in verse form) and the closet scene in *Hamlet* (1601).[20]

While many plays stage sins either behind or before the arras, others make reference to this theatrical iconography in ways similar to Donne. For example, the lead character, Tancred, in the Inns of Court play, *The Tragedie of Tancred and Gismund* (1591), describes how he witnessed his daughter having sex outside of marriage while he hid within the curtains. Rising from prayer, Tancred relates how his "fond delight" for his daughter Gismund resulted in him witnessing her in bed with her lover.[21] The shock that Tancred describes (and that the audience presumably shares to some degree) constitutes the kind of context informing how Donne sought to surprise through the nearness effect.

Such conscience effects inevitably bring to mind Hamlet's assertion "that guilty creatures sitting at a play / Have by the very cunning of the scene / Been struck so to the soul that presently / They have proclaimed their malefactions."[22] Like Hamlet's description of the effects of drama, Donne's scenario of the eavesdropping preacher recalls the existence of the character of Conscience that appears in Tudor interludes and morality plays. In plays such as *The World and the Child* (1522), Conscience plays opposite the Vice in leading heroes toward virtue rather than sin. Donne conceives of the preacher's role in terms evocative of Conscience's role in Tudor morality plays.[23] In this way, Donne's account of a good sermon is further proof of Brian Crockett's thesis that the stated goals of pulpit orators and early modern players were often difficult to distinguish. As Crockett observes, Perkins described preaching as an attempt "[t]o bind the conscience . . . either to accuse us or to excuse us of sin before God," just as the playwright and theatrical apologist Thomas Heywood argued "A play's a true transparent crystal mirror, / To shew good minds their mirth, the bad their terror."[24] Donne's description of how auditors should experience a sermon draws its force from the way stage and sermon cross-pollinated each other in the period.

If Donne's description of the nearness effect appears perturbing when cited in isolation from its immediate context in the 1620 sermon, it is even more so when read in relation to the sermon as a whole. The passage occurs in a sermon on Genesis 18:25, specifically Abraham's encounter with what Donne, following patristic and Reformation exegeses, interprets as three angels.[25] Donne focuses particular attention on the idea that Abraham was intrigued by one of the three angels because one angel appeared strangely, but inexpressibly, familiar to him. Donne claims that there was "[s]omething *Abraham* saw in this Angel above the rest, which drew him, which *Moses* does not expresse" (3.5.142). Abraham's mysterious reaction to the angel serves as an analogy for the auditor's response to the strangely proximal quality of an effective preacher's voice. Emphasizing the irreducible singularity of each man's conscience, Donne informs his auditors that often there is "[s]omething a man finds in one Preacher above another, which he cannot expresse" (3.5.142). Like the nearness of preacher and auditor, Abraham's sense of familiarity with the angel involves something so unique, something so individual, that it appears in the text only as a silence. This silence figures the mysteriousness of nearness as a phenomenon that is inherent to the sermon as a genre and to the experience of conscience that the genre seeks to effect.

The analogy between the Genesis text and Donne's idea of a well-executed sermon works by having his auditors project themselves into the pregnant silence Donne locates in Abraham's encounter with the angels. The silence generated by Donne's interpretation of the Genesis text is meant to be experienced rather than simply noted by an auditor; it should be felt not as an empty sign, a meaningless pause, but as a signifier of my private experience of guilt before my own conscience. Donne is not just speaking of Abraham's recognition, he is trying to make his auditors experience such a recognition for themselves. He is creating the space for a kind of penitential transference—the space in and through which an audience member might relive previously forgotten events in the present. It is in such a space that one can reencounter oneself in the light of the conscience and thus recognize the terrifying nearness of the preacher as an other who is both intimate and alien. In this respect, Donne uses Abraham's encounter with some familiar, yet difficult to articulate, aspect of the angel as an allegory of the auditor's relation to a preacher, who is presumed to know the sins one has committed. Through this process, Donne seeks to convert his auditors from what, in a different sermon on the penitential psalms, he defines as the deceitful silence of sin to the devout silence of obedience to God or *silentium subjectionis*.[26]

What makes the scene of Abraham's silence uncanny is its reflexive qualities: Donne's performance might affect us in the exact way as the allegory of sermonic experience in the sermon itself. This kind of rhetorical structure is analogous to a scenario in which a viewer is looking at a representation—say, a picture or a play—only to realize that he himself is *in the representation*. The nearness effect Donne seeks to generate unsettles the distinction between the familiar and the strange, inside and outside, self and other. The nearness effect thus names the oratorical desire to have auditors realize a Protestant version of the *de te fabula* principle—to understand that the story is about me in my private experience of guilt.

To accomplish such a goal, the preacher must take into account not only the irreducible singularity of each Christian's conscience but also the universality of sin as a shared dimension of human life. In a related sermon, Donne turns to the psalmist David in order to express the preacher's desire to have everyone in the audience identify themselves as sinners:

> His example is so comprehensive, so generall, that as a well made, and well placed Picture in a Gallery looks upon all that stand in severall places of the Gallery, in severall lines, in severall angles, so doth *Davids* history concerne and embrace all. (5.15.299)

The nearness effect consists of drawing auditors into such a frame by having them recognize themselves as objects of its gaze. Thus, where Abraham's experience expresses the irreducible singularity of an auditor's experience of sin, figured as a pregnant silence into which a listener projects his past transgressions, David's example expresses the universality of sin as a common human inheritance.

Donne expresses David's general relevance as a sinner by attributing to the portrait of his sins the omnivoyance that Nicholas of Cusa gives to God when the German theologian describes the divine gaze in the same way Donne describes David's. Just as Cusa's God sees everything at once, so David's sins encompass all possible acts of transgression.[27] Thus, Donne's use of these two figures, Abraham and David, indicates the rhetorical balancing act a preacher must accomplish to generate a nearness effect: a preacher must speak generally enough to encompass all possible sins but singularly enough to address an auditor's private transgression.

The figure of David provides Donne with his favorite vehicle for expressing the experience of conscience as an ecstatic phenomenon. In a sermon on Psalm 32.3–4, for example, Donne expresses how David's attempt to conceal his adultery from others and from himself resulted in an involuntary eruption of guilt. Donne expresses David's experience of conscience through the rhetoric of *copia*, an accumulation of greater and greater effects built up over time. The pattern of *amplificatio* re-creates the experience of a failed effort to contain an irrepressible sense of guilt and the inadvertent consequences resulting from its failed denial. Despite his best efforts, David cannot suppress his sins thoroughly enough to remain beyond the purview of his conscience as internal witness:

> He confesses his silence to have been *Ex doloso spiritu,* Out of a spirit, in which was deceit; And *David* did not hope, directly, and determinately to deceive God; But by endeavouring to hide his sin from other men, and from his owne conscience, he buried it deeper and deeper, but still under more and more sins. He silences his Adultery, but he smothers it, he buries it under a turfe of hypocrisie, of dissimulation . . . He silences this hypocrisie; but that must have a larger turfe to cover it; he buries it under the whole body of *Vriah,* treacherously murdered; He silences that murder, but no turfe was large enough to cover that, but the defeat of the whole army, and after all, the blaspheming of the name, and power of the Lord of Hosts, in the ruine of the army. That sin, which, if he would have carried it upward towards God, in Confession, would have vanished away, and evaporated, by silencing, by suppressing, by burying multiplied, as Corne buried in the earth, multiplies into many Eares. And, though he might (perchance for his farther punishment) overcome the remembrance of the first sin, he might have forgot the Adultery, and feele no paine of that, yet still being put to a new, and new sin, still the last sin that he did to cover the rest, could not chuse but appeare to his conscience. (9.12.287–288)

Like Donne's preacher behind the hangings, David's conscience speaks truth to the soul despite all efforts of concealing the past. While David silences his hypocrisy, his sins "could not chuse but appeare to his conscience" erupting in a kind of anagnorisis where his deceitful soul is exposed and his transgressions recalled.

In the following sermon on Psalm 32.5, Donne expresses David's terror as a sinner by emphasizing the terrifying gap between his self-perception
before and after experiencing the judgments of conscience. Once David is
confronted by the demonic face of his own otherness in the form of sin, he
returns to himself through the potentially salvific otherness of conscience.
In this way, Donne shifts our perception from the daimonic quality of conscience and the demonic quality of sin, both of which entail an experience of
becoming other to oneself. Donne enhances the sense of surprise attendant
upon David's confrontation with his daimonic conscience by shifting in the
middle of the passage from third-person to first-person pronouns. Though
subtle, this grammatical shift is existentially and dramatically consequential,
for it reminds us that just as the preacher is subject to the theme of sin that
he is sermonizing—so too are we:

> [H]ee sees his sinnes looke with other faces, and he heares his sins
> speak with other voyces, and hee findes them to call one another
> by other names: And when hee is thus come to that consideration,
> Lord! how have I mistaken my selfe, Am I, that thought my selfe,
> and passed with others, for a sociable, a pleasurable man, and good
> company; am I a leprous Adulterer . . . I mistooke my selfe all this
> while, so I may proceed to the *non operui*, to a perfit sifting of my
> conscience, in all corners. (9.13.300)

If the temporality of Donne's scene with the lurking preacher emphasizes the perturbation inspired by the knowledge that God forejudges our sins
by means of our conscience, the textual frame of this sermon emphasizes the
comfort inspired by the knowledge that God forgives sins before they have
actually been committed. This view of divine forgiveness as having always
already happened in the mind of God is grounded, Donne argues, in the
verbal tense of the word "forgavest" in line 5 of Psalm 32. Because the sermon is framed by the divine perspective of God's mercy, David's confession
is figured as comforting rather than terrifying: "I ACKNOWLEDGED MY SIN
UNTO THEE, AND MINE INIQUITY HAVE I NOT HID. I SAID, I *WILL* CONFESSE MY
TRANSGRESSIONS UNTO THE LORD, AND THOU *FORGAVEST* THE INIQUITY OF
MY SIN" (9.13.296, my emphasis). The retrospective temporality of forgiveness
vis-à-vis confession helps express Donne's thesis that we confess not to bring
something to God's attention, but to bring our soul in alignment with our
conscience and thus with God. In this respect, the otherness of sin and the
experience of self-alienation arising from such otherness are overcome in the
sermon through the ecstasis of conscience, which operates as a divine oracle.
In other words, while sin others oneself to oneself in a demonic way, a good
conscience others oneself to oneself in a salvific way. In this latter modality

of ecstasis, the uncanny encounter with conscience brings to light the self hidden within and by sin. Donne thus concludes this sequence by confessing that he will initiate a perfect "sifting of my conscience, in all corners," and like David "rip up that, and enter into the privatest, and most remote corners thereof" (9.13.300–301). The final result of this process is an avowal of sin, where Donne announces that "*I acknowledged my sin,* and I hid none, disguised none" (9.13.300). In the final analysis, such confession is the ultimate purpose of inspiring the nearness effect.

Whereas Donne dramatizes David's crisis of conscience in the sermons on Psalm 32, he offers a more fully theorized account of the role conscience plays in self-examination in a sermon on Mark 16:16. If Perkins describes the conscience as a notary who records all of our actions despite our desire to forget them, Donne figures the heart as a book in which all of our experiences are inscribed, despite our intention to overlook them. The role of the conscience is to recover our guilt and thereby render the heart legible again:

> The heart is a booke, legible enough, and intelligible in it selfe; but we have so interlined that booke with impertinent knowledge, and so clasped up that booke, for feare of reading our owne history, our owne sins, as that we are greatest strangers, and the least conversant with the examination of our owne hearts. (5.13.248)

For Donne, the experience of feeling other to oneself is part of an ameliorative but egotistically unsettling process of conversion—a dialectic, as he writes in the *Devotions,* between humiliation and restoration, terror and comfort.[28] In such an experience, it is God's overpresence in the soul, his nearness in the form of conscience, rather than his anxiety-inducing absence, that is perturbing. Donne's account of the lived experience of conscience as involving a dimension of the uncanny reveals both the genius and the limitations of Freud's thesis in "The Future of an Illusion" that religious thought is designed to make us "feel at home in the uncanny." For Freud, religious belief tames the uncanniness of life, giving us a "psychical means" of coping with the "senseless anxiety" of existence as such.[29] What Donne helps us to grasp is that Pauline Christianity marshals a certain form of the uncanny—using it as part of the process of destroying and re-creating individuals as subjects of Christ. To understand the literary power of Donne's representation of conscience is to recognize how this element of the uncanny is put to work.[30]

As we have seen, one of the ways Donne draws on the uncanny is by constructing rhetorical and dramatic scenarios in which he functions as both auditor and preacher, in which he is as much within the frame of God's judgment as we, his audience, are. This practice of including himself as both auditor and preacher is evinced in the 1620 sermon on Genesis 18, when Donne figures himself as the sinner whose transgression is being witnessed by the lurking preacher: "It is not the depth, nor the wit, nor the eloquence of the Preacher that pierces us, but his nearenesse; that hee speaks to my conscience, as though he had been behinde the hangings when I sinned, and as though he had read the book of the day of Judgement already" (*Sermons*, 3.5.142). Donne's sermons thus not only enact but also thematize this reflexive and potentially perturbing dimension of conscience. Most interestingly, they do so without diminishing their capacity to capture our conscience: just as the metadramatic quality of a Shakespeare play can enhance rather than deflate our sense of its magic, so too can the reflexive dimensions of a Donne sermon still surprise and catch us up in it.

## The Mitcham Letters

Donne's penchant for expressing the ecstatic dimensions of conscience often involves a pattern of rhetorical reflexivity, a kind of stylistic signature in which he moves from the outside to the inside, from the selfsame to the self-as-other. To use Donne's own terms, the nearness effect is often achieved through a rhetorical shift from the "foreign" to the "home-born," from the external to the intestine (*First Anniversary*, 80, 84).[31] John E. Parish notices this basic structure at work in "Batter My Heart," asserting that "as a whole, the poem is unified by a shifting viewpoint which produces the effect of God's boring from the outside into the very center of the human heart."[32] *An Anatomy of the World* operates according to a similar logic as readers are told at the outset that the experience of interpreting the poem will reveal one of two things: either they each have a soul who is able to "see, and Judge, and follow worthiness" or they each "[m]ay lodge an In-mate soule, but tis not his" (1–6). This commonly recurring pattern, and some of the key images often associated with it, are given a stunning articulation in a letter written to Donne's close friend Sir Henry Goodyer in 1608.[33] In this letter, as in the Lincoln's Inn sermon, the addressee finds himself represented by and inserted into the text in unexpected, even shocking, ways.

Like many of the letters written during the Mitcham years (1607–1610), this epistle addresses Donne's melancholy, particularly as it arises from his anxiety over the limitations of human reason in the confrontation with sin. What distinguishes the letter from others of the same period is its rigorous, if morbidly ironic, interrogation of the difficult nature of arriving at self-understanding through the diagnosis of mental disease. In the process of this letter's complex rhetorical performance, Donne presents a vision of human knowledge in which the human subject is not merely prone to disease but is constitutively diseased, a subject not simply threatened by external pressures but a subject vexed by internal, structurally determined limitations. In short, Donne's letter expresses the epistemological implications of Reformation views of the will as profoundly limited in scope. More precisely, Donne expresses what it feels like to live out the view that, as Luther puts it, "flesh . . . means everything that is born from the flesh, i.e., the entire self, body, and soul, including our reason and all our senses."[34]

Following on this view of the flesh as circumscribing both body and soul, Luther severely criticized the medieval habit of thinking analogically about the relations between humans and God. For Luther, the habits of mind which lead one to believe that divine justice can be understood by reference to human ideas of justice, or that one can understand the invisible things of God by means of empirically perceptible phenomena, are delusional—symptoms of what he calls the theology of glory *(theologia gloriae)*. Real faith, for Luther, opposes itself to analogical habits of thought that operate according to principles of similitude. A wise soul does not look for analogies between human perception and divine reality, as Augustine often did. On the contrary, the Reformed Christian seeks to understand God through the paradoxes of the cross or *(theologia crucis)*—the idea that God conceals his omnipotence in weakness, his greatness in suffering.[35] In the context of human self-understanding, this Reformation critique of the theological use of analogy can result in a "hermeneutical circle" in which one cannot know whether one is in a state of sinfulness or grace, spiritual illness or health. As Thomas McDonough remarks, for Luther the human will is "curved in on itself, *incurvatus in se,*" constitutively bent toward sinfulness and creatureliness.[36] If the only way out of such narcissistic incurving is faith, then how does one apply one's reason to ensure the status of the soul? How does one know one is spiritually healthy rather than spiritually ill? Such is Donne's problem in several of the Mitcham letters, especially the one dated March 1608.

Donne's letters during the Mitcham years are characterized by a pronounced sensitivity to the possibility that the will is *incurvatus in se,* that the will may be, as Luther and Calvin argue, bound within a hermeneutical circle precluding any transparent or even analogical understanding of how the self is an *imago Dei.* This anxiety over Reformation views of the will is expressed in the 1608 letter to Goodyer through a rhetorical pattern that emphasizes the helplessness of the sinner caught in a state of sin.[37] The letter begins with an inquiry into Goodyer's state of being before quickly turning into a confession: "I hope you are now welcome to London, and well, and well comforted in your father's health and love, and well contended that we ask you how you do and tell you how we are, which yet I cannot of myself."[38] Donne thus presents his letter as having been occasioned by a failed meditation on the Delphic dictum *nosce teipsum.* The letter proceeds not by correcting but by further dramatizing this failure.

Its analysis of the impossible art of self-understanding starts with an outline of a pre-Reformation trichotomic view of humans as divided between the soul, body, and mind:

> If I knew that I were ill, I were well, for we consist of three parts, a soul, and body and mind, which I call those thoughts and affections and passions which neither soul nor body hath alone but have been begotten by their communication, as music results out of our breath and a cornet. (30)

Assuming a homeopathic theory of disease in which elements of the affliction can be employed to cure the affliction itself, Donne asserts that "of all these the diseases are cures, if they be known" (30–31). Donne thus claims with apparent confidence that our knowledge of the body and the soul may be limited, but, on the whole, there is no need to be overly skeptical: in the case of the soul, disease is a function of sin, and so the "physic" comes in the form of confession and the self-knowledge derived in the process; and, in the case of the body, the rules of physic "are certain . . . if the matter be rightly applied to the rule" (31). The real problems come, Donne warns, with the mind:

> But of the diseases of the mind there is no criterion, no canon, no rule. For our own taste and apprehension and interpretation should be the judge, and that is the disease itself. (31)

Although Donne began his analysis by addressing the problem of how to diagnose particular diseases, he has been led to a diagnosis of something far more fundamental; he has been led to a structural limitation within the very process of knowing itself. The problem with diagnosing diseases of the mind, Donne says, is that we have to use the mind's powers to do it. The homeopathic paradox of curing disease with disease takes a perverse turn here as the mind's own methods become the very problem they are supposed to resolve.

By exposing the reflexive deadlocks inherent to self-understanding, Donne implicitly undermines the coherence of his original distinction between the diagnosable diseases of the soul and the nondiagnosable diseases of the mind. Because "thoughts and affections and passions" arise from the communication between soul, body, and mind all three are necessarily involved in the process of distinguishing amongst themselves. Expressing the reflexive circumvolutions of the tripartite soul, Donne's letter implies that while the three parts of the person may be distinguishable in trichotomic theory, they remain diffusely interwoven in epistemological practice. The letter thus suggests that the spiritual dimensions of the soul cannot stand outside of the fleshly dimensions of the mind long enough or thoroughly enough to properly see the difference between the two. By rendering illegible the differences between man as flesh and man as spirit, Donne is enacting the implications of Luther's view that the whole person *(totus homo),* rather than merely the *psyche* and *body,* stands under the sign of *caro,* of the creatureliness of the flesh.

While Donne's letter opens by enacting the limitations of human reason at the level of theory, it deepens its skeptical motions through a series of theologically loaded examples of cognitive corruption, each depicting some form of interpretive confusion. In one key example, Donne bemoans how a single phenomenon can inspire the best intellects to radically opposed interpretations:

> Augustine thought devout Antony to be . . . full of the Holy Ghost because, not being able to read, he could say the whole Bible and interpret it, and Thyreus the Jesuit, for the same reason, doth think all the Anabaptists to be possessed. And as often out of contrary things men draw one conclusion. (31)

Donne follows this by asserting that the only thing worse than disagreement among great men over theological matters is disagreement within the self: "[T]he mind, which is our natural guide here, chooses to every man a several way. Scarce any man likes what another doth, nor, advisedly, that which himself" (31). Here writ small is the rhetorical motion of the letter writ large: Donne begins by addressing an apparently external problem only to find that the problem is the psyche itself, its lack of the necessary resources for obtaining a clear method of self-analysis.

By this point in the letter, Donne has arrived at the terrifying recognition that if thoughts are a function of soul, body, and mind, then the diagnostic procedures for all three elements of the person are subject to the misprisions he originally located solely in the mind. Thus, the distinctions organizing Donne's line of thought become increasingly diffuse the further the analysis proceeds. In the face of such confusion, he cannot come to properly know himself: "I still vex myself with this because, if I know it not, nobody can know it" (31). Goodyer is thus witness to a rhetorical performance in which neither homeopathic nor heteropathic methods of physic can remedy human pathologies because human pathologies are a matter of inward corruption rather than an outward matter of infection.

The rhetorical structure organizing this performance unfolds by placing increasing pressure on the tripartite theory of the self grounding Donne's analysis. Such increasing pressure suggests that Donne is in the process of grappling with the implications of Luther's attack on tripartite views of the soul, particularly Origen's, which is the most influential. As Luther writes in his disputation with Erasmus, "I, too, am familiar with Origen's fable about the threefold disposition of flesh, soul, and spirit, with soul standing in the middle and being capable of turning either way, toward the flesh or toward the spirit. But these are dreams of his own; he states but does not prove them."[39] Donne signals the radically skeptical conclusion a reader must draw from his self-consciously erring speculations on the limits of self-consciousness in the letter's final and most remarkable paragraph:

> But, sir, I am beyond my purpose. I mean to write a letter, and I am fallen into a discourse, and I do not only take you from some business but I make you a new business by drawing you into these meditations, in which let my openness be an argument of such love as I would fain express in some worthier fashion. (31)

By exceeding his "purpose," Donne acknowledges that his line of thought has carried him beyond his "intention," "resolution," or discourse. And given the collapsing of distinctions at work in his effort to know himself, the conclusion implies that the process of exceeding one's purpose is a risk not limited to himself, but one inherent in the act of reasoning, indeed the act of "discourse" itself. Thus, when he says he has drawn Goodyer into these meditations, he seems to mean it quite literally. Just as the failure of diagnosing the mind necessarily leads to failures in diagnosing the soul and body, so Donne's failure to know himself is a result of limitations that extend to everyone else's capacity for self-analysis. By the end of the letter, then, an apparently external object, Donne's discourse, has been disclosed as uncannily interior: the letter not only discusses the mind's limitations, it exemplifies them. Thus, while his meditation began on solid trichotomic grounds, it ends in a state of Lutheran paralysis—a state in which both soul and mind are mired not just in moral corruption but in epistemological insufficiency. So much for wishing Goodyer well.

Read closely, the letter's sardonic "purpose" is a function of its reflexive structure, in the way Donne self-consciously gets caught up in self-consciousness. In this respect, the letter is more expressive than thematic, more performative than constative. Indeed, the letter performs the reflexive paradox that one of Donne's contemporary readers, his fellow churchman Godfrey Goodman, thematizes several years later in his treatise on original sin. In a remarkable passage in the treatise, Goodman declares "I forget my selfe, I forget my selfe, for, speaking of mans corruption, I am so far entangled, that I cannot easily release my selfe; being corrupted as wel as others, me thinkes whatsoeuer I see, whatsoeuer I heare, all things seeme to sound corruption."[40] By performing such delimitations, Donne's letter presumes that its reader is both the interpreter and the object being interpreted, just as it generates the effect that its own author is subject to the forces he himself has put into play: "I am fallen into a discourse," indeed. Thus, just as Donne's collapsing of preacher and auditor in the 1620 sermon on Genesis 18 produces the very nearness effect he is describing, so the letter of 1608 produces a similarly surprising effect by drawing the reader into its self-consuming motions.

By unexpectedly finding both himself and his addressee *in the letter*, Donne offers something of a parody of the form of ecstasis he elsewhere associates with epistles more generally. In a letter dated October 1607, Donne describes personal correspondence as "a kind of extasie, and a departure and secession and suspension of the soul, which doth then communicate it self to two bodies" (27). If this earlier letter theorizes a quasi-sacramental mingling of souls that is achieved through the spiritual power of material words—a theory John Carey argues is irreducible to classical and humanist thought on the topic—then the letter to Goodyer presents a more skeptical correspondence of souls.[41] In the letter of 1608, the shock of ecstasis arises not through the transcendence of soul from body, but from an encounter with the radical delimitations of mortal existence. Indeed, the "openness of love" that Donne would "fain express in some more worthier fashion" (31) does not occasion the mystically ecstatic experience Donne sees as characteristic of good letters; rather it involves a more humbling, kenotic experience of realizing one's mortal and epistemological limits.

The rhetorical force of the 1608 letter is thus similar to the force of Donne's later sermons: its power of fascination derives from the letter's capacity to express the feeling of being unable to control a phenomenon that happens within us. The letter voices the perturbing sensation of being overwhelmed by forces internal to us by tracing a reflexive movement from disease as an external threat to an internal condition. Through this pattern, Donne encourages Goodyer to experience the very delimitations being diagnosed by recognizing them as applying as much to himself as to the letter's author. So if the letter is a testament to what Donne calls, in his theoretical account of letters, "frendships sacraments," it is a sacrament only those souls predisposed to the stresses of skepticism will want to partake of.[42]

Donne pursues a parallel itinerary in the subsequent letter to Goodyer, which also takes the form of a self-diagnosis. This letter begins as a description of Donne's melancholy as a state of spiritual paralysis caused by external forces or "storms":

> [B]eing to pass more and more storms, I find that I have not only cast out all my ballast which nature and time gives (reason and discretion), and so am as empty and light as vanity can make me, but I have over-fraught myself with vice, and so am riddingly subject to two contrary wracks, sinking and oversetting. (32)

As the letter progresses, however, we learn that the disease corroding Donne's powers of discretion is not a "storm" battering him from the outside, but is an inward state that resists denomination. As such, his condition remains intransigently immune from diagnosis:

> as the earth and water, one sad, the other fluid, make but one body, so to air and vanity there is but one *centrum morbi* [centre of the disease], and that which later physicians say of our bodies is fitter for our minds. For that which they call destruction, which is a corruption and want of those fundamental parts whereof we consist, is vice, and that *collectio stercorum* [dungheap], which is but the excrement of that corruption, is our vanity and indiscretion. Both these have but one root in me, and must be pulled out at once, or never. But I am so far from digging to it, that I know not where it is, for it is not in mine eyes only, but in every sense, nor in my concupiscence only, but in every power and affection. (32–33)

Like the experience of conscience in the sermons, the state of sin is characterized in the Mitcham letters as a state of being subject to a power that is profoundly intimate and yet disturbingly alien. Donne's religious imagination is characterized by its profound sensitivity to such phenomena. Consequently, many of his key rhetorical strategies express an ambivalence about the ecstatic features of Christian life, especially as they are complicated in the post-Reformation period through the delimitation of the will under the sign of the flesh. Thus, while accounts of Donne's representation of conscience in relation to casuistry help explain some of the thematic concerns of his religious writing, along with some of the rhetorical structures employed therein, such accounts do not adequately explain how Donne expresses conscience as a phenomenon that is characterized by the way it temporally, spatially, and cognitively circumscribes a person. In other words, accounts of Donne's representation of conscience that focus primarily on casuistical features do not explain how Donne expresses the ecstatic dimensions of conscience by breaking down distinctions between text and reader, author and auditor, and words and Word. As I have argued, such dissolutions of apparent oppositions often unfold through a pattern in which the speaker moves from focusing on external (or "foreign") threats to internal (or "home-grown") harms. It is through such patterns that Donne generates various forms of the nearness effect so characteristic of his religious writing as a whole. Thus, to experience Donne's religious prose means historicizing not only its thematic messages but also its formal structures. Such structures, I have argued, both describe and evoke phenomenological dimensions of religious faith as lived within the context of early modern England.

## Notes

1. This distinction is implicit in Martin Luther's definition of conscience from his 1521 work on *Monastic Vows:* "[T]he conscience is not the power of acting but the power of judging which judges about works . . . Its purpose is not to do, but to speak about what has been done and what should be done" (cited in Randall C. Zachman, *The Assurance of Faith: Conscience in the Theology of Martin Luther and John Calvin* [Minneapolis: Fortress, 1993], 20–21).

2. All references to Donne's sermons are cited parenthetically in text by volume, sermon, and page number and are from *The Sermons of John Donne*, ed. and intro. George R. Potter and Evelyn M. Simpson (Berkeley: University of California Press, 1957).

3. To date, most studies of Donne's representation of conscience have focused on the discourse of casuistry. See, for example, A. E. Malloch, "John Donne and the Casuists," *Studies in English Literature* 2, no. 1 (1962): 57–76; Dwight Cathcart, *Doubting Conscience: Donne and the Poetry of Moral Argument* (Ann Arbor: University of Michigan Press, 1975); Camille Wells Slights, *The Casuistical Tradition in Shakespeare, Donne, Herbert, and Milton* (Princeton, NJ: Princeton University Press, 1981), 133–182; Jeanne M. Shami, "Donne's Protestant Casuistry: Cases of Conscience in the Sermons," *Studies in Philology* 80, no. 1 (1983): 53–66; Meg Lota Brown, *Donne and the Politics of Conscience in Early Modern England* (Leiden, The Netherlands: E. J. Brill, 1995); and Glen Bowman, "Every Man Is a Church in Himself: The Development of Donne's Ideas on the Relationship Between Individual Conscience and Human Authority," *Fides et Historia* 29, no. 1 (1997): 44–57. For a phenomenological approach to Donne's sermons that anticipates mine, see Gale H. Carrithers Jr., *Donne at Sermons: A Christian Existential World* (Albany: State University of New York Press, 1972). According to Jean M. Shami's "Donne on Discretion" (*English Literary History* 47, no. 1 [1980]: 48–66), Donne's nearness effect describes a mysterious but dramatic process of imposing God's presence on an audience by driving "the history recorded in Scriptures home to each one" of the members of his congregation (50). Dennis Quinn, in "Donne's Christian Eloquence" (*ELH* 27 [1960]: 276–293), contextualizes Donne's expressivity in relation to Augustine's theory that the preacher should imitate scriptural truths, pursuing a mimesis of scriptural reality rather than aiming for persuasion in the classical sense of the term.

4. For a discussion of William Perkins's claim that sermons should bind the conscience, see Brian Crockett, *The Play of Paradox: Stage and Sermon in Renaissance England* (Philadelphia: University of Pennsylvania Press, 1995), 42.

5. Michael G. Baylor, *Action and Person: Conscience in Late Scholasticism and the Young Luther* (Leiden, The Netherlands: E. J. Brill, 1977), 170.

6. According to Baylor in *Action and Person*, "Luther did assert that the Last Judgment is simply a confirmation of a judgment which the conscience has already made" (238).

7. See John Calvin, *Institutes of the Christian Religion*, trans. Henry Beveridge (Grand Rapids, MI: W. W. Eerdmans, 1989), 3.19.15.

8. *William Perkins, 1558–1602, English Puritanist: His Pioneer Works on Casuistry—"A Discourse of Conscience" and "The Whole Treatise of Cases of Conscience,"* ed. and intro. Thomas F. Merrill (The Hague: Nieuwkoop and B. De Graaf, 1966), 6–7. Subsequent references to this work are cited parenthetically in text.

9. Zachman, *Assurance of Faith*, 100.

10. As Zachman explains in *Assurance of Faith*, "Calvin not only distinguishes the conscience from the mind and understanding, but he also distinguishes the conscience from the will *(voluntas)*" (101). Perkins appears to differ from Calvin insofar as Perkins identifies conscience as a part of the understanding.

11. Cited in John S. Wilks, *The Idea of Conscience in Renaissance Tragedy* (New York: Routledge, 1990), 36. For a similar formulation in Calvin, see Calvin, *Institutes*, 3.19.15.

12. For this point, see Zachman, *Assurance of Faith*, 99.

13. The question of Donne's relation to Calvinism is highly vexed, and it is not my aim in this essay to delineate his notion of conscience in relation to Calvinist theories in precise theological terms. Suffice it to say, for now, that my analysis is generally consistent with Debora Shuger's observation that "Donne's understanding of the conscience . . . as accusatory and as the locus of divine presence . . . derives from Calvin, who defines the 'inward mind' as the 'forum of conscience', or the 'sense of divine judgment, as a witness . . . which does not allow them to hide their sins from being accused before the Judge's tribunal" (*Habits of Thought in the English Renaissance: Religion, Politics, and the Dominant Culture*, reprint of 1990 University of California Press edition [Toronto: University of Toronto Press, 1997], 181). Although Shuger's emphasis on the violent and absolutist aspects of Donne's Calvinism in the sermons has been tempered by Jeanne Shami's "Donne's *Sermons and the Absolutist Politics of Quotation*," in *John Donne's Religious Imagination Essays in Honor of John T. Shawcross* (ed. Raymond-Jean Frontain and Frances M. Malpezzi [Conway, AR: UCA, 1995], 380–412), her view that Donne articulates a moderately Calvinist notion of conscience in the sermons remains persuasive. A more systematic analysis of Donne's theology of conscience in the sermons might further clarify Donne's complex relation to the moderate Calvinism of the Jacobean Church.

14. For a discussion of such medieval accounts of conscience, see Wilks, *Idea of Conscience*, 36.

15. For an explanation of the Thomist view of conscience, see Baylor, *Action and Person*, 20–69.

16. *The Compact Oxford English Dictionary*, 2nd ed. (Oxford: Clarendon, 1998).

17. David F. Krell, "Das Unheimliche: Architectural Sections of Heidegger and Freud," *Research in Phenomenology* 22, no. 1 (1992): 43–61, quotation on 49.

18. Although Donne's nearness effect can be described as uncanny in this limited sense, it differs in important ways from the Freudian sense of the term. Whereas the psychoanalytic notion of the uncanny presupposes that what is returning unbeknownst to the subject is a thought that was repressed by unconscious elements of the ego, Donne is concerned with memories that are suppressed through a conscious act of will. For a study of the *unheimlich* dimensions of conscience in Shakespeare and Western philosophy more broadly, see Ned Lukacher, *Daemonic Figures: Shakespeare and the Question of Conscience* (Cornell, NY: Cornell University Press, 1994). Although Lukacher's study is essential reading for an understanding of

Platonic, Renaissance, modern, and postmodern ideas of conscience, the wide scope of his project results in a homogenizing account of Christian concepts of conscience. For a reading of Donne's representation of sin in the context of Calvinist soteriology, see John Stachniewski, *The Persecutory Imagination: English Puritanism and the Literature of Religious Despair* (Oxford: Clarendon, 1991). Whereas Stachniewski is concerned with demonstrating Donne's anxiety about predestination, I am concerned with his account of the phenomenology of conscience.

19. For accounts of the theatrical nature of Donne's sermons and poetry, see H. M. Richmond, "Donne's Master: The Young Shakespeare," *Criticism* 15 (1973): 126–144; Paul W. Harland, "Dramatic Technique and Personae in Donne's Sermons," *ELH* 53, no. 4 (1986): 709–26; and Crockett, *Play of Paradox*, chap. 7. Although Victor Harris, in "John Donne and the Theatre" (*Philological Quarterly* 41 [1962]: 257–269), makes a case for Donne's antipathy toward the theater, he offers substantial evidence for the more commonly held view that the theater had a significant impact on Donne's writing. For other discussions of the relations between the theater and pulpit, see Jeffrey Knapp, *Shakespeare's Tribe: Church, Nation, and Theatre in Renaissance England* (Chicago: University of Chicago Press, 2002); and Martha Tuck Rozett, *The Doctrine of Election and the Emergence of Elizabethan Tragedy* (Princeton, NJ: Princeton University Press, 1984).

20. For Donne's praising of *Volpone*, see Harris, "Donne and the Theatre," 258. According to Alan C. Dessen and Leslie Thomson (*A Dictionary of Stage Directions in English Drama, 1580–1642* [Cambridge: Cambridge University Press, 1999]), "roughly sixty plays have about ninety directions for a *curtain* of which seventy-eight call for the *curtains* to be opened or closed" (62). They also observe that the word "hangings," which Donne uses in place of curtains, was "an infrequently used alternative [in early modern stage directions] for the curtain or arras that hung just in front of the tiring-house wall" (110).

21. *The Tragedie of Tancred and Gismund* (London, 1591), 4.2.970–1000.

22. William Shakespeare, *Hamlet*, ed. Sylvan Barnet (New York: Signet, 1998), 2.2.601–604.

23. My understanding of the character of Conscience derives from Wilks, *Idea of Conscience*, chap. 2.

24. William Perkins and Thomas Heywood, cited in Crockett, *Play of Paradox*, 42.

25. See, for example, Origen, *Homilies on Genesis and Exodus*, trans. Ronald E. Heine (Washington, DC: Catholic University of America Press, 1981), 103–111; and Martin Luther, *Luther's Works*, ed. Jaroslav Pelikan, vol. 3: *Lectures on Genesis, Chapters 15–20* (St. Louis: Concordia, 1961), 176–238.

26. See *Sermons*, 9.12.

27. See Jasper Hopkins, *Nicholas of Cusa's Dialectical Mysticism: Text, Translation, and Interpretive Study of De Visione Dei* (Minneapolis, MN: Arthur J. Banning, 1985), 113–117.

28. See *Devotions upon Emergent Occasions*, ed. Anthony Raspa (New York: Oxford University Press, 1987), 39–40.

29. Sigmund Freud, "The Future of an Illusion (1927)," in *Civilization, Society, and Religion*, trans. James Strachey (New York: Penguin 1985), 179–180. For a discussion of Freud's theory of religion in light of the uncanny, see Nicholas Royle, *The Uncanny* (New York: Routledge, 2003), 20–21.

30. For further discussion of the uncanniness of Pauline thought as expressed in Donne's work, see my "Petrarchism and Repentance in John Donne's *Holy Sonnets*," *Modern Philology* 105, no. 3 (2008): 535–569, reprinted in *The Poetry of Religious Sorrow in Early Modern England* (Cambridge: Cambridge University Press, 2008), chap. 5. Also see the conclusion to my *Divine Subjection: The Rhetoric of Sacramental Devotion in Early Modern England* (Pittsburgh, PA: Duquesne University Press, 2005).

31. I have modernized the spelling of Donne's terms here. All citations to Donne's poems are from *The Complete English Poems of John Donne*, ed. C. A. Patrides (London: Dent and Sons, 1985), and are cited parenthetically by line numbers in text.

32. John E. Parish, "No. 14 of Donne's *Holy Sonnets*," in *John Donne's Poetry: Authoritative Texts and Criticism*, ed. Arthur L. Clements (New York: W. W. Norton, 1992), 331. See also my reading of Station XII in *Devotions upon Emergent Occasions*, in Kuchar, *Divine Subjection* (see note 32), 160–165.

33. Although the dating and addressing of this letter remain conjectural, it is consistent with other epistles of the period, and I see no reason to dispute Edmund Gosse's determinations (see Gosse's *The Life and Letters of John Donne* [Gloucester, England: Peter Smith, 1959], 1:183). In any case, my focus is on the internal rhetorical structure of the letter, not its biographical import per se. For clarification of this and other matters pertaining to Donne's correspondence, we anxiously await the Oxford edition of the letters currently in the works.

34. Martin Luther, "Preface to the Epistle of St. Paul to the Romans, 1522," in *Martin Luther: Selections From His Writings*, ed. John Dillenberger (New York: Anchor, 1962), 25.

35. For accounts of this aspect of Luther's thought, see Zachman, *Assurance of Faith*, 19; and Alister E. McGrath, *Luther's Theology of the Cross* (Oxford: Basil Blackwell, 1985), 135, 159; see also James Samuel Preus, *From Shadow to Promise: Old Testament Interpretation from Augustine to the Young Luther* (Cambridge, MA: Belknap Press of Harvard University Press, 1969), 252–253. I am especially indebted to Zachman's formulations of this aspect of Luther's theology.

36. Thomas M. McDonough, *The Law and the Gospel in Luther* (Oxford: Oxford University Press, 1963), 30.

37. To be clear, I am not arguing that Donne is a committed Lutheran on the point of the will at this or any other point in his life. I am simply suggesting that the rhetorical structure of this letter registers the phenomenological effects of Reformation soteriology. My interest here is with recurring rhetorical patterns and the effects they have on Donne's writing, not with biography.

38. References to Donne's letters are cited in the text by page numbers and are from John Donne, *John Donne Selected Letters*, ed. P. M. Oliver (New York: Routledge, 2002), 30.

39. Martin Luther, "Bondage of the Will," in *Luther and Erasmus: Free Will and Salvation*, ed. E. Gordon Rupp and Philip S. Watson (Philadelphia: Westminster John Kox, 1995), 317.

40. Goodman Godfrey, *The Fall of Man, or the Corruption of Nature* (London, 1616), 81. As several critics have noted, Godfrey's work shows clear signs of having been influenced by Donne's *The Anniversaries*. For the connection between Godfrey and Donne and for a larger bibliography on the topic, see Kuchar, *Poetry of Religious Sorrow*, chap. 6.

41. John Carey, "John Donne's Newsless Letters," *Essays and Studies* 34 (1981): 45–65.

42. For a discussion of Donne's phrase "frendships sacraments," see ibid., 54.

## ACKNOWLEDGMENT

Research for this article was made possible by the Social Sciences and Humanities Research Council of Canada.

# *Chronology*

| | |
|---|---|
| 1572 | John Donne born. |
| 1584 | Donne matriculates at Hart Hall, Oxford. |
| 1591 | Robert Herrick born. |
| 1592 | Donne admitted to Lincoln's Inn. |
| 1593 | George Herbert born. |
| 1596 | Donne sails with Essex in the English expedition to Cadiz. |
| 1597 | Donne sails on the Azores Expedition. |
| ca. 1598 | Donne becomes secretary to Sir Thomas Egerton. |
| 1601 | Donne marries Ann More, secretly, and is imprisoned by her father, Sir George More, the following year and dismissed from his post with Egerton. |
| 1605 | Herbert attends Westminster School. |
| 1609 | Herbert enters Trinity College, Cambridge. |
| 1610 | Donne publishes *Pseudo-Martyr*. |
| 1611 | Donne publishes *Ignatius His Conclave* and *The First Anniversarie*. |
| 1612 | Donne publishes *The Second Anniversarie*. Herbert publishes two memorial poems, in Latin, on the death of Prince Henry. |

| ca. 1612 | Richard Crashaw born. |
|---|---|
| 1613 | Herrick enters St. John's College, Cambridge; receives B.A in 1617, M.A. in 1620. |
| 1615 | Donne ordained as deacon and priest at St. Paul's Cathedral; appointed royal chaplain. |
| 1617 | Donne's wife Ann dies. |
| 1618 | Herbert appointed reader in rhetoric at Cambridge. |
| 1620 | Herbert elected public orator at Cambridge. |
| 1621 | Henry Vaughan born. Andrew Marvell born. Donne elected Dean of St. Paul's. |
| 1623 | Donne composes *Devotions Upon Emergent Occasions*. Herrick ordained as deacon and priest of the Church of England. |
| 1623–1627 | Herrick lives in London, associating with Jonson and other poets. |
| 1631 | Donne delivers *Death's Duel*, his last sermon; dies on March 31. Crashaw enters Pembroke College, Cambridge; receives B.A. in 1634, M.A. in 1638. |
| 1633 | Herbert dies; *The Temple* published posthumously. Donne's first collected edition of poems published. Marvell matriculates at Trinity College, Cambridge. |
| 1635 | Crashaw ordained as a priest in the Anglican Church. |
| 1637 | Thomas Traherne born. |
| 1638 | Vaughan studies at Jesus College, Oxford. |
| 1639 | Marvell receives B.A. from Cambridge. |
| 1640 | Vaughan in London studying law. |
| ca. 1642 | Marvell travels abroad in Holland, France, Italy, and Spain |
| 1643 | Crashaw flees from Cambridge before Cromwell's forces; he lives in exile on the continent. |
| 1645 | Crashaw converts to Catholicism. Vaughan serves in the Royalist army. |
| 1646 | Vaughan publishes *Poems, with the Tenth Satyre of Juvenal*. While in Rome, Crashaw's *Steps to the Temple* and *The Delights of the Muses* are published in London. |

| | |
|---|---|
| 1648 | Herrick publishes *Hesperides*. |
| 1649 | Crashaw dies. |
| 1650 | Vaughan publishes the first part of *Silex Scintillans*. Marvell writes "Tom May's Death" and "An Horatian Ode." |
| 1652 | Traherne enters Brasenose College, Oxford; receives B.A. in 1656. Marvell dedicates "Upon the Hill and Grove at Bill-borow" and "Upon Appleton House" to Thomas, Lord Fairfax. Crashaw's *Carmen Deo Nostro* published posthumously in Paris. |
| 1655 | Vaughan publishes the second part of *Silex Scintillans*. Marvell publishes "The First Anniversary of Government Under His Highness the Lord Protector." |
| 1657 | Marvell appointed Latin secretary. |
| 1659 | Marvell elected to a seat in Parliament for Hull, which he holds until 1678. |
| 1660 | Traherne ordained as deacon and priest. Marvell works to release Milton from prison. |
| ca. 1666–1670 | Traherne composes *Centuries of Meditations*. |
| 1667 | Marvell writes "Last Instructions to a Painter"; "Clarindon's House-Warming." |
| 1669 | Traherne receives Doctor of Divinity from Brasenose College, Oxford. |
| 1672 | Marvell publishes *The Rehearsal Transpros'd*. |
| 1673 | Traherne publishes *Roman Forgeries* anonymously. |
| 1674 | Herrick dies. Traherne dies. |
| 1678 | Marvell dies. |
| 1681 | Marvell's *Miscellaneous Poems* published. |
| 1695 | Vaughan dies. |

# Contributors

HAROLD BLOOM is Sterling Professor of the Humanities at Yale University. He is the author of 30 books, including *Shelley's Mythmaking* (1959), *The Visionary Company* (1961), *Blake's Apocalypse* (1963), *Yeats* (1970), *A Map of Misreading* (1975), *Kabbalah and Criticism* (1975), *Agon: Toward a Theory of Revisionism* (1982), *The American Religion* (1992), *The Western Canon* (1994), and *Omens of Millennium: The Gnosis of Angels, Dreams, and Resurrection* (1996). *The Anxiety of Influence* (1973) sets forth Professor Bloom's provocative theory of the literary relationships between the great writers and their predecessors. His most recent books include *Shakespeare: The Invention of the Human* (1998), a 1998 National Book Award finalist; *How to Read and Why* (2000); *Genius: A Mosaic of One Hundred Exemplary Creative Minds* (2002); *Hamlet: Poem Unlimited* (2003); *Where Shall Wisdom Be Found?* (2004); and *Jesus and Yahweh: The Names Divine* (2005). In 1999, Professor Bloom received the prestigious American Academy of Arts and Letters Gold Medal for Criticism. He has also received the International Prize of Catalonia, the Alfonso Reyes Prize of Mexico, and the Hans Christian Andersen Bicentennial Prize of Denmark.

DONALD RAMSAY ROBERTS wrote *Shakespeare and the Rhetoric of Stylistic Innovation* (1936).

PHOEBE S. SPINRAD is professor emerita at The Ohio State University. She wrote *The Summons of Death on the Medieval and Renaissance English Stage* (1987) and articles on Renaissance drama and poetry, medieval drama, and Vietnam War literature and history. She formerly edited *Discoveries: South Central Renaissance Conference Notes and Reviews*.

237

CAROL ANN JOHNSTON is associate professor of English and holds the Martha Porter Sellers Chair in rhetoric and the English language at Dickinson College. She wrote *Euroda Welty: A Study of the Short Fiction* (1997). She has also written on Thomas Traherne.

ROBERT WHALEN is associate professor of English at Northern Michigan University. He wrote *The Poetry of Immanence: Sacrament in Donne and Herbert* (2002).

MAUREEN SABINE is senior lecturer in history at the University of Hong Kong. She wrote *Feminine Engendered Faith: John Donne and Richard Crashaw* (1996) and *Maxine Hong Kingston's Broken Book of Life: An Intertextual Study of The Woman Warrior and China Men* (2004).

ANNE-MARIE MILLER BLAISE is associate professor at the University of Versailles Saint-Quentin-en-Yvelines and a member of the Study Center on the State, Society and Religion in Europe, the Middle Ages and Modern Times.

HOLLY FAITH NELSON is associate professor of English at Trinity Western University. She coedited *The Broadview Anthology of Seventeenth Century Verse and Prose, Of Paradise and Light: Essays on Henry Vaughan and John Milton in Honor of Alan Rudrum, Eikon Basilike with Selections from Eikonoklastes* (2000), *Of Paradise and Light: Essays on Henry Vaughan and John Milton in Honor of Alan Rudrum* (2004), and *James Hogg and the Literary Marketplace: Scottish Romanticism and the Working-class Author* (2009).

PIERS BROWN is a doctoral candidate at the University of Toronto, where he is preparing a dissertation on John Donne.

GARY KUCHAR is associate professor of English at the University of Victoria. He wrote *The Poetry of Religious Sorrow in Early Modern England* (2008).

# Bibliography

## John Donne

Aers, David, Bob Hodges, and Gunther Kress. *Literature, Language, and Society in England, 1580–1680.* Dublin: Gill and MacMillan, 1981.

Allen, Don Cameron. "Dean Donne Sets His Text," *ELH,* Volume 10 (1943): pp. 208–229.

———. "The Double Journey of John Donne," in *A Tribute to George Coffin Taylor,* ed. Arnold Williams (Chapel Hill: University of North Carolina Press, 1952), pp. 83–99.

Andreasen, N. J. C. *John Donne: Conservative Revolutionary.* Princeton: Princeton University Press, 1967.

Anselment, Raymond A. "'Ascensio Mendax, Descensio Crudelis': The Image of Babel I in the *Anniversaries,*" *ELH,* Volume 38 (1971): pp. 188–205.

Armstrong, Alan. "The Apprenticeship of John Donne: Ovid and the *Elegies,*" *ELH,* Volume 44 (1977): pp. 419–442.

Bennet, Joan. *Five Metaphysical Poets.* Cambridge: Cambridge University Press, 1963.

Benson, Donald R. "Platonism and Neoclassic Metaphor: Dryden's *Eleonora* and Donne's *Anniversaries,*" *Studies in Philology,* Volume 68 (1971): pp. 340–356.

Berman, Antoine, and Isabelle Berman. *Toward a Translation Criticism: John Donne.* Ed. Françoise Massardier-Kenney. Kent, Ohio: Kent State University Press, 2009.

Carrithers, Gale. *Donne at Sermons.* Albany: State University of New York Press, 1972.

Cathcart, D. *Doubting Conscience: Donne and the Poetry of Moral Argument.* Ann Arbor: University of Michigan Press, 1975.

Chambers, A. B. "'Good Friday, 1613. Riding Westward': The Poem and the Tradition," *ELH,* Volume 28 (1961): pp. 31–53.

Colie, Rosalie. *Paradoxica Epidemics: The Renaissance Tradition of Paradox.* Princeton: Princeton University Press, 1966.

Corthell, Ronald. *Ideology and Desire in Renaissance Poetry: The Subject of Donne.* Detroit, MI: Wayne State University Press, 1997.

Davies, Stevie. *John Donne.* Plymouth, England: Northcote House, with British Council, 1994.

DiPasquale, Theresa M. *Literature and Sacrament: The Sacred and the Secular in John Donne.* Pittsburgh, Penn.: Duquesne University Press, 1999.

Edwards, David L. *John Donne: Man of Flesh and Spirit.* Grand Rapids, Mich.: Eerdmans, 2001.

Elliot, Emory. "The Narrative and Allusive Unity of Donne's *Satyres,*" *Journal of English and Germanic Philology,* Volume 75 (1976): pp. 105–116.

Empson, William. "Donne and the Rhetorical Tradition," *Kenyon Review,* Volume 11 (1949): pp. 571–587.

Fiore, P. A., ed. *Just So Much Honor.* University Park: Pennsylvania State University Press, 1972.

Flynn, Dennis. *John Donne & the Ancient Catholic Nobility.* Bloomington: Indiana University Press, 1995.

Fowler, Alastair. *Triumphal Forms.* Cambridge: Cambridge University Press, 1970.

Fox, Ruth A. "Donne's *Anniversaries* and the Art of Living," *ELH,* Volume 38 (1971): pp. 528–541.

Gardner, Helen. "The Argument about the Ecstasy," in *Elizabethan and Jacobean Studies Presented to F. P. Wilson,* eds. H. Davies and H. Gardner. Oxford: Clarendon Press, 1959.

Guss, Donald L. *John Donne, Petrarchist: Italianate Conceits and Love Theory in the "Songs and Sonets."* Detroit: Wayne State University Press, 1966.

Hardison, O. B., Jr. *The Enduring Moment: A Study of the Idea of Praise in Renaissance Literary Theory and Practice.* Chapel Hill: University of North Carolina Press, 1962.

Henricksen, Bruce. "The Unity of Reason and Faith in John Donne's Sermons," *Papers on Language and Literature,* Volume 11 (1975): pp. 18–30.

Hodgson, Elizabeth M. A. *Gender and the Sacred Self in John Donne.* Newark: University of Delaware Press, 1999.

Hughes, Richard E. *The Progress of the Soul: The Interior Career of John Donne.* New York: Morrow, 1968.

Hunt, Clay. *Donne's Poetry.* New Haven, Conn.: Yale University Press, 1954.

Hurley, Ann Hollinshead. *John Donne's Poetry and Early Modern Visual Culture.* Selinsgrove, PA: Susquehanna University Press, 2005.

Johnson, Jeffrey. *The Theology of John Donne*. Cambridge, England: Brewer, 1999.

Klawitter, George. *The Enigmatic Narrator: The Voicing of Same-Sex Love in the Poetry of John Donne*. New York: Peter Lang, 1994.

Lauritsen, John R. "Donne's *Satyres*: The Drama of Self-Discovery," *Studies in English Literature*, Volume 16 (1976): pp. 117–130.

Leishman, J. B. *The Monarch of Wit: An Analytical and Comparative Study of the Poetry of John Donne*. London: Hutchinson, 1951.

Levine, Jay Arnold. "'The Dissolution': Donne's Twofold Elegy," *ELH*, Volume 28 (1961): pp. 301–315.

Love, Harold. "The Argument of Donne's *First Anniversary*," *Modern Philology*, Volume 64 (1966): pp. 125–131.

MacKenzie, Clayton G. *Emblem and Icon in John Donne's Poetry and Prose*. New York: Peter Lang, 2001.

Manley, Frank, ed. *John Donne:* The Anniversaries. Baltimore: Johns Hopkins University Press, 1963.

Mannani, Manijeh. *Divine Deviants: The Dialectics of Devotion in the Poetry of Donne and Rumi*. New York: Peter Lang, 2007.

Martz, Louis. *The Poetry of Meditation*. New Haven, Conn.: Yale University Press, 1954.

Maud, Ralph N. "Donne's *First Anniversary*," *Boston University Studies in English*, Volume 2 (1956): pp. 218–225.

Mazzaro, Jerome. *Tranformations in the Renaissance Lyric*. Ithaca, N.Y.: Cornell University Press, 1970.

Miller, Clarence H. "Donne's 'A Nocturnall Upon S. Lucies Day' and the Nocturne of Matins," *Studies in English Literature*, Volume 6 (1966): pp. 77–86.

Milward, Peter. *A Commentary on the Holy Sonnets of John Donne*. Tokyo: Renaissance Institute, Sophia University, 1988.

Miner, Earl Roy. *The Metaphysical Mode from Donne to Cowley*. Princeton: Princeton University Press, 1969.

Mueller, William R. *John Donne, Preacher*. Princeton: Princeton University Press, 1962.

Nellist, B. F. "Donne's 'Storm' and 'Calm' and the Descriptive Tradition," *Modern Language Review*, Volume 59 (1964): pp. 511–515.

Nelson, Brent. *Holy Ambition: Rhetoric, Courtship, and Devotion in the Sermons of John Donne*. Tempe: Arizona Center for Medieval and Renaissance Studies, 2005

Pebworth, Ted-Larry, Gary A. Stringer, Ernest W. Sullivan II, William A. McClung, and Jeffrey Johnson, eds. *The Variorum Edition of the Poetry of John Donne, VIII: The Epigrams, Epithalamions, Epitaphs, Inscriptions, and Miscellaneous Poems*. Bloomington: Indiana University Press, 1995.

Pebworth, Ted-Larry, Gary A. Stringer, Ernest W. Sullivan VI, William A. McClung, and Jeffrey Johnson, eds. *The Variorum Edition of the Poetry of John Donne, VIII: The Epigrams, Epithalamions, Epitaphs, Inscriptions, and Miscellaneous Poems.* Bloomington: Indiana University Press, 1995.

Pepperdene, Margaret W., ed. *That Subtle Wreath: Lectures Presented at Quartercentenary Celebration of the Birth of John Donne.* Atlanta: Agnes Scott College, 1973.

Praz, Mario. *The Flaming Heart.* New York: Doubleday, 1958.

Raspa, Anthony, ed. *Pseudo-Martyr/John Donne.* Montreal: McGill-Queen's University Press, 1993.

Ray, Robert H. *A John Donne Companion.* New York: Garland, 1990.

Roberts, John R. *John Donne: An Annotated Bibliography of Modern Criticism, 1979–1995.* Pittsburgh: Duquesne University Press, 2004.

Rooney, William J. "'The Canonization': The Language of Paradox Reconsidered," *ELH*, Volume 23 (1956): pp. 36–47.

Roston, Murray. *The Soul of Wit: A Study of John Donne.* Oxford: Clarendon Press, 1974.

Sackton, Alexander. "Donne and the Privacy of Verse," *Studies in English Literature*, Volume 7 (1967): pp. 67–82.

Sanders, Wilbur. *John Donne's Poetry.* Cambridge: Cambridge University Press, 1971.

Saunders, Ben. *Desiring Donne: Poetry, Sexuality, Interpretation.* Cambridge, Mass.: Harvard University Press, 2006.

Shami, Jeanne, ed. *John Donne's 1622 Gunpowder Plot Sermon: A Parallel Text Edition.* Pittsburgh: Duquesne University Press, 1996.

Sicherman, Carol M. "The Mocking Voices of Donne and Marvell," *Bucknell Review*, Volume 17 (1969): pp. 38–40.

Sleight, Richard. "John Donne: 'A Nocturnall Upon S. Lucies Day, Being The Shortest Day'," in *Interpretations*, ed. John Wain. London: Routledge & Kegan Paul, 1955.

Sloan, Thomas O. "The Rhetoric in the Poetry of John Donne," *Studies in English Literature*, Volume 3 (1963): pp. 31–44.

Smith A. J. *John Donne: The Songs and Sonnets.* London: Arnold, 1964.

——, ed. *John Donne: Essays in Celebration.* London: Methuen, 1972.

Smith, James. "Metaphysical Poetry," in *Determinations*, ed. F. R. Leavis. London: Folcroft Press, 1934.

Spencer, Theodore, ed. *A Garland for John Donne.* Cambridge, Mass.: Harvard University Press, 1931.

Stanwood, P. G. "'Essential Joye' in Donne's *Anniversaries*," *Texas Studies in Literature and Language*, Volume 13 (1971): pp. 227–238.

———, and Dennis Danielson. *John Donne and the Line of Wit: From Metaphysical to Modernist.* Vancouver, B.C.: Ronsdale, 2008.

Stein, Arnold. *John Donne's Lyrics: The Eloquence of Action.* Minneapolis: University of Minnesota Press, 1962.

Stringer, Gary A., and Paul A. Parrish II, eds. *The Variorum Edition of the Poetry of John Donne: The Elegies.* Bloomington: Indiana University Press, 2000.

Stubbs, John. John Donne: *The Reformed Soul.* New York: Norton, 2006.

Sugg, Richard. *John Donne.* Basingstoke, England: Macmillan, 2007.

Sullivan, Ernest W., II, ed. *The First and Second Dalhousie Manuscripts: Poems and Prose by John Donne and Others: A Facsimile Edition.* Columbia: University of Missouri Press, 1988.

———. *The Influence of John Donne: His Uncollected Seventeenth-Century Printed Verse.* Columbia: University of Missouri Press, 1993.

Tuve, Rosemond. *Elizabethan and Metaphysical Imagery.* Chicago: University of Chicago Press, 1947.

Webber, Joan. *Contrary Music: The Prose Style of John Donne.* Madison: University of Wisconsin Press, 1963.

Wiggins, Peter DeSa. *Donne, Castiglione, and the Poetry of Courtliness.* Bloomington: Indiana University Press, 2000.

Williamson, George. "The Design of Donne's *Anniversaries,*" *Modern Philology,* Volume 60 (1963): pp. 183–191.

———. "The Convention of 'The Exstasie'," in *Seventeenth Century Contexts.* London: Faber & Faber, 1960.

Wolfe, Heather. *John Donne's Marriage Letters in The Folger Shakespeare Library.* Eds. M. Thomas Hester, Robert Parker Sorlien, and Dennis Flynn. Washington, D.C.: Folger Shakespeare Library, 2005.

## Robert Herrick

Allen, Don Cameron. "Good Friday: Rex Tragicus, or Christ Going to His Crosse," in *Image and Meaning: Metaphoric Traditions in the Renaissance.* (Baltimore: The Johns Hopkins University Press, 1968), pp. 138–151

Asals, Heather. "King Solomon in the Land of the Hesperides," *Texas Studies in Literature and Language,* Volume 18 (1976): pp. 362–380.

Berman, Ronald. "Herrick's Secular Poetry," *English Studies,* Volume 52 (1971): pp. 20–30.

Braden, Gordon. *The Classics and English Renaissance Poetry: Three Case Studies.* New Haven, Conn.: Yale University Press, 1978.

Briggs, Katherine M. *The Anatomy of Puck: An Examination of Fairy Beliefs Among Shakespeare's Contemporaries and Successors.* London: Routledge & Kegan Paul, 1959.

Brooks, Cleanth. "What Does Poetry Communicate?" in *The Well Wrought Urn*. New York: Harcourt Brace Jovanovich, 1947.

Capwell, Richard L. "Herrick and the Aesthetic Principle of Variety and Contrast," *South Atlantic Quarterly*, Volume 71 (1972): pp. 488–495

Chambers, A. B. "Herrick and the Trans-Shifting of Time," *Studies in Philology*, Volume 72 (1975): pp. 85–114.

———. "Herrick, Corinna, Canticles, and Catullus," *Studies in Philology*, Volume 74 (1977): pp. 216–227.

Deming, Robert H. *Ceremony and Art: Robert Herrick's Poetry*. The Hague & Paris: Mouton, 1974.

DeNeef, A. Leigh. *"This Poetik Liturgie": Robert Herrick's Ceremonial Mode*. Durham, N.C.: Duke University Press, 1974.

Gertzman, Jay. "Robert Herrick's Recreative Pastoral," *Genre*, Volume 7 (1974): pp. 183–195.

Godshalk, William Leigh. "Art and Nature: Herrick and History," *Essays in Criticism*, Volume 17 (1967): pp. 121–124.

Holmer, Joan Ozark. "Religious Satire in Herrick's *The Faerie Temple: or, Oberons Chappell*," *Renaissance and Reformation*, Volume 17 (1981): pp. 40–57.

Jenkins, Paul R. "Rethinking What Moderation Means to Robert Herrick," *ELH*, Volume 39 (1972): pp. 49–65.

Kimmey, John L. "Order and Form in Herrick's *Hesperides*," *Journal of English and Germanic Philology*, Volume 70 (1971): pp. 255–268.

———. "Robert Herrick's Persona," *Studies in Philology*, Volume 67 (1970): pp. 221–236.

Malpezzi, Frances P. "The Feast of Circumcision: The Return to Sacred Time in Herrick's *Noble Numbers*," *Notre Dame English Journal*, Volume 14 (1981): pp. 29–40.

Marcus, Leah Sinanoglou. "Herrick's *Noble Numbers* and the Politics of Playfulness," *English Literary Renaissance*, Volume 7 (1977): pp. 108–126.

———. "Herrick's *Hesperides* and the 'Proclamation Made for May'," *Studies in Philology*, Volume 76 (1979): pp. 49–74.

Miller, Edmund. "Sensual Imagery in the Devotional Poetry of Robert Herrick," *Christianity and Literature*, Volume 28, Number 2 (1979): pp. 24–33.

Miner, Earl Roy. *The Cavalier Mode from Jonson to Cotton*. Princeton: Princeton University Press, 1971.

Patrick, J. Max, and Roger Rollin, eds., *Trust to Good Verses: Herrick Tercentenary Essays*. Pittsburgh: University of Pittsburgh Press, 1978.

Reed, Mark L. "Herrick among the Maypoles: Dean Prior and the *Hesperides*," *Studies in English Literature*, Volume 5 (1965): pp. 133–150.

Schleiner, Louise. "Herrick's Songs and the Character of *Hesperides*," *English Literary Renaissance*, Volume 6 (1976): pp. 77–91.

Schwenger, Peter. "Herrick's Fairy State," *ELH*, Volume 46 (1979): pp. 35–55.

Strakman, Miriam. *"Noble Numbers* and the Poetry of Devotion," in *Reason and the Imagination: Studies in the History of Ideas 1600–1800*, ed. J. A. Mazzeo. New York: Doubleday, 1962.

Summers, Joseph H. *The Heirs of Donne and Jonson*. New York: Oxford University Press, 1970.

Toliver, Harold. "Herrick's Books of Realms and Moments," *ELH*, Volume 49 (1982): pp. 429–448.

Warren, Austin. "Herrick Revisited," *Michigan Quarterly Review*, Volume 15 (1976): pp. 245–267.

Woodward, Daniel H. "Herrick's Oberon Poems," *Journal of English and Germanic Philology*, Volume 64 (1965): 270–284.

## George Herbert

Allen, Don Cameron. "George Herbert, 'The Rose'," in *Image and Meaning: Metaphoric Traditions in Renaissance Poetry* (Baltimore: Johns Hopkins University Press, 1968), pp. 102–114.

Asals, Heather. *Equivocal Predication: George Herbert's Way to God*. Toronto: University of Toronto Press, 1981.

Bell, Ilona. "'Setting Foot into Divinity': George Herbert and the English Reformation," *Modern Language Quarterly*, Volume 38 (1977): pp. 219–241.

Benet, Diana. *Secretary of Praise: The Poetic Vocation of George Herbert*. Columbia: University of Missouri Press, 1984.

Bloch, Chana. "George Herbert and the Bible: A Reading of 'Love (III)'," *English Literary Renaissance*, Volume 8 (1978): pp. 329–340.

Blunden, Edmund. "George Herbert's Latin Poems," *Essays and Studies*, Volume 19 (1923): pp. 29–39

Bowers, Fredson. "Herbert's Sequential Imagery: 'The Temper'," *Modern Philology*, Volume 59 (1962): pp. 202–213.

Carnes, Valerie. "The Unity of George Herbert's *The Temple*: A Reconsideration," *ELH*, Volume 35 (1968): pp. 505–526.

Carpenter, Margaret. "From Herbert to Marvell: Poetics in 'A Wreath' and 'The Coronet'," *Journal of English and Germanic Philology*, Volume 69 (1970): pp. 50–62.

Clark, Ira. "'Lord, in Thee the Beauty Lies in the Discovery': 'Love Unknown' and Reading Herbert," *ELH*, Volume 39 (1972): pp. 560–584.

Clements, A. L. "Theme, Tone, and Tradition in George Herbert," *English Literary Renaissance*, Volume 3 (1973): pp. 264–283.

Colie, Rosalie. *Paradoxia Epidemics: The Renaissance Tradition of Paradox*. Princeton: Princeton University Press, 1966.

Coolidge, John S. *The Pauline Renaissance in England: Puritanism and the Bible*. Oxford: Clarendon Press, 1970.

Eliot, T. S. *George Herbert*. London: Longmans, Green & Co., 1962.

Elsky, Marlin. "George Herbert's Pattern Poems and the Materiality of Language: A New Approach to Renaissance Hieroglyphics," *ELH*, Volume 50 (1983): pp. 245–260.

Empson, William. *Seven Types of Ambiguity*. New York: New Directions, 1955.

Endicott, Annabel M. "The Structure of George Herbert's *Temple:* A Reconsideration," *University of Toronto Quarterly*, Volume 34 (1965): pp. 226–237.

———. "'The Soul in Paraphrase': George Herbert's 'Library'," *Renaissance News*, Volume 19 (1966): pp. 14–16.

Fisch, Harold. *Jerusalem and Albion: The Hebraic Factor in Seventeenth-Century Literature*. New York: Schocken Books, 1964.

Fish, Stanley E. *The Living Temple: George Herbert and Catechizing*. Berkeley and Los Angeles: University of California Press, 1978.

Freeman, Rosemary. *English Emblem Books*. London: Chatto & Windus, 1948.

Freer, Coburn. *Music for a King: George Herbert's Style and the Metrical Psalms*. Baltimore: Johns Hopkins University Press, 1972.

Gallagher, Michael P. "Rhetoric, Style, and George Herbert," *ELH*, Volume 37 (1970): pp. 495–516.

Grant, Patrick. *The Transformation of Sin: Studies in Donne, Herbert, Vaughan, and Traherne*. Amherst: University of Massachusetts Press, 1974.

Halewood, William H. *The Poetry of Grace: Reformation Themes and Structures in English Seventeenth-Century Poetry*. New Haven, Conn.: Yale University Press, 1970.

Hart, Jeffrey. "Herbert's 'The Collar' Re-read," in *Seventeenth-Century Poetry: Modern Essays in Criticism*, ed. W. R. Keast. New York: Oxford University Press, 1971, pp. 248–256.

Hollander, John. *The Untuning of the Sky: Ideas of Music in English Poetry 1500–1700*. Princeton: Princeton University Press, 1961.

Johnson, Lee Ann. "The Relationship of 'The Church Militant' to *The Temple*," *Studies in Philology*, Volume 67 (1971): pp. 200–206.

Jones, Nicholas R. "Tests and Contests: Two Languages in George Herbert's Poetry," *Studies in Philology*, Volume 79 (1982): pp. 162–176.

Kelliher, W. Hilton. "The Latin Poetry of George Herbert," in *The Latin Poetry of English Poets*, ed. J. W. Binns. London: Routledge & Kegan Paul, 1974, pp. 26–57.

Klause, John L. "George Herbert's *Kenosis* and the Whole Truth," in *Allegory, Myth, and Symbol*, ed. Martin W. Bloomfield. Cambridge, Mass.: Harvard University Press, 1981, pp. 209–225.

Knieger, Bernard. "The Purchase-Sale: Patterns of Business Imagery in the Poetry of George Herbert," *Studies in English Literature*, Volume 6 (1966): pp. 11–24.

Kronenfeld, Judy Z. "Herbert's 'A Wreath' and Devotional Aesthetics: Imperfect Efforts Redeemed by Grace," *ELH*, Volume 48 (1981): pp. 290–309.

Levang, Dwight. "George Herbert's 'The Church Militant' and the Chances of History," *Philological Quarterly*, Volume 36 (1957): pp. 265–268.

McCanles, Michael. *Dialectical Criticism and Renaissance Literature*. Berkeley & Los Angeles: University of California Press, 1975.

McLaughlin, Elizabeth, and Gail Thomas. "Communion in *The Temple*," *Studies in English Literature*, Volume 15 (1975): pp. 110–124.

Mahood, M. M. "Something Understood: The Nature of Herbert's Wit," in *Metaphysical Poetry, Stratford Upon Avon Studies*, Volume 11. London: Edward Arnold, 1970, pp. 123–148.

Merrill, Thomas F. "Sacred Parody and the Grammar of Devotion," *Criticism*, Volume 23 (1981): pp. 195–210.

Mills, Jerry Leath. "Recent Studies in Herbert," *English Literary Renaissance*, Volume 6 (1976): pp. 105–118.

Miner, Earl Roy. *The Metaphysical Mode from Donne to Cowley*. Princeton: Princeton University Press, 1969.

Montgomery, Rupert. "The Province of Allegory in George Herbert's Verse," *Texas Studies in Literature and Language*, Volume 1 (1960): pp. 457–472.

Nardo, Anna K. "Play, Literary Criticism, and the Poetry of George Herbert," in *Play and Culture*, ed. Helen B. Schwartzman. West Point, NY: Leisure, 1980, pp. 30–38.

Ostriker, Alicia. "Song and Speech in the Metrics of George Herbert," *PMLA*, Volume 80 (1965): pp. 62–69.

Rickey, Mary Ellen. *Utmost Art: Complexity in the Verse of George Herbert*. Lexington: University of Kentucky Press, 1966.

Roberts, John R., ed. *Essential Articles for the Study of George Herbert's Poetry*. Hamden, Conn.: Archon Books, 1979.

Rubey, Daniel. "The Poet and the Christian Community: Herbert's Affliction Poems and the Structure of *The Temple*," *Studies in English Literature*, Volume 20 (1980): pp. 105–123.

Sanders, Wilbur. "'Childhood Is Health': The Divine Poetry of George Herbert," *Melbourne Critical Review*, Volume 5 (1962): pp. 3–15.

Sherwood, Terry G. "Tasting and Telling Sweetness in George Herbert's Poetry," *English Literary Renaissance*, Volume 12 (1982): pp. 319–340.

Stewart, Stanley. "Time and *The Temple*," *Studies in English Literature*, Volume 6 (1966): pp. 97–110.

Strier, Richard. *Love Known: Theology and Experience in George Herbert's Poetry.* Chicago: University of Chicago Press, 1983.

Summers, Claude J., and Ted-Larry Pebworth, eds. *"Too Rich-to Clothe the Sunne": Essays on George Herbert.* Pittsburgh: University of Pittsburgh Press, 1980.

Tuve, Rosemond. *A Reading of George Herbert.* Chicago: University of Chicago Press, 1952.

Walker, John. "The Architectonics of George Herbert's *The Temple*," *ELH*, Volume 29 (1962): pp. 289–305.

## Richard Crashaw

Adams, Robert M. "Taste and Bad Taste in Metaphysical Poetry: Richard Crashaw and Dylan Thomas," *Hudson Review*, Volume 8 (1955): pp. 60–77.

Bertonasco, Marc F. *Crashaw and the Baroque.* University: University of Alabama Press, 1971.

Chambers, Leland. "In Defense of 'The Weeper'," *Papers on Language and Literature*, Volume 3 (1967): pp. 11–21.

Collmer, Robert G. "Crashaw's 'Death More Misticall and High'," *Journal of English and Germanic Philology*, Volume 55 (1956): pp. 373–380.

Hollander, John. *The Untuning of the Sky: Ideas of Music in English Poetry, 1500–1700.* Princeton: Princeton University Press, 1961.

McCanles, Michael. "The Rhetoric of the Sublime in Crashaw's Poetry," in *The Rhetoric of Renaissance Poetry*, eds. Thomas O. Sloan and Raymond B. Waddington. Berkeley & Los Angeles: University of California Press, 1974, pp. 189–211.

Manning, Stephen. "The Meaning of 'The Weeper'," *ELH*, Volume 22 (1955): pp. 34–47.

Martz, Louis. *The Wit of Love.* Notre Dame: University of Notre Dame Press, 1969.

Miner, Earl Roy. *The Metaphysical Mode from Donne to Cowley.* Princeton: Princeton University Press, 1969.

Neill, Kerby. "Structure and Symbol in Crashaw's 'Hymn in the Nativity'," *PMLA*, Volume 63 (1948): pp. 101–113.

Peter, John. "Crashaw and 'The Weeper'," *Scrutiny*, Volume 19 (1953): pp. 258–273.

Praz, Mario. "The Flaming Heart: Richard Crashaw and the Baroque," in *The Flaming Heart.* New York: Doubleday, 1958.

Raspa, Anthony. "Crashaw and the Jesuit Poetic," *University of Toronto Quarterly*, Volume 36 (1966): pp. 37–54.

Schwenger, Peter. "Crashaw's Perspectivist Metaphor," *Comparative Literature*, Volume 28 (1976): pp. 65–74.

Strier, Richard. "Crashaw's Other Voice," *Studies in English Literature*, Volume 9 (1969): pp. 135–151.

Wallerstein, Ruth. *Richard Crashaw: A Study in Style and Poetic Development*. Madison: University of Wisconsin Press, 1935.

Warren, Austin. *Richard Crashaw: A Study in Baroque Sensibility*. University: Louisiana State University Press, 1939.

Williams, George Walton. *Image and Symbol in the Sacred Poetry of Richard Crashaw*. Columbia, S.C.: University of South Carolina Press, 1963.

Young, R. R. *Richard Crashaw and the Spanish Golden Age*. New Haven, Conn.: Yale University Press, 1982.

## Henry Vaughan

Allen, Don Cameron. "Vaughan's 'Cock Crowing' and the Tradition," *ELH*, Volume 21 (1954): pp. 94–106.

Bradford, Melvin E. "Henry Vaughan's 'The Night': A Consideration of Metaphor and Meditation," *Ariel: A Review of Literature*, Volume 1 (1968): pp. 209–222.

Brooks, Cleanth. "Henry Vaughan: Quietism and Mysticism," in *Essays Presented in Honor of Esmond Linworth Marilla*. Eds. Thomas Kirby and William John Olive. Baton Rouge: Louisiana State University Press, 1970, pp. 3–26.

Chambers, Leland H. "Henry Vaughan's Allusive Technique: Biblical Allusion in 'The Night'," *Modern Language Quarterly*, Volume 27 (1966): pp. 371–387.

———— . "Vaughan's 'The World': The Limits of Extrinsic Criticism," *Studies in English Literature*, Volume 8 (1968): pp. 137–150.

Farnham, Fern. "The Imagery of Henry Vaughan's 'The Night'," *Philological Quarterly*, Volume 38 (1959): pp. 425–435.

Grant, Patrick. *The Transformation of Sin: Studies in Donne, Herbert, Vaughan, and Traherne*. Amherst: University of Massachusetts Press, 1974.

Kermode, Frank. "The Private Imagery of Henry Vaughan," *Review of English Studies*, Volume 1 (1950): pp. 206–225.

Malpezzi, Frances M. "An Approach to Vaughan's 'Isaac's Marriage'," *English Language Notes*, Volume 14 (1976): pp. 112–117.

Marcus, Leah Sinanoglou. "Vaughan, Wordsworth, Coleridge, and the Encomioun Asini," *ELH*, Volume 42 (1974): pp. 224–241.

Murrin, Michael. *The Veil of Allegory*. Chicago: University of Chicago Press, 1969.

Olson, Paul. "Vaughan's 'The World': The Pattern of Meaning and the Tradition," *Comparative Literature*, Volume 13 (1961): pp. 26–32.

Pollock, John. "The Divided Consciousness of Henry Vaughn," *Papers on Language and Literature,* Volume 10 (1974): pp. 422–442.

Post, Jonathan F. S. *Henry Vaughan: The Unfolding Vision.* Princeton: Princeton University Press, 1982.

Rickey, Mary Ellen. "Vaughan, *The Temple* and Poetic Form," *Studies in Philology,* Volume 59 (1962): pp. 162–170.

Rudrum, A. W. "The Influence of Alchemy in the Poems of Henry Vaughan," *Philological Quarterly,* Volume 49 (1970): pp. 469–480.

———. "An Aspect of Vaughan's Hermeticism: The Doctrine of Cosmic Sympathy," *Studies in English Literature,* Volume 14 (1974): pp, 129–138.

Sandler, Florence. "The Ascent of Spirit: Henry Vaughan on the Atonement," *Journal of English and Germanic Philology,* Volume 73 (1974): pp. 209–226.

Shawcross, John T. "Vaughan's 'Amoret' Poems: A Jonsonian Sequence," in *Classic and Cavalier: Essays on Jonson and the Sons of Ben,* eds. Claude J. Summers and Ted-Larry Pebworth. Pittsburgh: University of Pittsburgh Press, 1982.

Simmonds, James D. *Masques of God: Form and Theme in the Poetry of Henry Vaughan.* Pittsburgh: University of Pittsburgh Press, 1972.

Summers, Claude J., and Ted-Larry Pebworth. "Vaughan's Temple in Nature and the Context of Regeneration," *Journal of English and Germanic Philology,* Volume 74 (1975): pp. 351–360.

Wyly, Thomas J. "Vaughan's 'Regeneration' Reconsidered," *Philological Quarterly,* Volume 55 (1976): pp. 340–353.

## Andrew Marvell

Allen, Don Cameron. *Image and Meaning: Metaphoric Traditions in Renaissance Poetry.* Baltimore: Johns Hopkins University Press, 1960, pp. 93–153.

Asp, Carolyn. "Marvell's Nymph: Unravished Bride of Quietness," *Papers on Language and Literature,* Volume 14 (1978): pp. 394–405.

Berek, Peter. "The Voices of Marvell's Lyrics," *Modern Language Quarterly,* Volume 32 (1971): pp. 143–157.

Berger, Harry, Jr. "Marvell's 'Garden': Still Another Interpretation," *Modern Language Quarterly,* Volume 28 (1967): pp. 290–309.

———. "Andrew Marvell: The Poem as Green World," *Forum for Modern Language Studies,* Volume 3 (1967): pp. 290–310.

Berthoff, Ann Evans. *The Resolved Soul: A Study of Marvell's Major Poems.* Princeton: Princeton University Press, 1970.

Bradbrook, M. C., and M. G. Lloyd Thomas. *Andrew Marvell.* Cambridge: Cambridge University Press, 1940.

Brett, R. L. "Andrew Marvell: The Voice of His Age," *The Critical Quarterly,* Volume 20 (1978): pp. 5–17.

———, ed. *Andrew Marvell: Essays on the Tercentenary of His Death*. Oxford: Oxford University Press, 1979.

Brooks, Cleanth. "Criticism and Literary History: Marvell's 'Horatian Ode'," *Sewanee Review*, Volume 55 (1947): pp. 199–222.

———. "Andrew Marvell: Puritan Authority with Classical Grace," in *Poetic Traditions of the English Renaissance*, eds. Maynard Mack and George deForest Lord. New Haven, Conn.: Yale University Press, 1982, pp. 219–228.

Carpenter, Margaret. "From Herbert to Marvell: Poetics in 'A Wreath' and 'The Coronet'," *Journal of English and Germanic Philology*, Volume 69 (1970): pp. 50–62.

Colie, Rosalie. *My Echoing Song: Andrew Marvell's Poetry of Criticism*. Princeton: Princeton University Press, 1970.

Cullen, Patrick. *Spenser, Marvell and Renaissance Pastoral*. Cambridge, Mass.: Harvard University Press, 1970.

Eliot, T. S. "Andrew Marvell," in *Selected Essays*. London: Faber & Faber, 1932.

Erickson, Lee. "Marvell's 'Upon Appleton House' and the Fairfax Family," *English Literary Renaissance*, Volume 9 (1979): pp. 158–168.

Evett, David. "'Paradices Only Map': The Topos of the Locus Amoenus and the Structure of Marvell's 'Upon Appleton House'," *PMLA*, Volume 85 (1970): pp. 504–513.

Fitzdale, Jay. "Irony in Marvell's 'Bermudas'," *ELH*, Volume 42 (1974): pp. 203–213.

Friedenrich, Kenneth, ed. *Tercentenary Essays in Honor of Andrew Marvell*. Hamden, Conn.: Archon Books, 1977.

Godshalk, William Leigh. "Marvell's 'Garden' and the Theologians," *Studies in Philology*, Volume 66 (1969): 50–62.

Goldberg, Jonathan. "Marvell's Nymph and the Echo of Voice," *Glyph*, Volume 8 (1981): pp. 19–39.

Gray, Allan. "The Surface of Marvell's 'Upon Appleton House'," *English Literary Renaissance*, Volume 9 (1979): pp. 169–182.

Guild, Nicholas. "Marvell's 'The Nymph Complaining for the Death of Her Faun'." *Modern Language Quarterly*, Volume 29 (1968): 385–394.

Hartman, Geoffrey. "Marvell, St. Paul and the Body of Hope," in *Beyond Formalism: Literary Essays 1958–1970*. New Haven, Conn.: Yale University Press, 1970.

Herron, Dale. "Marvell's 'Garden' and the Landscape of Poetry," *Journal of English and Germanic Philology*, Volume 73 (1974): pp. 328–337.

Hinz, Evelyn J., and John J. Tuenissen. "What Is the Nymph Complaining For?" *ELH*, Volume 45 (1978): 410–428.

Kermode, Frank. "The Argument of Marvell's 'Garden'," *Essays in Criticism*, Volume 1 (1952): pp. 225–241.

————— . "Marvell Transpros'd," *Encounter,* Volume 27 (1966): pp. 77–84.

Larkin, Philip. "The Changing Face of Andrew Marvell," *English Literary Renaissance,* Volume 9 (1979): pp. 149–157.

Legouis, Pierre. *Andrew Marvell, Poet, Puritan, Patriot.* Oxford: Clarendon Press, 1965.

Lord, George deForest. "From Contemplation to Action: Marvell's Poetic Career," *Philological Quarterly,* Volume 46 (1967): pp. 207–224.

Martz, Louis. *The Wit of Love.* Notre Dame: University of Notre Dame Press, 1969.

Miner, Earl Roy. *The Metaphysical Mode from Donne to Cowley.* Princeton: Princeton University Press, 1969.

Norford, Don Parry. "Marvell and the Arts of Contemplation and Action," *ELH,* Volume 41 (1974): pp. 50–73.

Patrides, C. A., ed. *Approaches to Andrew Marvell: The York Tercentenary Essays.* London: Routledge & Kegan Paul, 1978.

Reedy, Gerard. "'An Horatian Ode' and 'Tom May's Death'," *Studies in English Literature,* Volume 20 (1980): pp. 136–151.

Richards, Judith. "Literary Criticism and the Historian," *Literature and History,* Volume 7 (1981): pp. 25–47.

Schwenger, Peter. "'To Make His Saying True': Deceit in 'Appleton House'," *Studies in Philology,* Volume 77 (1980): pp. 84–104.

Siemon, James E. "Generic Limits in Marvell's 'Garden'," *Papers on Language and Literature,* Volume 8 (1972): pp. 261–272.

Spitzer, Leo. "Marvell's 'Nymph Complaining for the Death of Her Faun': Sources versus Meaning," *Modern Language Quarterly,* Volume 19 (1958): pp. 231–243.

Summers, Joseph H. *The Heirs of Donne and Jonson.* New York: Oxford University Press, 1970.

Toliver, Harold. *Marvell's Ironic Vision.* New Haven, Conn.: Yale University Press, 1965.

Warnke, Frank J. "Play and Metamorphosis in Marvell's Poetry," *Studies in English Literature,* Volume 5 (1965): pp. 23–30.

## Thomas Traherne

Botrall, Margaret. "Traherne's Praise of Creation," *Critical: Quarterly,* Volume 1 (1959): pp. 126–133.

Clements, A. L. *The Mystical Poetry of Thomas Traherne.* Cambridge, Mass.: Harvard University Press, 1969.

Dauber, Antoinette B. "Thomas Traherne and the Poetics of Object Relations," *Criticism,* Volume 23 (1981): pp. 103–125.

Day, Malcolm. "Traherne and the Doctrine of Pre-Existence," *Studies in Philology*, Volume 64 (1968): pp. 81–98.

——— . "'Naked Truth' and the Language of Thomas Traherne," *Studies in Philology*, Volume 68 (1971): pp. 305–325.

Drake, Ben. "Thomas Traherne's Songs of Innocence," *Modern Language Quarterly*, Volume 31 (1970): pp. 492–503.

Grant, Patrick. *The Transformation of Sin: Studies in Donne, Herbert, Vaughan, and Traherne*. Amherst: University of Massachusetts Press, 1974.

Hepburn, Ronald W. "Thomas Traherne: The Nature and Dignity of Imagination," *The Cambridge Journal*, Volume 6 (1953): pp. 725–734.

Hunter, C. Stuart. "Thomas Traherne and Francis Bacon: In Definition of Traherne's Poetic," *The Humanities Association Review Bulletin*, Volume 27 (1976): pp. 1–15.

Jordan, Richard. *The Temple of Eternity: Thomas Traherne's Philosophy of Time*. Port Washington: Kennikat, 1972.

Leishman, J. B. *The Metaphysical Poets: Donne, Herbert, Vaughan, Traherne*. Oxford: Clarendon Press, 1934.

Marks, Carol Louise. "Thomas Traherne and Cambridge Platonism," *PMLA*, Volume 81 (1966): pp. 521–534.

Marshall, William H. "Thomas Traherne and the Doctrine of Original Sin," *MLN*, Volume 73 (1958): pp. 161–165.

Sabine, Maureen. "'Stranger to the Shining Skies': Traherne's Child and His Changing Attitudes to the World," *Ariel: A Review of English Literature*, Volume 11 (1980): pp. 21–35.

Salter, Keith W. *Thomas Traherne: Mystic and Poet*. New York: Barnes & Noble, 1965.

Seelig, Sharon Cadman. *The Shadow of Eternity: Belief and Structure in Herbert, Vaughan, and Traherne*. Lexington: University Press of Kentucky, 1981.

Selkin, Carl M. "The Language of Vision: Traherne's Cataloguing Style," *English Literary Renaissance*, Volume 6 (1976): pp. 92–104.

Trimpey, John E. "An Analysis of Traherne's 'Thoughts (I)'," *Studies in Philology*, Volume 68 (1971): pp. 88–104.

Uphaus, Robert. "Thomas Traherne: Perception as Process," *University of Windsor Review*, Volume 2 (1968): pp. 19–27.

Wallace, John Malcolm. "Thomas Traherne and the Structure of Meditation," *ELH*, Volume 25 (1958): pp. 79–89.

# Acknowledgments

Donald Ramsay Roberts. "The Death Wish of John Donne," *PMLA*, Volume 62, Number 4 (December 1947): pp. 958–976. Copyright © 1947 Modern Language Association of America.

Phoebe S. Spinrad. "Death, Loss, and Marvell's Nymph," *PMLA*, Volume 97, Number 1 (January 1982): pp. 50–59. Copyright © 1982 Modern Language Association of America.

Carol Ann Johnston. "Heavenly Perspectives, Mirrors of Eternity: Thomas Traherne's Yearning Subject," *Criticism*, Volume 43, Number 4 (Fall 2001): pp. 377–405. Copyright © 2001 Wayne State University Press. Reprinted by permission of the publisher.

Robert Whalen. "George Herbert's Sacramental Puritanism," *Renaissance Quarterly*, Volume 54, Number 4, Part 1 (Winter 2001): pp. 1273–1307. Copyright © 2001 University of Chicago Press/Renaissance Society of America. Reprinted by permission of the author.

Maureen Sabine. "Crashaw and Abjection: Reading the Unthinkable in His Devotional Verse," *American Imago*, Volume 63, Number 4 (Winter 2006): pp. 423–443. Copyright © 2006 Johns Hopkins University Press.

Anne-Marie Miller Blaise. "George Herbert's Distemper: An Honest Shepherd's Remedy for Melancholy," *George Herbert Journal*, Volume 30,

Numbers 1 and 2 (Fall 2006/Spring 2007): pp. 59–82. Copyright © 2007 *George Herbert Journal*. Reprinted by permission of the publisher.

Holly Faith Nelson. "Historical Consciousness and the Politics of Translation in the Psalms of Henry Vaughan," *Studies in Philology*, Volume 104, Number 4 (Fall 2007): pp. 501–525. Copyright © 2007 University of North Carolina Press. Reprinted by permission of the publisher.

Piers Brown. "'Hac ex consilio meo via progredieris': Courtly Reading and Secretarial Mediation in Donne's *The Courtier's Library*," *Renaissance Quarterly*, Volume 61, Number 3 (Fall 2008): pp. 833–866. Copyright © 2008 University of Chicago Press/Renaissance Society of America. Reprinted by permission of the publisher.

Gary Kuchar. "Ecstatic Donne: Conscience, Sin, and Surprise in the *Sermons* and the Mitcham Letters," *Criticism*, Volume 50, Number 4 (Fall 2008): pp. 631–654. Copyright © 2008 Wayne State University Press. Reprinted by permission of the publisher.

# Index